Student Study Guide

to accompany

PSYCHOLOGY

CONTEXTS AND APPLICATIONS

Third Edition

Jane Halonen
Alverno College

John W. Santrock
University of Texas, Dallas

Prepared by
Steven A. Schneider
Pima Community College

Boston Burr Ridge, IL Dubuque, IA Madison, WI New York San Francisco St. Louis
Bangkok Bogotá Caracas Lisbon London Madrid
Mexico City Milan New Delhi Seoul Singapore Sydney Taipei Toronto

McGraw-Hill College

A Division of The McGraw-Hill Companies

Student Study Guide to accompany
PSYCHOLOGY: CONTEXTS AND APPLICATIONS, THIRD EDITION

4 5 6 7 8 9 0 CUS/CUS 9 0 9

ISBN 0-697-37667-2

www.mhhe.com

Contents

Preface

To the Student: Before You Begin

This *Student Study Guide* will assist you as you read *Psychology: The Contexts of Behavior,* by Jane Halonen and John Santrock. It will help you learn the essential concepts, facts, and theories covered in the text, but please remember, it is not intended to substitute for reading the text. This *Student Study Guide* should be used to help you identify essential information, review, indicate the gaps in your learning, stimulate your thinking about the ideas in the text, and test yourself. Each chapter in this guide contains the following features.

Learning Objectives

You can use the learning objectives in two different ways. First, examine them *before* you read the text chapter to get an overview of the major topics that will be covered. Pay special attention to the terms, concepts, and names mentioned in the objectives. Second, after you have read the text chapter, return to the objectives; you should be able to perform the activities listed. If an objective is unclear to you, return and reread that section of the text. The page numbers following each objective refer to the location of the material in the text.

The learning objectives are keyed to both sets of the multiple-choice questions at the end of each study guide chapter.

Outline

The extended outline will allow you to see how the material in the text is organized and how the parts of the chapter are related. It will be useful to review the extended outline both before and after you read the text.

Key Terms

To assist you in learning the key terms, this section provides a list of the terms, with space for you to write in definitions. You may compare your answers with the definitions that appear at the end of each chapter in the *Student Study Guide*.

Guided Review

The guided review is a challenging and comprehensive fill-in-the-blanks exercise. As you go through the exercise, try to resist the temptation to peek at the answers until you have provided them. This exercise will help point out the terms or sections of the text you need to review. When you have filled in all of the blanks correctly, you will have a thorough summary of the chapter for future reference and review.

Sociocultural Worlds/Applications in Psychology

This section asks you to summarize the material found in the "Sociocultural Worlds" and "Applications in Psychology" sections in the textbook and to relate them to the chapter material.

Concept Check

Tests your knowledge of key concepts within the chapter.

Multiple-Choice Questions

Each chapter of the *Student Study Guide* contains two sets of multiple-choice questions. These questions are similar to the type you might be asked to respond to on an exam. Remember that the multiple-choice questions are keyed to the learning objectives. At the end of each multiple choice question, the learning objective to which it refers is designated by "LO" and the learning objective number. If you incorrectly answer a multiple-choice question, you may want to review the material covered in the corresponding learning objective. You will find explanations for correct and incorrect answers to all multiple choice questions at the end of each chapter.

Tips for Successful Studying

Some students take an introductory psychology course because they are considering psychology as a major; others because it is a required course for another major; still others take psychology out of a general interest and curiosity about their fellow human beings. Whatever the reason, whatever your major, you are certain to find some topics in this course to be most interesting. Biology/pre-med students will find the chapters dealing with biological psychology and sensation and perception to be particularly interesting. Education majors, parents, and future parents will find the developmental psychology chapter applicable and interesting. Are you interested in health, diet, and exercise? If so, you will find the health psychology chapter to be intriguing. You don't have to be a social scientist to have wondered about whether intelligence tests are valid, how the human memory system works, what causes mental disorders, or what attracts people to each other. These issues and many others will be explored in your introductory psychology course.

I have taught several thousand introductory psychology students over the past 20 years, and I would like to share some observations about students who succeed in the course and those who fail to live up to their (and my) expectations in the course.

1. *Successful students are well organized.* Some of my most successful students have been some of my busiest students—those with part-time or full-time jobs, parents with many familial obligations, and students carrying an incredible courseload. Their ability to organize their lives and manage their time, however, allowed them to accomplish their tasks efficiently and effectively. In order to be well organized, you should make use of a semester calendar that clearly indicates deadlines for papers, exam dates, and other important dates. Keep your course outlines in a safe place so that you can refer to them during the semester. Be certain that you know the office hours and office phone numbers of your instructors. Make and adhere to a weekly schedule for yourself that builds in all the important activities, including class time, work time, study time, *and* relaxation time.

2. *Successful students come to class.* As you begin college, one difference you may note from your previous educational experiences is that your instructor may not take attendance. That doesn't signify a lack of concern on the part of your instructor—after all, its *your* tuition and textbook money. What it *does* mean is that you are responsible for the decision to come to class or not. Both casual observation and the results of research studies show that students who attend class do better than those who don't attend.

3. *Read the material before going to class.* My most successful students over the years generally read the text before coming to class. They had a pretty good idea what the lecture was going to be about. This also helped them organize their note taking while in class.

4. *Take good notes and review them.* In your efforts to be a good learner, it is usually a mistake to try to take down everything that is said in class. Instead, try to outline the lecture, using Roman numerals and letters for the major and minor points. This technique can be particularly effective if the instructor lectures from an outline. Review your notes as soon after class as possible. It is somewhat dismaying while studying for an exam to see notes in your handwriting that you don't even remember writing.

5. *Focus on key terms and concepts.* A large and important part of most introductory courses consists of learning the language of the field you are studying. This is necessary in order to communicate with and to think like the professionals in the field. The implication is that, when you study, you need to learn the language of psychology. You are likely to be tested on the terminology, and, even if you are not tested directly on the terms, you will almost certainly be expected to know and understand them.

6. *Allow time to read the material more than once.* How often have you seen a movie more than once and felt you got a lot more out the second or third viewing? The same principle will likely apply when you read the text. The biggest challenge, or course, is to find the time. But I feel certain you will find a second reading of the text to be time well invested.

7. *Consider using the SQ3R method for studying.* The SQ3R method of studying is a tried and tested technique. Research conducted with students who use this technique indicates significantly greater comprehension of text material. This is how it works:

Survey: Although the temptation when you begin studying is to open the text and begin reading, this technique suggests that you should first get an overview of the material. Read the chapter outline (found in the text) and the overview (found in this study guide). Skim through the text, noting the major headings as well as the charts and pictures. This activity will allow you to get a feel for the chapter, as well as to see how the chapter is organized.

Question: As you survey the chapter, begin noting questions about the material. You may use the Learning Objectives section in this study guide to help you formulate questions about the text. The questions that you formulate will help you pick out the most important parts of the text as you read.

Read: When you have formulated questions, reading the text now becomes purposeful; that is, you are reading in order to answer the questions. As you find the material that answers your questions, consider highlighting it or marking an *X* in the margin. Consider taking notes of the major points as you read the text.

Recite: After you have finished a section of the text, stop and state the answers to the questions in your own words (not the author's). This will help give you practice pronouncing some difficult terminology and will test whether the material you have just learned makes sense to you. Recitation is also a very efficient system; material that has been recited is remembered much longer than material not recited. Recitation is particularly effective when studying for essay exams, since it may simulate the questions you will receive on the exam.

Review: Virtually everybody who sees a movie for the second time comments that the experience was much different from the first viewing. People often say they ``got something completely different'' from seeing the movie a second time. A similar situation exists when reading a chapter of your text. Review the material soon after reading it. You may test yourself by working through the guided review for each chapter that is included in this study guide. Try to answer the multiple-choice questions in the study guide. These are keyed to the Learning Objectives, so, for example, if you miss multiple-choice question #5, you may need to review the material in Learning Objective #5.

8. *Prepare for exams.* The most widespread method for instructors to assess what you have learned is to give you an exam. Whereas some students welcome the challenge, for many it provides an exercise in terror. Test anxiety is widely recognized to be a major problem for many students. Some hints for preparing for and taking exams can help. Find out as much as you can about the exam beforehand (remaining, of course, within the bounds of conventional morality and the law!). What material will be covered? Will it be multiple-choice, essay, fill-in, or matching? How much time will be allotted? How much weight will be given to various topics? The answers to these questions should help guide your preparation for the exam. Try to study always in the same place and on a regular basis. It should be a quiet, well-lit area and should contain minimal distractions. Your study area should only be for studying. Generally speaking, you study more efficiently when you study alone. Take breaks when you study. Studying is a fatiguing activity, and most students can benefit from a short break every 20 minutes or so. It is certainly time to take a break when you reach the end of a page and then realize you haven't retained a word on the page. Take a break instead of fighting it. The type of test for which you are preparing should dictate how you prepare—for example, study for an essay exam by asking yourself essay questions and writing out good answers. Prepare for a multiple-choice exam by answering multiple-choice questions (be sure to review those in the study guide). Solid preparation, a good night's sleep the night before an exam, and relaxing instead of cramming just prior to the exam should help minimize test anxiety. If it starts to get out of hand for you, seek the advice of a counselor. Many colleges now offer courses designed to help deal with test anxiety.

I hope you enjoy and benefit from your psychology course. I also hope that you find this *Student Study Guide* to be a helpful resource. Many thanks to John Haley, Nancy Christie, and Sheila Hughes for their invaluable assistance in the preparation of this Study Guide. I welcome your comments, opinions, and suggestions for improvements. My address is Steve Schneider, c/o Psychology Department,
Pima Community College, 2202 W. Anklam Rd., Tucson AZ 85709.

Chapter 1 The Scope and Methods of Psychology

Learning Objectives

After studying this chapter, you should be able to:

1. Define psychology. (p. 5)

2 Discuss the contributions to psychology of the following: Socrates, Aristotle, Francis Bacon, Wilhelm Wundt, and William James. (p. 7)

3. Distinguish between the "hardheaded" and the "soft-hearted" approaches to psychology. (p. 7)

4. Describe the following contemporary perspectives in psychology: behavioral, psychoanalytic, humanistic, neurobiological, cognitive, evolutionary, and sociocultural. (p. 8)

5. Distinguish among the concepts of culture, ethnicity, ethnic identity, and gender. (p. 11)

6. Describe the following areas of specialization in psychology: clinical and counseling; neuroscience and physiological; developmental; social; cross-cultural; psychology of women; industrial and organizational; forensic; school and educational. (p. 13)

7. Identify the career possibilities that are offered by a degree in psychology. (p. 16)

8. Explain the following steps involved in using the scientific method: identifying and analyzing a problem; developing tentative explanations; collecting data; drawing conclusions; and confirming or revising theory. (p. 17)

9. Discuss the importance of carefully selecting participants for research. (p. 18)

10. Contrast laboratory research and naturalistic observation. (p. 18)

11. Describe each of the following assessment measures: direct observation, interviews and questionnaires, and standardized tests. (p. 19)

12. Distinguish among descriptive research methods, correlational research methods, and experimental research methods. (p. 20)

13. Distinguish between the experimental group and the control group; between the independent variable and the dependent variable. (p. 22)

14. Describe the challenges to researchers regarding the ethical treatment of human participants and the ethical treatment of research animals. (p. 24)

15. Discuss the importance of the following in making sense of claims about behavior: knowing how important terms are defined and measured; understanding the nature of the sample; avoiding predictions about individual behavior from group results; resisting the interpretation of results of a single study as definitive; differentiating correlational and experimental research; evaluating the credibility of the source; maintaining skepticism about simplistic claims. (p. 26)

16. Distinguish between psychology and pseudoscience. (p. 27)

Chapter 1 Outline

I. Introducing Psychology
  A. Definition of Psychology
  B. Exploring Psychology's History
    1. Wilhelm Wundt
    2. Edward Bradford Titchener
    3. William James
  C. Contemporary perspectives
    1. Behavioral
    2. Psychoanalytic
    3. Humanistic
    4. Neurobiological
    5. Cognitive
    6. Evolutionary
    7. Sociocultural
  D. Psychology's Specializations and Careers
    1. Major areas of specialization
      a. clinical and counseling
      b. experimental
      c. neuroscience and physiological
      d. developmental
      e. social
      f. cross-cultural
      g. psychology of women
      h. industrial and organizational
      I. forensic
      j. school and educational Psychology
    2. Careers in Psychology

II. Conducting Psychological Research
   A. The Scientific Method
      1. Identify and analyze a problem
      2. Develop tentative explanations
      3. Collect data
      4. Draw conclusions
      5. Confirm or revise theory
   B. Research Strategies in Psychology
      1. Selecting appropriate sample of participants
      2. Choosing a Research Setting
         a. Laboratory
         b. Naturalistic settings
      3. Selecting measures
         a. Direct observation
         b. Interviews and questionnaires
         c. Standardized tests
      4. Selecting a Strategy with Appropriate Depth of Explanation
         a. Descriptive Method
         b. Correlational Method
         c. Experimental Method
            (1) independent variable
            (2) dependent variable
            (3) experimenter bias
   C. Ethics in Research
      1. Human participants
      2. Animal Research
III. Thinking Critically about Behavior
   A. Making Sense of Behavior Claims
      1. How are important terms defined and measured?
      2. What is the nature of the sample?
      3. Was individual behavior predicted from group results?
      4. Was a single study put forth as resulting in a definitive conclusion?
      5. Was the research descriptive, correlational, or experimental?
      6. Are the sources credible?
      7. Is the claim too simplistic?
   B. Psychology vs. Pseudoscience

Who Am I?

Match the psychologists listed below with their contribution to psychology. Answers appear at the end of the chapter.

_____ 1. Aristotle
_____ 2. Titchener
_____ 3. Wilhelm Wundt
_____ 4. William James
_____ 5. Sigmund Freud

a. I am credited with developing the first scientific psychology laboratory.
b. As a philosopher, I believed that an empirical approach was superior to dialogue as a means of acquiring knowledge.
c. I opened a laboratory at Cornell university and advocated an approach that became known as structuralism.
d. I founded the psychoanalytic approach, which stresses that unlearned biological instincts influence behavior and mental processes.
e. I was one of the first American psychologists and I emphasized the changing, dynamic nature of mental activity.

Key Terms

Write a brief description for each of the following terms. Where relevant, provide an original example or illustration of the term. Then, compare your answers with those provided at the end of the Study Guide chapter. Review the text for those terms you don't know and those you define incorrectly.

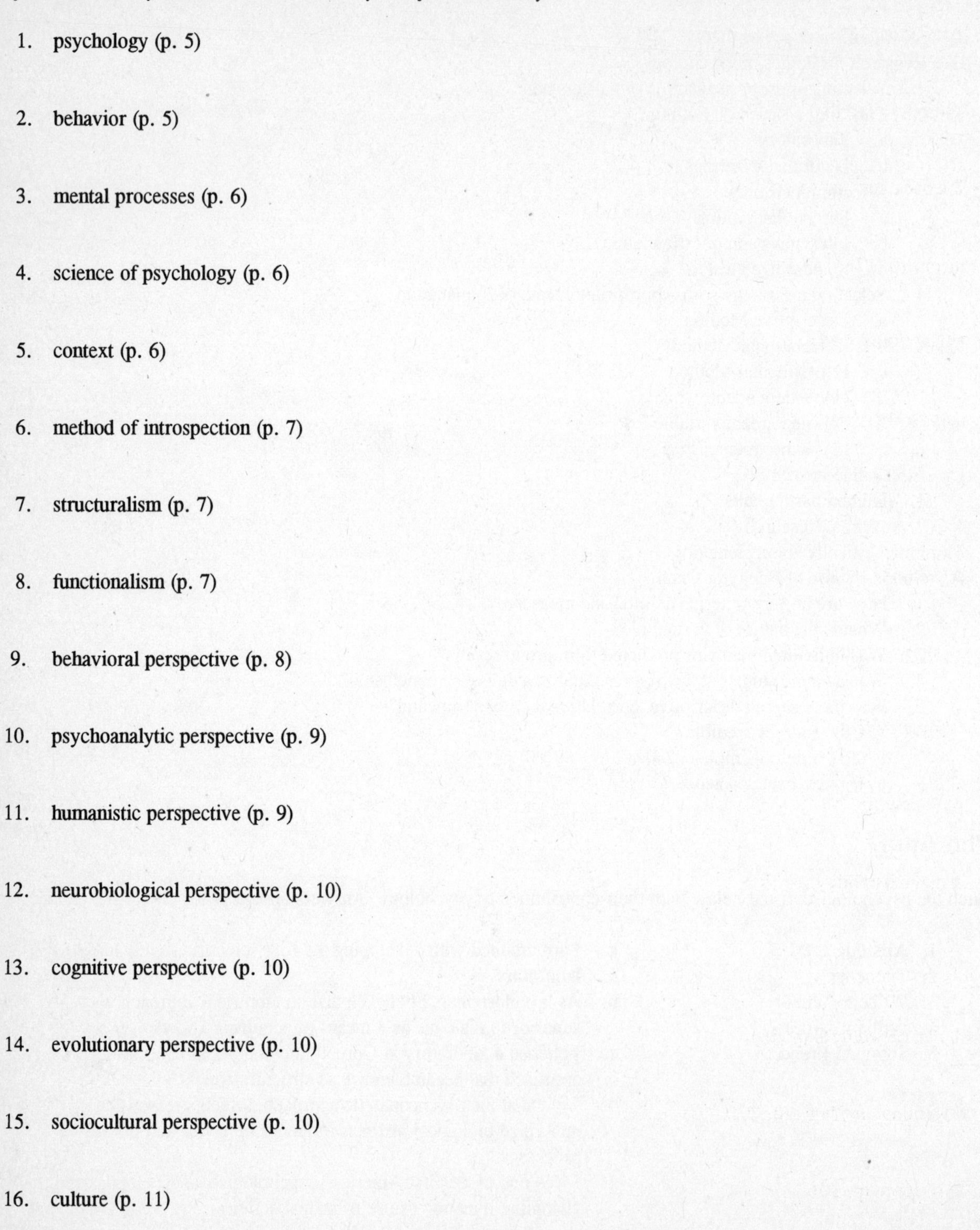

1. psychology (p. 5)

2. behavior (p. 5)

3. mental processes (p. 6)

4. science of psychology (p. 6)

5. context (p. 6)

6. method of introspection (p. 7)

7. structuralism (p. 7)

8. functionalism (p. 7)

9. behavioral perspective (p. 8)

10. psychoanalytic perspective (p. 9)

11. humanistic perspective (p. 9)

12. neurobiological perspective (p. 10)

13. cognitive perspective (p. 10)

14. evolutionary perspective (p. 10)

15. sociocultural perspective (p. 10)

16. culture (p. 11)

17. ethnicity (p. 11)

18. ethnic identity (p. 11)

19. gender (p. 11)

20. psychiatry (p. 13)

21. scientific method (p. 17)

22. theory (p. 17)

23. hypotheses (p. 17)

24. data (p. 17)

25. sample (p. 18)

26. population (p. 18)

27. random sample (p. 18)

28. laboratory (p. 18)

29. interview (p. 19)

30. social desirability (p. 19)

31. questionnaire (p. 19)

32. standardized tests (p. 20)

33. descriptive methods (p. 20)

34. case study (p. 20)

35. correlational method (p. 21)

36. experimental method (p. 21)

37. experiment (p. 22)

38. random assignment (p. 22)

39. experimental group (p. 22)

40. control group (p. 22)

41. baseline (p. 22)

42. independent variable (p. 22)

43. dependent variable (p. 22)

44. placebo effect (p. 23)

45. experimenter bias (p. 23)

46. double-blind study (p. 24)

47. replication (p. 24)

48. informed consent (p. 24)

49. deception (p. 24)

50. debriefing (p. 24)

51. skepticism (p. 26)

52. astrology (p. 27)

53. pseudopsychology (p. 28)

54. graphology (p. 28)

Guided Review

The following in-depth chapter review is a challenging and comprehensive fill-in-the-blanks exercise. The answers are found near the end of the chapter. As you go through the exercise, try to resist the temptation to look at the answers until you have provided them. When you have filled in all the blanks, you will have a thorough summary of the chapter for reference and review.

Psychology is the scientific study of ___(1)___ and ___(2)___ processes in context. "Behavior" is everything we do that can be directly ___(3)___. The private experiences of thoughts, feelings, and motives are referred to as ___(4)___ ________. The interpretations of observed behavior are called ___(5)___. As a science, psychology uses ___(6)___ methods to observe, describe, explain, and predict behavior. ___(7)___ refers to historical, economic, social, and cultural influences on behavior.

Psychology emerged as a science in the late nineteenth century, after being influenced by Greek philosophers such as ___(8)___ and Aristotle. In the sixteenth century, Francis Bacon promoted the need for scientific observations that could be ___(9)___.

In 1879, ___(10)___ ________ developed the first scientific psychology laboratory. Wundt advocated an approach in which trained people systematically observe and analyze their own mental experiences. This method is called ___(11)___. In the United States, Titchener advocated an approach that became known as ___(12)___. This approach emphasized the importance of conscious thought and classification of the mind's ___(13)___.

In the United States, William James promoted ___(14)___, an approach that emphasized the study of the functions of the mind and behavior in ___(15)___ to the environment.

Two distinct branches of psychology that evolved in the early twentieth century were (1) those emphasizing experimental psychology, referred to as "___(16)___," and (2) those emphasizing clinical and applied psychology, referred to as "___(17)___-________." A group of psychologists, including ___(18)___ ________, argued that psychologists should observe behavior directly and not make inferences about mental processes; this approach was called ___(19)___. In the early part of the twentieth century, soft-hearted psychologists became taken with the clinical methods of Sigmund ___(20)___.

Contemporary Perspectives

The following seven perspectives have dominated contemporary psychology: (1) the ___(21)___ perspective emphasizes the scientific study of observable behavioral responses and their environmental determinants; (2) the ___(22)___ perspective emphasizes the unconscious aspects of the mind, conflict between instincts and society's demands, and early family experiences; (3) the ___(23)___ perspective emphasizes the capacity for personal growth and personal freedom; (4) the ___(24)___ perspective emphasizes the importance of the brain and nervous system in understanding behavior, thought, and emotion; (5) the ___(25)___ perspective emphasizes the importance of adaptation, reproduction and "survival of the fittest."; (6) the cognitive perspective emphasizes the mental processes involved in ___(26)___; and (7) the ___(27)___ perspective emphasizes the importance of culture, ethnicity, and gender, as well as other sociocultural factors.

The behavior patterns, beliefs, and other products of a particular group of people are referred to as ___(28)___. ___(29)___ is based on cultural heritage, nationality characteristics, race, religion, and language. A sense of membership based on shared language, religion, customs, and so on is called ___(30)___ ________. ___(31)___ is the sociocultural dimension of being female or male.

Practicing Psychology

The most widely practiced specialization in psychology is clinical and ___(32)___ psychology. A branch of medicine that specializes in abnormal behavior and therapy is ___(33)___. Precise experimental strategies are followed by those in the fields of ___(34)___ psychology. Neuroscientists and ___(35)___ psychologists study the role of the brain and nervous system in determining behavior. Psychologists who study behavior and mental processes from conception to death are ___(36)___ psychologists. The study of people's interactions, relationships, attitudes, and group behavior is called ___(37)___ psychology. ___(38)___-________ psychology studies the role of culture in understanding behavior, thought, and emotion. The psychology of ___(39)___ promotes research and therapy with women. ___(40)___ and ______ psychology studies individuals and organizations in the workplace. Forensic psychologists work in the ___(41)___ arena. Children's learning and adjustment is a special concern of school and ___(42)___ psychology. A ___(43)___ degree is a marketable degree for a wide range of jobs.

The Scientific Method

The approach used in psychology to discover accurate information or establish meaningful relations about mind and behavior is the ___(44)___ ________. The following steps are used in the scientific method: ___(45)___ a problem, ___(46)___ a tentative explanation, collect ___(47)___, draw ___(48)___, and confirm or revise ___(49)___. A coherent set of ideas that helps to explain data and to make predictions is a ___(50)___. A theory has ___(51)___, which are assumptions that can be tested to determine their accuracy. Psychologists use the information they have collected from their systematic observations, called ___(52)___, to confirm or disconfirm a hypothesis.

Research Strategies in Psychology

An important research question relates to the selection of ___(53)___. The group actually being studied is called the ___(54)___. The complete group from which the sample is selected is called a ___(55)___. In conducting research, the participants must represent the group to be described. Psychologists accomplish this task by using a ___(56)___, a group of participants selected by a process in which every member of a population or group has an equal chance of being selected. If researchers do not use a random sample, they may not be able to ___(57)___ their results to the general population.

Conducting research in laboratories allows ___(58)___ of many of the complex factors of the real world. Among the drawbacks of laboratory research are these: Participants know they are being studied, the unnatural setting might cause the participants to behave ___(59)___, and some aspects of mind and behavior are difficult or impossible to examine in the laboratory. When behavior is observed in real-world settings, with no effort made to control the situation, this research method is called ___(60)___ observation.

Psychological researchers obtain systematic information through a variety of techniques, including direct ___(61)___ and asking questions in an interview. A possible shortcoming of an interview is the tendency of participants to tell the interviewer what they think is socially acceptable; this is referred to as ___(62)___ ________. A technique that is similar to interviews except that respondents read questions and mark their answers is called a ___(63)___ or survey. Standardized tests represent another technique to collect data. With these tests, an individual's overall score is totaled to produce a ___(64)___ score. Then the individual's score is compared to the scores of large numbers of others. Standardized scores are often reported in ___(65)___. Standardized tests provide information about ___(66)___ among people.

Descriptive research methods involve ___(67)___ and ___(68)___ descriptions of behavior. A descriptive technique used mainly by clinical psychologists is called the ___(69)___ ________. It is used when the unique aspects of a persons life cannot be ___(70)___. The goal of ___(71)___ research is to describe the strength of the relationship between two or more events or characteristics. When two variables correlate, it does not mean that one variable ___(72)___ the other. The only research methods that allow researchers to determine the cause of behavior are ___(73)___ research methods. A carefully regulated procedure in which researchers manipulate one or more of the factors and hold all the other factors constant is an ___(74)___. In experimental research, random assignment occurs when psychologists assign participants to experimental or control conditions by ___(75)___. The group whose experience is manipulated is the ___(76)___ group, while the comparison group is called the ___(77)___ group. In an experiment the manipulated, influential factor is called the ___(78)___ variable, while the factor that is measured is called the ___(79)___ variable. When participants' expectations rather than the experimental treatment produce the desired outcome, this is called the ___(80)___ effect. If the researcher's own expectations influence the outcome of the research, ___(81)___ ________ has occurred. A possible solution to expectancy effects is to conduct research in which neither the participants nor the researchers know which participants are in the experimental or control groups; this approach is called a ___(82)___-_______ study. In order to confirm original findings, research studies should be repeated; that is, results should be ___(83)___.

Ethics in Research

The ___(84)___ treatment of human participants dictates that the best interest of these participants be kept foremost in the researcher's mind. All participants must understand what their participation will involve and any risks that might occur; that is, participants must give their ___(85)___ ________. Participants also retain the right to ___(86)___ from a study at any time. In cases of ___(87)___, psychologists must ensure that it will not be harmful to participants, and participants must be ___(88)___ as soon as possible. Psychologists are also concerned about the ethical treatment of

__(89)__. Although it is true that animal researchers sometimes use procedures that would be unethical with __(90)__, they are guided by a stringent set of standards regarding such issues as the housing, feeding, and psychological well-being of animals.

Thinking Critically About Behavior

In the absence of research evidence, psychologists react to broad claims about behavior with __(91)__. In order to make sense of claims about behavior, it is important to: find out how important terms are __(92)__ and measured; understand the nature of the __(93)__ before generalizing; avoid predicting individual behavior from __(94)__ results; resist interpreting the results of a single study as being __(95)__; differentiate research that is correlational versus __(96)__; evaluate the __(97)__ of the source; be skeptical of __(98)__ claims. According to the text, astrology is an example of a __(99)__. Another example of a pseudopsychology, which uses handwriting analysis to describe, explain, and predict behavior, is __(100)__.

Sociocultural Worlds/Applications in Psychology

In your own words, summarize the material you have read in Sociocultural Worlds 1.1, "Women and Ethnic Minorities in Psychology," and Applications in Psychology 1.1, "The Changing Tapestry of American Culture." Briefly describe how each of these articles relates to the information contained in the chapter.

Concept Check

Perspectives in Psychology

1. The behavioral perspective — emphasizes scientific study of observable responses.

2. The psychoanalytic perspective — ______________________________.

3. The __________ perspective — emphasizes the capacity for personal growth and freedom.

4. The neurobiological perspective — ______________________________.

5. The __________ perspective — emphasizes the importance of mental processes.

6. The evolutionary perspective — ______________________________.

7. The __________ perspective — emphasizes the importance of culture, ethnicity, and gender.

Answers

2. emphasizes unconscious thought, early experiences, and conflict between instincts and society's demands
3. humanistic
4. emphasizes the importance of the brain and nervous system in understanding behavior
5. cognitive
6. emphasizes the importance of adaptation, reproduction, and survival of the fittest.
7. sociocultural

Research Concepts

1.	With descriptive research methods	the goal is ______________________.
2.	In ________ ________	the goal is to describe the strength of the relationship between two or more variables.
3.	Experimental research	uses methods that ____________________.
4.	The ________ ________	is the group whose experience is manipulated.
5.	The control group	is ______________________________.
6.	The ________ ________	is the factor manipulated in the experiment.

Answers

1. to provide a systematic and objective description of behavior
2. correlational research
3. allow us to determine the causes of behavior
4. experimental group
5. the comparison group, treated in every way like the experimental group except for the manipulated factor
6. dependent variable

Multiple-Choice Questions

Practice Test 1

After answering all the multiple-choice questions in Practice Test 1, compare your answers with the answer key provided at the end of the chapter. The answer key contains a brief explanation of both the correct and incorrect answers. Each of these questions is keyed to the Learning Objectives for the chapter. If you answer any questions incorrectly, review the corresponding Learning Objective and text material before you proceed to Practice Test 2.

1. Which of the following parts of the definition of psychology refers to thoughts, feelings, and motives that cannot be directly observed?
   a. scientific study
   b. behavior
   c. mental processes
   d. context

LO 1

2. Which of the following contributors to psychology advocated the method of introspection?
   a. Aristotle
   b. Socrates
   c. Wundt
   d. John Watson

LO 2

3. Each of the following is a "soft-hearted" approach to psychology *except:*
   a. experimental psychology
   b. clinical psychology
   c. school psychology
   d. industrial/organizational psychology

LO 3

4. Which of the following perspectives emphasizes unconscious thought?
   a. the behavioral perspective
   b. the psychoanalytic perspective
   c. the neurobiological perspective
   d. the cognitive perspective

LO 4

5. Which of the following perspectives emphasizes thinking, knowledge, and attention?
   a. neurobiological
   b. sociocultural
   c. evolutionary
   d. cognitive

LO 4

6. Culture, ethnicity, and gender are important components of which perspective?
   a. neurobiological
   b. sociocultural
   c. evolutionary
   d. cognitive

LO 5

7. The most widely practiced specialization in psychology is _________ psychology.
   a. developmental
   b. experimental
   c. clinical and counseling
   d. school and educational

LO 6

8. Regarding careers in psychology, each of the following is true *except*
   a. A graduate degree is required for a successful career in psychology.
   b. An undergraduate degree in psychology can be a prelude to graduate study in business or law.
   c. A variety of job possibilities exist for those with bachelor's degrees in psychology.
   d. Job opportunities are increasingly available for ethnic minority psychologists.

LO 7

9. Which of the following is the first step used in the scientific method?
   a. drawing conclusions
   b. revising theory
   c. analyzing a problem
   d. collecting data

LO 8

10. Each of the following is true of using random samples *except*
   a. Every member of the population has an equal chance of being selected.
   b. It is an alternative to measuring every member of the population.
   c. It is useful when researchers want to know about a large population of people.
   d. When random samples are used in research generalizations can never be made.

LO 9

11. Each of the following is a drawback of laboratory research *except*
   a. Participants know they are being studied.
   b. The laboratory setting might produce unnatural behavior.
   c. Some problems can't be studied in a laboratory.
   d. Laboratory settings do not permit control over participants.

LO 10

12. Social desirability is a potential problem associated with
   a. questionnaires.
   b. standardized tests.
   c. interviews.
   d. *a* and *c* above.

LO 11

13. Which of the following approaches attempts to yield information regarding individual differences?
   a. questionnaires
   b. surveys
   c. standardized tests
   d. naturalistic observation

LO 11

14. The strength of the relationship between two or more events can be determined by
   a. experimental research.
   b. correlational research.
   c. random assignment.
   d. controlling the dependent variable.

LO 12

15. When a psychologist conducts a case study, it is a special type of which of the following research methods?
    a. descriptive
    b. correlational
    c. experimental
    d. cause-and-effect

LO 12

16. An experiment is conducted to determine the effect of different methods of instruction on student performance. What is the dependent variable?
    a. student performance
    b. different methods of instruction
    c. not enough information is provided
    d. both *a* and *b*

LO 13

17. How does the control group differ from the experimental group?
    a. Only the control group receives the independent variable.
    b. Only the control group receives the dependent variable.
    c. The control group does not receive the manipulated factor.
    d. The control group should have older, more mature participants.

LO 13

18. Each of the following is true regarding ethics in research *except*
    a. Colleges and universities have review boards that must approve proposed research plans.
    b. Deceiving participants is not permitted in psychological research.
    c. The American Psychological Association has developed a code of ethics for its members.
    d. All research participants must give their informed consent to participate in research.

LO 14

19. Critical thinking implies that it is important to react to dramatic claims about behavior with
    a. acceptance.
    b. skepticism.
    c. informed consent.
    d. tolerance for those who find the scientific method to be cumbersome.

LO 15

20. The text would consider each of the following an example of pseudopsychology *except*
    a. astrology.
    b. the psychic hotline.
    c. graphology.
    d. correlational research.

LO 16

Practice Test 2

The following multiple-choice questions also are keyed to the chapter Learning Objectives. If you answer any questions incorrectly, be sure to review the corresponding Learning Objective and text material.

1. Which of the following parts of the definition of psychology refers to interest in historical, economic, social, and cultural factors?
    a. scientific study
    b. behavior
    c. mental processes
    d. context

LO 1

2. The first scientific laboratory was opened by
    a. Aristotle.
    b. Titchener.
    c. Wundt.
    d. William James.

LO 2

3. Experimental psychologists who engage in research in order to generate knowledge are sometimes referred to as
   a. hard-hearted.
   b. hard-headed.
   c. soft-hearted.
   d. soft-headed.

LO 3

4. Which of the following perspectives emphasizes the capacity for personal growth and the freedom to choose one's destiny?
   a. the behavioral approach
   b. the psychoanalytic approach
   c. the humanistic approach
   d. the neurobiological approach

LO 4

5. The role of the brain and nervous system in understanding behavior is of special interest to which perspective?
   a. the behavioral perspective
   b. the psychoanalytic perspective
   c. the humanistic perspective
   d. the neurobiological perspective

LO 4

6. The behavior patterns, beliefs, and other products of a group of people refers to
   a. culture.
   b. gender.
   c. ethnicity.
   d. ethnic identity.

LO 5

7. What is the difference between a psychologist and a psychiatrist?
   a. about $25 an hour
   b. They treat different people with widely different kinds of problems.
   c. Psychiatrists have medical backgrounds, whereas psychologists have graduate training in psychology.
   d. Clinical psychologists can prescribe medication, whereas psychiatrists cannot.

LO 6

8. An undergraduate degree in psychology can be useful to students who intend to
   a. pursue a graduate degree in business or law.
   b. work as a drug abuse counselor.
   c. work in sales.
   d. all of the above

LO 7

9. After developing a hypothesis, which of the following is the next step in using the scientific method?
   a. analyzing a problem
   b. collecting data
   c. drawing conclusions
   d. revising theories

LO 8

10. The procedure by which every member of a population has an equal chance of being selected is called
   a. a biased sample.
   b. a random sample.
   c. an independent variable.
   d. descriptive research.

LO 9

11. If you were to sit in the lobby of the student center and take notes on different students' hand gestures as they spoke, which research method would you be using?
   a. naturalistic observation
   b. case study
   c. correlational methods
   d. experimental methods

LO 10

12. The Stanford Binet and the MMPI are examples of
   a. questionnaires.
   b. surveys
   c. standardized tests.
   d. correlational research.

LO 11

13. Clinical psychologists, involved in the unique aspects of an individual's life, are most likely to use which method?
 a. case study
 b. correlational research
 c. survey
 d. casual observation

LO 12

14. Members of an experimental group
 a. receive the independent variable.
 b. receive the correlational variable.
 c. have been randomly assigned.
 d. both *a* and *c*

LO 13

15. Researchers who explain to participants any risks that might develop in the research are following the ethical principle of
 a. informed consent.
 b. avoiding deception.
 c. full disclosure.
 d. debriefing.

LO 14

16. According to Neal Miller, our knowledge about rehabilitating neuromuscular disorders can be attributed to the use of
 a. deceptive research techniques.
 b. completely debriefing participants.
 c. occasionally deceiving participants.
 d. research animals.

LO 14

17. When small samples are used in psychological research, consumers of the knowledge should avoid the temptation to
 a. confuse correlation with causation.
 b. overgeneralize.
 c. assume credibility from questionable sources.
 d. all of the above.

LO 15

18. Making sense out of claims about behavior includes distinguishing between correlational research as opposed to research that is
 a. experimental
 b. pseudoscientific.
 c. observational.
 d. descriptive.

LO 15

19. A pseudopsychology that uses handwriting analysis to describe, explain and predict behavior is called
 a. graphology.
 b. psychic analysis.
 c. clairvoyance.
 d. telepathy.

LO 16

20. According to the text, each of the following is a pseudopsychology *except*
 a. graphology.
 b. astrology.
 c. the psychic hotline.
 d. systematic observation.

LO 16

Answers to Who Am I? Quiz

1. b 2. c 3. a 4. e 5. d

Answers to Key Terms

1. **Psychology** is the scientific study of behavior and mental processes in context.
2. **Behavior** refers to everything we do that can be directly observed.
3. **Mental processes** are the private thoughts, feelings, and experiences each of us experiences.
4. The term **science of psychology** refers to the fact that psychologists use systematic methods to observe, explain, and predict behavior.

5. **Context** refers to the historical, economic, social, and cultural factors that influence mental processes and behavior.
6. **Introspection** is a technique used by Wundt and others in which specially trained people systematically observe and analyze their own mental experience.
7. **Structuralism** is an early theory of psychology developed by Wundt that emphasized classifying sensations in order to establish the mind's structures.
8. **Functionalism** is an early theory of psychology developed by William James. According to this theory, the role of psychology is to study the functions of the mind and behavior in adapting to the environment.
9. The **behavioral perspective** emphasizes the scientific study of observable behavior and the environmental conditions that produce behavior.
10. The **psychoanalytic perspective** emphasizes unconscious thought, conflict between biological instincts and the demands of society, and early family experiences.
11. The **humanistic perspective** emphasizes the individual's capacity for personal growth, freedom, and positive qualities.
12. The **neurobiological perspective** emphasizes the roles played by the brain and the central nervous system.
13. The **cognitive perspective** emphasizes the mental processes involved in knowing.
14. The **evolutionary perspective** emphasizes the importance of adaptation, reproduction and "survival of the fittest."
15. The **sociocultural perspective** emphasizes the roles played by culture, ethnicity, and gender in understanding behavior, thought, and emotion
16. **Culture** refers to the behavior patterns, beliefs, and other products of a particular group of people that are passed on from generation to generation.
17. **Ethnicity** is based on cultural heritage, nationality characteristics, race, religion, and language.
18. **Ethnic identity** refers to identification based on membership in an ethnic group.
19. **Gender** is the sociocultural dimension of being female or male.
20. **Psychiatry** is practiced by physicians (M.D.'s) who specialize in treating abnormal behavior and who engage in psychotherapy.
21. The **scientific method,** as employed in psychology, is used to discover accurate information about behavior. It incudes identifying and analyzing the problem, developing tentative explanations, collecting data, drawing conclusions, and confirming or revising theories.
22. A **theory** is a coherent set of ideas that helps to explain data and helps to make predictions.
23. **Hypotheses** are assumptions that can be tested to determine their accuracy.
24. **Data** is information gathered through systematic observation.
25. A **sample** is a group of organisms (human or animal) being studied.
26. A **population** is the complete group of organisms from which a sample is selected.
27. In a **random sample** every member of a population or group has an equal chance of being selected.
28. **Laboratories** are controlled settings where many of the complex factors of the "real world" have been removed.
29. An **interview** is a descriptive method in which questions are asked directly to an individual to find out about the person's experiences and attitudes.
30. **Social desirability** is a factor that leads interview participants to tell interviewers what they believe to be socially desirable rather than what they really think or feel.
31. A **questionnaire** is a type of structured interview in which respondents read questions and mark their answers on paper.
32. A **standardized test** yields a single score that tells something about the individual and compares that individual's scores to the scores of a large group.
33. **Descriptive methods** are techniques designed to provide an accurate portrayal of behavior using systematic and objective descriptipons of behavior.
34. A **case study** is an in-depth look at a single individual; it is mainly used by clinical psychologists.
35. The purpose of the **correlational method** is to describe the strength of the relationship between two or more events or characteristics.
36. The **experimental method** allows researchers to determine the causes of behavior.
37. An **experiment** is a carefully regulated procedure in which researchers manipulate one or more factors believed to influence the behavior being studied and hold all other factors constant.
38. **Random assignment** occurs when researchers assign subjects to experimental and control groups by chance.

39. The **experimental group** is the group in an experiment whose experience is manipulated.
40. The **control group** is a comparison group that is treated in every way like the experimental group except for the manipulated factor.
41. The **baseline** is used as a basis for comparison. It depicts behavior in the absence of the manipulated factor.
42. The **independent variable** is the manipulated factor in an experiment.
43. The **dependent variable** is the factor that is measured in an experiment.
44. The **placebo effect** occurs when participant's expectations, rather than the experimental treatment, produce the desired outcome.
45. **Experimenter bias** occurs when the researcher's own expectations influence the outcome of the research.
46 In a **double-blind study**, neither the participants nor the researchers are aware of which participants are in the experimental group or the control group.
47. **Replication** refers to repeating research studies in order to confirm the original research findings.
48. **Informed consent** means participants have the right to know what their participation will involve and whether there is any risk.
49. **Deception** refers to intentionally misleading a participant about the purpose of the research.
50. Researchers must provide a **debriefing** for participants, that is explain the complete nature of the study to participants as soon as possible.
51 **Skepticism** is the tendency to doubt the validity of claims in the absence of evidence.
52. **Astrology** uses the positions of the stars and planets at the time of a person's birth to describe, explain and predict his or her behavior.
53 **Pseudopsychology** is a nonscientific system that resembles psychology but lacks scientific support.
54 **Graphology** is the use of handwriting analysis to describe, explain and predict behavior.

Answers to Guided Review

1. behavior (p. 5)
2. mental (p. 5)
3. observed (p. 5)
4. mental processes (p. 5)
5. inferences (p. 6)
6. systematic (p. 6)
7. Context (p. 6)
8. Socrates (p. 7)
9. tested (p. 7)
10. Wilhelm Wundt (p. 7)
11. introspection (p. 7)
12. structuralism (p. 7)
13. structures (p. 7)
14. functionalism (p. 7)
15. adapting (p. 7)
16. hardheaded (p. 7)
17. soft-hearted (p. 7)
18. John Watson (p. 9)
19. behaviorism (p. 9)
20. Freud (p. 9)
21. behavioral (p. 9)
22. psychoanalytic (p. 9)
23. humanistic (p. 9)
24. neurobiological (p. 10)
25. evolutionary (p. 10)
26. knowing (p. 10)
27. sociocultural (p. 10)
28. culture (p. 11)
29. Ethnicity (p. 11)
30. ethnic identity (p. 11)
31. gender (p. 11)
32. counseling (p. 13)
33. psychiatry (p. 13)
34. experimental (p. 13)
35. physiological (p. 13)
36. developmental (p. 14)
37. social (p. 14)
38. cross-cultural (p. 15)
39. women (p. 15)
40. Industrial/organizational (p. 15)
41. legal (p. 15)
42. educational (p. 15)
43. bachelor's (p. 16)
44. scientific method (p. 17)
45. analyze (p. 17)
46. formulate (p. 17)
47. data (p. 17)
48. conclusions (p. 17)
49. theory (p. 17)
50. theory (p. 17)
51. hypotheses (p. 17)
52. data (p. 17)
53. participants (p. 18)
54. sample (p. 18)
55. population (p. 18)
56. random sample (p. 18)
57. generalize (p. 18)
58. control (p. 18)
59. unnaturally (p. 18)
60. naturalistic (p. 19)
61. observation (p. 19)
62. social desirability (p. 19)
63. questionnaire (p. 19)
64. single (p. 20)
65. percentiles (p. 20)
66. differences (p. 20)
67. systematic (p. 20)
68. objective (p. 20)
69. case study (p. 20)
70. duplicated (p. 20)
71. correlational (p. 21)

72. causes (p. 21)
73. experimental (p. 21)
74. experiment (p. 22)
75. chance (p. 22)
76. experimental (p. 22)
77. control (p. 22)
78. independent (p. 22)
79. dependent (p. 22)
80. placebo (p. 23)
81. experimenter bias (p. 23)
82. double-blind (p. 24)
83. replicable (p. 24)
84. ethical (p. 24)
85. informed consent (p. 24)
86. withdraw (p. 24)
87. deception (p. 24)
88. debriefed (p. 24)
89. animals (p. 25)
90. humans (p. 25)
91. skepticism (p. 26)
92. defined (p. 26)
93. sample (p. 26)
94. group (p. 26)
95. definitive (p. 26)
96. experimental (p. 26)
97. credibility (p. 27)
98. simplistic (p. 27)
99. pseudoscience (p. 28)
100. graphology (p. 28)

Answers to Multiple Choice Questions- Practice Test 1

1. a. Incorrect. Although "scientific study" is part of the definition of psychology, it refers to the fact that psychologists use systematic methods to observe, describe, explain, and predict behavior.
   b. Incorrect. Although "behavior" is part of the definition of psychology, it refers to everything we do that can be observed.
   c. **Correct.** Mental processes include thoughts, feelings and motives that are part of our private experiences.
   d. Incorrect. Although context is part of the definition of psychology, it refers to the historical, economic, social and cultural factors that influence mental processes and behavior.

2. a. Incorrect. Aristotle was a Greek philosopher who urged the use of logic in making inferences about behavior and the use of systematic observation.
   b. Incorrect. Socrates was a Greek philosopher who encouraged people to understand themselves.
   c. **Correct.** Wundt, considered by most historians to have opened the first scientific laboratory to study behavior, urged introspection, in which specially trained people systematically observe and analyze their own mental experiences.
   d. Incorrect. John Watson believed psychologists should focus on the direct observation of behavior, rather than inferences about behavior.

3. a. **Correct.** Experimental psychology, with its emphasis on research, represents a "hard-headed" approach to psychology.
   b. Incorrect. Clinical psychology is an example of a "soft-hearted" approach to psychology, which emphasizes helping others.
   c. Incorrect. School psychology is an example of a "soft-hearted" approach to psychology, which emphasizes helping others.
   d. Incorrect. I/O psychology is an example of a "soft-hearted" approach to psychology, which emphasizes helping others.

4. a. Incorrect. The behavioral perspective emphasizes the scientific study of observable behavior.
   b. **Correct.** The psychoanalytic perspective emphasizes unconscious thought, the conflict between biological instincts and societal demands, and the importance of early family experiences.
   c. Incorrect. The neurobiological perspective emphasizes the role of the brain and nervous system in behavior, thought and emotion.
   d. Incorrect. The cognitive perspective emphasizes the mental processes involved in "knowing": attentional processes, perceptual processes, memory processes, and so on.

5. a. Incorrect. The neurobiological perspective emphasizes the role of the brain and nervous system in behavior, thought and emotion.
   b. Incorrect. The sociocultural perspective emphasizes the role of culture, gender, and ethnicity in understanding behavior.
   c. Incorrect. The evolutionary perspective emphasizes the importance of adaptation, reproduction, and "survival of the fittest."
   d. **Correct.** A cognitive psychologist views the mind as an active and aware problem-solving system.

6. a. Incorrect. The neurobiological perspective emphasizes the role of the brain and nervous system in behavior, thought and emotion.
   b. **Correct.** The sociocultural perspective emphasizes the role of culture, gender, and ethnicity in understanding behavior.
   c. Incorrect. The evolutionary perspective emphasizes the importance of adaptation, reproduction, and "survival of the fittest."
   d. Incorrect. The cognitive perspective is primarily concerned with the processes involved in "knowing"; such processes include attention, perception and memory.

7. a. Incorrect. Developmental psychologists study the process of development from conception to death.
   b. Incorrect. Experimental psychologists engage in pure research, often in the areas of learning, memory, sensation and perception.
   c. **Correct.** This area of specialization involves diagnosing and treating people with psychological problems.
   d. Incorrect. This area is concerned with learning and adjustment in the school environment.

8. a. **Correct.** Although not absolutely necessary for a career in psychology, a graduate degree can greatly expand opportunities in psychology.
   b. Incorrect. Although this alternative is true, the question is asking for an *untrue* statement.
   c. Incorrect. Although this alternative is true, the question is asking for an *untrue* statement.
   d. Incorrect. Although this alternative is true, the question is asking for an *untrue* statement.

9. a. Incorrect. According to the text, this is the fourth step in the scientific method.
   b. Incorrect. According to the text, this is the final step in the scientific method.
   c. **Correct.** The first step consists of both identifying and analyzing a problem.
   d. Incorrect. According to the text, this is the third step in the scientific method.

10. a. Incorrect. Although this alternative is true, the question is asking for an *untrue* statement.
    b. Incorrect. Although this alternative is true, the question is asking for an *untrue* statement.
    c. Incorrect. Although this alternative is true, the question is asking for an *untrue* statement.
    d. **Correct.** Generalizations can be made, but the random sample must be carefully drawn.

11. a. Incorrect. This statement *does* reflect a drawback of laboratory research.
    b. Incorrect. This statement *does* reflect a drawback of laboratory research.
    c. Incorrect. This statement *does* reflect a drawback of laboratory research.
    d. **Correct.** The biggest advantage to laboratory research is the control it allows researchers.

12. a. Incorrect. Although this statement it true, it not the best alternative.
    b. Incorrect. Social desirability is not listed in the text as a problem with standardized tests.
    c. Incorrect. Although this statement is true, it is not the best alternative.
    d. **Correct.** Social desirability interferes with the ability of interviews or questionnaires to collect accurate information.

13. a. Incorrect. Questionnaires are typically designed to yield information about the beliefs or behavior of large numbers of people.
    b. Incorrect. Surveys are typically designed to yield information about the beliefs or behavior of large numbers of people.
    c. **Correct.** These tests compare an individual's score with the scores of large numbers of others.
    d. Incorrect. Naturalistic observation has as its goal the observation of behavior in natural settings.

14. a. Incorrect. The goal of experimental research is the cause-and-effect of behavior.
    b. **Correct.** The more closely two events are correlated, the more effectively one can predict the other.
    c. Incorrect. Random assignment refers to the manner in which participants are assigned to experimental groups.
    d. Incorrect. The dependent variable refers to the variable that is measured in an experiment.

15. a. **Correct.** Case studies are used mainly by clinical psychologists when the unique aspects of a person's life cannot be duplicated.
    b. Incorrect. Correlational research seeks to describe the relationship between two variables.
    c. Incorrect. Experimental research seeks to discover the cause-and-effect of behavior.
    d. Incorrect. The cause-and-effect of behavior is determined by using the experimental method.

16. a. **Correct.** The dependent variable is the factor that is measured. In this experiment, student performance depends on which method of instruction participants receive.
    b. Incorrect. In this experiment, different methods of instruction constitute the independent variable. This variable is controlled by the researchers.
    c. Incorrect. Review the material on independent and dependent variables.
    d. Incorrect. One of these alternatives is the independent variable and one is the dependent variable.

17. a. Incorrect. Actually, the control group does *not* receive the independent variable.
    b. Incorrect. All groups receive the dependent variable.
    c. **Correct.** The control group is a comparison group, treated like the experimental group in every way, except that members of the control group do not receive the independent variable.
    d. Incorrect. The control group, as well as the experimental group, should have its membership randomly assigned.

18. a. Incorrect. Although this alternative is true, the question is asking for an *untrue* answer.
    b. **Correct.** Deception is permitted, although participants must not be harmed in any way by the deception. Participants also have a right to be immediately debriefed.
    c. Incorrect. Although this alternative is true, the question is asking for an *untrue* answer.
    d. Incorrect. Although this alternative is true, the question is asking for an *untrue* answer.

19 a. Incorrect. According to the text, critical thinking implies that we not rush to accept claims, particularly dramatic claims about behavior.
    b. **Correct.** Skepticism is the tendency to doubt the validity of claims in the absence of evidence.
    c. Incorrect. Informed consent is a concept relating to ethical research, which gives participants the right to know what their participation involves.
    d. Incorrect. If the scientific method is cumbersome, critical thinkers believe it is a legitimate way to collect truthful information about behavior.

20. a. Incorrect. Although this alternative is true, the question is asking for an *untrue* answer.
    b. Incorrect. Although this alternative is true, the question is asking for an *untrue* answer.
    c. Incorrect. Although this alternative is true, the question is asking for an *untrue* answer.
    d. **Correct.** When it is properly conducted, and when the results are not confused with cause-and-effect, correlational research is a useful form of scientific inquiry.

Answers to Multiple Choice Questions- Practice Test 2

1. a. Incorrect. Scientific study implies psychologists use systematic methods to observe, describe, explain and predict behavior.
   b. Incorrect. Behavior refers to everything we do that can be observed.
   c. Incorrect. Mental processes encompass thoughts, feelings and motives; these cannot be observed directly.
   d. **Correct.** Context reminds us that our behavior and mental processes are influenced by where we come form, what has happened to us in the past, and what we think might happen to us in the future.

2. a. Aristotle was a Greek philosopher who urged the importance of systematic observation, but he never got around to opening a scientific laboratory.
   b. Incorrect. Titchener opened a laboratory at Cornell University, but, alas, it was not the *first* laboratory.
   c. **Correct.** In 1879, in Leipzig, Germany, Wundt opened the first scientific laboratory dedicated to studying behavior.
   d. Incorrect. William James is credited with authoring the first psychology textbook, published in 1890.

3. a. Incorrect. Hard-hearted people probably are not interested in learning much about other people and their behavior.
   b. **Correct.** This term is occasionally used to represent those who seek to generate knowledge through research.
   c. Incorrect. This term refers to psychologists who use the principles of psychology to help others in clinical and applied settings.
   d. Incorrect. I'm not sure what this term refers to, other than an insult!

4. a. Incorrect. The behavioral perspective emphasizes the scientific study of observable behavioral responses and their environmental determinants.
   b. Incorrect. This perspective emphasizes unconscious thought, the conflict between biological instincts and societal demands, and the importance of early family experiences.
   c. **Correct.** This perspective suggests people have the ability to control their lives rather than being manipulated by the environment.
   d. Incorrect. This perspective focuses on the physical basis of thoughts, behavior and emotion.

5. a. Incorrect. The behavioral perspective emphasizes the scientific study of observable behavioral responses and their environmental determinants.
   b. Incorrect. This perspective emphasizes unconscious thought, the conflict between biological instincts and societal demands, and the importance of early family experiences.
   c. Incorrect. This perspective suggests people have the ability to control their lives, rather than being manipulated by the environment.
   d. **Correct.** This perspective focuses on the physical basis of thoughts, behavior and emotion.

6. a. **Correct.** The culture of a group influences the identity, learning, and social behavior of its members.
   b. Incorrect. This refers to the sociocultural dimension of being a female or male.
   c. Incorrect. This is based on one's cultural heritage, nationality, race, religion, and language.
   d. Incorrect. This refers to identification based upon membership in an ethnic group.

7. a. Incorrect. Witty (at least in the opinion of the author), but incorrect.
   b. Incorrect. Actually, psychologists and psychiatrists tend to treat people with similar kinds of problems.
   c. **Correct.** One important consequence of this difference is that psychiatrists may prescribe medications for their patients.
   d. Incorrect. Actually, the reverse is true.

8. a. Incorrect. Although this alternative is correct, it is not the best answer.
   b. Incorrect. Although this alternative is correct, it is not the best answer.
   c. Incorrect. Although this alternative is correct, it is not the best answer.
   d. **Correct.** This supports the notion that, generally speaking, psychology is a marketable degree.

9. a. Incorrect. Identifying and analyzing a problem represent the first step in using the scientific method.
   b. **Correct.** After formulating hypotheses in the first step, collecting data to test the hypotheses forms the next step.
   c. Incorrect. After data are collected, the next step is to analyze the data and draw conclusions.
   d. Incorrect. The final step in using the scientific method involves confirming or revising theories.

10. a. Incorrect. Researchers seek to avoid any biases in the samples they use.
    b. **Correct.** A random sample implies that each member of the population has an equal chance of being drawn.
    c. Incorrect. This refers to the variable in an experiment that is controlled by the experimenter.
    d. Incorrect. Descriptive research involves techniques designed for the systematic and objective description of behavior.

11. a. **Correct.** Using naturalistic observation may help avoid the artificial behavior sometimes observed in a laboratory.
    b. Incorrect. Case studies involve an in depth look at one individual. This technique is used mainly by clinical psychologists.
    c. Incorrect. The goal of the correlational method is to describe the strength of the relation between two or more events.
    d. Incorrect. The experimental method allows psychologists to determine the causes of behavior. Since the research described in the question involves observation, rather than the manipulation of variables, this could not be the correct answer.

12. a. Incorrect. The Stanford-Binet is an intelligence test, and the MMPI is a personality test. These tests are used to compare an individual's score to the scores of large numbers of others.
    b. Incorrect. The Stanford-Binet is an intelligence test, and the MMPI is a personality test. These tests are used to compare an individual's score to the scores of large numbers of others.
    c. **Correct.** Another example of a standardized test is the Beck Depression Inventory.
    d. Incorrect. The Stanford-Binet is an intelligence test, and the MMPI is a personality test. These tests are used to compare an individual's score to the scores of large numbers of others.

13. a. **Correct.** This type of descriptive research is used when the unique aspects of an individual's life cannot be duplicated.
    b. Incorrect. The goal of the correlational method is to describe the relation between two or more events or characteristics.
    c. Incorrect. Surveys are structured interviews. A major advantage of surveys is that they can be given easily to large numbers of people.
    d. Incorrect. Casual observation is no more likely to be used by clinical psychologists than by any other type of psychologists.

14. a. Incorrect. Although this answer is true, it is not the best alternative.
    b. Incorrect. The correlational method is not used in conjunction with experimental groups.
    c. Incorrect. Although this answer is true, it is not the best alternative.
    d. **Correct.** Members of the experimental group are the ones whose experience is manipulated. Thus, they are randomly selected and they receive the independent variable.

15. a. **Correct.** Informed consent also implies participants have the right to know what their participation involves.
    b. Incorrect. Although this is an ethical principle, it does not apply to this question.
    c. Incorrect. Although this term may sound correct, researchers use a different term to describe the potential risks to participants.
    d. Incorrect. This refers to disclosing to participants the complete nature of the study as soon as possible after it is over.

16. a. Incorrect. According to Miller, our knowledge about treating neuromuscular disorders can be attributed to a different type of research technique.
    b. Incorrect. According to Miller, our knowledge about treating neuromuscular disorders can be attributed to a different type of research technique.
    c. Incorrect. According to Miller, our knowledge about treating neuromuscular disorders can be attributed to a different type of research technique.
    d. **Correct.** Among other areas where animal research has benefitted humans are alleviating the effects of stress and pain, testing drugs for anxiety and mental illness, and understanding drug addiction and relapse.

17. a. Incorrect. Although this is important for consumers of research to avoid, it doesn't apply specifically to the "small sample" problem.
    b. **Correct.** This caution applies particularly when the participants represent a narrowly defined sample.
    c. Incorrect. Although this is important for consumers of research to avoid, it doesn't apply specifically to the "small sample" problem.
    d. Incorrect. Although all the other choices represent important cautions, one choice in particular applies to the problem of small sample size.

18. a. **Correct.** Correlational research is often confused with experimental research. Only experimental research yields information about cause-and-effect.
    b. Incorrect. Although it is important to distinguish pseudoscientific claims from legitimate scientific claims, correlational research is most often confused with another type of research.
    c. Incorrect. Correlational research is most often confused with another type of research.
    d. Incorrect. Correlational research is most often confused with another type of research.

19. a. **Correct.** Although the there has been an increase in the use of graphology as a selection measure for employee screening, according to the text, graphology's claims are not supported by scientific evidence.
    b. Incorrect. This sounds like a pseudopsychology, but it has no real meaning.
    c. Incorrect. This is a psychic "skill", but is not related to handwriting analysis.
    d. Incorrect. This is a psychic "skill", but is not related to handwriting analysis.

20. a. Incorrect. Although this alternative is true, the question is asking for an *untrue* answer.
    b. Incorrect. Although this alternative is true, the question is asking for an *untrue* answer.
    c. Incorrect. Although this alternative is true, the question is asking for an *untrue* answer.
    d. **Correct.** Systematic observation is the hallmark of the scientific method, and therefore, is not a pseudopsychology.

Chapter **2** **Biological Foundations and the Brain**

Learning Objectives

After studying this chapter you should be able to:

1. Distinguish between nature and nurture and discuss the interaction between the two factors. (p. 36)

2. Describe the genetic perspective and explain the dominant-recessive genes principle. (p. 38)

3. Describe the evolutionary perspective and explain the concept of natural selection. (p. 41)

4. Distinguish between the following nervous system divisions: the central and the peripheral; the somatic and the autonomic; and the sympathetic and the parasympathetic. (p. 42)

5. Distinguish among afferent nerves, interneurons, and efferent nerves. (p. 43)

6. Describe the structure of a neuron, including the cell body, the dendrite, the axon, and the myelin sheath. (p. 44)

7. Discuss the transmission of a nerve impulse. (p. 46)

8. Describe synapses and discuss the significance of neurotransmitters. (p. 47)

9. Describe the structures and functions of areas within the hindbrain, the midbrain and the forebrain. (p. 50)

10. Identify the major structures of the cerebral cortex. (p. 54)

11. Describe the results of research regarding the split-brain, hemispheric specialization, and male-female brain differences. (p. 55)

12. Discuss the localization and integration of functions within the brain. (p. 61)

13. Describe the brain's plasticity and discuss the research on brain tissue implants. (p. 64)

14. Identify the techniques used by neuroscientists to study the brain. (p. 66)

Chapter Outline

I. Perspectives on Nature and Nurture
   A. The Genetic Perspective
      1. DNA
      2. Genes
   B. The Evolutionary Perspective
      1. Natural selection
      2. Evolutionary Psychology
II. The Brain and Nervous System
   A. Elegant Organization
      1. Central Nervous System (CNS)
         a. brain
         b. spinal cord
      2. Peripheral Nervous System (PNS)
         a. somatic nervous system
         b. autonomic nervous system
   B. Neural Transmission
      1. Neuron Pathways
         a. afferent nerves
         b. efferent nerves
         c. interneurons
      2. Structure of the Neuron
         a. cell body
         b. dendrite
         c. axon
         d. myelin sheath
      3. The Nerve Impulse
         a. resting potential
         b. action potential
         c. all-or-none principle
      4. Synapses
      5. Neurotransmitters
         a. dopamine
         b. serotonin
         c. endorphins
III. The Central Nervous System
   A. Hindbrain
      1. Medulla
      2. Cerebellum
      3. Pons
   B. Midbrain
      1. Reticular formation
      2. Basal ganglia
   C. Forebrain
      1. Thalamus
      2. Hypothalamus
      3. Endocrine system
      4. Limbic system
         a. amygdala
         b. hippocampus
      5. Cortex
         a. occipital lobe
         b. temporal lobe
         c. parietal lobe
         d. frontal lobe
   D. Split-brain Research and the Cerebral Hemispheres
      1. Hemispheric specialization
      2. His brain and her brain
   E. Localization and integration of function
IV. Brain Damage, Plasticity, and Repair
   A. The brain's Plasticity and Capacity for Repair
   B. Brain Tissue Implants
IV. Techniques to Study the Brain
   A. Electroencephalograph (EEG)
   B. Computer-assisted Tomography (CAT scan)
   C. Positron-emission tomography (PET scan)
   D. Magnetic Resonance Imaging (MRI)
   E. Superconducting quantum interference device (SQUID)

Key Terms

Write a brief description for each of the following terms. Where relevant, provide an original example or illustration of the term. Then, compare your answers with those provided at the end of the Study Guide chapter. Review the text for those terms you don't know and those you define incorrectly.

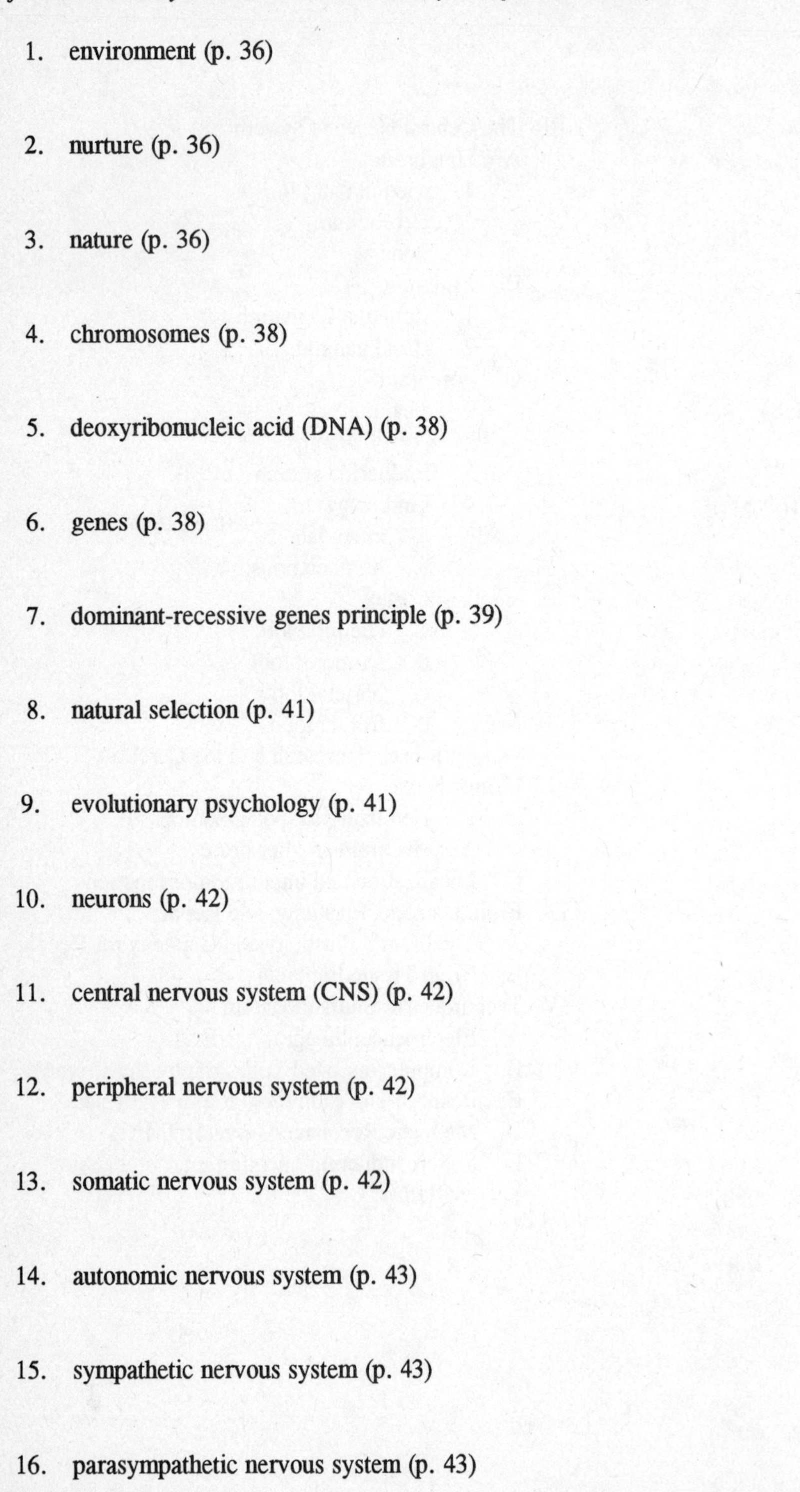

1. environment (p. 36)
2. nurture (p. 36)
3. nature (p. 36)
4. chromosomes (p. 38)
5. deoxyribonucleic acid (DNA) (p. 38)
6. genes (p. 38)
7. dominant-recessive genes principle (p. 39)
8. natural selection (p. 41)
9. evolutionary psychology (p. 41)
10. neurons (p. 42)
11. central nervous system (CNS) (p. 42)
12. peripheral nervous system (p. 42)
13. somatic nervous system (p. 42)
14. autonomic nervous system (p. 43)
15. sympathetic nervous system (p. 43)
16. parasympathetic nervous system (p. 43)

17. afferent nerves (p. 43)

18. efferent nerves (p. 43)

19. interneurons (p. 43)

20. cell body (p. 44)

21. dendrite (p. 46)

22. axon (p. 46)

23. myelin sheath (p. 46)

24. ions (p. 46)

25. resting potential (p. 46)

26. action potential (p. 47)

27. all-or-none principle (p. 47)

28. synapses (p. 47)

29. neurotransmitters (p. 47)

30. dopamine (p. 48)

31. serotonin (p. 48)

32. endorphins (p. 48)

33. hindbrain (p. 50)

34. medulla (p. 50)

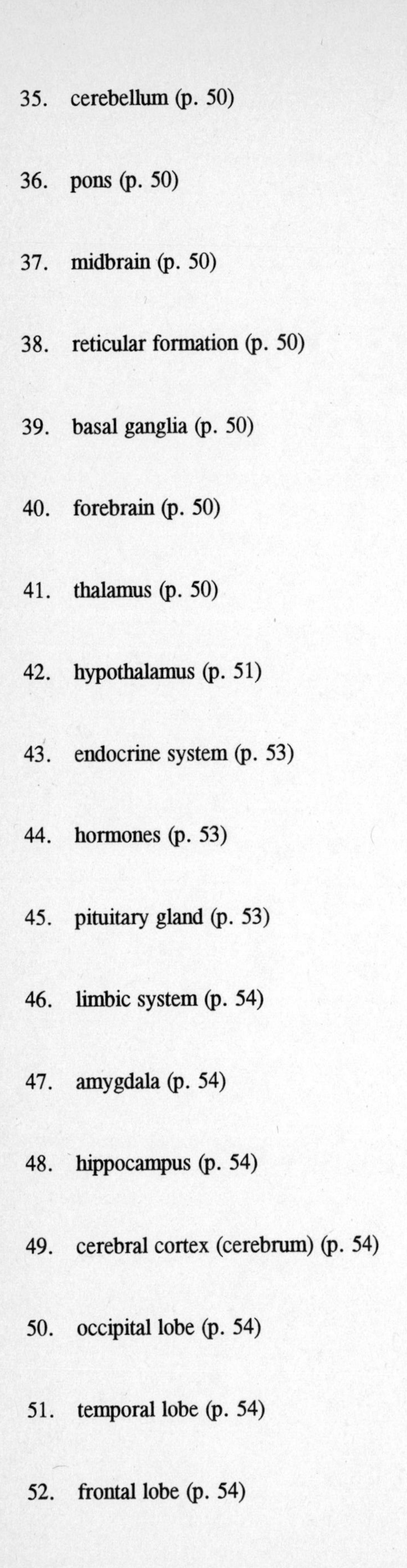

35. cerebellum (p. 50)

36. pons (p. 50)

37. midbrain (p. 50)

38. reticular formation (p. 50)

39. basal ganglia (p. 50)

40. forebrain (p. 50)

41. thalamus (p. 50)

42. hypothalamus (p. 51)

43. endocrine system (p. 53)

44. hormones (p. 53)

45. pituitary gland (p. 53)

46. limbic system (p. 54)

47. amygdala (p. 54)

48. hippocampus (p. 54)

49. cerebral cortex (cerebrum) (p. 54)

50. occipital lobe (p. 54)

51. temporal lobe (p. 54)

52. frontal lobe (p. 54)

53. parietal lobe (p. 54)

54. association cortex (p. 55)

55. corpus callosum (p. 55)

56. aphasia (p. 60)

57. phrenology (p. 61)

58. plasticity (p. 64)

59. brain implant (p. 64)

60. electroencephalograph (p. 66)

61. computer-assisted axial tomography (CAT scan) (p. 66)

62. positron-emission tomography (PET scan) (p. 66)

63. magnetic resonance imaging (MRI) (p. 67)

64. superconducting quantum interference device (SQUID) (p. 67)

Guided Review

The following in-depth chapter review is a challenging and comprehensive fill-in-the-blanks exercise. The answers are found near the end of the chapter. As you go through the exercise, try to resist the temptation to look at the answers until you have provided them When you have filled in all the blanks, you will have a thorough summary of the chapter for reference and review.

The surrounding conditions and influences that affect the development of living things is referred to as the ____(1)____. Psychologists refer to an organism's environmental experiences as ____(2)____ and an organism's biological inheritance as ____(3)____. Both nature and nurture ____(4)____with each other.

The study of the passage of inheritance from one generation to the next is ____(5)____. The nucleus of each human cell has 46 ____(6)____. Chromosomes are composed of molecules called ____(7)____. The units of hereditary information, found on DNA molecules, are called ____(8)____. According to the dominant-recessive genes principle, the ____(9)____ gene exerts its influence. A recessive gene exerts its influence only when the two genes of a pair are both ____(10)____. Each of us has at least ____(11)____ genes in our chromosomes. An international project designed to unlock the mysteries of human genetics is called the Human ____(12)____ Project.

Darwin referred to the evolutionary process that favors genes that are best adapted to survive and reproduce in a particular environment as ____(13)____ ________.

A contemporary perspective that emphasizes both evolution and psychological mechanisms in adaptive behavior is called ____(14)____ psychology. According to evolutionary psychologists, the human mind evolved as a collection of mechanisms that serve ____(15)____ functions.

The Nervous System

Scientists refer to the nerve cell, the basic unit of the nervous system, as a ____(16)____. The nervous system is divided into two parts: the central nervous system and the ____(17)____ nervous system. The central nervous system consists of the brain and ____(18)____ ________; the peripheral nervous system connects the brain and spinal cord to other parts of the body.

The peripheral nervous system consists of two major divisions: one, which contains both sensory nerves and motor nerves, is called the ____(19)____ nervous system. The other, which monitors breathing, heart rate, and digestion, is the ____(20)____ nervous system. The autonomic nervous system is divided into the sympathetic nervous system, which helps ____(21)____ the body, and the parasympathetic nervous system, which helps ____(22)____ the body.

The cells that carry input to the brain are called ____(23)____ neurons; the cells that carry the output from the brain are referred to as ____(24)____ neurons. Most of the brain consists of cells called ____(25)____.

The nucleus of a neuron can be found in the ____(26)____ ________. Information is collected for the neurons by the ____(27)____. Information is carried away from the cell body by the ____(28)____. Most axons are covered with a layer of insulating fat cells called the ____(29)____ ________. The axon terminates in small knobs called ____(30)____ buttons.

Neurons create electrical signals as electrically charged particles called ____(31)____ move back and forth through their membranes. ____(32)____ ________ refers to the stable, negative charge of an inactive neuron. Neurons send messages by creating a brief wave of electrical charge called an ____(33)____ ________. This charge conforms to the ____(34)____ principle.

As neural impulses reach the end of the axon, they face a gap between neurons called a ____(35)____. Impulses are able to cross the synapse by acting on a group of chemical substances called ____(36)____. A neurotransmitter that is related to movement, attention, learning and mental health is ____(37)____. An excess of the neurotransmitter dopamine is associated with ____(38)____. A neurotransmitter that is involved in the regulation of sleep is ____(39)____. Neurotransmitters that are involved in pleasure and in the control of pain are called ____(40)____.

The Central Nervous System

During embryological development, the central nervous system begins as a long, hollow ___(41)___.

The portion of the brain located at the rear of the skull is called the ___(42)___. The hindbrain contains the ___(43)___, which helps control breathing, and the ___(44)___, which is believed to help control movement. The ___(45)___ is a bridge in the hindbrain involved in sleep and arousal.

The midbrain is involved in the relay of information between the brain and the ___(46)___ and ___(47)___. Two important midbrain structures are the ___(48)___ formation and the ___(49)___ ganglia.

The highest region of the brain is called the ___(50)___. A forebrain structure that serves mainly as a relay station is called the ___(51)___. The forebrain structure that monitors eating, drinking, and sex is called the ___(52)___. Olds and Milner's rat research in the 1950s suggested the existence of a ___(53)___ ______ in the hypothalamus. Today, researchers agree that other areas of the brain are also involved in pleasure.

The hypothalamus also governs the release of chemical messengers called ___(54)___ via the endocrine system. The glands of the endocrine system release hormones directly into the ___(55)___. The endocrine gland that controls and regulates the other glands is the ___(56)___ gland.

The ___(57)___ system, a loosely connected network of structures under the cerebral cortex, plays important roles in memory and emotion. The limbic system consists of the amygdala and the ___(58)___. The amygdala is involved in ___(59)___; the hippocampus plays a role in the storage of ___(60)___.

The largest part of the brain is the ___(61)___ ______. The cerebral cortex is divided into two halves, called ___(62)___, and each is divided into four ___(62)___. The occipital lobe is involved with ___(64)___; hearing is associated with the ___(65)___ lobe; control of voluntary muscles is associated with the ___(66)___ lobe; the ___(67)___ lobe is involved in body sensations.

The research of Penfield and others has indicated that there is a point-to-point relation between a part of the body and a location on the ___(68)___.

More than 75 percent of the cerebrum is made up of the ___(69)___ ______. Association areas are responsible for thinking and ___(70)___ solving.

The two brain hemispheres are connected by the ___(71)___ ______. Researchers have found that the two hemispheres function somewhat independently. The left hemisphere mainly controls the ability to use ___(72)___.

Although many misconceptions exist regarding the functions of the left and right hemispheres, researchers believe that complex thinking involves ___(73)___ sides of the brain.

One theory suggests the male brain is more ___(74)___, while females use both hemispheres more ___(75)___. Support for this idea comes from the research finding that males are far more likely to develop ___(76)___ after strokes that cause damage to the left-hemisphere. Although some anatomical differences exist in the brains of males and females, there are far more ___(77)___ than differences.

An approach developed by Gall that argued that bumps on the skull were associated with personality and intelligence was called ___(78)___. Although different brain regions do have different functions, Gall assigned incorrect brain ____(79)____ to the different regions. Scientists today believe there is considerable ____(80)____ of function in the brain.

Brain Damage, Plasticity and Repair

The brain's capacity to modify and reorganize itself following damage is called ____(81)____. The brain shows the most plasticity in ____(82)____ ________before brain functions become entirely fixed. although neurons can't be regenerated, brain repair mechanisms include collateral ____(83)____ and ____(84)____ of function. Brain ____(85)____involve the implanting of healthy tissue into damaged brains. Brain grafts have a higher degree of success when brain tissue from the ____(86)____ stage is used. Brain grafts may hold promise in treating ____(87)____ disease and ____(88)____ disease.

Techniques for Studying the Brain

The use of high-powered microscopes allows scientists to study the ____(89)____ in great detail. The electrical activity of the brain is recorded by the ____(90)____. A three-dimensional image of the brain is provided by ____(91)____-________ ________, known as a CAT scan. The amount of specially treated glucose in various areas of the brain is measured by ____(92)____-________ tomography, or a PET scan. Another technique, which uses radio waves to construct images of brain tissues and biochemical activity, is called ____(93)____ ________ ________ (MRI). A brain-scanning device that sense tiny changes in magnetic fields is called the superconducting quantum ____(94)____ device (SQUID).

Sociocultural Worlds/Applications in Psychology

In your own words, summarize the material you have read in Sociocultural Worlds 2.1, "Race and Ethnicity," and Applications in Psychology 2.1, "The Brains of the Mankato Nuns." Briefly describe how each of these articles relates to the information in the chapter.

Concept Check

1. The central nervous system ______________________.
2. The ________ ________ ________ connects the brain and spinal cord to the rest of the body.
3. The somatic nervous system ______________________.
4. The ________ ________ ________ monitors breathing, heart rate, and digestion.
5. The sympathetic nervous system ______________________.
6. The ________ ________ ________ helps calm the body.
7. The hindbrain ______________________.
8. The ________ consists of ascending and descending nerve fiber systems, connecting the higher and lower portions of the brain.
9. The forebrain ______________________.

Answers

1. consists of the brain and spinal cord
2. peripheral nervous system
3. contains both sensory nerves and motor nerves
4. autonomic nervous system
5. helps arouse the body
6. parasympathetic nervous system
7. is the lowest part of the brain and contains the hindbrain, medulla, cerebellum, and pons
8. midbrain
9. is the highest region of the brain, containing the thalamus, hypothalamus and endocrine system, the limbic system, and the cerebrum.

Multiple-Choice Questions

Practice Test 1

After answering all the multiple choice questions in Practice Test 1, compare your answers with the answer key provided at the end of the chapter. The answer key contains a brief explanation of both the correct and incorrect answers. Each of these questions is keyed to the Learning Objectives for each chapter. If you answer any questions incorrectly, review the corresponding Learning Objective and text material before you proceed to Practice Test 2.

1. The term *nature* as used by psychologists, refers to
   a. genetics.
   b. biological inheritance.
   c. environmental experiences.
   d. both *a* and *b*

LO 1

2. Two far-sighted parents have a child who is near-sighted. How is this possible?
   a. Both parents carry dominant genes for near-sightedness.
   b. Only one parent carries dominant genes for near-sightedness.
   c. Only one parent carries recessive genes for near-sightedness.
   d. Both parents carry recessive genes for near-sightedness.

LO 2

3. Which of the following is correct?
   a. Genes are short segments of DNA.
   b. DNA contains only dominant genes.
   c. The nucleus of each human cell contains at least 50 chromosomes.
   d. Some chromosomes do not carry any DNA.

LO 2

4. Each of the following is part of the process of natural selection *except*
   a. an intense struggle for survival among the young.
   b. survival of the fittest.
   c. dramatic, sudden changes in the populations of most species.
   d. changes in the environment that alter the process.

LO 3

5. According to the evolutionary perspective, the mind evolved as a collection of
   a. random mechanisms.
   b. overlapping mechanisms.
   c. independent mechanisms.
   d. localized structures.

LO 3

6. The physiological arousal that you feel as you enter a classroom to take an exam is produced by the _________ nervous system.
   a. parasympathetic
   b. sympathetic
   c. somatic
   d. central

LO 4

7. Which of the following types of neurons carries input to the brain?
   a. afferent neurons
   b. efferent neurons
   c. interneurons
   d. All types of neurons are likely to be involved.

LO 5

8. Neural messages are collected by the
   a. axon.
   b. synapse.
   c. cell body.
   d. dendrite.

LO 6

9. Which of the following serves to insulate a nerve cell?
   a. the axon
   b. the dendrite
   c. the myelin sheath
   d. the synapse

LO 6

10. The neural membrane is in a semipermeable state, with sodium outside the membrane and potassium generally inside. This situation describes
    a. the all-or-none principle.
    b. a resting potential.
    c. an action potential.
    d. a synaptic transmission.

LO 7

11. Each of the following is true regarding neurotransmitters *except*
    a. they allow neural messages to "jump" across synapses.
    b. they may be excitatory or inhibitory.
    c. they are stored in the terminal buttons of axons.
    d. approximately 10 neurotransmitters have been identified.

LO 8

12. Which of the following neurotransmitters acts as a natural opiate?
    a. serotonin
    b. dopamine
    c. endorphins
    d. acetylcholine

LO 8

13. A hindbrain structure thought to play a major role in motor control is the
    a. cerebellum.
    b. medulla.
    c. cerebral cortex.
    d. pons.

LO 9

14. The forebrain structure that monitors eating, drinking, and sexual behavior is called the
    a. thalamus.
    b. hypothalamus.
    c. cerebral cortex.
    d. cerebellum.

LO 9

15. The "master gland" is the
    a. adrenal gland.
    b. pituitary gland.
    c. testes.
    d. hypothalamus.

LO 9

16. Vision is controlled by which lobe of the cerebral cortex?
    a. occipital
    b. temporal
    c. frontal
    d. parietal

LO 10

17. The brain structure that allows the hemispheres to communicate with each other is called the
    a. corpus callosum.
    b. occipital lobe.
    c. frontal lobe.
    d. temporal lobe.

LO 11

18. According to Gall's approach called phrenology, personality and intelligence could be predicted by
    a. the size of a person's brain relative to their body.
    b. the bumps on a person's skull.
    c. the weight of a person's brain.
    d. the size of a person's corpus callosum.

LO 12

19. An important brain repair mechanism occurs when the axons of healthy neurons grow new branches. This process is called
    a. collateral sprouting.
    b. substitution of function.
    c. brain grafting.
    d. SQUID growth.

LO 13

20. A technique for studying the brain that involves passing X rays through the brain is called
    a. PET scan.
    b. CAT scan.
    c. magnetic resonance imaging.
    d. electroencephalography (EEG).

LO 14

Practice Test 2

The following multiple-choice questions also are keyed to the chapter Learning Objectives. If you answer any questions incorrectly, be sure to review the corresponding Learning Objective and text material.

1. Psychologists believe that personality is determined
   a. primarily by nature.
   b. primarily by nurture.
   c. by the interaction of nature and nurture.
   d. by the interaction of nurture and environmental factors.

LO 1

2. If you inherit a recessive gene from one parent, which of the following occurs?
   a. You will show the trait.
   b. You may or may not show the trait.
   c. You will not show the trait.
   d. The trait may partially appear.

LO 2

3. Which of the following is correct?
   a. Genes help to determine only physical characteristics.
   b. Certain behavioral characteristics may involve a genetic component.
   c. Recessive genes always exert their influence.
   d. Recessive genes never exert their influence.

LO 2

4. According to Darwin, changes in a species can be explained by
   a. natural selection.
   b. random change.
   c. survival of the fittest.
   d. both *a* and *c*.

LO 3

5. As you are driving your car, another car cuts in front of you without signaling, almost causing an accident. As an astute observer of behavior, you notice that your physical reaction takes place almost immediately, but it seems to take longer to calm down. This is because
   a. your parasympathetic nervous system takes longer to act than your sympathetic nervous system.
   b. your sympathetic nervous system takes longer to act than your parasympathetic nervous system.
   c. your somatic nervous system takes longer to act than your autonomic nervous system.
   d. your peripheral nervous system takes longer to act than your autonomic nervous system.

LO 4

6. The brain and the spinal cord comprise the
   a. central nervous system.
   b. peripheral nervous system.
   c. autonomic nervous system.
   d. parasympathetic nervous system.

LO 4

7. The majority of the brain consists of which type of neurons?
   a. afferent neurons
   b. efferent neurons
   c. interneurons
   d. axons

LO 5

8. Information is carried to other cells by the
   a. axons.
   b. cell bodies.
   c. dendrites.
   d. myelin sheaths.

LO 6

9. The nucleus of a neuron is found in the
   a. axon.
   b. cell body.
   c. dendrite.
   d. myelin sheath.

LO 6

10. What occurs when the sodium gates on the axon are open?
    a. a resting potential
    b. a synaptic transmission
    c. an action potential
    d. an all-or-none potential

LO 7

11. A neurotransmitter that, in excess, is associated with schizophrenia is
    a. dopamine.
    b. serotonin.
    c. an endorphin.
    d. norepinephrine.

LO 8

12. A neurotransmitter involved in the regulation of sleep and mood is
    a. dopamine.
    b. serotonin.
    c. an endorphin.
    d. acetylcholine.

LO 8

13. A brain structure responsible for relaying information between the brain and the eyes and ears is the
    a. hindbrain.
    b. midbrain.
    c. forebrain.
    d. cerebellum.

LO 9

14. The hypothalamus is involved in each of the following activities *except*
    a. eating
    b. emotions
    c. drinking
    d. motor control

LO 9

15. A limbic structure that plays an important role in the storage of memories is the
    a. amygdala.
    b. basal ganglia.
    c. hippocampus.
    d. thalamus.

LO 9

16. Which structure is involved in the control of voluntary muscles and intelligence?
    a. temporal lobe
    b. parietal lobe
    c. frontal lobe
    d. occipital lobe

LO 10

17. Sperry's research found that the left brain is superior at
    a. intuitive thought.
    b. music and art.
    c. everyday logic.
    d. abstract logic.

LO 11

18. Although the details of Gall's theory are no longer accepted, which of Gall's notions still prevails?
    a. localization of brain function
    b. the integration of brain function
    c. wide anatomical differences between the brains of males and females
    d. bumps on the skull as predictors of personality

LO 12

19. Collateral sprouting and substitution of function are examples of
    a. brain grafting.
    b. the plain's plasticity.
    c. brain imaging techniques.
    d. phrenology.

LO 13

20. A technique for studying the brain that measures the amount of glucose in various areas of the brain is called
    a. PET scan.
    b. CAT scan.
    c. magnetic resonance imaging.
    d. electroencephalography.

LO 14

Answers to Key Terms

1. **Environment** refers to all of the surrounding conditions and influences that affect the development of living things.
2. **Nurture** refers to an organism's environmental experiences.
3. **Nature** refers to an organism's biological inheritance.
4. **Chromosomes** are threadlike structures found in the cell nucleus and, in humans, come in 23 pairs, one member of each pair coming from each parent.
5. **DNA** is a complex molecule that contains genetic information.
6. **Genes** are short segments of DNA that contain the hereditary information; they act as a blueprint for cells to reproduce themselves, and they manufacture the proteins essential to life.
7. According to the **dominant-recessive genes principle,** the dominant gene exerts its influence, and a recessive gene exerts its influence only when both genes of a pair are recessive.
8. **Natural selection** is an evolutionary process that favors those individuals who are best adapted to survive and reproduce.
9. **Evolutionary psychology** emphasizes the roles of both evolution and psychological mechanisms in adaptive behavior.
10. **Neurons,** or nerve cells, are the basic units of the nervous system.
11. The **central nervous system** consists of the brain and the spinal cord.
12. The **peripheral nervous system** is a network of nerves connecting the brain and spinal cord to other parts of the body.
13. The **somatic nervous system** consists of sensory nerves, which connect the skin and muscles to the central nervous system, and motor nerves, which inform muscles when to act.
14. The **autonomic nervous system** takes messages to and from the body's internal organs.
15. The **sympathetic nervous system** is a division of the autonomic nervous system that arouses the body.
16. The **parasympathetic nervous system** is a division of the autonomic nervous system that calms the body.
17. **Afferent nerves,** also called sensory nerves, carry information to the brain.
18. **Efferent nerves** carry the brain's output.
19. **Interneurons,** which make up most of the neurons of the brain, are the neurons that mediate sensory input and motor input.
20. The **cell body** of the neuron contains the cell's nucleus.
21. The **dendrite** is the part of the neuron that receives information and orients it toward the cell body.
22. The **axon** is the part of the neuron that carries information away from the cell body to other cells.
23. The **myelin sheath** is a layer of fat cells that insulates the axon and helps the nerve impulse travel faster.
24. **Ions** are electrically charged particles that allow the neuron to create electrical signals.
25. **Resting potential** refers to the stable, negative charge of an inactive neuron.
26. **Action potential** is the brief wave of electrical charge that sweeps down the axon.
27. The **all-or-none principle** means that when the electrical impulse reaches a certain level, it causes an electrical charge to move down the axon, remaining at the same strength throughout its travel.
28. **Synapses** are tiny gaps between neurons.
29. **Neurotransmitters** are chemicals that carry information across the synaptic gap to the next neuron.
30. **Dopamine** is a neurotransmitter related to mental health; excessive dopamine is associated with schizophrenia.
31. **Serotonin** is a neurotransmitter that is involved in the regulation of sleep as well as depression.
32. **Endorphins** are neurotransmitters that are involved in pleasure and in the control of pain; they are natural opiates.
33. The **hindbrain** is located at the rear of the skull and consists of the spinal cord, lower brain stem (pons and medulla), and cerebellum.
34. The **medulla** helps to control breathing and posture.
35. The **cerebellum** is believed to play important roles in motor control.
36. The **pons** is a bridge located in the hindbrain that contains fibers involved in sleep and arousal.
37. The **midbrain** helps to relay information between the brain and the ears and eyes.

38. The **reticular formation** is a diffuse collection of neurons involved in such behaviors as walking, sleeping, or turning to attend to a sudden noise.
39. **Basal ganglia** are small groups of neurons in the midbrain that send their axons to a variety of brain regions.
40. The **forebrain** is the region of the brain that governs its highest functions; it contains the thalamus, the hypothalamus and endocrine system, the limbic system, and the cerebral cortex.
41. The **thalamus** is located at the top of the brain stem and serves as an essential relay station.
42. The **hypothalamus** monitors eating, drinking, and sex; directs the endocrine system through the pituitary gland; and is involved in emotion, stress, and reward.
43. The **endocrine system** is a set of glands that release their chemical products directly into the bloodstream.
44. **Hormones** are the chemical messengers manufactured by the endocrine glands.
45. The **pituitary gland** sits at the base of the skull; it controls growth and regulates other glands.
46. The **limbic system** is a loosely connected network of structures under the cerebral cortex that plays an important role in memory and emotion.
47. The **amygdala,** a structure located in the base of the temporal lobe, is involved in the discrimination of objects that are important for an organism's survival, such as appropriate food, mates, and social rivals.
48. The **hippocampus** is a limbic system structure that plays an important role in the storage of memories.
49. The **cerebral cortex,** the most recently evolved part of the brain, makes up about 80 percent of the brain's volume.
50. The **occipital lobe** of the cerebral cortex is involved in vision.
51. The **temporal lobe** of the cerebral cortex is involved in hearing.
52. The **frontal lobe** of the cerebral cortex is involved in controlling voluntary muscles and in intelligence.
53. The **parietal lobe** of the cerebral cortex is involved in body sensations.
54. The **association cortex** is involved in our highest intellectual functions, such as problem solving and thinking.
55. The **corpus callosum** is a large bundle of axons that connect the brain's two hemispheres.
56. **Aphasia** is the inability to recognize or express language; it occurs after left-hemisphere damage.
57. **Phrenology** was an approach that linked bumps on the skull to personality and intelligence.
58. **Plasticity** is the brains' ability to modify and reorganize itself following damage.
59. **Brain implants** involve implanting healthy tissue into damaged brains.
60. The **electroencephalograph** records the electrical activity of the brain.
61. **Computer-assisted axial tomography (CAT scan)** is an imagining device that passes X rays through the brain; a computer then assembles the individual pictures into a composite.
62. **Positron-emission tomography (PET scan)** measures brain activity by measuring the amount of glucose in various areas of the brain.
63. **Magnetic resonance imaging (MRI)** is a technique that involves creating a magnetic field around a person's body and using radio waves to construct images the person's tissues (such as brain tissues) and biochemical activity.
64. **Superconducting quantum interference device (SQUID)** is a brain-scanning device that senses tiny changes in magnetic fields.

Answers to Guided Review

1. environment (p. 36)
2. nurture (p. 36)
3. nature (p. 36)
4. interact (p. 38)
5. genetics (p. 38)
6. chromosomes (p. 38)
7. DNA (p. 38)
8. genes (p. 38)
9. dominant (p. 39)
10. recessive (p. 39)
11. 50,000 (p. 40)
12. Genome (p. 40)
13. natural selection (p. 41)
14. evolutionary (p. 41)
15. adaptive (p. 41)
16. neuron (p. 42)
17. peripheral (p. 42)
18. spinal cord (p. 42)
19. somatic (p. 42)
20. autonomic (p. 43)
21. arouse (p. 43)
22. calm (p. 43)
23. afferent (p. 43)
24. efferent (p. 43)
25. interneurons (p. 43)
26. cell body (p. 44)
27. dendrites (p. 46)
28. axon (p. 46)
29. myelin sheath (p. 46)
30. terminal (p. 46)
31. ions (p. 46)
32. Resting potential (p. 46)
33. action potential (p. 47)
34. all-or-none (p. 47)
35. synapse (p. 47)
36. neurotransmitters (p. 47)
37. dopamine (p. 48)
38. schizophrenia (p. 48)
39. serotonin (p. 48)
40. endorphins (p. 48)
41. tube (p. 49)
42. hindbrain (p. 50)
43. medulla (p. 50)
44. cerebellum (p. 50)
45. pons (p. 50)
46. eyes (p. 50)
47. ears (p. 50)
48. reticular (p. 50)
49. basal (p. 50)
50. forebrain (p. 50)
51. thalamus (p. 50)
52. hypothalamus (p. 51)
53. pleasure center (p. 52)
54. hormones. (p. 53)
55. bloodstream (p. 53)
56. pituitary (p. 53)
57. limbic (p. 54)
58. hippocampus (p. 54)
59. emotion (p. 54)
60. memories (p. 54)
61. cerebral cortex (p. 54)
62. hemispheres (p. 54)
63. lobes (p. 78)
64. vision (p. 54)
65. temporal (p. 54)
66. frontal (p. 54)
67. parietal (p. 54)
68. cerebrum (p. 54)
69. association cortex (p. 54)
70. problem (p. 54)
71. corpus callosum (p. 54)
72. language (p. 57)
73. both (p. 57)
74. lateralized (p. 59)
75. symmetrically (p. 59)
76. aphasia (p. 60)
77. similarities (p. 61)
78. phrenology (p. 61)
79. functions (p. 62)
80. integration (p. 62)
81. plasticity (p. 64)
82. young children (p. 64)
83. sprouting (p. 64)
84. substitution (p. 64)
85. grafts (p. 64)
86. fetal (p. 64)
87. Parkinson's (p. 65)
88. Alzheimer's (p. 65)
89. neuron (p. 66)
90. electroencephalograph (p. 66)
91. computer-assisted tomography (p. 66)
92. positron-emission (p. 66)
93. magnetic resonance imaging (p. 66)
94. interference (p. 66)

Answers to Multiple Choice Questions- Practice Test 1

1. a. Incorrect. This answer is partially correct; another answer is a better alternative.
   b. Incorrect. This answer is partially correct; another answer is a better alternative.
   c. Incorrect. Environmental experiences are referred to as nurture.
   d. **Correct.** Genetics controls one's biological inheritance.

2. a. Incorrect. If this were the case, both parents would be near-sighted rather than far-sighted.
   b. Incorrect. We know that both parents are far-sighted and that far-sightedness is dominant. Therefore, both parents must carry at least one set of "far-sighted" genes.
   c. Incorrect. Since near-sightedness is a recessive trait, we know that it takes two parents to contribute "near-sighted" genes.
   d. **Correct.** If both parents contribute recessive "near-sighted" genes, their offspring will be near-sighted.

3. a. **Correct.** Genes are the units of hereditary information.
   b. Incorrect. DNA contains both recessive and dominant genes.
   c. Incorrect. The nucleus of each human cell contains 46 chromosomes, arranged in 23 pairs.
   d. Incorrect. All chromosomes contain DNA.

4. a. Incorrect. This struggle characterizes the "survival of the fittest," and is part of natural selection.
   b. Incorrect. This is an important part of the process of natural selection.
   c. **Correct.** Darwin proposed that evolution proceeds at a very slow pace.
   d. Incorrect. Changes in the environment can change the rules for survival, and are thus part of the process of natural selection.

5. a. Incorrect. This perspective views the mind as a collection of mechanisms that serve adaptive functions.
   b. Incorrect. This perspective does not view these mechanisms as overlapping.
   c. **Correct.** These independent mechanisms exist to serve important adaptive functions.
   d. Incorrect. According to the evolutionary view, the mind serves important adaptive functions; it evolved as a series of independent mechanisms.

6. a. Incorrect. This nervous system helps to calm the body.
   b. **Correct.** This system involves breathing, heart rate and digestion.
   c. Incorrect. This system conveys information to the CNS from the skin and muscles about matters such as pain and temperature.
   d. Incorrect. The central nervous system consists of the brain and spinal cord.

7. a. **Correct.** These are sometimes referred to as sensory nerves.
   b. Incorrect. These carry the brain's output; they are also called motor nerves.
   c. Incorrect. These neurons, which make up most of the brain, help mediate the afferent and efferent neurons.
   d. Incorrect. One specific type of neuron is designed to carry out this function.

8. a. Incorrect. This part of the neuron carries information away from the cell body and toward other cells.
   b. Incorrect. This refers to the gap between neurons.
   c. Incorrect. This part of the neuron contains the nucleus, which helps to maintain the neuron.
   d. **Correct.** Most neurons have a number of dendrites, but only one axon.

9. a. Incorrect. This part of the neuron carries information away from the cell body and toward other cells.
   b. Incorrect. This part of the neuron collects information and orients it toward the cell body.
   c. **Correct.** This is actually a layer of fat cells that also help nerve impulses to travel faster.
   d. Incorrect. This is the gap between the axon of one neuron and the dendrite of another neuron.

10. a. Incorrect. This refers to the idea that electrical impulses will fire only when they reach a certain level of intensity; at that point the neural message travels all the way down the axon.
    b. **Correct.** This refers to the stable, negative charge of an inactive neuron.
    c. Incorrect. This refers to the brief wave of electrical charge that sweeps down the axon.
    d. Incorrect. Synaptic transmissions involve neurotransmitters helping to connect an electrical impulse to an adjacent neuron.

11. a. Incorrect. This *is* characteristic of neurotransmitters.
    b. Incorrect. This *is* characteristic of neurotransmitters.
    c. Incorrect. This *is* characteristic of neurotransmitters.
    d. **Correct.** More than 50 neurotransmitters have been identified so far.

12. a. Incorrect. This neurotransmitter is involved in the regulation of sleep, mood, arousal, and pain.
    b. Incorrect. This neurotransmitter is related to learning, movement, and mental health .
    c **Correct.** These are involved in pleasure and in the control of pain.
    d. Incorrect. This neurotransmitter (not mentioned in the text) is related to movement.

13. a. **Correct.** This area is located just above the medulla.
    b. Incorrect. This structure helps to control breathing and is involved in posture.
    c. Incorrect. This forebrain structure is involved in much of our high-level thinking.
    d. Incorrect. This structure is involved in sleep and arousal.

14. a. Incorrect. This structure serves as a relay station, between the cortex and the reticular formation.
    b. **Correct.** In short, the hypothalamus is both a regulator and a motivator.
    c. Incorrect. The cortex is the covering that contains the lobes of the brain.
    d. Incorrect. This is a forebrain structure believed to play important roles in motor control.

15. a. Incorrect. This gland is part of the sympathetic nervous system and affects organs by releasing adrenaline and noradrenaline.
    b. **Correct.** This gland sits at the base of the skull; it controls growth and regulates other glands.
    c. Incorrect. This gland regulates the sex hormones in males.
    d. Incorrect. The hypothalamus is a brain structure that actually regulates the "master gland."

16. a. **Correct.** This lobe is located at the back of the head.
    b. Incorrect. This lobe is responsible for hearing.
    c. Incorrect. This lobe is involved in the control of voluntary muscles and in intelligence.
    d. Incorrect. This lobe is involved in processing body sensations.

17. a. **Correct.** This structure consists of a large bundle of axons.
    b. Incorrect. This lobe, located at the back of the head, is responsible for vision.
    c. Incorrect. This lobe is involved in the control of voluntary muscles and in intelligence.
    d. Incorrect. This is a lobe of the cortex and is responsible for processing auditory information.

18. a. Incorrect. Gall's approach focused on attributes of the skull.
    b. **Correct.** He believed these bumps were associated with personality and intelligence.
    c. Incorrect. Gall's approach focused on attributes of the skull.
    d. Incorrect. Gall's approach focused on attributes of the skull.

19. a. **Correct.** The regeneration of new neurons does not occur in humans.
    b. Incorrect. This occurs when the damaged region's function is taken over by another region.
    c. Incorrect. This procedure involves implanting healthy brain tissue into damaged brains.
    d. Incorrect. SQUID refers to a brain-scanning device that senses changes in magnetic fields.

20. a. Incorrect. This technique involves measuring the amount of glucose in various areas of the brain.
    b. **Correct.** These X rays help to create a three-dimension image of the brain.
    c. Incorrect. This approach involves creating a magnetic field around a person's body and using radio waves to construct images of the person's brain.
    d. Incorrect. This technique uses electrodes to record the electrical activity of the brain.

Answers to Multiple Choice Questions- Practice Test 2

1. a. Incorrect. Psychologists believe nature is an important factor in determining personality, but not that it is the primary factor.
   b. Incorrect. Psychologists believe nurture is an important factor in determining personality, but not that it is the only factor.
   c. **Correct.** Note the importance of the term *interaction*; the two forces cannot simply be added to understand personality.
   d. Incorrect. Nurture and environment refer to the same basic forces.

2. a. Incorrect. You will inherit the trait only if the second parent also contributes a recessive gene.
   b. **Correct.** If the second parent contributes a recessive gene, you will inherit the trait; if the second parent contributes a dominant gene, then the dominant gene will exert its influence.
   c. Incorrect. It depends on whether the second parent contributes a recessive gene.
   d. Incorrect. If the second parent contributes a recessive gene, then the trait will appear; if the second parent contributes a dominant gene, then the dominant gene will exert its influence.

3. a. Incorrect. Many researchers believe the influence of genetics goes beyond physical characteristics.
   b. **Correct.** Researchers believe that many personality traits may have a genetic component.
   c. Incorrect. Recessive genes exert their influence only when paired with another recessive gene.
   d. Incorrect. Recessive genes exert their influence when paired with another recessive gene.

4. a. Incorrect. This answer is partially true; another alternative is a better answer.
   b. Incorrect. Changes in a species result from adapting to changes in the environment.
   c. Incorrect. This answer is partially true; another alternative is a better answer
   d. **Correct.** Natural selection, the evolutionary process that favors genes that code for design feature most likely to lead to reproduction and survival, is also referred to as natural selection.

5. a. **Correct.** The activating nervous system is the sympathetic nervous system. The "calming" nervous system is the parasympathetic nervous system. You have demonstrated that the sympathetic system kicks in faster than the parasympathetic. Do you see the evolutionary advantage?
   b. Incorrect. Your behavior has demonstrated just the opposite.
   c. Incorrect. The somatic nervous system conveys information from the skin and muscles to the CNS. The primary activity in the driving experience is in the sympathetic and parasympathetic nervous systems.
   d. Incorrect. The peripheral nervous system is a network that consists of the somatic and autonomic nervous systems. Therefore, the autonomic nervous system is actually part of the peripheral nervous system.

6. a. **Correct.** More than 99 percent of all neurons in the body are in the CNS.
   b. Incorrect. The peripheral nervous system is a network that consists of the somatic and autonomic nervous systems.
   c. Incorrect. The autonomic nervous system consists of the sympathetic and parasympathetic nervous systems.
   d. Incorrect. The parasympathetic nervous system is the division of the autonomic nervous system that helps calm the body.

7. a. Incorrect. These sensory nerves carry information to the brain. The do not comprise a majority of the neurons of the brain.
   b. Incorrect. These motor neurons carry the brain's output. They do not comprise a majority of the brain's neurons.
   c. **Correct.** These central nervous system neurons mediate sensory input and motor output.
   d. Incorrect. This refers to a structure on neurons, rather than a type of neuron.

8. a. **Correct.** These may be as long as three feet.
   b. Incorrect. Cell bodies contain the nucleus of the neuron, which aids in the growth and maintenance of the neuron.
   c. Incorrect. The dendrites are the receiving parts of neurons, collecting information and orienting the information toward the cell body.
   d. Incorrect. Myelin sheaths are layers of fat cells that insulate nerve cells and help messages to travel faster.

9. a. Incorrect. The axon carries information away from the cell body and toward other neurons.
   b. **Correct.** The nucleus directs the manufacture of the substances used by the neuron for growth and maintenance.
   c. incorrect. The dendrite is the receiving part of the neuron; it collects information and orients the information toward the cell body.
   d. Incorrect. The myelin sheath is a layer of fat cells that insulates the neuron and allows messages to travel faster.

10. a. Incorrect. During a resting potential, the sodium gates are closed.
    b. Incorrect. A synaptic transmission refers to the events that take place as a neural message reaches the end of an axon.
    c. **Correct.** During an action potential, the sodium gates are briefly opened, and sodium ions, with their positive electrical charge, rush into the axon.
    d. Incorrect. All-or-none refers to the principle that an electrical impulse must reach a certain level of intensity before the neuron "fires."

11. a. **Correct.** Dopamine is also related to movement, attention, and learning.
    b. Incorrect. Serotonin is involved in the regulation of sleep, mood, arousal, and pain.
    c. Incorrect. Endorphins are involved in pleasure and in the control of pain.
    d. Incorrect. Norepinephrine, a neurotransmitter not mentioned in the text, is involved in regulating sleep, moods and learning.

12. a. Incorrect. Dopamine is related to movement, learning, attention, and mental health.
    b. **Correct.** Serotonin is also involved in the regulation of pain and arousal.
    c. Incorrect. Endorphins are involved in pleasure and in the control of pain.
    d. Incorrect. Acetylcholine, not mentioned in the text, is involved in the regulation of movement and memory.

13. a. Incorrect. The hindbrain is generally involved in housekeeping chores. It consists of the medulla, the cerebellum and the pons.
    b. **Correct.** The midbrain connects the lower and higher portions of the brain.
    c. Incorrect. The forebrain controls the highest functions of the brain; it consists of the thalamus, the endocrine system, the limbic system and the cerebral cortex.
    d. Incorrect. The cerebellum is a midbrain structure thought to play important roles in motor control.

14. a. Incorrect. The hypothalamus is involved in hunger and in satiation.
    b. Incorrect. The hypothalamus is involved in our emotional reactions to the world.
    c. Incorrect. The hypothalamus helps regulate drinking.
    d **Correct.** The peripheral nervous system is a network that consists of the somatic and autonomic nervous systems. This is not one of the primary functions of the hypothalamus. The hypothalamus is best thought of as a regulator and a motivator.

15. a. Incorrect. This limbic structure is involved in emotions and in discriminating important objects in the environment.
    b. Incorrect. These are small group of midbrain neurons involved in high-level integrative functions.
    c. **Correct.** Injuries to this structure lead to an inability to store new memories.
    d. Incorrect. The thalamus is a forebrain structure that acts as a relay between the cortex and the reticular formation.

16. a. Incorrect. This lobe is involved in processing auditory information.
    b. Incorrect. This lobe is involved in processing bodily sensations.
    c. **Correct.** This area is located behind the forehead.
    d. Incorrect. This lobe processes visual information.

17. a. Incorrect. This is not consistent with Sperry's findings.
    b. Incorrect. This is not consistent with Sperry's findings.
    c. Incorrect. In solving these problems, we integrate information from both hemispheres of the brain.
    d. **Correct.** Sperry found that the left hemisphere is superior in processing this type of logic.

18. a. **Correct.** Gall's theory that brain functions are localized has withstood the test of time; his details were slightly off.
    b. Incorrect. Neuroscientists now appreciate that, although areas of the brain are specialized, the brain functions as an integrated whole.
    c. Gall's theory focused on bumps on the head as predictors of personality, not wide differences between male and female brains.
    d. Incorrect. Although this was an important part of Gall's theory, scientists have abandoned this notion.

19. a. Incorrect. This refers to the process of implanting healthy tissue into damaged brains.
    b. **Correct.** Plasticity refers to the brain's capacity to modify and reorganize itself following damage.
    c. Incorrect. Sprouting and substitution of function refer to ways the brain copes with damage.
    d. Incorrect. Phrenology is Gall's long-ago disproved theory of bumps on the head as predictors of personality.

20. a. **Correct.** The glucose levels serve as a measure of activity levels in the brain.
    b. Incorrect. A CAT scan is a three-dimensional image obtained from X rays and assembled by a computer.
    c. Incorrect. An MRI creates a magnetic field around a person's body and uses radio waves to construct images of tissues and activities.
    d. Incorrect. An EEG is a record of electrical activity of the brain obtained by placing electrodes on the scalp.

Chapter 3 Sensation and Perception

Learning Objectives

After studying this chapter, you should be able to:

1. Distinguish between the processes of sensation and perception. (p. 75)

2. Distinguish between the absolute threshold and the difference threshold. (p. 76)

3 Describe signal detection theory and distinguish between conservative and liberal responders. (p. 77)

4. Discuss the controversies surrounding subliminal perception. (p. 78)

5. Distinguish among sensory adaptation, sensation seeking and sensory deprivation. (p. 79)

6. Identify the major structural components of the eye. (p. 82)

7. Discuss the functions of rods and cones located in the retina. (p. 83)

8. Describe the processing of visual information by the optic nerve and the visual cortex. (p. 84)

9. Distinguish among a color's hue, saturation, and brightness. (p. 86)

10. Distinguish between the trichromatic and opponent-process theories of color vision. (p. 88)

11. Distinguish among a sound's pitch, loudness and, complexity. (p. 90)

12. Identify the major structural components of the ear. (p. 91)

13. Describe the process by which the ear converts sound waves into neural impulses. (p. 92)

14. Distinguish among place theory, frequency theory and volley theory. (p. 93)

15. Discuss the processes by which the skin senses pressure, temperature and pain. (p. 94)

16. Describe the gate-control theory of pain. (p. 95)

17. Describe the kinesthetic and vestibular senses. (p. 97)

18. Explain how the chemical senses (taste and smell) process information. (p. 100)

19. Identify and discuss the four characteristics of the perceptual process. (p. 102)

20. Discuss the processes by which we perceive shape. (p. 103)

21. Distinguish between monocular and binocular cues used in depth perception. (p. 106)

22. Discuss the processes involved in the perception of motion. (p. 106)

23. Describe three types of perceptual constancy. (p. 107)

24. Discuss the reasons visual illusions occur. (p. 109)

25. Discuss various research efforts to determine whether perception is innate or learned. (p. 110)

26. Distinguish among the following types of extrasensory perception: telepathy, precognition, clairvoyance, and psychokinesis. (p. 113)

27. Discuss the controversies surrounding the claims of ESP enthusiasts. (p. 114)

Chapter 2 Outline

I. Detecting and Perceiving the World
  A. Definition of Sensation
  B. Definition of Perception
  C. Sensory Thresholds
    1. Absolute threshold
    2. Difference threshold
    3. Signal Detection
    4. Subliminal Perception
  D. Sensory Reactions
    1. Sensory adaptation
    2. Sensation-seeking
    3. Sensory deprivation
II. Sensation
  A. The Visual System
    1. Properties of light
    2. Major structures of the eye
      a. sclera
      b. iris
      c. pupil
      d. cornea
      e. lens
      f. retina
      g. rods
      h. cones
    3. Color vision
      a. Why things have color
        (1) hue
        (2) saturation
        (3) brightness
      b. Theories of Color vision
        (1) trichromatic theory
        (2) opponent-process theory
  B. The Auditory System
  C. The Haptic System
  D. The Chemical System
III. Perception
  A. Principles of Perception
  B. Perceptual Illusions
  C. Is Perception Innate or Learned
  D. Extrasensory Perception
    1. Telepathy
    2. Precognition
    3. Clairvoyance
    4. Psychokinesis

Key Terms

Write a brief description for each of the following terms. Where relevant, provide an original example or illustration of the term. Then, compare your answers with those provided at the end of the Study Guide chapter. Review the text for those terms you don't know and those you define incorrectly.

1. sensation (p. 75)

2. perception (p. 75)

3. psychophysics (p. 75)

4. difference threshold (p. 76)

5. Weber's Law (p. 76)

6. absolute threshold (p. 76)

7. signal detection theory (p. 77)

8. subliminal perception (p. 78)

9. sensory adaptation (p. 79)

10 sensation seeking (p. 79)

11 sensory deprivation (p. 79)

12. light (p. 81)

13. wavelength (p. 81)

14. sclera (p. 82)

15. iris (p. 82)

16. pupil (p. 82)

17. cornea (p. 83)

18. lens of the eye (p. 83)

19. accommodation (p. 83)

20. retina (p. 83)

21. rods (p. 83)

22. cones (p. 83)

23. fovea (p. 83)

24. blind spot (p. 84)

25. hue (p. 86)

26. saturation (p. 86)

27. brightness (p. 86)

28. additive mixture (p. 86)

29. subtractive mixture (p. 87)

30. trichromatic theory (p. 88)

31. dichromats (p. 89)

32. trichromats (p. 89)

33. afterimages (p. 89)

34. opponent-process theory (p. 89)

35. sounds (p. 90)

36. frequency (p. 90)

37. pitch (p. 90)

38. amplitude (p. 90)

39. loudness (p. 90)

40. complex sounds (p. 91)

41. timbre (p. 91)

42. outer ear (p. 91)

43. middle ear (p. 92)

44. inner ear (p. 93)

45. cochlea (p. 93)

46. basilar membrane (p. 93)

47. organ of Corti (p. 93)

48. place theory (p. 93)

49. frequency theory (p. 93)

50. volley theory (p. 93)

51. auditory nerve (p. 93)

52. pain threshold (p. 95)

53. gate-control theory (p. 95)

54. acupuncture (p. 95)

55. kinesthetic senses (p. 97)

56. vestibular sense (p. 97)

57. semicircular canals (p. 97)

58. papillae (p. 100)

59. olfactory epithelium (p. 100)

60. perceptual set (p. 103)

61. contour (p. 103)

62. figure-ground relationship (p. 103)

63. Gestalt psychology (p. 104)

64. depth perception (p. 105)

65. binocular cues (p. 106)

66. monocular cues (p. 106)

67. retinal or binocular disparity (p. 106)

68. convergence (p. 106)

69. apparent movement (p. 106)

70. stroboscopic motion (p. 106)

71. movement aftereffects (p. 106)

72. size constancy (p. 107)

73. shape constancy (p. 107)

74. brightness constancy (p. 108)

75. visual illusion (p. 109)

76. carpentered-world hypothesis (p. 111)

77. extrasensory perception (p. 113)

78. telepathy (p. 113)

79. precognition (p. 113)

80. clairvoyance (p. 113)

81. psychokinesis (p. 113)

Guided Review

The following in-depth chapter review is a challenging and comprehensive fill-in-the-blanks exercise. The answers are found near the end of the chapter. As you go through the exercise, try to resist the temptation to look at the answers until you have provided them. When you have filled in all the blanks, you will have a thorough summary of the chapter for reference and review.

Detecting and Perceiving the World

The process of detecting and encoding stimulus energy is called ___(1)___. The process of organizing and interpreting sensory information to give it meaning is referred to as ___(2)___. Most contemporary psychologists refer to these processes as a unified ___(3)___-______ system.

The minimum amount of a sensory energy we are able to detect 50 percent of the time is called the ___(4)___. The formal study of psychological reactions to physical stimulation is called ___(5)___.

The difference threshold, or ___(6)___ ______, is the point at which a person detects the difference between two stimuli 50 percent of the time. ___(7)___ law states that, regardless of their magnitude, two stimuli must differ by a constant proportion to be detected. According to ___(8)___ ______ theory, no absolute thresholds exist. This theory states sensitivity to stimuli depends on the strength of the sensory stimulus, the respondent's sensory abilities and on a variety of psychological and ___(9)___ factors. Signal detection researchers have found that people vary in how conservative or ___(10)___ they are in detecting signals. The perception of stimuli below the threshold of awareness is referred to as ___(11)___ perception.

Prolonged exposure to a sensory stimulus may lead to weakened sensitivity to the stimulus; this is referred to as ___(12)___ ______. Sensory adaptation is also called ___(13)___.

The need for varied, novel, and complex situations is called ___(14)___ ___(15)___.People with high sensation seeking needs can seek thrills in either constructive or ___(16)___ ways. Individuals who undergo extended periods of time in which normal external stimulation is prevented experience the effects of ___(17)___ ______.

Sensation

Light is a form of electromagnetic energy that can be described in terms of ____(18)____. The distance from the peak of one wave of light to the next is a ____(19)____. The white part of the eye, which helps maintain the shape of the eye and protects it from injury, is called the ____(20)____. The ring of muscles in the eye, which ranges in color from light blue to dark brown, is the ____(21)____. The opening in the center of the iris, whose main purpose is to control the amount of light that enters the eye, is called the ____(22)____. The clear membrane that bends light rays as they enter the eye is called the ____(23)____. The part of the eye that changes shape to bring objects into focus is called the ____(24)____. In order to focus on objects that are close to us, the lens changes its curvature, a process called ____(25)____.

The light-sensitive surface in the back of the eye is the ____(26)____. The retina contains two kinds of light receptors, called the ____(27)____ and ____(28)____. In the center of the retina, where vision is the sharpest, is a structure called the ____(29)____. Also on the retina is an area where the optic nerve leaves on its way to the brain; this is called the ____(30)____ ________. The receptors in the retina that are especially important in night vision are the ____(31)____. The cones are sensitive to color and important in ____(32)____ vision.

Information is carried out of the eye toward the brain by the____(33)____ ________. Most of the fibers cross over at a point called the ____(34)____ ________. Therefore, what we see on the left side of our visual field ends up on the____(35)____ side of the brain. Visual information is processed in the brain in the____(36)____ ________.

Objects appear colored because they reflect certain ____(37)____ of light to our eyes. Three important properties of color are hue, ____(38)____ , and brightness. A mixture of beams of light from different parts of the color spectrum is referred to as an ____(39)____ mixture. A subtractive mixture is a mixture of ____(40)____ . Color television is an example of ____(41)____ mixing, whereas an artist's painting is an example of ____(42)____ mixing.

A theory of color perception based on the existence of three types of receptors is the ____(43)____ theory. Dichromats refer to people with two kinds of cones, whereas people with normal color vision are referred to as ____(44)____. Although trichromatic theory helps explain color blindness, it cannot adequately explain ____(45)____. The phenomenon of afterimages led Hering to propose that the visual system treats colors as complementary pairs. The theory that cells in the retina respond to pairs of colors is called the ____(46)____-________ theory.

The Auditory System

Sounds, or sound waves, are ____(47)____ in the air that are processed by our auditory system. One way in which sound waves differ from each other is in ____(48)____. The ear detects the frequency of a sound wave as ____(49)____. Sound waves also vary in ____(50)____, which is the change of pressure created by sound waves. The amplitude of a sound wave is measured in ____(51)____. The blending of numerous sound waves refers to _____(52)_____. We experience the different qualities of sound as _____(53)_____.

The outer ear is made up of the _____(54)_____, which helps us localize sounds, and the external auditory canal, which funnels sounds to the _____(55)_____ _____. In the middle ear, the first structure touched by sound is the _____(56)_____. The eardrum's vibrations then touch the three tiny bone structures, the hammer, the _____(57)_____, and the stirrup. In the inner ear, sound waves travel to the _____(58)_____, a structure that contains the organ of Corti. Sensory receptors in the organ of Corti are stimulated by vibrations of the _____(59)_____ _____. These vibrations generate neural impulses. How does the inner era register the frequency of sound? According to the place theory, each frequency produces vibrations at a particular place on the _____(60)_____ _____. Another theory suggests that the perception of sound is due to how often the _____(61)_____ _____ fires. This is called _____(62)_____theory. A theory that attempts to explain high-frequency sounds is called _____(63)_____ theory. Neural impulses are carried to the brain's auditory areas by the_____(64)_____ _____.

The Haptic System

Our largest sensory system is the_____(65)_____. The skin contains receptors for pressure,_____(66)_____, and pain. The stimulation level at which pain is first perceived is called the pain _____(67)_____. A pain message begins with the release of chemicals that sensitize the _____(68)_____ _____ and help transmit pain messages to the brain. The pain's intensity and location are identified in the _____(69)_____ _____. A theory of pain that suggests that neural "gates" determine whether or not we experience pain is called the _____(70)_____-_____theory. A technique for relieving pain that involves the insertion of thin needles into the body is called _____(71)_____.

Information about movement, posture, and orientation is provided to the brain by the _____(72)_____ _____. Information about balance and movement is provided by the _____(73)_____ sense. The kinesthetic senses are located in the cells of our muscles, _____(74)_____, and tendons. An important part of the vestibular sense is the semicircular canals, which lie in the _____(75)_____ ear. This sense is sometimes called the _____(76)_____ sense.

The Chemical System

The senses of taste and smell differ from other senses because they react to _____(77)_____ rather than energy. Taste buds are found in the tongue on the _____(78)_____. Taste buds respond to four main qualities: sweet, _____(79)_____, bitter, and _____(80)_____.

Located at the top of the nasal cavity is a sheet of receptor cells called the _____(81)_____ _____. Preferences for smell are learned from consequences or by _____(82)_____.

Perception

The process of organizing and interpreting information is called _____(83)_____. Perceptual processes have four characteristics: they are automatic, _____(84)_____, contextual and _____(85)_____. The expectations that influence how perceptual elements will be interpreted are called _____(86)_____ _____. We are able to perceive shapes because they are marked off from the rest of what we see by _____(87)_____. The principle that organizes our perceptual field into stimuli that stand out and those that do not stand out is called the ____(88)____ - ________relationship. An area of psychology that studies how people organize their perceptions is called ____(89)____ psychology. In addition to figure-ground, other Gestalt principles include closure, ____(90)____, and similarity.

The ability to perceive objects three-dimensionally is called ____(91)____ ________. The cues that we use for depth perception are both ____(92)____ and ____(93)____. When an individual perceives a single scene even though the two images on the eye are slightly different, this is called retinal, or ____(94)____, disparity. A binocular cue for depth perception is called ____(95)____. Monocular cues, which can be perceived by only one eye, are also called ____(96)____ cues.

The phenomenon that occurs when we perceive a stationary object to be moving is called ____(97)____ ________. The illusion of movement created when an image is flashed off and on rapidly at slightly different places on the retina is referred to as ____(98)____ motion. When we watch continuous movement in one direction and then look at a stationary surface, it appears to move in the opposite direction; this phenomenon is called ____(99)____ ________.

We perceive three types of perceptual constancy: The recognition that an object remains the same size even though the retinal image changes is called ____(100)____ constancy. The perception that an object is the same even though its orientation to us changes is called ____(101)____ constancy. The recognition that an object retains the same degree of brightness even though different amounts of light fall on it is called ____(102)____ constancy.

When two objects produce exactly the same retinal image but are perceived as being different images, a ____(103)____ ________ occurs.

Researchers have attempted to answer whether perception is innate through (a) experiments with infants, using a structure called a ____(104)____ ________; (b) studies of individuals who recover from ____(105)____; and (c) ____(106)____ - ________ studies. The ____(107)____ - ________hypothesis illustrates the influence of cultural experiences on perception.

Perception that occurs without the use of known sensory processes is called ____(108)____ ________. One type of ESP, the transfer of thought from one person to another, is called ____(109)____. The perception of events before they occur is called ____(110)____. The ability to perceive remote events is ____(111)____. The ability to move objects without touching them is called ____(112)____. Many ESP phenomena have not been ____(113)____ when rigorous experimental standards have been applied.

Sociocultural Worlds/Applications in Psychology

In your own words, summarize the material you have read in Sociocultural Worlds, "Cultural and Ethnic Differences in Reactions to Pain," and Applications in Psychology, "Debunking Psychics' Claims." Briefly describe how each of these articles relates to the information contained in the chapter.

Concept Check

Eyes and Ears

1. The pupil is ______________________________.
2. The __________ is the clear membrane in front of the eye that helps bend light.
3. The retina is ______________________________.
4. The __________ are highly light-sensitive receptors, not useful for color vision.
5. The cones are ______________________________.
6. The __________ __________ leads out of the eye toward the brain, carrying information about light.
7. The outer ear consists of ______________________________.
8. The __________ __________ consists of the eardrum and three tiny bones, the hammer, anvil, and stirrup.
9. The inner ear consists of ______________________________.

Answers:

1. the opening in the center of the iris
2. cornea
3. the light-sensitive structure at the back of the eye that contains the rods and cones
4. rods
5. highly light-sensitive receptors, useful for color vision
6. optic nerve
7. the pinna and the external auditory canal
8. middle ear
9. the oval window, cochlea, and organ of Corti

Multiple-Choice Questions

Practice Test 1

After answering all the multiple-choice questions in Practice Test 1, compare your answers with the answer key provided at the end of the chapter. The answer key contains a brief explanation of both the correct and incorrect answers. Each of these questions is keyed to the Learning Objectives for the chapter. If you answer any questions incorrectly, review the corresponding Learning Objective and text material before you proceed to Practice Test 2.

1. The process of detecting and encoding stimuli is
   a. sensation.
   b. perception.
   c. Gestalt psychology.
   d. accommodation.

LO 1

2. Experimentally, the absolute threshold is defined as the minimum value of stimulus intensity that can be detected
   a. by the average person.
   b. by an individual half the time.
   c. by half the people tested.
   d. when amplified by Weber's constant.

LO 2

3. The context of a situation influences a person's sensitivity to stimuli, according to
   a. Weber's law.
   b. subliminal perception.
   c. signal detection theory.
   d. the absolute threshold.

LO 3

4. Advertisers who attempted to influence moviegoers by sending visual messages at rates too fast to be consciously detected were testing
   a. subliminal perception.
   b. Weber's law
   c. signal detection theory
   d. sensory adaptation

LO 4

5. Getting used to the cold water in a swimming pool is known as
   a. subliminal perception.
   b. the difference threshold.
   c. Weber's law.
   d. sensory adaptation.

LO 5

6. The part of the eye that "bends" light rays as they enter the eye is called the
   a. sclera.
   b. retina.
   c. pupil.
   d. cornea.

LO 6

7. Each of the following statements regarding the rods in the retina is true *except*
   a. Rods are sensitive to black, white, and gray.
   b. Rods function well under low illumination.
   c. Rods especially function in night vision.
   d. Rods are found in dense concentration at the fovea.

LO 7

8. The visual cortex, which is responsible for processing visual information, is located in the _________ lobe.
   a. occipital
   b. parietal
   c. temporal
   d. frontal

LO 8

9. Which of the following is based on the intensity of a color?
   a. hue
   b. saturation
   c. brightness
   d. strength

LO 9

10. Which theory of color vision does the best job of explaining afterimages?
    a. the trichromatic theory
    b. the opponent-process theory
    c. the additive-subtractive theory
    d. no theory currently explains afterimages

LO 10

11. The perceived pitch of a tone is a reflection of the _________ of the sound waves entering the ear.
    a. frequency
    b. timbre
    c. complexity
    d. amplitude

LO 11

12. The eardrum, hammer, anvil, and stirrup are important structures found in the
    a. outer ear.
    b. middle ear.
    c. inner ear.
    d. basilar membrane.

LO 12

13. The hairlike cells that translate sound waves into neural impulses are found in the
    a. eardrum.
    b. oval window.
    c. basilar membrane.
    d. organ of Corti.

LO 13

14. Which theory of sound states that each frequency of sound produces vibrations at a particular spot on the basilar membrane?
    a. place theory
    b. frequency theory
    c. volley theory
    d. none of the above

LO 14

15. The pain message is initiated when chemicals released in the skin sensitize
    a. the cerebral cortex.
    b. the pain threshold.
    c. the spinal cord.
    d. nerve endings in the skin.

LO 15

16. According to the gate-control theory of pain, a neural gate is located in
    a. the spinal cord.
    b. the pain receptors in the skin.
    c. the brain stem.
    d. both *a* and *c*.

LO 16

17. The semicircular canals are found in
    a. Venice.
    b. the inner ear.
    c. the outer ear.
    d. the middle ear.

LO 17

18. Each of the following is a basic quality of taste *except*
    a. sweet.
    b. bitter.
    c. salty.
    d. spicy.

LO 18

19. Each of the following is a characteristic of perceptual processes *except*
    a. purposeful
    b. selective
    c. contextual
    d. creative

LO 19

20. The tendency to mentally "fill in the spaces" in order to see figures as complete refers to the Gestalt principle of
    a. closure.
    b. figure-ground.
    c. proximity.
    d. similarity.

LO 20

21. As objects get closer to us, our eyes turn inward. This principle is called
    a. convergence, a monocular cue.
    b. convergence, a binocular cue.
    c. linear perspective, a monocular cue.
    d. liner perspective, a binocular cue.

LO 21

22. Paul said to Diane, "If you're free on Saturday, would you like to participate in an illusion of movement created when an object is flashed on a screen in rapid succession at different places on the retina?" Paul is probably
    a. asking Diane to go dancing.
    b. asking Diane out for a lunch date.
    c. asking Diane out for a movie date.
    d. spending too much time studying psychology.

LO 22

23. We continue to perceive that a penny is round, regardless of the angle from which it is perceived. This is an example of
    a. perceptual constancy.
    b. stroboscopic motion.
    c. movement aftereffects.
    d. a figure-ground relationship

LO 23

24. When two objects produce the same retinal image but are perceived as being different images, what has occurred?
    a. telepathy
    b. psychokinesis
    c. a visual illusion
    d. perceptual constancy

LO 24

25. Research conducted with the visual cliff indicated that
    a. 6-month-old infants are not able to perceive depth, but year-old infants are able to perceive depth.
    b. neither 6-month-old infants nor year-old infants are able to perceive depth.
    c. 6-month-old infants are able to perceive depth.
    d. adults from some different cultures have difficulty in perceiving depth.

LO 25

26. Clair believes she can predict events before they actually occur. Which type of ESP does Clair believe she possesses?
    a. clairvoyance
    b. precognition
    c. psychokinesis
    d. telepathy

LO 26

27. According to the text, which of the following has hindered the acceptance of ESP in the scientific community?
    a. excessive publicity
    b. the subjective nature of ESP
    c. the inability to replicate research
    d. the inability to precisely define the phenomena

LO 27

Practice Test 2

The following multiple-choice questions also are keyed to the chapter Learning Objectives. If you answer any questions incorrectly, be sure to review the corresponding Learning Objective and text material.

1. The process of organizing and interpreting sensory information in order to give it meaning is
    a. sensation.
    b. perception.
    c. Gestalt psychology.
    d. both *a* and *b*.

LO 1

2. A painter who is able to tell the difference between two similar shades of paint is demonstrating
    a. the absolute threshold.
    b. the difference threshold.
    c. Weber's law.
    d. sensory adaptation.

LO 2

3. Each of the following is consistent with signal detection theory *except*
   a. liberal responders say a stimulus is present even with a faint indication
   b. conservative responders say a stimulus is present only when they are very sure
   c. psychological factors are important in determining sensitivity to stimuli
   d. absolute thresholds are an integral part of signal detection theory

LO 3

4. People can be influenced by sensations that are too faint to be detected at a conscious level, according to
   a. signal detection theory.
   b. Weber's law.
   c. subliminal perception.
   d. sensory adaptation.

LO 4

5. Weber's law relates to which of the following?
   a. the absolute threshold
   b. sensory adaptation
   c. subliminal perception
   d. the difference threshold

LO 5

6. The rods and cones are found in what part of the eye?
   a. the sclera
   b. the retina
   c. the cornea
   d. the fovea

LO 6

7. Each of the following statements regarding the cones in the retina is true *except*
   a. Under good illumination, cones can detect color.
   b. Cones are primarily located at the fovea.
   c. Cones have a long, cylindrical shape.
   d. Cones actively function in daytime vision.

LO 7

8. Messages from the retina "cross over" at the
   a. optic chiasm.
   b. visual cortex.
   c. retina.
   d. fovea.

LO 8

9. The intensity of light is perceived as
   a. vividness.
   b. brightness.
   c. color.
   d. hue.

LO 9

10. The opponent-process view
    a. states that the cones are sensitive to one of three colors.
    b. helps to explain afterimages.
    c. states that the cells respond to red-green and blue-yellow colors.
    d. both *b* and *c*.

LO 10

11. Decibels are a measure of a sound wave's
    a. frequency.
    b. timbre.
    c. complexity.
    d. amplitude.

LO 11

12. The oval window, the cochlea, and the organ of Corti are located in the
    a. outer ear.
    b. external auditory canal.
    c. middle ear.
    d. inner ear.

LO 12

13. The ear's sensory receptors are located in
    a. the inner ear.
    b. the organ of Corti.
    c. the cochlea.
    d. all of the above.

LO 13

14. Which theory of hearing suggests that high-frequency tones are explained by a team of neurons, with each neuron firing at a different time?
    a. place theory
    b. frequency theory
    c. volley theory
    d. both *a* and *c*

LO 14

15. Which of the following is involved in the sensation of pain?
    a. the peripheral nervous system
    b. the central nervous system
    c. the thalamus
    d. all of the above

LO 15

16. The neural gate for pain can be closed by
    a. a signal from the brain.
    b. neurotransmitters.
    c. emotions.
    d. any of the above.

LO 16

17. Which of the following is responsible for information about movement?
    a. the vestibular sense
    b. the semicircular canals
    c. the kinesthetic sense
    d. all of the above

LO 17

18. In what ways are the papillae and the olfactory epithelium related?
    a. Both are necessary for the sense of taste.
    b. Both are necessary for the sense of smell.
    c. They both contain receptor cells.
    d. Both *a* and *c*.

LO 18

19. Which of the following characterizes the perceptual process?
    a. automatic
    b. selective
    c. creative
    d. all of the above

LO 19

20. The principle by which we organize perception into those stimuli that stand out and those that are left over is called
    a. figure-ground.
    b. closure.
    c. similarity.
    d. proximity.

LO 20

21. An object that partially conceals another or overlaps another object is perceived as being closer, according to the monocular cue called
    a. linear perspective.
    b. texture gradient.
    c. relative size.
    d. interposition.

LO 21

22. Movement aftereffects are an example of
    a. apparent movement.
    b. stroboscopic movement.
    c. real movement.
    d. shape constancy.

LO 22

23. Each of the following is an example of perceptual constancy *except*
    a. size constancy.
    b. shape constancy.
    c. dimensional constancy.
    d. brightness constancy.

LO 23

24. The devil's tuning fork produces a visual illusion because of
    a. ambiguous depth cues.
    b. ambiguous size cues.
    c. ambiguous brightness cues.
    d. both *a* and *b*.

LO 24

25. Research on individuals who recover from blindness
    a. conclusively proves that perception is innate.
    b. conclusively proves that perception is learned.
    c. has conclusively demonstrated the interaction of learning and innate perception.
    d. is inconclusive regarding the issue of whether perception is innate or learned.

LO 25

26. Which of the following skills might allow you to transfer your thoughts to somebody else?
    a. precognition
    b. clairvoyance
    c. psychokinesis
    d. telepathy

LO 26

27. Although ESP demonstrations are dramatic, according to scientific researchers, ESP experiments thus far have lacked
    a. precision of definition.
    b. replication.
    c. the necessary instruments to measure ESP phenomena.
    d. widespread acceptance by the public.

LO 27

Answers to Key Terms

1. **Sensation** is the process of detecting and encoding stimulus energy in the world.
2. **Perception** is the brain's process of organizing and interpreting sensory information to give it meaning.
3. **Psychophysics** is the formal study of psychological reactions to physical stimulation.
4. The **difference threshold** is the smallest difference in stimulation required to discriminate one stimulus from another 50 percent of the time.
5. According to **Weber's law,** the difference threshold is a constant percentage (rather than a constant amount).
6. The **absolute threshold** is the minimum amount of energy an individual can detect 50 percent of the time.
7. **Signal detection theory** states that no absolute thresholds exist. According to this theory a variety of psychological and contextual factors also affect sensitivity to sensory stimuli.
8. **Subliminal perception** is the perception of stimuli below the threshold of awareness.
9. **Sensory adaptation** is weakened sensitivity due to prolonged stimulation.
10. **Sensation seeking** refers to the need for varied, novel, and complex sensations and experiences.
11. **Sensory deprivation** refers to extended periods of time in which normal external stimulation is prevented.
12. **Light** is a form of electromagnetic energy that can be described in terms of wavelengths.
13. A **wavelength** is the distance from the peak of one wave to the peak of the next.
14. The **sclera** is the white part of the eye. It helps maintain the shape of the eye and protects it from injury.
15. The **iris** is a ring of muscles in the eye; they range in color from light blue to dark brown.
16. The **pupil** is the dark opening in the center of the iris; it helps reduce glare from high illumination.
17. The **cornea** is a clear membrane in front of the iris that bends light rays as they enter the eye.
18. The **lens of the eye** helps bring objects into focus by bending light to focus it at the back of the eye.
19. **Accommodation** is the action of the lens of the eye to increase its curvature.
20. The **retina** is the light-sensitive surface in the back of the eye containing the rods and cones.
21. The **rods** are receptors that especially function in night vision; they are sensitive to white, black, and gray.
22. The **cones** are receptors that especially function in the daytime; they are sensitive to color.
23. The **fovea** is a minute area in the center of the retina where vision is at its best.
24. The **blind spot** is the area of the retina where the optic nerve leaves the eye. We cannot see anything at this spot.
25. **Hue** is a characteristic of color based on its wavelength. It is what we usually think of as "color."
26. The **saturation** of a color is its purity, or the amount of white light added to a single wavelength of color.
27. The **brightness** of a color refers to the intensity of light; white has most brightness, and black has the least.
28. An **additive mixture** of color is a mixture of beams of light from different parts of the color spectrum; television is an example.
29. A **subtractive mixture** is a mixture of pigments, as on an artist's canvas.
30. The **trichromatic theory** suggests that each receptor on the retina is maximally sensitive to different, but overlapping wavelengths.
31. **Dichromats** are people with only two kinds of cones.
32. **Trichromats** are people with normal color vision; that is, they have three kinds of cone receptors.
33. **Afterimages** are sensations that remain after a stimulus is removed.
34. The **opponent-process theory** states that cells in the retina respond to red or green and to blue or yellow colors.
35. **Sounds** are vibrations in the air that are processed by our auditory system.

36. The **frequency** of a sound wave is the number of cycles (full wavelengths) that pass through a point in a given amount of time.
37. **Pitch** is the perceptual interpretation of a sound's frequency.
38. **Amplitude,** measured in decibels, is the amount of pressure produced by a sound wave.
39. **Loudness** is the perception of a sound wave's amplitude.
40. **Complex sounds** are those in which numerous frequencies of sound blend together.
41. **Timbre** is the tone color or perceptual quality of a sound.
42. The **outer ear** contains the pinna and the external auditory canal. The pinna helps localize sound; waves are the funneled through the canal.
43. The **middle era** contains the eardrum, hammer, anvil, and stirrup. Its structures translate the sound waves in air into sound waves in fluid.
44. The **inner ear** contains the oval window, cochlea, and organ of Corti. The inner ear changes the sound waves into neural impulses.
45. The **cochlea** is a fluid-filled, tubular, coiled structure in the inner ear.
46. The **basilar membrane** is housed inside the cochlea and runs its entire length.
47. The **organ of Corti** contains the ear's sensory receptors, which convert the energy of the sound waves into nerve impulses.
48. **Place theory** states that each frequency produces vibrations at a particular spot on the basilar membrane.
49. **Frequency theory** states that the perception of a sound's frequency is due to how often the auditory nerve fires.
50. **Volley theory** expands frequency theory to account for high-frequency sounds in terms of offset firing times of neurons.
51. The **auditory nerve** carries neural impulses to the brain's auditory areas.
52. The **pain threshold** is the stimulation level at which pain is first perceived.
53. The **gate-control theory** of pain suggests that the spinal cord has a neural gate that can be opened (allowing the perception of pain) or closed (blocking the perception of pain).
54. **Acupuncture** is a technique involving the insertion of needles at specific points in the body to produce specific effects.
55. The **kinesthetic senses** provide information about movement, posture, and orientation.
56. The **vestibular sense** provides information about balance and movement.
57. The **semicircular canals** are located in the inner ear and contain receptors that detect body motion.
58. **Papillae** are the bumps on the tongue that contain taste buds.
59. The **olfactory epithelium** is tissue located at the top of the nasal cavity that contains the receptors for smell.
60. **Perceptual set** refers to expectations that influence how we interpret stimuli.
61. **Contour** is a perceptual term; it refers to a location at which a sudden change in brightness occurs.
62. **Figure-ground relationship** is the principle by which we organize the perceptual field into stimuli that stand out (figure) and those that are left over (ground).
63. **Gestalt psychology** suggests that people naturally organize their perceptions according to certain patterns.
64. **Depth perception** is the ability to perceive objects three-dimensionally.
65. **Binocular cues** are depth cues based on both eyes working together.
66. **Monocular cues** are depth cues based on each eye working independently.
67. **Retinal or binocular disparity** is perception in which the individual sees a single scene, even though the retinal images are slightly different.
68. **Convergence** is a binocular cue for depth perception in which the eyes turn inward as the object gets closer.
69. **Apparent movement** occurs when an object is stationary, but we perceive it to be moving.
70. **Stroboscopic motion** is the illusion of movement created when the image of an object is flashed on and off rapidly in succession at different places on the retina.
71. **Movement aftereffects** occur when we watch continuous movement in one direction and then look at a stationary surface, which appears to move in the opposite direction.
72. **Size constancy** is the recognition that an object stays the same size even though the retinal image of the object changes.
73. **Shape constancy** is the recognition that an object remains the same shape even though its orientation to us changes.

74. **Brightness constancy** is the recognition that an object retains the same degree of brightness even when different amounts of light fall on it.
75. A **visual illusion** occurs when two objects produce the same retinal image but are perceived as different images.
76. The **carpentered-world hypothesis** states that people who live in cultures in which straight lines, right angles, and rectangles predominate should be more susceptible to illusions, such as the Müller-Lyer illusion, involving straight lines, right angles, and rectangles than are people who live in noncarpentered worlds.
77. **Extrasensory perception** is perception that occurs without the use of any known sensory process.
78. **Telepathy** involves the transfer of thought from one person to another.
79. **Precognition** involves "knowing" events before they occur.
80. **Clairvoyance** involves the ability to perceive remote events that are not in sight.
81. **Psychokinesis** is the ability to move objects without touching them.

Answers to Guided Review

1. sensation (p. 95)
2. perception (p. 95)
3. information-processing (p. 95)
4. absolute threshold (p. 95)
5. psychophysics
6. just noticeable difference (p. 97)
7. Weber's (p. 97)
8. signal detection
9. contextual
10. liberal
11. subliminal (p. 97)
12. sensory adaptation (p. 97)
13. habituation (p. 97)
14. sensation
15. seeking
16. destructive
17. sensory deprivation
18. wavelengths (p. 98)
19. wavelength (p. 98)
20. sclera (p. 99)
21. iris (p. 99)
22. pupil (p. 99)
23. cornea (p. 99)
24. lens (p. 99)
25. accommodation (p. 100)
26. retina (p. 100)
27. rods (p. 100)
28. cones (p. 100)
29. fovea (p. 100)
30. blind spot (p. 100)
31. rods (p. 100)
32. daytime (p. 100)
33. optic nerve (p. 101)
34. optic chiasm (p. 101)
35. right (p. 101)
36. visual cortex (p. 102)
37. wavelengths (p. 102)
38. saturation (p. 102)
39. additive (p. 103)
40. pigments (p. 103)
41. additive (p. 103)
42. subtractive (p. 103)
43. trichromatic (p. 104)
44. trichromats
45. afterimages (p. 104)
46. opponent-process (p. 105)
47. vibrations (p. 106)
48. frequency (p. 106
49. pitch (p. 106)
50. amplitude (p. 106)
51. decibels (p. 106)
52. complexity (p. 106)
53. timbre (p. 106)
54. pinna (p. 107)
55. middle ear (p. 108)
56. eardrum (p. 108)
57. anvil (p. 108)
58. cochlea (p. 108)
59. basilar membrane (p. 108)
60. basilar (p. 108)
61. auditory nerve (p. 108)
62. frequency (p. 108)
63. volley (p. 108)
64. auditory nerve (p. 108)
65. skin (p. 109)
66. temperature (p. 109)
67. threshold (p. 109)
68. nerve endings (p. 109)
69. cerebral cortex (p. 109)
70. gate-control (p. 110)
71. acupuncture (p. 111)
72. kinesthetic senses (p. 112)
73. vestibular (p. 112)
74. joints (p. 112)
75. inner (p. 113)
76. equilibratory (p. 113)
77. chemicals (p. 114)
78. papillae (p. 114)
79. sour (p. 114)
80. salty (p. 114)
81. olfactory epithelium (p. 114)
82. modeling (p. 114)
83. perception (p. 116)
84. selective (p. 117)
85. creative (p. 117)
86. perceptual set (p. 117)
87. contour (p. 117)
88. figure-ground (p. 117)
89. Gestalt (p. 117)
90. proximity (p. 118)
91. depth perception (p. 118)
92. binocular (p. 118)
93. monocular (p. 118)
94. binocular (p. 119)
95. convergence (p. 119)
96. pictorial (p. 119)
97. apparent movement
98. stroboscopic
99. movement aftereffects
100. size (p. 120)
101. shape (p. 120)
102. brightness (p. 121)
103. visual illusion (p. 121)
104. visual cliff (p. 122)
105. blindness (p. 123
106. cross-cultural (p. 123)
107. carpentered-world (p. 123)
108. extrasensory perception (p. 124)
109. telepathy (p. 124)
110. precognition (p. 124)
111. clairvoyance (p. 124)
112. psychokinesis (p. 124)
113. reproducible (p. 127)

Answers to Multiple-Choice Questions- Practice Test 1

1. a. **Correct.** The process of perception begins when stimuli are detected by receptor cells in the sense organs.
   b. Incorrect. Perception is the process of organizing and interpreting sensory information.
   c. Incorrect. Gestalt psychology is an approach that attempts to understand how people organize their perceptions.
   d. Incorrect. Accommodation is a process that helps the eye to focus on stimuli.

2. a. Incorrect. It would be a difficult task, indeed, to find the "average" person.
   b. **Correct.** The absolute threshold is also referred to as "limen."
   c. Incorrect. If this were true, what happens to the detection abilities of the other half of the people tested?
   d. Incorrect. This may sound impressive, but I'm not sure what it means!

3. a. Incorrect. Weber's law states that two stimuli must differ by a constant proportion in order to detect a difference.
   b. Incorrect. Subliminal perception refers to the perception of stimuli below the threshold of awareness.
   c. **Correct.** Signal detection theory suggests that no absolute thresholds exist. Rather, sensitivity to stimuli is based on psychological and contextual factors.
   d. Incorrect. The absolute threshold is the minimum amount of sensation we are able to detect 50 per cent of the time.

4. a. **Correct.** Although this idea has caused a great deal of debate and concern, according to the text there is little evidence that subliminal messages influence behavior.
   b. Incorrect. Weber's law deals with absolute thresholds that *are* detected.
   c. Incorrect. Signal detection theory is concerned with the psychological and contextual components involved in detecting stimuli.
   d. Incorrect. Sensory adaptation involves weakened sensitivity to a stimulus as a result of prolonged stimulation. It is also referred to as habituation.

5. a. Incorrect. Subliminal perception is the perception of stimuli below the threshold of awareness. When you step into the cold water, you are definitely aware of the stimulus.
   b. Incorrect. Although you may be aware of the difference between being in the pool and not being in the pool, the question asks about habituation to the cold water.
   c. Incorrect. Weber's law states that two stimuli must differ by a constant proportion to detect a difference.
   d. **Correct**. Sensory adaptation is also referred to as "habituation."

6. a. Incorrect. The sclera helps to maintain the shape of the eye and to protect it from injury.
   b. Incorrect. The retina is the light-sensitive surface in the back of the eye that contains the rods and cones.
   c. Incorrect. The pupil is the opening in the center of the iris.
   d. **Correct.** Both the cornea and the lens of the eye help to "bend" light as it enters the eye.

7. a. Incorrect. The statement is true; the question is looking for an *untrue* statement.
   b. Incorrect. The statement is true; the question is looking for an *untrue* statement.
   c. Incorrect. The statement is true; the question is looking for an *untrue* statement.
   d. **Correct.** It is the cones that are found at the fovea.

8. a. **Correct.** Messages are carried to the occipital lobe by the optic nerve.
   b. Incorrect. The parietal lobe is involved in detecting body sensations.
   c. Incorrect. The temporal lobe is involved in hearing.
   d. Incorrect. The frontal lobe is involved in controlling involuntary movements, and in intelligence.

9. a. Incorrect. A color's hue is based on its wavelength.
   b. Incorrect. A color's saturation is based on its purity.
   c. **Correct.** White has the most brightness, black the least.
   d. Incorrect. "Strength" is not considered a variation of color, whereas hue, saturation and brightness are considered variations.

10. a. Incorrect. The trichromatic theory is best at explaining dichromats and trichromats, but not at explaining afterimages.
    b. **Correct.** Proposed initially by Hering, the red-blue and yellow-green opposites help to explain afterimages.
    c. Incorrect. The additive mixture and subtractive mixture refer to mixing colors to get different variations.
    d. Incorrect. One of the other alternatives is a better answer.

11. a. **Correct.** Frequency refers to the number of wavelengths that pass through a point at a given time.
    b. Incorrect. Timbre is the perceptual *quality* of a sound.
    c. Incorrect. Complexity is the number of frequencies of a sound that blend together.
    d Incorrect. Amplitude is the amount of pressure produced by a sound wave. Loudness is the perception of amplitude.

12. a. Incorrect. The outer ear, consisting of the pinna and the external auditory canal, is designed to help us localize the sound.
    b. **Correct.** The tiny bones help to amplify the sound waves before they reach the fluid-filled inner ear.
    c. Incorrect. The inner ear contains the oval window, cochlea and the organ of Corti.
    d. Incorrect. The basilar membrane is found inside the cochlea; it is part of the inner ear.

13. a. Incorrect. The eardrum is a structure in the middle ear that vibrates in response to sound.
    b. Incorrect. Although the oval window is located in the inner ear, it is a membrane that transmits the soundwaves to the cochlea.
    c. Incorrect. The basilar membrane is housed inside the cochlea, but does not contain the hairlike cells.
    d. **Correct.** The organ of Corti also runs the length of the cochlea.

14. a. **Correct.** Although place theory explains high-frequency sounds, it does not adequately explain low-frequency sounds.
    b. Incorrect. Frequency theory states that the perception of a sound's frequency is due to how often the auditory nerve fires.
    c. Incorrect. Volley theory states that high frequencies can be signaled by teams of neurons that fire at different offset times, and thus signal a high frequency.
    d. Incorrect. One of the other alternatives is the correct answer. Hint: the theory is particularly effective at explaining high-frequency sounds.

15. a. Incorrect. The cerebral cortex is the last stop in a pain message's journey to the brain.
    b. Incorrect. The pain threshold refers to the amount of pain message necessary to feel pain.
    c. Incorrect. The spinal cord is not the structure sensitized by the chemicals.
    d. **Correct.** Two examples of chemicals are substance P and bradykinin.

16. a. **Correct.** If the gate is opened it allows the perception of pain; if closed, the pain message is blocked.
    b. Incorrect. These receptors are stimulated by chemicals, but this is not the location of the neural gate.
    c. Incorrect. The brain stem is not the location of the neural gate.
    d. Incorrect. The correct location is actually one of those mentioned in this answer.

17. a. Incorrect. I believe there are different types of canals located in Venice.
    b. **Correct.** The canals are three circular tubes that lie in different planes of the body.
    c. Incorrect. The outer ear consists of the pinna and external auditory canal.
    d. Incorrect. The canals are found in one of the other divisions of the ear.

18. a. Incorrect. This *is* one of the basic qualities of taste.
    b. Incorrect. This *is* one of the basic qualities of taste.
    c. Incorrect. This *is* one of the basic qualities of taste.
    d. **Correct.** The fourth quality is sour.

19. a. **Correct.** The perceptual process missing is *automatic*.
    b. Incorrect. This *is* one of the characteristics of perceptual processes.
    c. Incorrect. This *is* one of the characteristics of perceptual processes.
    d. Incorrect. This *is* one of the characteristics of perceptual processes.

20. a. **Correct.** This is an important Gestalt principle.
    b. Incorrect. This is the principle by which we organize perceptions into stimuli that stand out and those that are background.
    c. Incorrect. This is the principle that when we see objects close together, we mentally group them together.
    d. Incorrect. This is the principle that we are more likely to group together items that are similar.

21. a. Incorrect. Convergence is a binocular cue.
    b. **Correct**. Another binocular cue is called retinal disparity.
    c. Incorrect. Linear perspective tells us that the farther an object is from view, the less space it takes up in the visual field.
    d. Incorrect. Linear perspective is a monocular cue.

22. a. Incorrect. Unless, that is, Paul is dancing in a movie.
    b. Incorrect. If it's an offer for lunch, it sounds most unappetizing!
    c. **Correct**. The formal name for it is stroboscopic motion.
    d. Incorrect. One can *never* spend too much time studying psychology!

23. a. **Correct.** Two examples of perceptual constancy are shape constancy and size constancy.
    b. Incorrect. Stroboscopic motion is an illusion of movement.
    c. Incorrect. Movement aftereffects are an illusion of movement.
    d. Incorrect. Figure-ground is an example of shape perception.

24. a. Incorrect. This refers to the extrasensory transfer of thought from one person to another.
    b. Incorrect. This refers to the extrasensory ability to move objects without touching them.
    c. **Correct.** Although illusions are incorrect perceptions, according to the text they are not abnormal.
    d. Incorrect. Perceptual constancy refers to our ability to see objects as constant although the visual images of them are changing.

25. a. Incorrect. Research suggests that children are able to perceive depth before their first birthday.
    b. Incorrect. Research found that infants develop depth perception at an early age.
    c. **Correct.** This research didn't answer the question of whether depth perception is innate.
    d. Incorrect. Although culture shapes perception, the visual cliff research was conducted on infants.

26. a. Incorrect. Clair is not demonstrating clairvoyance, which is the ability to perceive remote events not in sight.
    b. **Correct**. Perhaps Clair has a career waiting for her as a fortune teller.
    c. Incorrect. This skill involves moving objects without touching them.
    d. Incorrect. This type of extrasensory perception involves transferring thought from one person to another.

27. a. Incorrect. Although there has been much publicity given to ESP phenomena, this has not hindered the acceptance of ESP in the scientific community.
    b. Incorrect. This has not hindered the acceptance of ESP in the scientific community.
    c. **Correct**. According to the text, when vigorous experimental standards have been applied, ESP phenomena have not been demonstrated.
    d. Incorrect. This has not hindered the acceptance of ESP in the scientific community.

Answers to Multiple Choice Questions- Practice Test 2

1 a. Incorrect. Sensation is the process of detecting and encoding stimuli.
  b. **Correct.** Perception organizes and interprets what is sensed.
  c. Incorrect. Gestalt psychologists try to understand the ways in which people organize their perceptions.
  d. Incorrect. This does not define sensation.

2. a. Incorrect. The absolute threshold would determine whether or not the painter can detect the presence of a color.
   b. **Correct.** The difference threshold is the smallest magnitude of difference between two stimuli that can be detected 50 percent of the time.
   c. Incorrect. According to this law, the difference threshold is a constant percentage rather than a constant amount.
   d. Incorrect. This refers to weakened sensitivity to a stimulus due to prolonged stimulation.

3. a. Incorrect. This statement *is* consistent with signal detection theory.
   b. Incorrect. This statement *is* consistent with signal detection theory.
   c. Incorrect. This statement *is* consistent with signal detection theory.
   d. **Correct.** Signal detection theory states that absolute thresholds do not exist.

4. a. Incorrect. Signal detection theory is concerned with the psychological and contextual factors in detecting signals.
   b. Incorrect. Weber's law states that the difference threshold is a constant percentage.
   c. **Correct.** Subliminal perception remains a controversial topic.
   d. Incorrect. Sensory adaptation refers to weakened sensitivity to a stimulus due to prolonged stimulation.

5. a. Incorrect. The absolute threshold refers to the minimum amount of energy an individual can detect 50 percent of the time.
   b. Incorrect. Sensory adaptation refers to weakened sensitivity to a stimulus due to prolonged stimulation.
   c. Incorrect. Subliminal perception is the perception of stimuli below the threshold of awareness.
   d. **Correct.** Weber's law states that the difference threshold is a constant percentage.

6. a. Incorrect. The sclera helps maintain the shape of the eye and protects it from injury.
   b. **Correct.** The rods and cones are the light-sensitive cells on the retina.
   c. Incorrect. The cornea is the clear membrane in front of the iris that bends light rays as they enter the eye.
   d. Incorrect. The fovea is a minute area in the center of the retina where vision is at its best.

7. a. Incorrect. This statement regarding cones is true.
   b. Incorrect. This statement regarding cones is true.
   c. **Correct**. Cones are shorter and fatter than rods.
   d. Incorrect. This statement regarding cones is true.

8. a. **Correct.** It is at this point that the optic nerve fibers divide on their way to the brain.
   b. Incorrect. This section of the occipital lobe is responsible for processing visual information.
   c. Incorrect. The blind spot is the location on the retina where the optic nerve leaves on its way to the brain.
   d. Incorrect. The fovea is an area on the retina where vision is at its best.

9. a. Incorrect. Saturation is based on the purity of a color.
   b. **Correct**. White has the most brightness, whereas black has the least brightness.
   c. Incorrect. The colors we perceive are based upon the specific wavelengths reflected.
   d. Incorrect. A color's hue is based on its wavelength.

10. a. Incorrect. This statement is consistent with the trichromatic theory of color vision.
    b. Incorrect. This statement is true, but is not the best alternative.
    c. Incorrect. This statement is true, but is not the best alternative.
    d. **Correct.** The opponent process view contrasts with the trichromatic theory of color vision.

11. a. Incorrect. Frequency is a measure of the number of sound waves that pass through a point at a given time.
    b. Incorrect. Timbre is the tone color or perceptual quality of a sound.
    c. Incorrect. Complexity is a measure of the number of frequencies blending together.
    d. **Correct.** Decibels measure the amount of pressure produced by a sound.

12. a. Incorrect. The outer ear consists of the pinna and the external auditory canal.
    b. Incorrect. The external auditory canal is located in the pinna.
    c. Incorrect. The middle ear consists of the eardrum, hammer, anvil and stirrup.
    d. **Correct**. This is where sound is finally transformed into neural impulse.

13. a. Incorrect. This statement is true, but is not the best alternative.
    b Incorrect. This statement is true, but is not the best alternative.
    c. Incorrect. This statement is true, but is not the best alternative.
    d. **Correct.** The organ of Corti is located in the cochlea, which forms the inner ear.

14. a. Incorrect. Place theory states that each frequency produces vibrations at a particular spot on the basilar membrane.
    b. Incorrect. Frequency theory states that the perception of a sound's frequency is due to how often the auditory nerve fires.
    c. **Correct.** Volley theory is actually a modification of place theory.
    d. Incorrect. Place theory does not adequately explain low-frequency sounds.

15. a. Incorrect. This statement is true, but is not the best alternative.
    b. Incorrect. This statement is true, but is not the best alternative.
    c. Incorrect. This statement is true, but is not the best alternative.
    d. **Correct.** The sensation of pain flows through each of the alternatives.

16. a. Incorrect. Signals from the brain *can* close the pain gate.
    b. Incorrect. Neurotransmitters can close the pain gate.
    c. Incorrect. Emotions can influence the opening or closing of the neural pain gate.
    d. **Correct.** Chemicals released in the skin do not influence the opening or closing of the neural pain gate.

17. a. Incorrect. The vestibular sense provides feedback about whether the body is slowing down, speeding up, titling or moving.
    b. Incorrect. The semicircular canals are located in the inner ear and contain receptors that detect motion such as tilting the head or body.
    c. Incorrect. The kinesthetic sense provides information about movement, posture and orientation.
    d. **Correct.** Papillae are the bumps on the tongue that contain the taste buds.

18. a. Incorrect. The olfactory epithelium is not necessary for the sense of taste.
    b. Incorrect. The papillae are receptor cells for the taste sense.
    c. **Correct.** The papillae are taste buds and the olfactory epithelium is a sheet of receptor cells for the sense of smell.
    d. Incorrect. The papillae are taste buds, located on the tongue.

19 a. Incorrect. Although this answer is true, it is not the best alternative.
    b. Incorrect. Although this answer is true, it is not the best alternative.
    c. Incorrect. Although this answer is true, it is not the best alternative.
    d. **Correct.** An additional characteristic of the perceptual process is *contextual.*

20 a. **Correct.** An ambiguous demonstration of this principle is demonstrated by the goblet/silhouetted faces pattern in the text.
    b. Incorrect. Closure refers to our tendency to mentally "fill in the gaps" when we see a disconnected or incomplete picture.
    c. Incorrect. The principle of similarity refers to our tendency to group similar items together.
    d. Incorrect. The principle of proximity refers to our tendency to group together objects that are physically close together.

21. a. Incorrect. According to this cue, objects that are farther from the viewer take up less space in the visual field. As objects recede in the distance, parallel lines begin to converge.
    b. Incorrect. According to this cue, the texture of objects become denser the farther away they are from a viewer.
    c. Incorrect. According to this cue, objects farther away create a smaller retinal image than objects that are closer.
    d. **Correct**. Remember that monocular cues are depth cues based on each eye working independently.

22. a. **Correct.** Apparent movement refers to situations when an object is stationary but we perceive them to be moving. Another example is stroboscopic movement.
    b. Incorrect. Stroboscopic movement is another example of movement aftereffects.
    c. Incorrect. Actually, movement aftereffects are the *perception* of movement, not real movement.
    d. Incorrect. Shape constancy is the recognition that an object remains the same shape even though we may look at it from different distances, angles, and so on.

23. a. Incorrect. Although this answer is true, it is not the best alternative.
    b. Incorrect. Although this answer is true, it is not the best alternative.
    c. **Correct**. Dimensional constancy (whatever it is) is not an example of perceptual constancy.
    d. Incorrect. Although this answer is true, it is not the best alternative.

24. a. **Correct.** Can you think of other visual illusions produced by ambiguous depth cues?
    b. Incorrect. Other illusions, including the Ponzo illusion, are produced by ambiguous size cues.
    c Incorrect. The devil's tuning fork is produced by ambiguous cues, but not ambiguous brightness cues.
    d. Incorrect. One of the two alternatives mentioned in this alternative is correct.

25. a. Incorrect. According to the text, research on individuals who recover from blindness is inconclusive.
    b. Incorrect. According to the text, research on individuals who recover from blindness is inconclusive.
    c. Incorrect. According to the text, research on individuals who recover from blindness is inconclusive.
    d. **Correct.** The wide variety of reactions to recovery from blindness has not permitted researchers to conclusively answer the question regarding whether perception is learned or innate.

26. a. Incorrect. Precognition involves "knowing" events before they occur.
    b. Incorrect. Clairvoyance involves the ability to perceive remote events that are not in sight.
    c. Incorrect. Psychokinesis involves the ability to move objects without touching them.
    d. **Correct**. A high degree of telepathy would be useful during exams!

27. a. Incorrect. Precision in defining terms is not cited in the text as a problem for scientific researchers.
    b. **Correct.** According to the text, scientists have been unable to replicate the work of ESP enthusiasts.
    c. Incorrect. Instrumentation is not mentioned in the text as a problem for scientific researchers.
    d. Incorrect. Public support or lack thereof is not mentioned in the text as an issue for scientific researchers.

Chapter 4 States of Consciousness

Learning Objectives

After studying this chapter, you should be able to:

1. Define consciousness. (p. 122)

2. Contrast William James's concept of "stream of consciousness" and Freud's unconscious thought. (p. 122)

3. Distinguish between controlled processes and automatic processes. (p. 123)

4. Define and describe altered states of consciousness. (p. 123)

5. Describe circadian rhythms. (p. 125)

6. Describe the four stages of sleep and REM sleep. (p. 125)

7. Distinguish between the repair theory and the ecological theory of sleep. (p. 130)

8. Identify the following sleep disorders: insomnia, sleepwalking and sleeptalking, nightmares and night terrors, narcolepsy, and sleep apnea. (p. 131)

9. Distinguish among the major theories of dreaming. (p. 133)

10. Define hypnosis; describe the four steps used to induce hypnosis. (p. 137)

11. Distinguish between the special-process theory and the nonstate view of hypnosis. (p. 138)

12. Discuss the reasons why humans are attracted to psychoactive drugs. (p. 139)

13. Distinguish among drug tolerance, drug addiction, drug withdrawal, and psychological dependence on drugs. (p. 140)

14. Discuss the physical and psychological effects of the following: alcohol, barbiturates, tranquilizers, and opiates. (p. 140)

15. Describe the physical and psychological effects of stimulants such as amphetamines and cocaine. (p. 144)

16. Describe the physical and psychological effects of marijuana and hallucinogens such as LSD. (p. 145)

Chapter 4 Outline

I. The Nature of Consciousness
   A. Consciousness
      1. Controlled processes
      2. Automatic processes
      3. Daydreaming
   B. Altered states of consciousness
II. Sleep and Dreams
   A. Cycles of sleep and wakefulness
      1. Circadian rhythms
      2. Sleep cycles
         a. beta waves
         b. alpha waves
         c. delta waves
         d. theta waves
         e. sleep spindles
         f. REM sleep
   B. Why we sleep
      1. Repair theory
      2. Ecological theory
   C. Sleep deprivation
   D. Sleep Disorders
      1. Insomnia
      2. Somnambulism
      3. Nightmare/Night terror
      4. Narcolepsy
      5. Sleep apnea
   E. Dreams
      1. Why we dream
         a. wish fulfillment
         b. problem solving
         c. entertainment
         d. meaningless brain states
      2. The nature of dreams
III. Hypnosis
   A. Features of the hypnotic state
      1. Minimize distractions and increase comfort level
      2. Focus attention
      3. Hypnotist describes sensations to expect
      4. Hypnotist suggests events or feelings that are occurring or are highly likely to occur
   B. Individual differences in hypnosis
   C. Theories of hypnosis
      1. Special cognitive state
      2. Nonstate view
   D. Applications of hypnosis
IV. Psychoactive Drugs and Application
   A. Psychoactive drugs
   B. Addiction
      1. Tolerance
      2. Addiction
      3. Withdrawal
      4. Psychological dependence
   C. Alcohol
   D. Other Psychoactive drugs
      1. Barbiturates
      2. Tranquilizers
      3. Opiates
      4. Stimulants
      5. Cocaine/Crack
      6. Marijuana
      7. Hallucinogens

Key Terms

Write a brief description for each of the following terms. Where relevant, provide an original example or illustration of the term. Then, compare your answers with those provided at the end of the Study Guide chapter. Review the text for those terms you don't know and those you define incorrectly.

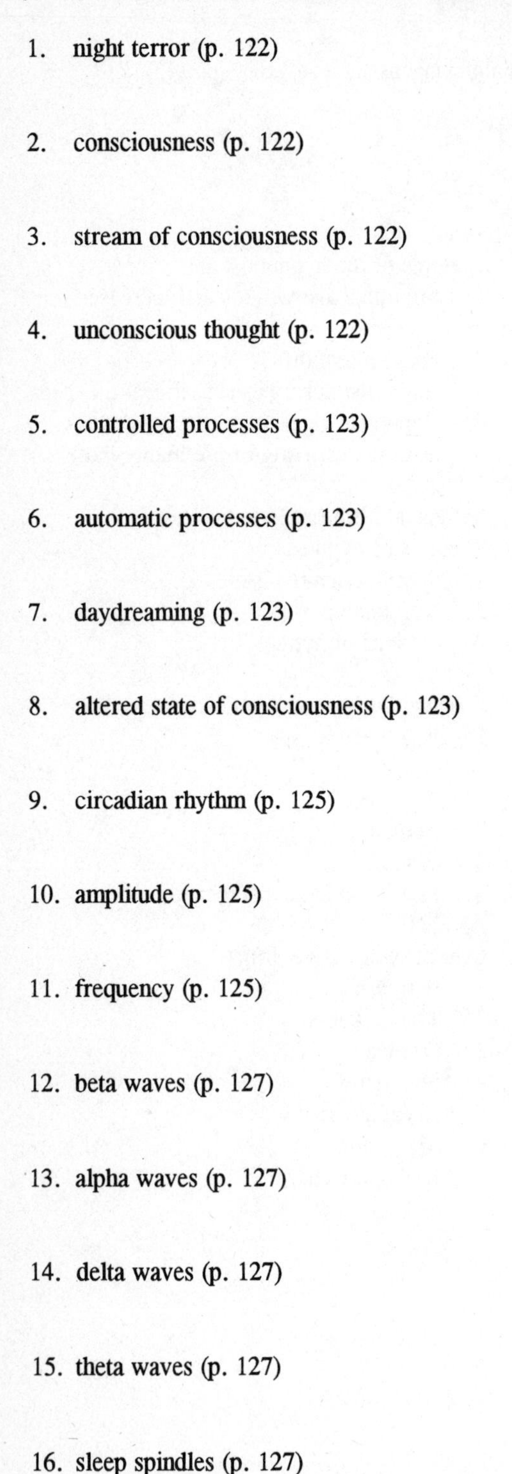

1. night terror (p. 122)

2. consciousness (p. 122)

3. stream of consciousness (p. 122)

4. unconscious thought (p. 122)

5. controlled processes (p. 123)

6. automatic processes (p. 123)

7. daydreaming (p. 123)

8. altered state of consciousness (p. 123)

9. circadian rhythm (p. 125)

10. amplitude (p. 125)

11. frequency (p. 125)

12. beta waves (p. 127)

13. alpha waves (p. 127)

14. delta waves (p. 127)

15. theta waves (p. 127)

16. sleep spindles (p. 127)

17. REM sleep (p. 128)

18. repair theory (p. 130)

19. ecological theory (p. 130)

20. insomnia (p. 131)

21. somnambulism (p. 131)

22. nightmare (p. 132)

23. narcolepsy (p. 132)

24. sleep apnea (p. 132)

25. lucid dreams (p. 136)

26. activation-synthesis view (p. 136)

27. hypnosis (p. 137)

28. posthypnotic suggestion (p. 137)

29. posthypnotic amnesia (p. 137)

30. hidden observer (p. 139)

31. special process theory (p. 138)

32. nonstate view (p. 139)

33. psychoactive drugs (p. 139)

34. tolerance (p. 140)

33. psychoactive drugs (p. 139)

34. tolerance (p. 140)

35. addiction (p. 140)

36. withdrawal (p. 140)

37. psychological dependence (p. 140)

38. barbiturates (p. 144)

39. tranquilizers (p. 144)

40. opiates (p. 144)

41. stimulants (p. 144)

42. crack (p. 144)

43. hallucinogens (p. 145)

Guided Review

The following in-depth chapter review is a challenging and comprehensive fill-in-the-blanks exercise. The answers are found near the end of the chapter. As you go through the exercise, try to resist the temptation to look at the answers until you have provided them. When you have filled in all the blanks, you will have a thorough summary of the chapter for reference and review.

The Nature of Consciousness

When individuals experience sudden arousal from sleep and intense fear, this is referred to as a ___(1)___ ________. The external and internal stimuli we are aware of at any given time is called ___(2)___. William James described consciousness as a continuous flow called a ___(3)___ ________ ________. Freud believed that most of our thoughts are contained in a reservoir of unacceptable wishes; he referred to this as ___(4)___ ________.

Consciousness comes in different forms and levels. The most alert state of consciousness, in which individuals are actively focused on a goal, is referred to as ___(5)___ ________. Activities that require minimal attention are called ___(6)___ processes. Another form of consciousness that involves a low level of conscious effort is called ___(7)___.

A mental state that is noticeably different from normal awareness, produced by drugs, meditation, trauma, fatigue, hypnosis, or sensory deprivation, is called an ___(8)___ ________ of consciousness.

Sleep and Dreams

On the average, sleep takes up about ___(9)___-________ of our lives. The human sleep/wake cycle is an example of a ___(10)___ ________. These rhythms can become ___(11)___ when we take a cross-country flight or change our working hours. The ___(12)___ allows researchers to measure the brain's electrical activity. Periods of concentration are characterized by an EEG pattern of ___(13)___ waves. When we are in a relaxed or drowsy state, individuals produce an EEG pattern of ___(14)___ waves. Slower waves, characteristic of deepening sleep, are called ___(15)___ waves.

As we fall asleep, we begin to produce theta waves; these are characteristic of ___(16)___ sleep. During stage 2 sleep, we periodically produce brief bursts of high-frequency waves called ___(17)___ ________. In stage 3 sleep, ___(18)___-wave activity becomes prominent. During stage 4 sleep, we continue to produce ___(19)___ waves. After about 70 minutes of sleep, the sleeper enters ___(20)___ sleep. Dreams often occur during ___(21)___sleep. *REM* stands for ___(22)___ ________ ________. The amount of deep (stage 4) sleep is greater in the ___(23)___ half of a night's sleep, where the majority of REM sleep takes place during the ___(24)___ part of a night's sleep.

Two theories exist about why we sleep. One, which states that sleep restores or replenishes our brains and bodies, is called ___(25)___ ________. The other theory, which says that sleep helps keep us from wasting energy and from risking harm during those times for which we are not adapted, is called ___(26)___ ________.

Although the exact amount of sleep a person needs varies, some researchers believe almost all adults need to get at least ___(27)___ hours of sleep every night.

A common sleep disorder, characterized by the inability to fall asleep, is ___(28)___. A sleep disorder in which individuals walk in their sleep is called ___(29)___. A frightening dream that awakens a sleeper from REM sleep is called a ___(30)___. Nightmares occur more often than ___(31)___ ________. Some individuals have a sleep disorder in which they experience an overpowering urge to fall asleep; this is called ___(32)___. Some individuals have a sleep disorder in which they stop breathing while they are asleep; this is called ___(33)___ ________.

Throughout history, dreams have had historical, personal, and religious significance. According to psychoanalysts, the sexual and aggressive content of dreams represent ___(34)___ ________. Freud suggested that we disguise our wish fulfillment through the use of ___(35)___. Some dream researchers have studied the role of dreams in ___(36)___ solving. Dreams in which we are aware that the dream is taking place are called ___(37)___ dreams.

A different view of dreaming that suggests that dreams have no inherent meaning is suggested by the ___(38)___-______ view. This view holds that dreams are the way in which the brain tries to make sense out of ___(39)___ activity.

Although some people claim they dream only in black and white, virtually everyone's dreams contain ___(40)___.

Hypnosis

A psychological state of altered attention in which the individual is very receptive to suggestions is called ___(41)___. In the eighteenth century, physician Anton Mesmer credited his success in curing problems to "___(42)___ ________"; we sometimes refer to a hypnotized person as being "___(43)___." There are four steps used to induce hypnosis: (1) the hypnotist makes the subject feel ___(44)___; (2) the hypnotist tells the subject to ___(45)___ on one specific thing; (3) the hypnotist gives the subject ___(46)___ about what to expect; (4) the hypnotist suggests certain events that will occur or are occurring.

Some subjects carry out suggestions after they emerge from the hypnotic state; this is called ___(47)___ ________. Some subjects forget everything that occurred while they were in a hypnotic state; this is called ___(48)___ ________. Individuals vary widely in their ability to be hypnotized.

Two general theories try to explain how hypnosis works. According to Hilgard, hypnosis creates a ___(49)___ ________ in which the person is fully aware but maintains passive involvement. This approach is referred to as the ___(50)___ ________ ________. A different perspective suggests that hypnosis is similar to other forms of social behavior; this is referred to as the ___(51)___ view. Psychotherapy, medicine, dentistry, criminal investigations, and sports have all made use of ___(52)___.

Psychoactive Drugs and Addiction

Drugs that act on the nervous system to alter our state of consciousness, modify our perceptions, and alter our moods are called ___(53)___ drugs. The users of many psychoactive drugs find that they need increasing amounts of the drug for its effect to be produced; they have developed ___(54)___. When the body becomes physically dependent on a drug, this condition is called ___(55)___. When users stop taking some psychoactive drugs, they experience intense pain and craving for the drug, a condition called ___(56)___. The psychological need to take a drug is called psychological ___(57)___.

The most widely used drug in our society is ___(58)___. Alcohol is the substance most abused by adolescents and ___(59)___ students. A number of experts have concluded that heredity plays an important role in some forms of alcoholism; however, although family, twin, and adoption studies reveal a genetic influence, they also implicate ___(60)___ factors.

___(61)___ are depressant drugs that induce sleep or reduce anxiety; tranquilizers, another type of depressant drug, are widely used and can produce ___(62)___ symptoms when a person stops taking them. Opiates, which consist of ___(63)___ and its derivatives, depress the activity of the ___(64)___ nervous system.

Drugs that increase the central nervous system's activity are called ___(65)___. A widely prescribed group of stimulants are ___(66)___. Amphetamines increase the release of the neurotransmitter ___(67)___. A stimulant derived from the coca plant is ___(68)___. An intensified form of cocaine, believed to be one of the most addictive substances known, is ___(69)___. Treating cocaine ___(70)___ has not been very successful.

Derived from the hemp plant, marijuana disrupts the membranes of ___(71)___ and affects the functioning of a variety of ___(72)___ and hormones.

Psychoactive drugs that modify a person's perceptual experiences and produce visual images that are not real are called ___(73)___. An example of a hallucinogen is lysergic acid diethylamide, more commonly known as ___(74)___.

Sociocultural Worlds/Applications in Psychology

In your own words, summarize the material you have read in Sociocultural Worlds, "Altered States of Consciousness and the World's Religions," Applications in Psychology, "Contrasting Views on Treating Alcoholism." Briefly describe how each of these articles relates to the material contained in the chapter.

Concept Check I

Consciousness and Sleep

1. Controlled processes are ________________.
2. ______ ______ are a form of consciousness that requires minimal attention and does not interfere with ongoing activities.
3. A circadian rhythm is ________________.
4. ______ ______ states that sleep restores, replenishes, and rebuilds our brains and bodies, which get worn out by the day's activities.
5. Ecological theory is ________________.

Answers

1. the most alert state of consciousness, in which individuals actively focus their effort toward a goal
2. Automatic processes
3. a daily behavioral or physiological cycle
4. Repair theory
5. an evolution-based view of sleep that suggests that the main purpose of sleep is to prevent animals from wasting their energy and harming themselves during the times of day to which they have not adapted.

Concept Check II

Addiction and Drugs

1.	The disease model of addiction	________________.
2.	_____ _______-_______ _______ ___ _______	suggests that addiction is not a disease but a habitual response and source of gratification or security that can be understood only in the context of social relationships and experiences.
3.	Barbiturates are	________________.
4.	_______ are	depressant drugs, like Valium, that reduce anxiety and induce relaxation.
5.	Opiates	________________.
6.	_______	increase the activity of the central nervous system.
7.	Marijuana is	________________.
8.	_______ is	lysergic acid diethylamide, a hallucinogen that causes striking perceptual changes.

Answers

1. views addictions as biologically based, lifelong diseases that require medical and/or spiritual treatment for recovery
2. The life-process model of addiction
3. depressant drugs, such as Seconal, that induce sleep or reduce anxiety
4. Tranquilizers
5. consist of opium and its derivatives; they depress the central nervous system's activity
6. Stimulants
7. derived from the hemp plant; this drug disrupts the membranes of neurons and affects the functioning of a variety of neurotransmitters and hormones.
8. LSD

Multiple-Choice Questions

Practice Test 1

After answering all the multiple-choice questions in Practice Test 1, compare your answers with the answer key provided at the end of the chapter. The answer key contains a brief explanation of both the correct and incorrect answers. Each of these questions is keyed to the Learning Objectives for the chapter. If you answer any questions incorrectly, review the corresponding Learning Objective and text material before you proceed to Practice Test 2.

1. Each of the following is a component of the definition of consciousness *except*
   a. awareness
   b. external stimuli
   c. internal stimuli
   d. unconscious thought

LO 1

2. William James described the mind as a
   a. series of controlled processes.
   b. series of automatic processes.
   c. stream of consciousness.
   d. series of unconscious thoughts.

LO 2

3. At the beginning of his lecture class, Mike, a student, finds that he is alert, attentive, and focused on the lecture. In which state of consciousness is Mike?
   a. controlled processes
   b. automatic processes
   c. hypnotized
   d. stream of consciousness

LO 3

4. According to the text, an altered state of consciousness widely practiced around the world is
   a. hypnosis.
   b. ritual possession.
   c. sensory deprivation.
   d. caffeine-induced alertness.

LO 4

5. A circadian rhythm is
   a. a popular Latin dance.
   b. a daily cycle.
   c. a body rhythm based upon the moon's phases.
   d. both *b* and *c*.

LO 5

6. Delta waves dominate the deep sleep in
   a. REM sleep.
   b. stage 1 sleep.
   c. stage 2 sleep.
   d. stage 4 sleep.

LO 6

7. The body appears to be temporarily "paralyzed" during
   a. REM dreaming.
   b. non-REM dreaming.
   c. stage 1 sleep.
   d. stage 4 sleep.

LO 6

8. Which theory suggests that sleep is necessary to restore and replenish our bodies?
   a. ecological theory
   b. repair theory
   c. neural theory
   d. circadian theory

LO 7

9. Joe was upset when his date kept falling asleep, until she explained that she is
   a. experiencing posthypnotic amnesia.
   b. bored.
   c. somnambulistic.
   d. narcoleptic.

LO 8

10. A sleep disorder in which individuals stop breathing while they are asleep is called
    a. night terror.
    b. narcolepsy.
    c. sleep apnea.
    d. somnambulism.

LO 8

11. A young man dreams about going home for the holidays, and in his dream he sees himself entering his parents' home through the front door. He describes his dream to a psychology major, who tells him he has unresolved sexual feelings. The psychology major is reflecting the theory of dreaming we know as
   a. lucid dreaming.
   b. the activation-synthesis theory.
   c. Freud's psychoanalytic approach.
   d. the problem-solving approach.

LO 9

12. When hypnosis is induced, the hypnotist
   a. tries to keep the subject distracted.
   b. discourages the subject from concentrating on anything specific.
   c. suggests to the subject what will be experienced in the hypnotic state.
   d. is careful to prevent posthypnotic amnesia.

LO 10

13. According to Hilgard, the "hidden observer" in hypnosis
   a. is consistent with the special-process theory.
   b. describes a part of the mind that is aware of what is happening.
   c. is consistent with the nonstate view.
   d. both *a* and *b*.

LO 11

14. Each of the following is true about psychoactive drugs *except*
   a. They have become popular only recently.
   b. They act on the nervous system.
   c. They produce tolerance
   d. In the short run, they help relieve tension and frustration.

LO 12

15. When he first started to use drugs, Jim needed only a small amount to feel euphoric. Now, six months later, he requires almost three times as much to produce the same feeling. Jim
   a. is addicted to the drug.
   b. has developed a psychological dependence.
   c. has developed a tolerance for the drug.
   d. is trying to avoid withdrawal.

LO 13

16. According to the text, the most widely used drug in our society is
   a. marijuana.
   b. amphetamines.
   c. alcohol.
   d. opiates.

LO 14

17. Which of the following drugs is *not* a depressant?
   a. amphetamines.
   b. alcohol.
   c. barbiturates.
   d. opiates.

LO 14

18. Stimulants produce each of the following effects *except*
   a. increases in heart rate.
   b. increases in appetite.
   c. increases in energy.
   d. increases in body temperature.

LO 15

19. A drug widely prescribed as a diet pill is (are)
   a. opiates.
   b. amphetamines.
   c. barbiturates.
   d. tranquilizers.

LO 15

20. Increases in heart rate, reddening of eyes, and dryness of the mouth characterize reactions to
   a. LSD.
   b. cocaine.
   c. marijuana.
   d. all of the above.

LO 16

Practice Test 2

The following multiple-choice questions also are keyed to the chapter Learning Objectives. If you answer any questions incorrectly, be sure to review the corresponding Learning Objective and text material.

1. "An awareness of external and internal stimuli" defines
   a. altered states of consciousness.
   b. consciousness.
   c. controlled processes.
   d. unconscious thought.

LO 1

2. According to Freud, "a reservoir of unacceptable wishes and feelings" describes
   a. controlled processes.
   b. automatic processes.
   c. a stream of consciousness.
   d. unconscious thought.

LO 2

3. A form of consciousness that requires minimal attention is
   a. controlled processes.
   b. automatic processes.
   c. stream of consciousness.
   d. unconscious thought.

LO 3

4. According to the text, each of the following is an altered state of consciousness *except*
   a. hypnosis.
   b. meditation.
   c. LSD-induced hallucination.
   d. caffeine-induced alertness.

LO 4

5. Which of the following is a circadian rhythm?
   a. the stream of consciousness
   b. the four stages of sleep
   c. REM sleep
   d. the sleep/wake cycle

LO 5

6. Which of the following statements regarding sleep is *true?*
   a. We spend more time in stage 4 and REM sleep during the first half of our sleep cycle.
   b. We spend more time in stage 4 and REM sleep during the second half of our sleep cycle.
   c. We spend more time in stage 4 in the first half of our sleep cycle.
   d. We spend more time in stage 4 in the second half of our sleep cycle.

LO 6

7. The longest REM periods occur during
   a. the early stages of sleep.
   b. the latter stages of sleep.
   c. the middle stages of sleep.
   d. stage 1 sleep.

LO 6

8. Which theory suggests that sleep helps prevent animals from wasting energy and harming themselves during those periods for which they are not adapted?
   a. ecological theory
   b. repair theory
   c. neural theory
   d. circadian theory

LO 7

9. One result of using sedatives to help fall asleep may be
   a. increased REM sleep.
   b. increased stage 4 sleep.
   c. decreased REM sleep.
   d. increased nightmares.

LO 8

10. Each of the following may be a problem in using sedatives to sleep *except*
   a. danger of overdose
   b. decreased REM sleep
   c. increased chance of sleep apnea
   d. decreased effectiveness of the drug over time

LO 8

11. According to the activation-synthesis view,
    a. dreams represent wish fulfillment.
    b. dreams have no inherent meaning.
    c. dreams are a way to solve problems and think creatively.
    d. dreams are merely entertainment.

LO 9

12. Each of the following is a requirement for hypnosis to succeed *except*
    a. distractions are minimized.
    b. the subject is told to concentrate on something specific.
    c. the participant is told what to expect.
    d. the participant is tested to see if he or she is truly relaxed.

LO 10

13. According to the nonstate view of hypnosis,
    a. hypnotic behavior is substantially different from other forms of behavior.
    b. hypnotic behavior can be explained without resorting to special processes.
    c. dissociations in cognitive systems take place.
    d. hypnosis creates a hidden observer.

LO 11

14. Each of the following is a consequence of psychoactive drugs *except*
    a. altered consciousness.
    b. modified perceptions.
    c. changed moods.
    d. increased intelligence levels.

LO 12

15. Which of the following produces withdrawal?
    a. addiction
    b. tolerance
    c. psychological dependence
    d. hypnosis

LO 13

16. Family studies on alcoholism consistently find
    a. little or no genetic component in alcoholism.
    b. a high frequency of alcoholism in close relatives of alcoholics.
    c. strong genetic evidence of alcoholism if grandparents were alcoholic.
    d. a precise genetic mechanism linked to alcoholism.

LO 14

17. Which of the following dramatically affects the neurotransmitters called endorphins?
    a. alcohol
    b. barbiturates
    c. opiates
    d. tranquilizers

LO 15

18. Which of the following is a stimulant?
    a. amphetamines
    b. alcohol
    c. barbiturates
    d. opiates

LO 15

19. Each of the following characterizes marijuana or marijuana use *except*
    a. It is derived from the hemp plant.
    b. The use of marijuana increased in the 1980s.
    c. It produces increases in pulse rate and in blood pressure.
    d. It can alter sperm count.

LO 16

20. The drug LSD primarily acts upon which neurotransmitter?
    a. endorphins
    b. acetylcholine
    c. melatonin
    d. serotonin

LO 16

Answers to Key Terms

1. A **night terror** is characterized by sudden arousal from sleep and intense fear.
2. **Consciousness** is awareness of both external and internal stimuli or events.
3. **Stream of consciousness** is a term first used by William James to describe a continuous flow of changing sensations, thoughts, images, and feelings.
4. **Unconscious thought** is Freud's concept of a reservoir of unacceptable wishes, feelings, and thoughts beyond conscious awareness.
5. **Controlled processes** are the most alert states of consciousness, in which a person is actively focused.
6. **Automatic processes** are a form of consciousness that requires minimal attention and does not interfere with other activities.
7. **Daydreaming** is a form of consciousness that requires a low level of conscious effort. Daydreaming keeps our minds active while helping us to cope, to create, and to fantasize.
8. An **altered state of consciousness** is a mental state that is noticeably different from normal awareness. Drugs, meditation, traumas, fatigue, hypnosis, and sensory deprivation all can induce such states.
9. A **circadian rhythm** is any daily behavioral or physiological cycle, an example of which is the sleep/awake cycle.
10. **Amplitude** refers to the height of a wave.
11. **Frequency** refers to the number of wave cycles per second.
12. **Beta waves** are high-frequency electrical activity in the brain characteristic of periods of concentration.
13. **Alpha waves** are the type of EEG pattern produced by people in a relaxed state.
14. **Delta waves** are the EEG pattern characteristic of deepening sleep and progressive muscle relaxation.
15. **Theta waves** are low-frequency, low-amplitude EEG waves that characterize stage 1 sleep.
16. **Sleep spindles** are brief bursts of higher-frequency brain waves during sleep.
17. **REM sleep** is a periodic stage of sleep during which dreaming occurs.
18. **Repair theory** is the theory that sleep restores, replenishes, and rebuilds our brains and bodies.
19. **Ecological theory** suggests that the purpose of sleep is to prevent animals from wasting energy and harming themselves during those times of the day or night to which they have not adapted.
20. **Insomnia** is the inability to fall asleep or to stay asleep.
21. **Somnambulism** is the formal term for sleepwalking.
22. A **nightmare** is a frightening dream that wakes a sleeper from REM sleep.
23. **Narcolepsy** is the overpowering urge to fall asleep.
24. **Sleep apnea** is a sleep disorder in which individuals stop breathing while they are asleep.
25. In **lucid dreams,** a person "wakes up" mentally but remains in a dream.
26. The **activation-synthesis view** of sleep states that dreams are the brain's efforts to make sense out of the neural activity that takes place during REM sleep, and that dreams have no inherent meaning.
27. **Hypnosis** is a psychological state of altered attention and awareness in which the individual is unusually receptive to suggestions.
28. **Posthypnotic suggestion** is a suggestion, made by the hypnotist while the subject is in a hypnotic state, that the subject carries out after emerging from the hypnotic state.
29. **Posthypnotic amnesia,** induced by the hypnotist's suggestion, is the subject's inability to remember what took place during hypnosis.
30. The **hidden observer** is Hilgard's term for a part of the hypnotized individual's mind that is completely aware of what is happening. This part remains passive or hidden until called upon to comment.
31. **Special process theory** states that hypnotic behavior is fundamentally different from nonhypnotic behavior.
32. The **nonstate view** states that hypnotic behavior is similar to other forms of behavior and can be explained without appealing to special processes.
33. **Psychoactive drugs** act on the nervous system to alter our state of consciousness, modify our perceptions, and alter our moods.
34. **Tolerance** is a state in which a greater amount of a drug is needed to produce the same effect.
35. **Addiction** is physical dependence on a drug.
36. **Withdrawal** is the undesirable intense pain and craving for an addictive drug when the drug is withdrawn.

37. **Psychological dependence** is the need to take a drug to cope with problems and stresses.
38. **Barbiturates** are depressant drugs, such as Nebutal and Seconal, that reduce anxiety and induce sleep.
39. **Tranquilizers** are depressant drugs that induce relaxation and reduce anxiety.
40. **Opiates** are derived from the opium poppy; they depress the central nervous system's activity.
41. **Stimulants** are psychoactive drugs that increase the central nervous system's activity.
42. **Crack** is a highly addictive intensified form of cocaine.
43. **Hallucinogens** are psychoactive drugs that modify a person's perceptual experiences and produce visual images that are not real.

Answers to Guided Review

1. night terror (p. 122)
2. consciousness (p. 122)
3. stream of consciousness (p. 122)
4. unconscious thought (p. 122)
5. controlled processes (p. 123)
6. automatic (p. 123)
7. daydreaming (p. 123)
8. altered state (p. 123)
9. one-third (p. 125)
10. circadian rhythm (p. 125)
11. desynchronized (p. 125)
12. electroencephalogram (EEG) (p. 125)
13. beta (p. 127)
14. alpha (p. 127)
15. delta (p. 127)
16. stage 1 (p. 127)
17. sleep spindles (p. 127)
18. delta (p. 127)
19. delta (p. 127)
20. REM (p. 127)
21. REM (p. 127)
22. rapid eye movement (p. 128)
23. first (p. 129)
24. latter (p. 129)
25. repair theory (p. 129)
26. ecological theory (p. 129)
27. 7 (p. 131)
28. insomnia (p. 131)
29. somnambulism (p. 131)
30. nightmare (p. 132)
31. night terrors (p. 132)
32. narcolepsy (p. 132)
33. sleep apnea (p. 132)
34. wish fulfillment (p. 134)
35. symbolism (p. 135)
36. problem (p. 135)
37. lucid (p. 136)
38. activation-synthesis (p. 136)
39. neural (p. 136)
40. color (p. 136)
41. hypnosis (p. 137)
42. animal magnetism (p. 137)
43. mesmerized (p. 137)
44. comfortable (p. 137)
45. concentrate (p. 137)
46. suggestions (p. 137)
47. posthypnotic suggestion (p. 137)
48. posthypnotic amnesia (p. 137)
49. hidden-observer (p. 138)
50. special process theory (p. 138)
51. nonstate (p. 139)
52. hypnosis (p. 139)
53. psychoactive (p. 139)
54. tolerance (p. 140)
55. addiction (p. 140)
56. withdrawal (p. 140)
57. dependence (p. 140)
58. alcohol (p. 140)
59. college (p. 141)
60. environmental (p. 142)
61. Barbiturates (p. 144)
62. withdrawal (p. 144)
63. opium (p. 144)
64. central (p. 144)
65. stimulants (p. 144)
66. amphetamines (p. 144)
67. dopamine (p. 144)
68. cocaine (p. 144)
69. crack (p. 144)
70. addiction (p. 144)
71. neurons (p. 145)
72. neurotransmitters (p. 145)
73. hallucinogens (p. 145)
74. LSD (p. 145)

Answers to Multiple Choice Questions-Practice Test 1

1. a. Incorrect. Consciousness is defined as awareness of both external and internal stimuli or events.
   b. Incorrect. Consciousness is defined as awareness of both external and internal stimuli or events.
   c. Incorrect. Consciousness is defined as awareness of both external and internal stimuli or events.
   d. **Correct.** Unconscious thought is Freud's concept of a reservoir of unacceptable wishes, feelings, and thoughts that are beyond conscious awareness.

2. a. Incorrect. Controlled processes represent the most alert state of consciousness in which individuals actively focus their effort toward a goal.
   b. Incorrect. Automatic processes are a form of consciousness that require minimal attention and do not interfere with other ongoing activities.
   c. **Correct.** William James described the mind as a stream of consciousness--a continuous flow of changing sensations, images, thoughts, and feelings.
   d. Incorrect. Unconscious thought is Freud's concept of a reservoir of unacceptable wishes, feelings, and thoughts that are beyond conscious awareness.

3. a. **Correct.** Controlled processes represent the most alert state of consciousness in which individuals actively focus their effort toward a goal.
   b. Incorrect. Automatic processes are a form of consciousness that requires minimal attention and does not interfere with other ongoing activities.
   c. Incorrect. Hypnosis is a psychological state of altered attention and awareness in which the individual is usually receptive to suggestions.
   d. Incorrect. Stream of consciousness is a continuous flow of changing sensations, images, thoughts, and feelings.

4. a. Incorrect. Hypnosis is recognized as a legitimate process in psychology and medicine, although it is not practiced as widely as ritual possession.
   b. **Correct.** Ritual possession appears to be widely practiced all over the globe.
   c. Incorrect. Sensory deprivation is any major reduction in the amount or variety of sensory stimulation. It is obviously not practiced as widely as ritual possession.
   d. Incorrect. Caffeine-induced alertness is so common, it is considered a normal state of consciousness rather than an altered state.

5. a. Incorrect. It is Latin, but its not a dance!
   b. **Correct.** A circadian rhythm is a daily behavioral or physiological cycle; an example is the 24-hour sleep-wake cycle.
   c. Incorrect. Circadian rhythm is based on a daily cycle, the moon's phases are based on a monthly cycle.
   d. Incorrect. Since "c" is incorrect, this answer is incorrect also.

6. a. Incorrect. REM sleep is a periodic stage of sleep during which dreaming occurs. During REM sleep, the EEG pattern shows fast, high-intensity waves similar to those of the alpha waves of relaxed wakefulness.
   b. Incorrect. Theta waves, low-frequency and low-amplitude EEG patterns, characterize stage 1 sleep.
   c. Incorrect. In stage 2 sleep, the EEG pattern reflects the presence of sleep spindles, brief bursts of higher-frequency waves.
   d. **Correct.** Although delta waves begin to emerge and intensify throughout the four stages of sleep, delta wave patterns dominate the deep sleep that occurs in stage 4.

7. a. **Correct.** While dreaming in REM, the body is severely limited in its capacity of execute voluntary behavior.
   b. Incorrect. Someone dreaming in a non-REM period does not have the motor paralysis protection found during REM periods.
   c. Incorrect. Someone dreaming in a non-REM period does not have the motor paralysis protection found during REM periods.
   d. Incorrect. Someone dreaming in a non-REM period does not have the motor paralysis protection found during REM periods.

8. a. Incorrect. This evolution-based approach argues that the main purpose of sleep is to prevent animals from wasting their energy and harming themselves during the part of the day or night to which they have not adapted.
   b. **Correct.** Repair theory states that sleep restores, replenishes, and rebuilds our brains and bodies, which somehow are worn out or used up by the day's waking activities.
   c. Incorrect. This theory attempts to explain why we dream.
   d. Incorrect. Circadian rhythm has to do with the full daily cycle.

9. a. Incorrect. Posthypnotic amnesia is the subject's inability to remember what took place during hypnosis.
   b. Incorrect. If his date told him this, Joe would probably still be upset.
   c. Incorrect. Somnambulism is the formal term for sleepwalking.
   d. **Correct.** Narcolepsy is the overpowering urge to fall asleep.

10. a. Incorrect. Night terrors are characterized by sudden arousal from sleep and intense fear, usually accompanied by a number of physiological reactions.
   b. Incorrect. Narcolepsy is the overpowering urge to fall asleep.
   c. **Correct**. Sleep apnea is a sleep disorder in which individuals stop breathing while they are asleep because their windpipe fails to open or brain processes involved in respiration fail to work properly.
   d. Incorrect. Somnambulism is the formal term for sleepwalking.

11. a. Incorrect Lucid dreams are a class of dreams in which a person "wakes up" mentally but remains in the sensory landscape of the dream world.
   b. Incorrect. The activation-synthesis view states that dreams are powered by the spontaneous firing of neurons.
   c. **Correct.** Freud contended that dreams are unconscious attempts to fulfill needs, especially those involving sex and aggression, that cannot be expressed, or that go ungratified during waking hours.
   d. Incorrect. Those supporting this approach believe that dreams are a mental realm where we can solve problems and think creatively.

12. a. Incorrect. Minimizing distraction is the first step in hypnosis.
   b. **Correct.** In the second step of hypnosis, the hypnotist tells the subject to concentrate on something specific.
   c. Incorrect. In the third step of hypnosis, the hypnotist describes what to expect in the hypnotic state.
   d. Incorrect. Posthypnotic amnesia is the subject's inability to remember what took place during hypnosis. Some hypnotists purposely induce posthypnotic amnesia through suggestion.

13. a. Incorrect. According to the special process theory, hypnotic responses are involuntary and involve a hidden observer, but it is also true that the hidden observer describes a part of the mind that is aware of what is happening.
   b. Incorrect. The hidden observer allows a person to be fully aware of what is happening yet maintain passive involvement, but it is also true that the special process theory is consistent with the concept of the hidden observer.
   c. Incorrect. The nonstate view says that hypnotic behavior is similar to other forms of social behavior and can be explained without resorting to special processes. This perspective conflicts with the idea of the hidden observer.
   d. **Correct.** The hidden observer is consistent with the special-process theory and the hidden observer describes a part of the mind that is aware of what is happening.

14. a. **Correct.** Ever since our ancient ancestors first sat entranced in front of a communal fire, humans have searched for substances that would produce pleasurable sensations and alter their states of consciousness.
    b. Incorrect. Psychoactive drugs alter the balance of the chemicals in our nervous system.
    c. Incorrect. As a person continues to take a psychoactive drug, the body develops a tolerance, which means that a greater amount of the drug is needed to produce the same effect.
    d. Incorrect. Smoking, drinking, and taking drugs reduce tension and frustration.

15. a. Incorrect. Addiction is a physical dependence on a drug.
    b. Incorrect. Psychological dependence is the need to take a drug to cope with problems and stress.
    c. **Correct.** As a person continues to take a psychoactive drug, the body develops a tolerance, which means that a greater amount of the drug is needed to produce the same effect.
    d. Incorrect. Withdrawal is the undesirable intense pain and craving that an addicted person feels when the addicting drug is withdrawn.

16. a. Incorrect. According to the text, alcohol is the most widely used drug in our society.
    b. Incorrect. According to the text, alcohol is the most widely used drug in our society.
    c. **Correct.** According to the text, alcohol is the most widely used drug in our society.
    d. Incorrect. According to the text, alcohol is the most widely used drug in our society.

17. a. **Correct.** Amphetamines are stimulants and stimulants are psychoactive drugs that increase the central nervous system's activity.
    b. Incorrect. Alcohol acts upon the body primarily as a depressant and slows down the brain's activities.
    c. Incorrect. Barbiturates are depressant drugs that induce sleep or reduce anxiety.
    d. Incorrect. Opiates depress the central nervous system's activity.

18. a. Incorrect. Stimulants are psychoactive drugs that increase the central nervous system's activity, which would include increases in heart rate.
    b. **Correct.** Diet pills are usually stimulants and they obviously decrease appetite.
    c. Incorrect. Stimulants are psychoactive drugs that increase the central nervous system's activity, which would include increases in energy.
    d. Incorrect. Stimulants are psychoactive drugs that increase the central nervous system's activity, which would include increases in body temperature.

19. a. Incorrect. Opiates depress the central nervous system's activity. Generally appetite is suppressed when nervous system activity is increased.
    b. **Correct.** Amphetamines are widely prescribed, often in the form of diet pills.
    c. Incorrect. Barbiturates are a depressant and do not generally suppress appetite. Stimulants suppress appetite.
    d. Incorrect. Tranquilizers are depressants and do not generally suppress appetite. Stimulants suppress appetite.

20. a. Incorrect. LSD is a hallucinogen that even in low doses produces striking perceptual changes.
    b. Incorrect. Cocaine produces a rush of euphoric feelings.
    c. **Correct.** The physical effects of marijuana include increases in pulse rate and blood pressure, reddening of the eyes, coughing, and dryness of mouth.
    d. Incorrect. Marijuana is the only psychoactive drug among these three that produces this combination of effects.

Answers to Multiple Choice Questions- Practice Test 2

1. a. Incorrect An altered state of consciousness occurs when a person is in a mental state that noticeably differs from normal awareness.
   b. **Correct.** This is the definition of consciousness.
   c. Incorrect. Controlled processes represent the most alert state of consciousness in which individuals actively focus their effort toward a goal.
   d. Incorrect. Unconscious thought is Freud's concept of a reservoir of unacceptable wishes, feelings, and thoughts that are beyond conscious awareness.

2. a. Incorrect. Controlled processes represent the most alert state of consciousness in which individuals actively focus their effort toward a goal.
   b. Incorrect Automatic processes are a form of consciousness that require minimal attention and do not interfere with other ongoing activities.
   c. Incorrect A stream of consciousness is a continuous flow of changing sensations, images, thoughts, and feelings.
   d. **Correct**. Unconscious thought is Freud's concept of a reservoir of unacceptable wishes, feelings, and thoughts that are beyond conscious awareness.

3. a. Incorrect. Controlled processes represent the most alert state of consciousness in which individuals actively focus their effort toward a goal.
   b. **Correct**. Automatic processes are a form of consciousness that require minimal attention and do not interfere with other ongoing activities.
   c. Incorrect. A stream of consciousness is a continuous flow of changing sensations, images, thoughts, and feelings.
   d. Incorrect. Unconscious thought is Freud's concept of a reservoir of unacceptable wishes, feelings, and thoughts that are beyond conscious awareness.

4. a. Incorrect. Hypnosis is a psychological state of altered attention and awareness in which the individual is unusually receptive to suggestions.
   b. Incorrect. Meditation is a mental technique for quieting the mind and body. It is considered an altered state of consciousness.
   c. Incorrect. LSD is a psychoactive drug. Psychoactive drugs act on the nervous system to alter our state of consciousness, modify our perceptions and change our moods.
   d. **Correct.** Caffeine-induced alertness is so common, it is considered a normal state of consciousness rather than an altered state.

5. a. Incorrect. A stream of consciousness is a continuous flow of changing sensations, images, thoughts, and feelings.
   b. Incorrect. A circadian rhythm is a daily behavioral or physiological cycle; an example is the 24-hour sleep-wake cycle. The four stages of dreaming only have to do with the sleep part of the sleep-wake cycle.
   c. Incorrect. A circadian rhythm is a daily behavioral or physiological cycle; an example is the 24-hour sleep-wake cycle. REM sleep is only one part of the sleep portion of the sleep-wake cycle.
   d. **Correct.** A circadian rhythm is a daily behavioral or physiological cycle; an example is the 24-hour sleep-wake cycle.

6. a. Incorrect. The amount of deep sleep (stage 4) is much greater in the first half of a night's sleep than in the second half. The majority of REM sleep, however, takes place during the latter part of a night's sleep when the REM period becomes progressively longer.
   b. Incorrect. The majority of REM sleep takes place during the latter part of a night's sleep when the REM period becomes progressively longer. The amount of deep sleep (stage 4), however, is much greater in the first half of a night's sleep.
   c. **Correct.** The amount of deep sleep (stage 4) is much greater in the first half of a night's sleep than in the second half.
   d. Incorrect. The amount of deep sleep (stage 4) is much greater in the first half of a night's sleep than in the second half.

7. a. Incorrect. The majority of REM sleep takes place during the latter part of a night's sleep when the REM period becomes progressively longer.
   b. **Correct.** The majority of REM sleep takes place during the latter part of a night's sleep when the REM period becomes progressively longer.
   c. Incorrect. The majority of REM sleep takes place during the latter part of a night's sleep when the REM period becomes progressively longer.
   d. Incorrect. The majority of REM sleep takes place during the latter part of a night's sleep when the REM period becomes progressively longer.

8. a. **Correct.** This evolution-based theory argues just this point.
   b. Incorrect. Repair theory states that sleep restores, replenishes, and rebuilds our brains and bodies, which somehow are worn out or used up by the day's waking activities.
   c. Incorrect. This theory attempts to explain why we dream.
   d. Incorrect. Circadian rhythm has to do with the full daily cycle.

9. a. Incorrect. Sedatives reduce the amount of time a person spends in stage 4 and REM sleep and may disrupt the restfulness of sleep.
   b. Incorrect. Sedatives reduce the amount of time a person spends in stage 4 and REM sleep and may disrupt the restfulness of sleep.
   c. **Correct.** Sedatives reduce the amount of time a person spends in stage 4 and REM sleep and may disrupt the restfulness of sleep.
   d. Incorrect. Nightmares are dreams and dreams occur during REM sleep. Since REM sleep is reduced when sedatives are used, nightmares are probably also reduced.

10. a. Incorrect. There is a danger of overdose with sedatives and over time they lose their effectiveness, requiring ever greater doses to achieve the same effect.
    b. Incorrect. Sedatives reduce the amount of time a person spends in stage 4 and REM sleep and may disrupt the restfulness of sleep.
    c. **Correct**. Sleep apnea is a sleep disorder in which individuals stop breathing while they are asleep. Sedatives do not increase the chances of developing this sleep disorder.
    d. Incorrect. Over time sedatives lose their effectiveness, requiring ever greater doses to achieve the same effect.

11. a. Incorrect. Freud is the one who claimed that dreams are unconscious attempts to fulfill wishes.
    b. **Correct.** The activation synthesis view states that dreams are powered by the random and spontaneous firing of neurons and have no real meaning.
    c. Incorrect. Those who support the problem-solving approach believe that dreams are a mental realm where we can solve problems and think creatively.
    d. Incorrect. Since those supporting the activation synthesis view believe that dreams have no real meaning, it is doubtful that they believe dreams could serve as entertainment.

12. a. Incorrect. Minimizing distractions is one of the four steps of hypnosis.
    b. Incorrect. In the second step of hypnosis, the hypnotist tells the participant to concentrate on something specific.
    c. Incorrect. In the third step of hypnosis, the hypnotist describes what to expect in the hypnotic state.
    d. **Correct.** Testing to see if the person being hypnotized is truly relaxed is not one of the four steps of hypnosis.

13. a. Incorrect. The nonstate view says that hypnotic behavior is similar to other forms of social behavior.
    b. **Correct.** This is one of the main tenants of the non-state view.
    c. Incorrect. This idea is asserted by the special process theory.
    d. Incorrect. Supporters of the special process theory believe that hypnotic responses are involuntary and involve a hidden observer.

14. a. Incorrect. Psychoactive drugs act on the nervous system to alter our state of consciousness, modify our perceptions and change our moods.
    b. Incorrect. Psychoactive drugs act on the nervous system to alter our state of consciousness, modify our perceptions and change our moods.
    c. Incorrect. Psychoactive drugs act on the nervous system to alter our state of consciousness, modify our perceptions and change our moods.
    d. **Correct.** Psychoactive drugs generally impair activities requiring intellectual functioning.

15. a. Correct. Withdrawal is the undesirable intense pain and craving that an addicted person feels when the addicting drug is withdrawn.
    b. Incorrect. Tolerance means that a greater amount of the drug is needed to produce the same effect.
    c. Incorrect. Psychological dependence is the need to take a drug to cope with problems and stress.
    d. Incorrect. Hypnosis is a psychological state of altered attention and awareness in which the individual is unusually receptive to suggestions.

16. a. Incorrect. Family studies consistently find a high frequency of alcoholism in the first-degree relatives of alcoholics.
    b. **Correct.** Family studies consistently find a high frequency of alcoholism in the first-degree relatives of alcoholics.
    c. Incorrect. The genetic evidence has found a high frequency of alcoholism in the parents of alcoholics rather than the grandparents.
    d. Incorrect. The precise genetic mechanism for alcoholism has not yet been identified.

17. a. Incorrect. Alcohol acts upon the body primarily as a depressant and slows down the brain's activities.
    b. Incorrect. Barbiturates are depressant drugs that induce sleep or reduce anxiety.
    c. **Correct.** The most common opiate drugs--morphine and heroin--affect synapses in the brain that use endorphins as their neurotransmitter.
    d. Incorrect. Tranquilizers are depressant drugs that reduce anxiety and induce relaxation.

18. a. **Correct.** Amphetamines are among the most widely used stimulants.
    b. Incorrect. Alcohol acts upon the body primarily as a depressant and slows down the brain's activities.
    c. Incorrect. Barbiturates are depressant drugs that induce sleep or reduce anxiety.
    d. Incorrect. Opiates depress the central nervous system's activity.

19. a. Incorrect. Marijuana is the dried leaves and flowers of the hemp plant.
    b. **Correct.** Marijuana use declined during the 1980s, but an upsurge in its use has occurred in the 1990s.
    c. Incorrect. The effects of marijuana include increases in pulse rate and blood pressure.
    d. Incorrect. When used daily in large amounts, Marijuana can alter sperm counts.

20. a. Incorrect. Opiates affect synapses in the brain that use endorphins as their neurotransmitter. LSD is not an opiate.
    b. Incorrect. Acetylcholine, a neurotransmitter released by neurons to activate muscles, is not affected by LSD.
    c. Incorrect. Melatonin, a hormone produced by the pineal gland in response to cycles of light and dark, is not affected by LSD.
    d. **Correct.** LSD acts primarily on the neurotransmitter serotonin.

Chapter 5 Learning

Learning Objectives

After studying this chapter, you should be able to:

1. Define learning. (p. 153)

2. Explain the terminology and the process of classical conditioning. (p. 153)

3. Distinguish among generalization, discrimination, extinction, and spontaneous recovery as they relate to classical conditioning. (p. 155)

4. Describe classical conditioning in humans. (p. 158)

5. Contrast Pavlov's view of classical conditioning with the contemporary point of view. (p. 160)

6. Distinguish between Thorndike's law of effect and Skinner's operant conditioning. (p. 162)

7. Distinguish among positive reinforcement, negative reinforcement, and punishment. (p. 163)

8. Identify the following operant conditioning principles: time interval, shaping and chaining, and primary and secondary reinforcement. (p. 166)

9. List and describe the various schedules of reinforcement. (p. 169)

10. Distinguish among extinction, generalization , and discrimination as they relate to operant conditioning. (p. 171)

11. Describe how behavior modification is used to change human behavior. (p. 172)

12. Discuss the criticisms of operant conditioning. (p. 173)

13. Describe Bandura's model of observational learning. (p. 174)

14. Identify the S-O-R model of learning. (p. 179)

15. Define the following concepts: cognitive maps and insight learning. (p. 180)

16. Discuss biological and cultural factors in learning. (p. 183)

Chapter 5 Outline

I. Definition of Learning
II. Classical Conditioning
    A. How classical conditioning works
        1. Unconditioned stimulus (US)
        2. Unconditioned response (UR)
        3. Conditioned stimulus (CS)
        4. Conditioned response (CR)
    B. Classical conditioning phenomena
        1. Generalization
        2. Discrimination
        3. Extinction
        4. Spontaneous recovery
    C. Applications of human classical conditioning
        1. Phobias
        2. Counterconditioning
    D. Evaluation of classical conditioning
        1. Stimulus substitution
        2. Information theory
III. Operant Conditioning
    A. Thorndike's law of effect
    B. Skinner's operant conditioning
        1. Reinforcement
            a. positive reinforcement
            b. negative reinforcement
        2. Punishment
        3. Shaping and chaining
        4. Primary and secondary reinforcement
        5. Schedules of reinforcement
            a. fixed-ratio
            b. variable-ratio
            c. fixed-interval
            d. variable-interval
        6. Extinction
        7. Generalization
        8. Discrimination
    C. Applications of operant conditioning
    D. Evaluation of operant conditioning
IV. Observational Learning
    A. Bandura's model of observational learning
        1. Attention
        2. Retention
    B. Role models and mentors
    C. Evaluation of observational learning
V. Cognitive Factors in Learning
    A. Bandura's cognitive model
    B. Expectations and cognitive maps
    C. Insight learning
VI. Biological and cultural factors in learning
    A. Biological factors
        1. Preparedness
        2. Instinctive drift
    B. Cultural factors

Key Terms

Write a brief description for each of the following terms. Where relevant, provide an original example or illustration of the term. Then, compare your answers with those provided at the end of the Study Guide chapter. Review the text for those terms you don't know and those you define incorrectly.

1. learning (p. 153)

2. classical conditioning (p. 153)

3. fixed action patterns (p. 153)

4. reflexes (p. 153)

5. unconditioned stimulus (US) (p. 153)

6. unconditioned response (UR) (p. 153)

7. conditioned stimulus (CS) (p. 154)

8. conditioned response (CR) (p. 154)

9. generalization (classical conditioning) (p. 155)

10. discrimination (classical conditioning) (p. 155)

11. extinction (classical conditioning) (p. 157)

12. spontaneous recovery (p. 157)

13. phobias (p. 158)

14. counterconditioning (p. 158)

15. stimulus substitution (p. 160)

16. information theory (p. 160)

17. latent learning (p. 160)

18. operant conditioning (p. 161)

19. law of effect (p. 162)

20. reinforcement (p. 163)

21. positive reinforcement (p. 163)

22. negative reinforcement (p. 164)

23. punishment (p. 164)

24. shaping (p. 167)

25. chaining (p. 168)

26. primary reinforcement (p. 168)

27. secondary reinforcement (p. 168)

28. partial reinforcement (p. 169)

29. schedules of reinforcement (p. 169)

30. fixed-ratio schedule (p. 170)

31. variable-ratio schedule (p. 170)

32. fixed-interval schedule (p. 170)

33. variable-interval schedule (p. 170)

34. extinction (operant conditioning) (p. 171)

35. generalization (operant conditioning) (p. 171)

36. discrimination (operant conditioning) (p. 172)

37. discriminative stimuli (p. 172)

38. behavior modification (p. 172)

39. observational learning (p. 174)

40. mentor (p. 176)

41. S-O-R model (p. 179)

42. self-efficacy (p. 180)

43. cognitive map (p. 180)

44. insight learning (p. 183)

45. preparedness (p. 183)

46. instinctive drift (p. 183)

47. taste aversion (p. 184)

Guided Review

The following in-depth chapter review is a challenging and comprehensive fill-in-the-blanks exercise. The answers are found near the end of the chapter. As you go through the exercise, try to resist the temptation to look at the answers until you have provided them. When you have filled in all the blanks, you will have a thorough summary of the chapter for reference and review.

Defining Learning/Classical Conditioning

Learning is a relatively permanent change in ____(1)____ that occurs through ____(2)____.

In the early 1900s, Pavlov described principles of ____(3)____ ________. Classical conditioning consists of the following components: a stimulus that produces a response without prior learning, called an ____(4)____ ________;

an unlearned response, called the ____(5)____ response; a previously neutral stimulus that eventually elicits the conditioned response, called the ____(6)____ stimulus; and a learned, or ____(7)____, response. When a stimulus similar to the CS produces a CR, this is called ____(8)____. When an organism is conditioned to respond to one stimulus and not another, this is called ____(9)____. Repeatedly presenting the CS without the US will cause the CR to disappear; this process is called ____(10)____. When a CR recurs without further conditioning, this is called ____(11)____ ________.

Many psychologists believe that, in humans, irrational fears, or ____(12)____, are caused by classical conditioning. A procedure for weakening a classically conditioned fear response is called ____(13)____. Behaviors associated with health problems or mental disorders can involve ____(14)____ conditioning.

While Pavlov explained that classical conditioning works by stimulus ____(15)____, the contemporary explanation of classical conditioning is referred to as ____(16)____ ________. Tolman's research suggested learning can take place without direct experience; he referred to this as ____(17)____ learning.

Operant Conditioning

A form of learning in which the consequences of behavior lead to changes in the probability of the behavior's occurrence is called ____(18)____ conditioning. The concept of operant conditioning was developed by ____(19)____. Operant conditioning generally does a better job than classical conditioning of explaining ____(20)____ behavior. Whereas the stimuli that govern classically conditioned behavior ____(21)____ the behavior, in operant conditioning the stimuli that govern behavior ____(22)____ the behavior. According to Thorndike, behavior followed by positive outcomes is____(23)____, and behavior followed by negative outcomes is ____(24)____. Thorndike referred to these concepts as the ____(25)____ ________ ________. Skinner has extensively studied animals in the laboratory, in the belief that the principles of learning are the same for all ____(26)____. Skinner studied organisms under ____(27)____ circumstances to understand the relationship between ____(28)____ and their consequences. Skinner developed an apparatus for studying animals that has become known as the ____(29)____ ________. According to Skinner, consequences that increase the probability that a behavior will occur are called ____(30)____; consequences that decrease a behavior's probability are labeled ____(31)____. When the frequency of a behavior increases because it is followed by a pleasant stimulus, it is a ____(32)____ reinforcement. Negative reinforcement increases the frequency of a response either by removing an ____(33)____ stimulus or by allowing the individual to ____(34)____ the stimulus.

According to Richard Solomon, punishment can be effective when it is immediate, ____(35)____ and severe enough to alter the targeted behavior. Punishment may be effective if ____(36)____ positive reinforcement has not worked; also, when the behavior is more ____(37)____ than the punishment. When punishment is reduced, it is wise to ____(38)____ an alternative behavior, so that ____(39)____ behavior doesn't replace the ____(40)____ response. Less severe punishment may create a negative consequence by removing opportunities for ____(41)____. A procedure that involves removing a child from a rewarding circumstance is called ____(42)____ ________. Another punishment technique is called ____(43)____ ________. Skinner viewed ____(44)____ reinforcement as preferable to punishment.

Several factors are relevant to the effectiveness of operant conditioning; for example, learning is more efficient when the time interval is ___(45)___. Also, behaviors are learned more rapidly if approximations to the desired behavior are rewarded; this is called ___(46)___. A related technique, which begins by shaping the final response and working backward, is known as ___(47)___.

Positive reinforcements that are innately rewarding are called ___(48)___ reinforcements; those reinforcements that acquire their positive value through experience are called ___(49)___ reinforcements. Money and other objects that can be exchanged for another reinforcer eventually acquire reinforcing value as well; these are referred to as ___(50)___ reinforcers.

Often, reinforcements do not follow every occurrence of a response. This is called ___(51)___ reinforcement and occurs in four different ___(52)___ of reinforcement. When a behavior must occur a set number of times before it is rewarded, this is referred to as a ___(53)___-________ schedule. On the other hand, slot machines give out rewards on a

___(54)___-________ schedule. Behaviors that are rewarded after the passage of a fixed amount of time are on ___(55)___-________ schedules, whereas behaviors that are rewarded after differing amounts of time are referred to as ___(56)___-________ schedules. Generally, behaviors are learned most rapidly on ___(57)___ reinforcement schedules; however, the intermittent schedules are effective for ___(58)___ behavior.

In operant conditioning, a decrease in the tendency to perform a behavior that results in neither a positive nor a negative consequence is called ___(59)___. Giving the same response to similar stimuli is called ___(60)___. When a response occurs in the presence of one stimulus that is reinforced but not in the presence of another stimulus, this is called ___(61)___. Discriminative ___(62)___ signal that a response will be reinforced.

Applying the principles of operant conditioning to changing human behavior is called ___(63)___ ________. Behavior modification has been applied to maladaptive behavior, to teach couples to improve their ___(64)___, and to improve a person's ___(65)___ skills.

Among the criticisms of operant conditioning are these: Skinner's adherence to operant explanations was ___(66)___; many psychologists believe that operant conditioning only explains ___(67)___ behaviors; and operant techniques are ___(68)___.

Observational Learning

When an individual learns by imitation or modeling, psychologists refer to this as ___(69)___ ________. Observational learning allows us to learn without having to go through ___(70)___-________-________. Albert Bandura's research on ___(71)___ showed that aggressive behavior was just as extensive whether or not the modeled aggressive behavior was ___(72)___. Even though the modeled behavior might not be performed by the subject, it still might have been ___(73)___. Bandura believes that the following processes influence an observer's behavior after being exposed to a model: (a) ___(74)___, (b) retention, © ___(75)___ reproduction, and (d) reinforcement or ___(76)___ conditions. A practical aspect of observational learning involves the importance of role models and

(77)___ in modeling appropriate behavior. According to Bandura, observational learning is an ___(78)___-processing activity.

Cognitive, Biological, and Cultural Influences on Learning

Many contemporary psychologists believe that learning involves more than stimulus-response connections; a view that includes cognitive factors is the ___(79)___ model. The "O" is sometimes referred to as the ___(80)___ ________. According to Bandura's recent learning model, behavioral, cognitive, and other personal factors and environmental factors all operate ___(81)___.Bandura believes an important factor in learning is the expectation one can master a situation and produce positive outcomes; he calls this ___(82)___-________.

According to Tolman, when classical and operant conditioning are occurring, the organism acquires ___(83)___. Tolman wrote that individuals select information from the environment and develop a ___(84)___ ________ of their world.

Wolfgang Kohler's work with apes led him to conclude that humans and other animals engage in ___(85)___ ________.

Organisms also bring a biological background to the learning context. Thus, some animals learn readily in one situation but have great difficulty in others; this biological predisposition to learn has been termed ___(86)___. When animals are being trained, they tend to revert to instinctive behavior, a concept called ___(87)___ ________. Another biological constraint on learning involves the conditioned avoidance of substances that have produced nausea; this is termed ___(88)___ ________.

Culture can influence the ___(89)___ to which learning processes occur and often determines the ___(90)___ of learning.

Sociocultural Worlds/Applications in Psychology

In your own words, briefly summarize the material you have read in Sociocultural Worlds, "Ethnicity and Role Models," and Applications in Psychology, "How Immediate and Delayed Consequences Influence Your Self-Control." Briefly describe how each of these articles relates to the information contained in the chapter.

Concept Check I

Classical Conditioning

1. An unconditioned stimulus is ______________________________.
2. _____ __________ _________ is an unlearned response that is automatically associated with the US.
3. A conditioned stimulus is ______________________________.
4. _____ __________ _________ is the learned response to the conditioned stimulus that occurs after being paired with the unconditioned stimulus.
5. Generalization is ______________________________.
6. __________ is the process of learning to respond to certain stimuli but not to others.
7. Extinction is ______________________________.
8. __________ __________ is the process by which a conditioned response can appear again without further conditioning.
9. Counterconditioning is ______________________________.

Answers

1. a stimulus that produces a response without prior learning
2. An unconditioned response
3. a previously neutral stimulus that elicits the conditioned response after being paired with the unconditioned stimulus.
4. A conditioned response
5. the tendency of a stimulus similar to the original CS to elicit a response similar to the CR
6. Discrimination
7. the weakening of the conditioned response in the absence of the unconditioned stimulus
8. Spontaneous recovery
9. a process for weakening a conditioned response of fear

Concept Check II

Operant Conditioning

1. In positive reinforcement, ________________________________.
2. ________ ________ is an increase in the frequency of a response because the response either removes a negative consequence or lets the individual avoid the circumstance.
3. Extinction is ________________________________.
4. ________ is the process of rewarding successive approximations of desired behavior.
5. Chaining is ________________________________.
6. ________ ________ involves reinforcers that are innately satisfying, i.e., require no previous learning.
7. Secondary reinforcement involves ________________________________.
8. A ________-________ ________ reinforces a behavior after a set number of responses.
9. A variable-ratio schedule is ________________________________.
10. A ________-________ ________ reinforces the first response after a fixed amount of time has elapsed.
11. A variable-interval schedule ________________________________.
12. ________ is giving the same response to similar stimuli.
13. Discriminative stimuli are ________________________________.

Answers

1. the frequency of a response increases because it is followed by a pleasant stimulus
2. Negative reinforcement
3. a decrease in the tendency to perform a behavior that receives neither a positive nor a negative consequence
4. Shaping
5. an operant technique used to teach a complex sequence of behaviors
6. Primary reinforcement
7. reinforcers that acquire their positive value through experience
8. A fixed-ratio schedule
9. a timetable in which responses are rewarded on an unpredictable basis
10. A fixed-interval schedule
11. reinforces a response after a variable amount of time has elapsed
12. Generalization
13. stimuli that signal that a response will be reinforced

Multiple-Choice Questions

Practice Test 1

After answering all the multiple-choice questions in Practice Test 1, compare your answers with the answer key provided at the end of the chapter. The answer key contains a brief explanation of both the correct and incorrect answers. Each of these questions is keyed to the Learning Objectives for the chapter. If you answer any questions incorrectly, review the corresponding Learning Objective and text material before you proceed to Practice Test 2.

1. Each of the following is a part of the definition of learning *except*
   a. relatively permanent.
   b. change of behavior.
   c. maturation.
   d. experience.

LO 1

2. A 12-year-old child has a bedwetting problem, so the parents buy a special trainer. The child sleeps on a pad; when the first drop of urine touches the pad, an alarm goes off. After 2 weeks, the child wakes up before the first drop of urine is expressed, gets up, and goes to the bathroom to urinate. This classical conditioning exercise was a success. You explain to the parents that
   a. the sensations of a full bladder were the CS and waking up was the CR.
   b. since urinating is an automatic response, the CS-US interval could be very short.
   c. shaping is not always successful.
   d. the alarm was the CS and the urine was the CR.

LO 2

3. You volunteer to participate in an experiment in classical conditioning, and the experimenter conditions your eye-blink reflex to the sound of a bell. The next day, you notice that you blink whenever the phone rings. You are not upset because you know that
   a. this UR will be extinguished soon.
   b. stimulus discrimination will readily develop.
   c. spontaneous recovery is not dangerous or long-lasting.
   d. without the US, extinction will naturally occur.

LO 3

4. Pavlov found that dogs continued to salivate, even after the conditioned response had been extinguished. This phenomenon is called
   a. spontaneous recovery
   b. generalization
   c. discrimination
   d. unextinction

LO 3

5. When a child disagrees with another child of a different ethnic background, classical conditioning may help to explain the learning of prejudices through the process of
   a. extinction.
   b. generalization.
   c. spontaneous recovery.
   d. fixed action patterns.

LO 4

6. The contemporary explanation of classical conditioning is called
   a. information theory.
   b. operant conditioning.
   c. stimulus substitution.
   d. cognitive theory.

LO 5

7. According to Thorndike's law of effect,
   a. a conditioned stimulus ultimately produces a conditioned response.
   b. behaviors followed by positive outcomes are strengthened.
   c. behavior learned on variable-interval schedules is difficult to extinguish.
   d. reinforcers should be given immediately after a desired response.

LO 6

8. Which of the following describes negative reinforcement?
   a. teaching your dog to "shake hands" by giving him a dog biscuit every time he does so
   b. punishing a 3-year-old child for writing on the walls with crayons
   c. getting home early from a date to avoid getting yelled at by your parents
   d. developing a phobic response to anyone who looks like your mean third-grade teacher

LO 7

9. What technique(s) do animal trainers use to teach animals complex or unusual behavior?
   a. shaping
   b. chaining
   c. primary reinforcement
   d. all of the above

LO 8

10. Amanda is learning a complex gymnastics routine. Her coach has suggested she learn the final part of the routine first. Amanda's coach is using
    a. shaping
    b. chaining
    c. partial reinforcement
    d. extinction

LO 8

11. Which of the following schedules rewards behavior on an unpredictable basis?
    a. fixed-interval
    b. variable-interval
    c. fixed-ratio
    d. continuous ratio

LO 9

12. On which reinforcement schedule is gambling typically reinforced?
    a. fixed-ratio
    b. variable-ratio
    c. fixed-interval
    d. variable-interval

LO 9

13. Little Jennifer has learned to throw a temper tantrum in front of Dad (who often gives in). Jennifer has learned, however, that this same behavior is not effective with Mom. Jennifer has demonstrated
    a. discrimination.
    b. instinctive drift.
    c. generalization.
    d. superstitious behavior.

LO 10

14. Advocates of behavior modification believe emotional and behavioral problems are caused by inappropriate
    a modeling
    b response consequences
    c discriminative stimuli
    d generalization

LO 11

15. According to its critics, behavior modification works only on
    a. simple behaviors
    b. behaviors involving free will
    c. complex behaviors
    d. depression

LO 12

16. Which of the following is at work in observational learning?
    a. imitation
    b. modeling
    c. unconditioned responses
    d. both *a* and *b*

LO 13

17. In the S-O-R model of learning, which is occasionally referred to as the "black box"?
    a. S
    b. O
    c. R
    d. all of the above

LO 14

18. Each of the following is a component of Bandura's cognitive model of learning *except*
    a. person and cognitive factors
    b. modeling
    c. behavior
    d. environment

LO 14

19. Kohler contended that insight learning is different from other forms of learning in that it does not involve
    a. an active organism operating on the environment.
    b. a change in behavior as a result of experience.
    c. trial-and-error or S-R connections.
    d. the use of incentives for a new behavior.

LO 15

20. Kellor and Marion Breland found that training animals to perform behaviors at fairs was limited by
    a. taste aversion.
    b. physical characteristics.
    c. preparedness.
    d. instinctive drift.

LO 16

Practice Test 2

The following multiple-choice questions also are keyed to the chapter Learning Objectives. If you answer any questions incorrectly, be sure to review the corresponding Learning Objective and text material.

1. Each of the following is true regarding learning *except*
    a. It is a relatively permanent change in behavior.
    b. It is acquired through experience
    c. It involves reflexive behaviors.
    d. It promotes successful adaptation to the environment.

LO 1

2. In Pavlov's experiment, the bell was a previously neutral stimulus that became a(n)
    a. conditioned stimulus.
    b. conditioned response.
    c. unconditioned response.
    d. unconditioned stimulus.

LO 2

3. The classical conditioning process by which little Albert learned to fear a rabbit, a dog, and a sealskin coat is called
    a. extinction.
    b. generalization.
    c. spontaneous recovery.
    d. discrimination.

LO 3

4. The process of responding to certain stimuli while not responding to others stimuli is called
    a. generalization.
    b. discrimination.
    c. extinction.
    d. spontaneous recovery.

LO 3

5. A classical conditioning process that helps eliminate conditioned fear responses is called
    a. counterconditioning.
    b. superstitious behavior.
    c. operant conditioning.
    d. spontaneous recovery.

LO 4

6. Each of the following characterizes the contemporary view of classical conditioning *except*
    a. The organism is viewed as an active information seeker.
    b. Contiguity between the CS and the US is important.
    c. The information provided by the CS and US is important.
    d. The CS and US bond together and the CS eventually substitutes for the US.

LO 5

7. According to Thorndike's law of effect,
    a. behavior followed by positive outcomes is strengthened.
    b. behavior can be conditioned either by operant or classical conditioning.
    c. behaviors followed by negative outcomes are weakened.
    d. both *a* and *c* are true.

LO 6

8. If the frequency of a response increases because it is followed by a pleasant stimulus, then it is an example of
   a. the law of effect.
   b. positive reinforcement.
   c. negative reinforcement.
   d. punishment.

LO 7

9. In which operant technique does the trainer begin by reinforcing the final response in the sequence and then work backward?
   a. chaining
   b. primary reinforcement
   c. secondary reinforcement
   d. shaping

LO 8

10. Reinforcement delivered after a set number of responses is on which of the following schedules?
    a. fixed-interval
    b. fixed-ratio
    c. variable-interval
    d. variable-ratio

LO 9

11. According to the text, which reinforcement schedule usually produces the highest response rate?
    a. fixed-interval
    b. fixed-ratio
    c. variable-ratio
    d. variable-interval

LO 9

12. Food, water, and sexual satisfaction are examples of
    a. primary reinforcement.
    b. secondary reinforcement.
    c. partial reinforcement.
    d. learned reinforcement.

LO 10

13. The frequency of little Johnny's temper tantrums decreased sharply after his parents began to ignore the behavior. In the language of operant conditioning, Johnny's tantrum behavior was undergoing
    a. generalization.
    b. extinction.
    c. discrimination.
    d. superstition.

LO 11

14. Monitoring daily moods and learning more effective coping skills are recommended behavior modification techniques for learning to deal with
    a. incontinence
    b. depression
    c. losing weight
    d. phobias

LO 11

15. According to proponents of operant conditioning, which of the following is true?
    a. Each organism experiences a distinctive reinforcement history.
    b. A stimulus is a positive reinforcer only if it strengthens the response it follows.
    c. Operant techniques are manipulative.
    d. Both *a* and *b* above.

LO 12

16. Each of the following is an important component of observational learning *except*
    a. attention.
    b. retention.
    c. reinforcement.
    d. the distinction between learning and performance.

LO 13

17. The S-O-R model of learning emphasizes the importance of
    a. the environment.
    b. cognitive factors.
    c. stimulus-response connections.
    d. operant conditioning.

LO 14

18. According to Bandura, the expectation that a person can master a situation and produce positive outcomes is called
    a. self-control
    b. self-efficacy
    c. self-esteem
    d. self-awareness

LO 14

19. According to Tolman, our mental awareness of physical space and the elements in it is called
    a. insight learning.
    b. S-O-R learning.
    c. expectational learning.
    d. a cognitive map.

LO 15

20. How can culture influence learning?
    a. Classical and operant conditioning are not used in some cultures.
    b. Culture can influence the degree to which operant and classical conditioning are used.
    c. Culture often determines the content of learning.
    d. both *b* and *c*.

LO 16

Answers to Key Terms

1. **Learning** is a relatively permanent change in behavior that occurs due to experience.
2. In **classical conditioning,** a neutral stimulus acquires the ability to elicit a response that was originally elicited by another stimulus.
3. **Fixed action patterns** are behaviors that are driven by genetic inheritance and are species-specific.
4. **Reflexes** are automatic stimulus-response connections.
5. An **unconditioned stimulus (US)** is a stimulus that produces a response without prior learning. In Pavlov's classic experiment, food was the US.
6. An **unconditioned response (UR)** is an unlearned response that is automatically associated with the US. In Pavlov's experiment, salivation was the UR to the food.
7. A **conditioned stimulus (CS)** is a previously neutral stimulus that comes to elicit the conditioned response after being paired with the unconditioned stimulus. Pavlov used a bell as the CS.
8. The **conditioned response (CR)** is the learned response to the conditioned stimulus that occurs after the CS-US association. When Pavlov's dogs salivated in response to the bell, they had acquired a CR.
9. **Generalization,** in classical conditioning, occurs when a stimulus similar to the original conditioned stimulus produces a response similar to the conditioned response.
10. **Discrimination,** in classical conditioning, is the process of learning to respond to certain stimuli and not to others.
11. **Extinction,** in classical conditioning, is the weakening of the conditioned response in the absence of the unconditioned stimulus.
12. **Spontaneous recovery** is the process by which a conditioned response can reappear without further conditioning.
13. **Phobias** are irrational fears.
14. **Counterconditioning** is a classical conditioning procedure for weakening a CR of fear by associating the fear-provoking stimulus with a new response that is incompatible with fear.
15. **Stimulus substitution** was Pavlov's explanation for how classical conditioning works. According to this theory, the CS and US bond together, and eventually the CS substitutes for the US.
16. **Information theory** is the contemporary explanation of how classical conditioning works. According to this theory, the important factor is the information the individual obtains from the situation.
17. **Latent learning** refers to changes in behavior that occur without direct experience.
18. **Operant conditioning (instrumental conditioning)** is a form of learning in which the consequences of behavior produce changes in the probability of the behavior's occurrence.
19. The **law of effect** is the hypothesis, developed by Thorndike, that behaviors followed by positive outcomes are strengthened, whereas behaviors followed by negative outcomes are weakened.

20. **Reinforcement** is a consequence that increases the probability that a behavior will occur.
21. In **positive reinforcement** the frequency of a response increases because the response is followed by a pleasant stimulus.
22. In **negative reinforcement** the frequency of the response increases because the response either removes an unpleasant stimulus or allows the individual to avoid the stimulus.
23. **Punishment** is a consequence that decreases the probability that a behavior will occur.
24. **Shaping** is the process of rewarding approximations of the desired behavior.
25. **Chaining** is an operant conditioning technique used to teach a complex sequence, or chain, of behaviors. The process begins by shaping the final response and then working backward until a chain of behaviors is learned.
26. **Primary reinforcement** is the use of reinforcers, such as food, water, and sexual satisfaction, that are innately satisfying. No learning is required to make them pleasurable.
27. **Secondary reinforcement** is the use of reinforcers that acquire their reinforcing value through experience. These are learned, or conditional, reinforcers.
28. **Partial reinforcement** occurs when behaviors are not reinforced each time they occur.
29. **Schedules of reinforcement** are timetables that determine when a behavior will be reinforced.
30. A **fixed-ratio schedule** reinforces a behavior after a set number of responses.
31. A **variable-ratio schedule** rewards behaviors an average number of times, but on an unpredictable basis.
32. A **fixed-interval schedule** reinforces the first appropriate response after a fixed amount of time has elapsed.
33. A **variable-interval schedule** reinforces a response after an unpredictable amount of time has elapsed.
34. **Extinction,** in operant conditioning, is a decrease in the tendency to perform a behavior when it receives neither a positive nor a negative consequence.
35. **Generalization,** in operant conditioning, means giving the same response to similar stimuli.
36. **Discrimination,** in operant conditioning, is the process of responding in the presence of another stimulus that is not reinforced.
37. **Discriminative stimuli** are signals that a response will be reinforced.
38. **Behavior modification** is the application of operant conditioning principles to changing human behavior.
39. **Observational learning** occurs when a person observes and imitates another person's behavior.
40. A **mentor** is a role model who acts as an advisor, coach and/or confidant.
41. The **S-O-R model** of learning stresses the importance of cognitive factors in learning. *S* stands for stimulus, *O* for organism, and *R* for response.
42. **Self-efficacy**, according to Bandura, is the expectation that one can master a situation and produce positive outcomes.
43. A **cognitive map** is an organism's mental representation of the structure of physical space.
44. **Insight learning** is a form of problem solving in which the organism develops a sudden understanding of how to solve a problem.
45. **Preparedness** is the species-specific biological predisposition to learn in certain ways but not in others.
46. **Instinctive drift** is the tendency of animals to revert to instinctive behavior that interferes with learning.
47. **Taste aversion** is the conditioned avoidance of ingesting substances that cause nausea or other unpleasant reactions.

Answers to Guided Review

1. behavior (p. 153)
2. experience (p. 153)
3. classical conditioning (p. 153)
4. unconditioned stimulus (p. 153)
5. unconditioned (p. 153)
6. conditioned (p. 154)
7. conditioned (p. 154)
8. generalization (p. 155)
9. discrimination (p. 155)
10. extinction (p. 157)
11. spontaneous recovery (p. 157)
12. phobias (p. 158)
13. counterconditioning (p. 158)
14. classical (p. 159)
15. substitution (p. 160)
16. information theory (p. 160)
17. latent (p. 160)
18. operant (p. 161)
19. Skinner (p. 161)
20. voluntary (p. 161)
21. precede (p. 162)
22. follow (p. 162)
23. strengthened (p. 162)
24. weakened (p. 162)
25. law of effect (p. 162)
26. species (p. 163)
27. controlled (p. 163)
28. operants (p. 163)
29. Skinner box (p. 163)
30. reinforcements (p. 163)
31. punishments (p. 163)
32. positive (p. 164)
33. unpleasant (p. 164)
34. avoid (p. 164)
35. consistent (p. 164)
36. positive (p. 164)
37. destructive (p. 165)
38. reinforce (p. 165)
39. undersirable (p. 165)
40. punished (p. 165)
41. reward (p. 165)
42. time out (p. 165)
43. response cost (p. 165)
44. positive (p. 165)
45. brief (p. 166)
46. shaping (p. 167)
47. chaining (p. 168)
48. primary (p. 168)
49. secondary (p. 168)
50. token (p. 169)
51. partial (p. 169)
52. schedules (p. 169)
53. fixed-ratio (p. 170)
54. variable-ratio (p. 170)
55. fixed-interval (p. 170)
56. variable-interval (p. 170)
57. continuous (p. 170)
58. maintaining (p. 170)
59. extinction (p. 171)
60. generalization (p. 171)
61. discrimination (p. 172)
62. stimuli (p. 172)
63. behavior modification (p. 172)
64. communication (p. 173)
65. interpersonal (p. 173)
66. reductionistic (p. 173)
67. simple (p. 173)
68. manipulative (p. 173)
69. observational learning (p. 174)
70. trial-and-error (p. 174)
71. modeling (p. 175)
72. reinforced (p. 175)
73. learned (p. 175)
74. attention (p. 175)
75. motor (p. 175)
76. incentive (p. 176)
77. mentors (p. 176)
78. information (p. 179)
79. S-O-R (p. 179)
80. black box (p. 179)
81. interactively (p. 179)
82. self-efficacy (p. 180)
83. expectations (p. 180)
84. cognitive map (p. 180)
85. insight learning (p. 183)
86. preparedness (p. 183)
87. instinctive drift (p. 183)
88. taste aversion (p. 184)
89. degree (p. 185)
90. content (p. 185)

Answers to Multiple-Choice Questions- Practice Test 1

1. a. Incorrect. Learning is defined as a relatively permanent change in behavior that occurs through experience.
   b. Incorrect. Learning is defined as a relatively permanent change in behavior that occurs through experience.
   c. **Correct.** Maturation is not a part of the definition of learning. Maturation is defined as the physical growth and development of the body and nervous system.
   d. Incorrect. Learning is defined as a relatively permanent change in behavior that occurs through experience.

2. a. **Correct.** In this case, the US is the alarm and the UR is waking up. A full bladder is associated with the alarm long enough so that it becomes the CS and waking to the full bladder becomes the CR.
   b. Incorrect. The fact that urinating is an automatic response is irrelevant in this case because it is not the UR.
   c. Incorrect. Shaping is the process of rewarding successive approximations of desired behavior.
   d. Incorrect. The CS is the full bladder and the CR is waking up.

3. a. Incorrect. Blinking when the phone rings is the CR not the UR.
   b. Incorrect. Discrimination in classical conditioning is the process of learning to respond to certain stimuli and not to others. Further conditioning would have to take place in order for stimulus discrimination to occur.
   c. Incorrect. Spontaneous recovery in classical conditioning is the process by which a conditioned response can appear again without further conditioning. Extinction would have to occur before spontaneous recovery could take place.
   d. **Correct.** Extinction in classical conditioning is the weakening of the conditioned response in the absence of the US. Without further conditioning, you would eventually stop blinking at the sound of a bell.

4. a. **Correct.** Spontaneous recovery is the process in classical conditioning by which a conditioned response can appear again without further conditioning.
   b. Incorrect. Generalization in classical conditioning is the tendency of a new stimulus that is similar to the original CS to elicit a response that is similar to the CS.
   c. Incorrect. Discrimination in classical conditioning is the process of learning to respond to certain stimuli and not to others.
   d. Incorrect. Unextinction is not a term used to describe any classical conditioning process.

5. a. Incorrect. Extinction in classical conditioning is the weakening of the CR in the absence of the US.
   b. **Correct.** Through the process of classical conditioning, the child could generalize the unpleasant association with the child of a different ethnicity to other similar children.
   c. Incorrect. Spontaneous recovery in classical conditioning is the process by which a CR can appear again without further conditioning.
   d. Incorrect. Fixed action patterns are behaviors that are driven by genetic inheritance and are species specific.

6. a. **Correct.** The key to understanding classical conditioning is in the information the organism obtains from the situation. Information theory is the contemporary explanation of how classical conditioning works.
   b. Incorrect. Operant conditioning is a different kind of conditioning. It is defined as a form of learning in which the consequences of behavior produce changes in the probability of the behavior's occurrence.
   c. Incorrect. Stimulus substitution was Pavlov's theory of how classical conditioning works; it states that the nervous system is structured in such a way that the CS and US bond together and eventually the CS substitutes for the US. More recently we have discovered that classical conditioning does not always happen this way.

d. Incorrect. Cognitive psychology is the study of human thinking, understanding, knowing and anticipation.

7. a. Incorrect. This statement is related to classical conditioning not Thorndike's law of effect.
   b. **Correct.** Thorndike's law of effect states that behavior followed by positive outcomes are strengthened whereas behaviors followed by negative outcomes are weakened.
   c. Incorrect. A variable-interval schedule is a timetable in which a response is reinforced after a variable amount of time has elapsed. The fact that behavior learned under these conditions is difficult to extinguish is not a part of Thorndike's law.
   d. Incorrect. Although this is true, it is not part of Thorndike's law of effect.

8. a. Incorrect. This is an example of positive reinforcement. In positive reinforcement the frequency of a response increases because it is followed by a positive stimulus.
   b. Incorrect. This is an example of punishment. Punishment is a consequence that decreases the probability that a behavior will occur.
   c. **Correct.** Getting home early is reinforcing because it involves avoiding a negative stimulus (getting yelled at). In negative reinforcement the frequency of response increases because the response either removes a negative stimulus or involves avoiding a negative stimulus.
   d. Incorrect. Phobias (irrational fears) can be learned through the process of classical conditioning. Negative reinforcement is a process in operant conditioning.

9. a. Incorrect. Shaping is the process of rewarding approximations of behavior. Chaining is the term used for the complex process animal trainers use to teach complex behaviors. However, shaping and primary reinforcement are a part of the chaining process.
   b. Incorrect. Chaining is the operant conditioning technique used to teach a complex sequence or chain of behaviors. But shaping and primary reinforcement are both part of this technique.
   c. Incorrect. Primary reinforcement involves the use of reinforcers that are innately satisfying. Chaining is the operant conditioning technique used to teach a complex sequence or chain of behaviors. However, shaping and primary reinforcement are a part of the chaining process.
   d. **Correct.** Chaining is the operant conditioning technique used to teach a complex sequence or chain of behaviors. The procedure begins by shaping the final response in the sequence. Shaping usually involves the use of primary reinforcers. Therefore, chaining, shaping and primary reinforcers are all part of animal trainers' techniques for teaching complex behaviors.

10. a. Incorrect. Shaping is the process of rewarding approximations of behavior. It does not necessarily begin by shaping the final response in the desired sequence.
    b. **Correct.** Chaining begins by shaping the final response in the desired sequence.
    c. Incorrect. Partial reinforcement simply means that responses are not reinforced each time they occur.
    d. Incorrect. Extinction is the weakening of the conditioned response in the absence of the US.

11. a. Incorrect. A fixed-interval schedule reinforces the first appropriate response after a fixed (predictable) amount of time has elapsed.
    b. **Correct.** A variable-interval schedule is a timetable in which a response is reinforced after a variable (unpredictable) amount of time has elapsed.
    c. Incorrect. A fixed-ratio schedule reinforces behavior after a set (predictable) number of responses.
    d. Incorrect. A continuous ratio schedule reinforces the appropriate response every time it occurs.

12. a. Incorrect. A fixed-ratio schedule reinforces behavior after a set number of responses. A slot machine might pay off an average of every twentieth time, but unlike the fixed-ratio schedule, the gambler does not know when this payoff will be.
    b. **Correct.** Slot machines are on a variable-ratio schedule, a timetable in which responses are rewarded an average number of times, but on an unpredictable basis.
    c. Incorrect. Interval schedules are determined by time elapsed since the last behavior was reinforced. Reinforcement from slot machines is based on number of responses rather than time elapsed.
    d. Incorrect. Interval schedules are determined by time elapsed since the last behavior was reinforced. Reinforcement from slot machines is based on number of responses not time elapsed.

13. a. **Correct.** Discrimination in operant conditioning is the tendency to respond only to those stimuli that are correlated with reinforcement. Dad reinforced little Jennifer's tantrums (by giving in) and Mom did not.
    b. Incorrect. Instinctive drift is the tendency of animals to revert to instinctive behavior that interferes with learning.
    c. Incorrect. Generalization in operant conditioning means giving the same response to similar stimuli.
    d. Incorrect. A superstitious behavior is behavior repeated because it seems to produce reinforcement, even though it is actually unnecessary.

14. a. Incorrect. Observational learning or modeling is learning that occurs when a person observes and imitates someone's behavior. Advocates of behavior modification are more interested in learning that occurs through consequences than through observation.
    b. **Correct.** Behavior modification is the application of operant conditioning principles to changing human behavior. Advocates of this technique believe that many emotional and behavioral problems are caused by inadequate (or inappropriate) response consequences.
    c. Incorrect. Discriminative stimuli signal that a response will be reinforced.
    d. Incorrect. Generalization in operant conditioning means giving the same response to similar stimuli.

15. a. **Correct.** Critics of operant conditioning and its applications, such as behavior modification, argue that it is reductionistic and is only effective in explaining simple behaviors.
    b. Incorrect. The concepts behind operant conditioning and behavior modification were developed by B.F. Skinner who insisted that humans have no free will.
    c. Incorrect. Critics of behavior modification claim that explanations of complex behaviors require a more complex understanding of cognitive processes than the reductionistic theories behind behavior modification can provide.
    d. Incorrect. Critics of behavior modification probably consider depression too complex to be treated effectively with behavior modification.

16. a. Incorrect. Observational learning is also known as imitation <u>or</u> modeling.
    b. Incorrect. Observational learning is also known as imitation <u>or</u> modeling.
    c. Incorrect. Unconditioned responses are part of the theory of classical conditioning, not observational learning.
    d. **Correct.** Observational learning is also known as imitation or modeling.

17. a. Incorrect. In the S-O-R model, S stands for stimulus.
    b. **Correct.** In the S-O-R model, O stands for organism. It is sometimes referred to as the "black box" because the mental activities of the organism cannot be seen, and, therefore, must be inferred.
    c. Incorrect. In the S-O-R model, R stands for response.
    d. Incorrect. The only part of the S-O-R model that is referred to as the "black box" is the O.

18. a. Incorrect. These are important factors in Bandura's cognitive model.
    b. **Correct.** The essential part of Bandura's model is that behavior, cognition, and the environment all mutually influence each other.
    c. Incorrect. This is an important component of Bandura's cognitive model.
    d. Incorrect. This is an important component of Bandura's cognitive model.

19. a. Incorrect. Insight learning does involve the organism's interaction with the environment.
    b. Incorrect. This is the definition of learning and insight is a form of learning.
    c. **Correct.** Kohler claims that insight learning does not involve things as simplistic as trial and error or mere connections between stimuli and responses. Insight learning is a form of problem solving in which the organism develops a sudden insight or understanding of a problem's solution.
    d. Incorrect. Reinforcers have been used for incentive to demonstrate insight learning.

20. a. Incorrect. Taste aversion is the conditioned avoidance of substances that cause nausea.
    b. Incorrect. Physical characteristics can interfere with training animals to perform physical feats that are not within their physical capacity, but this is not what Kellor and Marion Breland discovered while training animals for fairs.
    c. Incorrect. Preparedness is the species-specific biological predisposition to learn in certain ways but not in others.
    d. **Correct.** Instinctive drift is the tendency of animals to revert to instinctive behavior that interferes with learning. After Keller and Marion Breland taught raccoons to cart large wooden nickels to a piggy bank and deposit them, the raccoons eventually started to engage in an instinctive food-washing response with the coins instead of depositing them. Their instinctive drift interfered with learning.

Answers to Multiple Choice Questions- Practice Test 2

1. a. Incorrect. Learning is defined as a relatively permanent change in behavior that occurs through experience.
   b. Incorrect. Learning is defined as a relatively permanent change in behavior that occurs through experience.
   c. **Correct.** Reflexive behaviors, such as swallowing, are innate and do not have to be taught.
   d. Incorrect. Learning does promote our adaptation to the environment.

2. a. **Correct.** After being associated with the food (US) long enough, the bell (CS) alone eventually elicited salivation (CR) from the dogs.
   b. Incorrect. In Pavlov's experiment, salivation was the CR.
   c. Incorrect. In this experiment, salivation was the UR.
   d. Incorrect. In this experiment, food was the US.

3. a. Incorrect. Extinction in classical conditioning is the weakening of the CR in the absence of the US.
   b. **Correct.** Generalization in classical conditioning is the tendency of a new stimulus that is similar to the original CS to elicit a response that is similar to the CS. Little Albert generalized his conditioned fear of the laboratory rat (CS) to similar furry stimuli such as rabbits, dogs and fur coats.
   c. Incorrect. Spontaneous recovery is the process in classical conditioning by which a conditioned response can appear again without further conditioning.
   d. Incorrect. Discrimination in classical conditioning is the process of learning to respond to certain stimuli and not to others.

4. a. Incorrect. Generalization in classical conditioning is the tendency of a new stimulus that is similar to the original CS to elicit a response that is similar to the CS.
   b. **Correct.** Discrimination in classical conditioning is the process of learning to respond to certain stimuli and not to others.
   c. Incorrect. Extinction in classical conditioning is the weakening of the CR in the absence of the US.
   d. Incorrect. Spontaneous recovery is the process in classical conditioning by which a conditioned response can appear again without further conditioning.

5. a. **Correct.** Counterconditioning is a classical conditioning procedure for weakening a conditioned response of fear by associating the fear-producing stimulus with a new response that is incompatible with the fear.
   b. Incorrect. A superstitious behavior is behavior repeated because it seems to produce reinforcement, even though it is actually unnecessary.
   c. Incorrect. Operant conditioning is a different kind of conditioning. It is defined as a form of learning in which the consequences of behavior produce changes in the probability of the behavior's occurrence.
   d. Incorrect. Spontaneous recovery is the process in classical conditioning by which a conditioned response can appear again without further conditioning.

6. a. Incorrect. The contemporary view of classical conditioning sees the organism as an information seeker using logical and perceptual relations among events, along with preconceptions, to form a representation of the world.
   b. Incorrect. The contemporary view still recognizes contiguity between the CS and the US as important in classical conditioning.
   c. Incorrect. The contemporary view emphasizes that what is important about the CS-US connection is the information the stimuli give the organism.
   d. **Correct.** This describes the process of stimulus substitution. Contemporary psychologists have realized, however, that the process of classical conditioning cannot always happen this way.

7. a. Incorrect. Thorndike's law of effect states that behaviors followed by positive outcomes are strengthened and behaviors followed by negative outcomes are weakened.
   b. Incorrect. Thorndike's law of effect is related more closely to operant conditioning than to classical conditioning.
   c. Incorrect. Thorndike's law of effect states that behaviors followed by positive outcomes are strengthened and behaviors followed by negative outcomes are weakened.
   d. **Correct.** Thorndike's law of effect states that behaviors followed by positive outcomes are strengthened and behaviors followed by negative outcomes are weakened.

8. a. Incorrect. Thorndike's law of effect states that behaviors followed by positive outcomes are strengthened and behaviors followed by negative outcomes are weakened.
   b. **Correct.** This is the definition of positive reinforcement.
   c. Incorrect. In negative reinforcement the frequency of response increases because the response either removes a negative stimulus or involves avoiding a negative stimulus.
   d. Incorrect. Punishment is a consequence that decreases the probability that a behavior will occur.

9. a. **Correct.** This is the definition of chaining.
   b. Incorrect. Primary reinforcement involves the use of reinforcers that are innately satisfying.
   c. Incorrect. Secondary reinforcement acquires its positive value through experience; secondary reinforcers are learned or conditioned reinforcers.
   d. Incorrect. Shaping is the process of rewarding approximations of behavior. It does not necessarily begin by shaping the final response in the desired sequence.

10. a. Incorrect. A fixed-interval schedule reinforces the first appropriate response after a fixed (predictable) amount of time has elapsed.
    b. **Correct.** A fixed-ratio schedule reinforces behavior after a set number of responses.
    c. Incorrect. A variable-interval schedule is a timetable in which a response is reinforced after a variable amount of time has elapsed.

d. Incorrect. On a variable ratio schedule, responses are rewarded an average number of times, but on an unpredictable basis.

11. a. Incorrect. The interval schedules produce behavior at a lower rate than the ratio schedules do.
    b. Incorrect. The fixed ratio schedule produces a high rate of behavior with a pause occurring between the reinforcer and the behavior, but the variable ratio schedule usually produces the highest response rate of all four schedules.
    c. **Correct.** The variable ratio schedule usually produces the highest response rate of all four schedules.
    d. Incorrect. The interval schedules produce behavior at a lower rate than the ratio schedules do.

12. a. **Correct.** Primary reinforcement involves the use of reinforcers that are innately satisfying, that is, they do not take any learning on the organism's part to make them pleasurable. Food, water, and sexual satisfaction are primary reinforcers.
    b. Incorrect. Secondary reinforcement acquires its positive value through experience; secondary reinforcers are learned or conditioned reinforcers.
    c. Incorrect. Partial reinforcement simply means that responses are not reinforced each time they occur.
    d. Incorrect. Learned reinforcement is the same as secondary reinforcement where reinforcers are learned or conditioned.

13. a. Incorrect. Generalization in operant conditioning means giving the same response to similar stimuli.
    b. **Correct.** Extinction in operant conditioning is a decrease in the tendency to perform a behavior that results in neither a positive nor a negative consequence. Johnny's parents are helping the decrease his tantrums by providing no consequence, positive or negative.
    c. Incorrect. Discrimination in operant conditioning is the tendency to respond only to those stimuli that are correlated with reinforcement.
    d. Incorrect. A superstitious behavior is repeated because it seems to produce reinforcement, even though it is actually coincidental.

14. a. Incorrect. A behavior modification program designed for incontinence includes things like monitoring toileting behaviors and scheduling going to the toilet.
    b. **Correct.** A behavior modification program designed for depression includes monitoring daily moods and developing more efficient coping skills.
    c. Incorrect. A behavior modification program designed for losing weight might include monitoring daily food intake and exercise.
    d. Incorrect. Phobias are most successfully treated with classical conditioning techniques. Behavior modification is the application of operant conditioning.

15. a. Incorrect. Proponents of operant conditioning do recognize that each organism experiences a distinct reinforcement history, but they also believe that a stimulus is a positive reinforcer only if it strengthens the response it follows.
    b. Incorrect. Proponents of operant conditioning do believe that a stimulus is a positive reinforcer only if it strengthens the response it follows, but they also recognize that each organism experiences a distinct reinforcement history.
    c. Incorrect. Although critics of operant conditioning believe this to be true, proponents of operant conditioning do not believe that it is manipulative.
    d. **Correct.** Proponents of operant conditioning recognize that each organism experiences a distinct reinforcement history <u>and</u> that a stimulus is a positive reinforcer only if it strengthens the response it follows.

16. a. Incorrect. Bandura claimed that before a person can imitate (through observational learning) a model's actions, she must attend to what the model is doing or saying.
    b. Incorrect. Bandura claimed that to reproduce a model's actions (part of observational learning), you must code the information and keep it in memory so that it can be retrieved.
    c. **Correct.** Experiments with Bobo dolls have demonstrated that observational learning occurs just as extensively when modeled behavior is not reinforced as when it is reinforced.
    d. Incorrect. Proponents of observational learning claim that just because an organism does not perform a response does not mean it was not learned.

17. a. Incorrect. Bandura's model of reciprocal influences on behavior emphasizes environmental factors.
    b. **Correct.** The S-O-R model is a model of learning that gives some importance to cognitive factors.
    c. Incorrect. Operant conditioning theories emphasize the importance of stimulus-response connections.
    d. Incorrect. Operant conditioning gives no room to the possibility that cognitive factors might be might be important in the learning process.

18. a. Incorrect. Self-control is defined as the restraint exercised over one's own impulses, emotions or desires.
    b. **Correct.** This is the definition of self-efficacy.
    c. Incorrect. Self-esteem has to do with regarding oneself as a worthwhile person.
    d. Incorrect. Self-awareness is consciousness of oneself as a person.

19. a. Incorrect. Insight learning is a form of problem solving in which the organism develops a sudden insight or understanding of a problem's solution.
    b. Incorrect. The S-O-R model is a model of learning that gives some importance to cognitive factors.
    c. Incorrect. Expectational learning has to do with Bandura's Cognitive Model. In this model, expectations can change the environment and the environment can change expectations.
    d. **Correct.** A cognitive map is an organism's mental representation of the structure of physical space.

20. a. Incorrect. Most psychologists agree that the principles of classical conditioning, operant conditioning, and observational learning are universal and powerful learning processes in every culture.
    b. Incorrect. Although culture can influence the degree to which these learning processes are used, it can also determine the content of learning.
    c. Incorrect. Although culture can determine the content of learning, it can also influence the degree to which classical and operant conditioning are used.
    d. **Correct.** Culture can determine the degree to which classical and operant conditioning are use and the content of learning.

Chapter **6** **Memory**

Learning Objectives

After studying this chapter, you should be able to:

1. Define memory. (p. 192)

2. List and describe the three different memory systems and their corresponding time frames. (p. 192)

3. Distinguish between echoic memory and iconic memory. (p. 193)

4. Describe the effects of chunking and maintenance rehearsal on working memory. (p. 194)

5. Distinguish between declarative memory and procedural memory and between episodic memory and semantic memory. (p. 196)

6. Contrast the traditional and contemporary memory models. (p. 197)

7. Describe the following encoding processes: attention, automatic and effortful processing, elaboration, organization, and imagery. (p. 200)

8. Describe how the network theories and the schema theories explain the representation of knowledge in memory. (p. 204)

9. Describe the process of retrieval from long-term memory, including the tip-of-the-tongue phenomenon and the serial position effect. (p. 208)

10. Distinguish between recall and recognition. (p. 209)

11. Distinguish between proactive and retroactive interference. (p. 210)

12. Distinguish between anterograde amnesia and retrograde amnesia. (p. 213)

13. Discuss the search for the neurobiological basis of memory. (p. 214)

14. Describe the importance of cultural factors in memory. (p. 216)

15. Distinguish between the strategies for improving practical memory and academic memory. (p. 216)

Chapter 6 Outline

- I. The Nature of Memory
  - A. Time frames of memory
    - 1. Sensory memory
      - a. echoic memory
      - b. iconic memory
    - 2. Working memory
    - 3. Long-term memory
  - B. Contents of memory
    - 1. Declarative memory
    - 2. Procedural memory
    - 3. Episodic memory
    - 4. Semantic memory
  - C. Traditional and contemporary memory models
    - 1. Atkinson and Shiffrin (information processing model)
    - 2. Baddeley (redefined working memory)
- II. The Processes of Memory
  - A. Encoding
    - 1. Attention
    - 2. Automatic and effortful processing
    - 3. Depths of processing
    - 4. Organization
    - 5. Imagery
  - B. Representation
    - 1. Network theories
    - 2. Schema theories
  - C. Retrieval and Forgetting
    - 1. Serial position effect
    - 2. Recall
    - 3. Recognition
    - 4. Cue-dependent forgetting
    - 5. Interference
      - a. proactive interference
      - b. retroactive interference
    - 6. Decay theory
    - 7. Amnesia
      - a. anterograde amnesia
      - b. retrograde amnesia
    - 8. Repression of memories
- III. The Biological and Cultural Contexts of Memory
  - A. The neurobiological origins of memory
  - B. Cultural influences on memory
- IV. Improving Memory
  - A. Improving practical memory
  - B. Improving academic memory

Key Terms

Write a brief description for each of the following terms. Where relevant, provide an original example or illustration of the term. Then, compare your answers with those provided at the end of the Study Guide chapter. Review the text for those terms you don't know and those you define incorrectly.

1. memory (p. 192

2. sensory memory (p. 192)

3. echoic memory (p. 193)

4. iconic memory (p. 193)

5. working memory (p. 193)

6. memory span (p. 193)

7. chunking (p. 194)

8. maintenance rehearsal (p. 194)

9. eidetic memory (p. 194)

10. long-term memory (p. 195)

11. declarative memory (p. 196)

12. procedural memory (p. 196)

13. episodic memory (p. 196)

14. semantic memory (p. 196)

15. traditional information-processing model (p. 197)

16. contemporary model of working memory (p. 198)

17. memory processes (p. 199)

18. encoding (p. 199)

19. selective attention (p. 200)

20. effortful processing (p. 200)

21. automatic processing (p. 200)

22. levels of processing theory (p. 200)

23. elaboration (p. 201)

24. schema (p. 205)

25. script (p. 207)

26. tip-of-the-tongue phenomenon (TOT state) (p. 208)

27. serial position effect (p. 208)

28. primacy effect (p. 208)

29. recency effect (p. 208)

30. recall (p. 209)

31. recognition (p. 209)

32. cue-dependent forgetting (p. 210)

33. interference theory (p. 210)

34. proactive interference (p. 210)

35. retroactive interference (p. 210)

36. decay theory (p. 212)

37. amnesia (p. 213)

38. anterograde amnesia (p. 213)

39. retrograde amnesia (p. 213)

40. culture specificity hypothesis (p. 216)

41. mnemonics (p. 219)

42. method of loci (p. 219)

43. pegword method (p. 219)

Guided Review

The following in-depth chapter review is a challenging and comprehensive fill-in-the-blanks exercise. The answers are found near the end of the chapter. As you go through the exercise, try to resist the temptation to look at the answers until you have provided them. When you have filled in all the blanks, you will have a thorough summary of the chapter for reference and review.

The Nature of Memory

Memory is the retention of ___(1)___ over time. The part of the memory system that retains sensory information very briefly is called ___(2)___ ________. In the sensory registers, auditory images are referred to as ___(3)___ memory and visual images are called ___(4)___ memory. Information is stored up to 30 seconds in ___(5)___ memory. George Miller wrote that the capacity of working memory was ___(6)___ items, plus or minus ___(7)___. An example of the 7+/− phenomenon, involving the number of digits an individual can report back in order after a single presentation, is the ___(8)___ ________. The capacity of working memory can be expanded by grouping information into higher-order units, a technique called ___(9)___.

The conscious repetition of information, which increases the length of time it stays in short-term memory is called ___(10)___ ________. Although rehearsal is often verbal, it can also be visual or ___(11)___. Some people have

___(12)___ memory, or photographic memory. A contemporary view of ___(13)___ memory views it as a place to manipulate and assemble information. One view suggests that working memory contains an "executive" and two "slave" systems, consisting of (1) the ___(14)___ loop, which is specialized to process language, and (2) the ___(15)___-________ scratch pad, which processes spatial imagery information.

The relatively permanent memory system that holds information for long periods of time is called ___(16)___-________ memory. Information in long-term memory that can be verbally communicated is called ___(17)___ memory. A more recent term for declarative memory is ___(18)___ memory. Information regarding skills, which is difficult or impossible to communicate verbally, is called ___(19)___ memory. A more recent term for procedural memory is ___(20)___ memory.

One type of declarative memory, which focuses on the where and when of events and episodes, is called ___(21)___ memory; another type, which reflects our general knowledge about the world, is called ___(22)___ memory. Semantic memory is independent of the individual's ___(23)___ identity with the past.

Two models attempt to explain how the memory systems work together. According to the ___(24)___ information-processing model, memory involves a sequence of three stages-sensory registers, ___(25)___-term memory and long-term memory. According to the contemporary working model, ___(26)___-term memory often precedes ___(27)___ memory. Also, working memory uses long-term memory in ___(28)___ ways.

The Processes of Memory

The encoding of new information, the representation of information, and its retrieval are referred to as ___(29)___ ________. The transformation of information into a memory system is called ___(30)___. A key ingredient in the encoding process is the ability to focus mentally on certain stimuli, while excluding other stimuli; this is paying ___(31)___. The ability to focus and concentrate on a narrow band of information is called ___(32)___ attention. Attention not only is selective, it also is ___(33)___.

An important aspect of encoding information is the degree of ___(34)___ required. ___(35)___ processing requires capacity or resources to encode information, whereas ___(36)___ processing does not require capacity, resources, or effort to encode information into memory.

The view that memory is on a continuum from shallow to deep is referred to as the ___(37)___ ________ ________ theory. In this view, the physical or sensory features of stimuli are memorized at the ___(38)___ level, more details are added at the ___(39)___ level, and the greatest number of details is added at the ___(40)___ level. Research indicates that memory improves when people make ___(41)___ associations to stimuli.

As memory is processed more extensively—that is, ___(42)___-memory improves. Elaboration produces processing that is more ___(43)___ and allows for the storage of more information.

Our memory is ____(44)____; one important feature of memory's organization is that it sometimes is ____(45)____. Researchers have found that memory can also be improved through the use of ____(46)____.

Two approaches have been advanced to explain the representation of knowledge in memory: network theories and schema theories. Network theories view memory as a network of ____(47)____. A ____(48)____ is information that exists in a person's mind. Schema theories suggest that our long-term memory search is not very exact and we ____(49)____ the past. A schema for an event is called a ____(50)____.

The process we use to get information out of memory storage is called ____(51)____. In some cases, we are confident we know something, but we can't quite "pull" it out of memory. This is called the ____(52)____-________-________-________ phenomenon. One of the most important aspects of retrieval is the use of good ____(53)____.

Recall of items is superior at the beginning and the end of a list, according to the ____(54)____ ________ effect. The better recall for items at the beginning of a list is called the ____(55)____ effect, whereas the better recall at the end of the list is called the ____(56)____ effect. Generally, items in the middle of a list produce a ____(57)____ level of recall.

Two important factors involved in retrieval are (1) the ____(58)____ of the cues and (2) the retrieval ____(59)____ required. A memory measure that requires retrieval of previously learned information is called ____(60)____. By contrast, a memory measure that requires only identification is called ____(61)____.

____(62)____-________ forgetting is a form of forgetting information due to the failure to use effective retrieval cues. This principle is consistent with a theory of forgetting called ____(63)____ theory. When material that has been learned earlier interferes with the recall of material learned later, this is called ____(64)____ interference; when material learned later interferes with material learned earlier, it is termed ____(65)____ interference.

Decay theory suggests that, when something is learned, a ____(66)____ ________ is formed. With the passage of time, however, the memory trace ____(67)____.

The loss of memory is referred to as ____(68)____. A type of amnesia that affects the retention of new information is called ____(69)____ amnesia. A type of amnesia involving memory loss for a segment of the past but not for new events is called ____(70)____ amnesia. Recently, some cognitive psychologists have investigated the relationship between ____(71)____ and memory.

The Biological and Cultural Contexts of Memory

The last several decades have seen extensive investigation of the biological basis of memory. Many neuroscientists believe that memory is located in discrete sets of ____(72)____. Some researchers claim that memories may be clustered in groups of about ____(73)____ neurons. Although ____(74)____ neurons are involved in memory, neurons must work together. Research with the sea slug suggests that memories are written in ____(75)____. Research into the role played by brain structures in memory impairment has implicated the following: the amygdala, the hippocampus, the thalamus, the ____(76)____ body, the ____(77)____ forebrain, and the ____(78)____ cortex.

The ____(79)____ ________ hypothesis states that cultural experiences determine what an individual is most likely to remember.

Improving Memory

The following strategies are recommended to help improve your general memory: pay close ___(80)___; rehearse and ___(81)___; make a ___(82)___ and check it twice; organize yourself to jog your memory; give yourself additional memory ___(83)___; when your memory fails, ___(84)___ what went wrong. Two strategies that may help improve memory for people's names are to repeat the name several times and try to make additional ___(85)___ to the name.

Specific techniques designed to help improve academic memory include organizing the material ___(86)___ and elaborating the meaning. Techniques that make memory more efficient are called ___(87)___. Two techniques that make use of imagery are the method of ___(88)___ and the ___(89)___ method. Other recommendations include consolidating your learning, minimizing ___(90)___ and organizing yourself.

Sociocultural Worlds/Applications in Psychology

In your own words, summarize the material you have read in Sociocultural Worlds , "Eyewitness Testimony," and Applications in Psychology, "Repressed Memories, Child Abuse, and Reality." Briefly describe how each of these articles relates to the information contained in the chapter.

Concept Check

1. Echoic memory involves ______________________________.
2. ________ ________ involves visual sensory registers, which retain information for about one-quarter of a second.
3. Working memory is ______________________________.
4. ________ ________ is the conscious recollection of information; can be verbally communicated; also called explicit memory.
5. Procedural memory involves ______________________________.
6. ________ ________ is the retention of information about the where and when of life's occurrences.
7. Semantic memory involves ______________________________.
8. ________ ________ occurs when material learned previously interferes with the recall of material learned later.
9. Retroactive interference occurs when ______________________________.

Answers

1. auditory sensory registers, which retain information up to several seconds
2. Iconic memory
3. a limited-capacity system in which information is retained for up to 30 seconds; also called short-term memory
4. Declarative memory
5. knowledge of skills and is difficult to communicate verbally
6. Episodic memory
7. knowledge about the world, including one's areas of expertise, school knowledge, and everyday knowledge
8. Proactive interference
9. material learned later interferes with material that has been previously learned

Multiple-Choice Questions

Practice Test 1

After answering all the multiple-choice questions in Practice Test 1, compare your answers with the answer key provided at the end of the chapter. The answer key contains a brief explanation of both the correct and incorrect answers. Each of these questions is keyed to the Learning Objectives for the chapter. If you answer any questions incorrectly, review the corresponding Learning Objective and text material before you proceed to Practice Test 2.

1. Each of the following is an aspect of memory studied by psychologists *except*
   a. the encoding of memory.
   b. the storage of memory.
   c. the decoding of memory.
   d. the retrieval of memory.

LO 1

2. Which of the following can store information for up to 30 seconds?
   a. sensory memory
   b. working memory
   c. long-term memory
   d. iconic memory

LO 2

3. Which of the following can store the largest amount of information?
   a. sensory memory
   b. working memory
   c. echoic memory
   d. long-term memory

LO 2

4. Visual images that are stored in the sensory registers are called __________ memory.
   a. iconic
   b. echoic
   c. semantic
   d. procedural

LO 4

5. The capacity of working memory can be expanded by grouping information into higher-order units. This technique is called
   a. maintenance rehearsal.
   b. eidetic imagery.
   c. chunking.
   d. the articulatory loop.

LO 4

6. Each of the following refers to the concept of working memory *except*
   a. manipulation and assembling of information.
   b. the phonological loop.
   c. "slave" systems.
   d. permanent memory.

LO 4

7. The reason basketball star Shaquille O'Neal might have trouble verbally explaining his movements on the basketball court is that these movements are based on __________ memory.
   a. episodic
   b. semantic
   c. declarative
   d. procedural

LO 5

8. According to the text, "everyday" knowledge is an example of which type of memory?
   a. episodic
   b. semantic
   c. declarative
   d. procedural

LO 5

9. Long-term memory often precedes working memory, according to
   a. the contemporary model.
   b. the traditional model.
   c. the Atkinson-Shiffrin model.
   d. levels of processing theory.

LO 6

10. Thinking of examples of a concept is a good way to help yourself understand the concept. This approach is referred to as
    a. deep processing.
    b. automatic processing.
    c. imagery.
    d. elaboration.

LO 7

11. Which of the following kinds of theories is consistent with reconstructive memory?
    a. network theories
    b. schema theories
    c. levels of processing theories
    d. none of the above

LO 8

12. Which of the following underscores the importance of good cues in the process of retrieval?
    a. the serial position effect
    b. the tip-of-the-tongue phenomenon
    c. the primacy effect
    d. the recency effect

LO 9

13. Which part of a list of items is recalled most effectively?
    a. the beginning
    b. the middle
    c. the end
    d. both *a* and *c*

LO 9

14. Multiple-choice questions measure which type of memory?
    a. recognition
    b. recall
    c. serial position
    d. sensory memory

LO 10

15. The expression "You can't teach an old dog new tricks" describes
    a. retroactive interference.
    b. proactive interference.
    c. cue-dependent forgetting.
    d. anterograde interference.

LO 11

16. In retrograde amnesia, there is memory loss
    a. only for new information.
    b. only for segments of new information.
    c. for the complete past.
    d. only for a segment of the past.

LO 12

17. Each of the following is believed to be true about the neurobiological basis of memory *except*
    a. Many researchers believe that memory is located in discrete sets of neurons.
    b. Single neurons are at work in memory.
    c. Research on the sea slug has demonstrated the importance of endorphins in memory.
    d. The amygdala and the hippocampus are two of the most important brain regions related to memory.

LO 13

18. According to Bartlett, the way a person reconstructs events reveals much about the person's
    a. intelligence.
    b. sensory memory.
    c. cultural background.
    d. amygdala.

LO 14

19. Mnemonic devices include which of the following?
    a. method of loci
    b. rote memory
    c. peg method
    d. both *a* and *c*

LO 15

20. Students who improve their learning by finding personal connections in the material they study are engaging in
    a. organization.
    b. elaboration.
    c. rote memory.
    d. the peg method.

LO 15

Practice Test 2

The following multiple-choice questions also are keyed to the chapter Learning Objectives. If you answer any questions incorrectly, be sure to review the corresponding Learning Objective and text material.

1. The encoding of memory refers to how information is
    a. retained.
    b. retrieved.
    c. initially placed.
    d. maintained.

LO 1

2. Which memory system can retain information in its original form for only an instant?
    a. sensory memory
    b. working memory
    c. long-term memory
    d. semantic memory

LO 2

3. Which of the following types of memory benefits from maintenance rehearsal?
    a. sensory memory
    b. working memory
    c. echoic memory
    d, long-term memory

LO 2

4. Auditory information that is stored in the sensory registers is referred to as
    a. iconic memory.
    b. echoic memory.
    c. semantic memory.
    d. memory span.

LO 3

5. Which technique can help increase the length of time information stays in short-term memory?
    a. chunking
    b. iconic memory
    c. maintenance rehearsal
    d. both *a* and *c*

LO 4

6. According to one working memory model, the phonological loop
    a. processes language.
    b. processes spatial skills.
    c. is important in visualization.
    d. is the general "executive" of short-term memory.

LO 4

7. According to Tulving, which of the following is a type of declarative memory?
    a. procedural memory
    b. episodic memory
    c. semantic memory
    d. both *b* and *c*

LO 5

8. Declarative memory is to explicit memory as procedural is to
    a. implicit.
    b. episodic.
    c. semantic.
    d. traditional.

LO 5

9. Working memory uses long-term memory in flexible ways according to
    a. the contemporary model.
    b. the traditional model.
    c. the Atkinson-Shiffrin model.
    d. the implicit memory model.

LO 6

10. Which of the following is a type of automatic processing?
    a. elaboration
    b. mental imagery
    c. organization
    d. none of the above

LO 7

11. The schema theories suggest
    a. that memory is represented as networks.
    b. that our memory search is not very exact.
    c. that we reconstruct information.
    d. both *b* and *c*

LO 8

12. You are more likely to remember items at the end of a list than those in the middle of the list, according to the
    a. recency effect.
    b. tip-of-the-tongue phenomenon.
    c. primacy effect.
    d. network theories.

LO 9

13. Which of the following demonstrates the primacy effect?
    a. superior recall for items at the beginning of a list
    b. superior recall for items in the middle of the list
    c. superior recall for items at the end of the list
    d. superior recall for items both at the beginning and end of a list

LO 9

14. Essay tests measure
    a. recall.
    b. recognition.
    c. the primacy effect.
    d. the recency effect.

LO 10

15. Adam took a Spanish course during his first semester at college; during his second semester, he took a French course. Retroactive interference would suggest that Adam
    a. should now consider taking German.
    b. is going to have a difficult time learning French.
    c. is not going to remember his Spanish very well.
    d. is going to have a difficult time with both Spanish and French.

LO 11

16. In anterograde amnesia there is memory loss
    a. only for new information.
    b. only for segments of new information.
    c. for the complete past.
    d. only for a segment of the past.

LO 12

17. Mishkin's research on monkeys found the most severe memory impairments when there was damage to the amygdala and the
    a. hypothalamus.
    b. reticular formation.
    c. basal ganglia.
    d. hippocampus.

LO 13

18. According to the cultural specificity hypothesis, culture influences
    a. brain neurochemistry.
    b. memory.
    c. the duration of sensory memory.
    d. the capacity of working memory.

LO 14

19. Imagery techniques include the method of loci and
    a. the pegword method.
    b. ARESIDORI.
    c. organization.
    d. elaboration.

LO 15

20. Each of the following is advice for improving academic performance *except*
    a. organize the material
    b. minimize distraction
    c. avoid elaboration
    d. avoid cramming

LO 15

Answers to Key Terms

1. **Memory** is the retention of information over time.
2. **Sensory memory** holds information in its original sensory form for only an instant.
3. **Echoic memory** is the name given to the auditory sensory registers. (Remember the word *echo.*)
4. **Iconic memory** is the name given to the visual sensory registers.
5. **Working memory** is also called short-term memory. It is a limited-capacity system in which information is retained for up to 30 seconds. With rehearsal, the information can be retained longer.
6. **Memory span** is the number of digits an individual can report back in order after a single presentation of them.
7. **Chunking** is a technique for expanding the capacity of the short-term memory by grouping information into higher-order units.
8. **Maintenance rehearsal** is the conscious repetition of material; this increases the length of time it stays in working memory.
9. **Eidetic memory** is also called photographic memory. This type of memory allows some people to recall significantly more visual details than most people.
10. **Long-term memory** is the relatively permanent memory system that holds huge amounts of information for a long period of time.
11. **Declarative memory** is the conscious recollection of information, such as specific facts or events, that can be verbally communicated. It is sometimes referred to as "knowing that."
12. **Procedural memory** is knowledge of skills and cognitive operations, or "knowing how."
13. **Episodic memory** is the retention of information about the where and when of life's happenings.
14. **Semantic memory** is a type of declarative memory, involving a person's general knowledge about the world.
15. The **traditional information-processing model** holds that memory involves a sequence of three stages- sensory registers, short-term memory and long-term memory.
16. **The contemporary model of working memory** emphasizes that long-term memory often precedes working memory and that working memory uses long-term memory in flexible ways.
17. **Memory processes** involve the encoding of information into memory, the representation of information, and the retrieval of what was previously stored.
18. **Encoding** is the transformation of information in, or transfer of information into, a memory system.
19. **Selective attention** is the focusing of attention on a narrow band of information.
20. **Effortful processing** requires capacity or resources to encode information in memory.
21. **Automatic processing** does not require capacity, resources, or effort to encode information.
22. **Levels of processing** theory is Craik and Lockhart's theory that memory processing is on a continuum from shallow to deep. Deeper processing produces better memory.
23. **Elaboration** is the extensiveness of processing at any given depth in memory.
24. A **schema** is information in the form of concepts, events, and knowledge that already exists in a person's mind.
25. A **script** is a schema for an event.
26. The **tip-of-the-tongue phenomenon** is a type of effortful retrieval that occurs when people are confident they know something but are unable to retrieve it.
27. **Serial position effect** is the effect of an item's position in a list on our recall of it; recall is superior for items at the beginning and at the end of a list.
28. The **primacy effect** refers to superior recall for items at the beginning of a list.
29. The **recency effect** refers to superior recall for items at the end of a list.
30. **Recall** is a memory measure in which the individual must retrieve previously learned material. An essay test is a test of recall.
31. **Recognition** is a memory measure that requires the individual to identify (recognize) learned items. A multiple-choice test is a test of recognition.
32. **Cue-dependent forgetting** is a form of forgetting due to failure to use effective retrieval cues.
33. **Interference theory** suggests that we forget because other information gets in the way of what we want to remember.
34. **Proactive interference** occurs when material that was previously learned disrupts the recall of material learned later.

35. **Retroactive interference** occurs when material that is learned disrupts the retrieval of material that was previously learned.
36. **Decay theory** states that when something new is learned, a "memory trace" is created; over time, this memory trace can disintegrate.
37. **Amnesia** is the loss of memory.
38. **Anterograde amnesia** affects the retention of new information or events. Previously learned material is not affected.
39. **Retrograde amnesia** is the loss of memory for a segment of the past, but not for new events.
40. The **culture specificity hypothesis** states that cultural experiences determine what is socially relevant in a person's life and, therefore, what the person is most likely to remember.
41. **Mnemonics** are techniques designed to make memory more efficient.
42. The **method of loci** is a mnemonic strategy in which information is associated with a well-known sequence of activities or locations.
43. The **pegword method** is a mnemonic strategy that involves using a set of mental pegwords associated with numbers.

Answers to Guided Review

1. information (p. 192)
2. sensory memory (p. 192)
3. echoic (p. 193)
4. iconic (p. 193)
5. working (p. 193)
6. seven (p. 193)
7. two (p. 193)
8. memory span (p. 193)
9. chunking (p. 194)
10. maintenance rehearsal (p. 194)
11. spatial (p. 194)
12. eidetic (p. 194)
13. working (p. 194)
14. phonological (p. 195)
15. visuo-spatial (p. 195)
16. long-term (p. 195)
17. declarative (p. 196)
18. explicit (p. 196)
19. procedural (p. 196)
20. implicit (p. 196)
21. episodic (p. 196)
22. semantic (p. 196)
23. personal (p. 196)
24. traditional (p. 197)
25. short (p. 197)
26. long (p. 197)
27. working (p. 198)
28. flexible (p. 198)
29. memory processes (p. 199)
30. encoding (p. 199)
31. attention (p. 200)
32. selective (p. 200)
33. shiftable (p. 200)
34. effort (p. 200)
35. Effortful (p. 200)
36. automatic (p. 200)
37. levels of processing (p. 200)
38. shallow (p. 200)
39. intermediate (p. 200)
40. deepest (p. 200)
41. semantic (p. 201)
42. elaborated (p. 201)
43. distinctive (p. 202)
44. organized (p. 202)
45. hierarchical (p. 202)
46. imagery (p. 203)
47. nodes (p. 204)
48. schema (p. 205)
49. reconstruct (p. 205)
50. script (p. 207)
51. retrieval (p. 208)
52. tip-of-the-tongue (p. 208)
53. cues (p. 208)
54. serial position (p. 208)
55. primacy (p. 208)
56. recency (p. 208)
57. low (p. 208)
58. nature (p. 209)
59. task (p. 209)
60. recall (p. 209)
61. recognition (p. 209)
62. Cue-dependent (p. 210)
63. interference (p. 210)
64. proactive (p. 210)
65. retroactive (p. 210)
66. memory trace (p. 212)
67. disintegrates (p. 212)
68. amnesia (p. 213)
69. anterograde (p. 213)
70. retrograde (p. 213)
71. repression (p. 213)
72. neurons (p. 214)
73. 1000 (p. 214)
74. single (p. 215)
75. chemicals (p. 215)
76. mammillary (p. 215)
77. basal (p. 215)
78. prefrontal (p. 215)
79. culture specificity (p. 216)
80. attention (p. 216)
81. practice (p. 216)
82. list (p. 216)
83. cues (p. 217)
84. analyze (p. 217)
85. associations (p. 217)
86. hierarchically (p. 219)
87. mnemonics (p. 219)
88. loci (p. 219)
89. pegword (p. 219)
90. distractions (p. 220)

Answers to Multiple Choice Questions- Practice Test 1

1. a. Incorrect. Psychologists study how information is initially placed, or encoded, into memory; how it is retained, or stored, after being encoded; and how it is found, or retrieved, for a specific purpose later.
   b. Incorrect. Psychologists study how information is initially placed, or encoded, into memory; how it is retained, or stored, after being encoded; and how it is found, or retrieved, for a specific purpose later.
   c. **Correct.** Psychologists study how memory is encoded, stored and retrieved, not how it is decoded.
   d. Incorrect. Psychologists study how information is initially placed, or encoded, into memory; how it is retained, or stored, after being encoded; and how it is found, or retrieved, for a specific purpose later.

2. a. Incorrect. Sensory memory holds information from the world in its original sensory form for only an instant, not much longer than the brief time for which one is exposed to the visual, auditory, and other sensations.
   b. **Correct.** Working memory is a limited capacity memory system in which information is retained for as long as 30 seconds.
   c. Incorrect. Long-term memory is a type of memory that holds huge amounts of information for a long period of time.
   d. Incorrect. Information is held in iconic memory for only about 1/4 second.

3. a. Incorrect. Sensory memory holds information from the world in its original sensory form for only an instant, not much longer than the brief time for which one is exposed to the visual, auditory, and other sensations.
   b. Incorrect. Working memory is a limited capacity memory system in which information is retained for as long as 30 seconds.
   c. Incorrect. Echoic memory is the name given to the auditory sensory registers in which information is retained for up to several seconds.
   d. **Correct.** Long-term memory is a type of memory that holds huge amounts of information for a long period of time.

4. a. **Correct.** Iconic memory is the name given to the visual sensory registers.
   b. Incorrect. Echoic memory is the name given to the auditory sensory registers in which information is retained for up to several seconds.
   c. Incorrect. Semantic memory is a person's general knowledge about the world.
   d. Incorrect. Procedural memory refers to knowledge in the form of skills and cognitive operations about how to do something.

5. a. Incorrect. Maintenance rehearsal expands working memory through the conscious repetition of information.
   b. Incorrect. Eidetic memory is the same thing as photographic memory.
   c. **Correct.** Chunking is the grouping or "packing" of information into higher-order units that can be remembered as single units.
   d. Incorrect. The method of loci is a mnemonic strategy in which information is associated with a well-known sequence of activities or locations.

6. a. Incorrect. Working memory is a kind of mental "workbench" that lets us manipulate and assemble information when we make decisions, solve problems, and comprehend written and spoken language.
   b. Incorrect. The phenomenological loop is one of the slave systems of the working memory. This system is specialized to process language information.
   c. Incorrect. One model of working memory proposes that it consists of a general "executive" and two "slave" systems that help the executive do its job.
   d. **Correct.** Permanent memory is a concept of long-term memory.

7. a. Incorrect. Episodic memory is the retention of information about the where and when of life's happenings.
   b. Incorrect. Semantic memory is a person's general knowledge about the world.
   c. Incorrect. Declarative memory is the conscious recollection of information, such as specific facts or events that can be verbally communicated.
   d. **Correct.** Procedural memory refers to knowledge in the form of skills and cognitive operations about how to do something. Procedural memory cannot be consciously recollected, at least not in the form of specific events or facts. This makes procedural memory difficult if not impossible to communicate verbally.

8. a. Incorrect. Episodic memory is the retention of information about the where and when of life's happenings.
   b. **Correct.** Semantic memory is a person's general knowledge about the world. It includes "everyday" knowledge about meanings of words, famous individuals, important places, and common things.
   c. Incorrect. Declarative memory is the conscious recollection of information, such as specific facts or events that can be verbally communicated.
   d. Incorrect. Procedural memory refers to knowledge in the form of skills and cognitive operations about how to do something.

9. a. **Correct.** According to the contemporary model, long-term memory often precedes working memory and working memory uses long-term memory in flexible ways.
   b. Incorrect. According to the traditional model, long-term memory never precedes short-term memory.
   c. Incorrect. This is another name for the traditional model and according to this model, long-term memory never precedes short-term memory.
   d. Incorrect. The level of processing theory has more to do with the quality of encoding information than the interplay between short- and long-term memory.

10. a. Incorrect. Deep processing has to do with memorizing information with great detail.
    b. Incorrect. Automatic processing occurs regardless of how people focus their attention.
    c. Incorrect. Imagery is used to aid memory by picturing the information to be remembered.
    d. **Correct.** Elaboration is the extensiveness of information processing at any given depth in memory. Thinking of examples of a concept is an example of elaboration.

11. a. Incorrect. Network theories claim that our memories consist of a hierarchical network of nodes that stand for labels or concepts. If all memory is stored perfectly in these kinds of networks, reconstructing memories would not be necessary.
    b. **Correct.** According to schema theories, we often reconstruct information we are trying to remember, fitting it into information that already exists in our mind.
    c. Incorrect. This theory deals with the effect of processing depth on the quality of memory rather than memory reconstruction.
    d. Incorrect. Schema theories are consistent with reconstructive memory.

12. a. Incorrect. The serial position effect refers to the effect of an item's position in a list on our recall of that item.
    b. **Correct.** The tip-of-the-tongue phenomenon suggests that without good retrieval cues, information encoded in memory can be difficult to find.
    c. Incorrect. Primacy effect refers to better recall for items at the beginning of a list.
    d. Incorrect. Recency effect refers to better recall for items at the end of a list.

13. a. Incorrect. According to the serial position effect, recall of a list is greatest for items at the beginning <u>and</u> end of a list.
    b. Incorrect. Many items from the middle of a list drop out of working memory before being encoded into long-term memory.
    c. Incorrect. According to the serial position effect, recall of a list is greatest for items at the beginning <u>and</u> end of a list.
    d. **Correct.** According to the serial position effect, recall of a list is greatest for items at the beginning <u>and</u> end of a list.

14. a. **Correct.** Recognition is a memory measure in which the individual only has to identify learned items, as on a multiple choice test.
   b. Incorrect. Recall is a memory measure in which the individual must retrieve previously learned information, as on an essay test.
   c. Incorrect. The serial position effect refers to the effect of an item's position in a list on our recall of that item.
   d. Incorrect. Sensory memory holds information from the world in its original sensory form for only an instant.

15. a. Incorrect. Retroactive interference occurs when material learned later disrupts retrieval of information learned earlier.
   b. **Correct.** Proactive interference occurs when retrieval of information that was learned earlier disrupts recall of material learned later.
   c. Incorrect. Cue-dependent forgetting is a form of forgetting information because of failure to use effective retrieval cues.
   d. Incorrect. Anterograde amnesia is the loss of the ability to form or retrieve memories for events that occur after injury or trauma.

16. a. Incorrect. Retrograde amnesia involves memory loss of past information not memory loss of new information.
   b. Incorrect. Retrograde amnesia involves memory loss of past information not memory loss of new information.
   c. Incorrect. Retrograde amnesia is a memory disorder that involves memory loss for a segment of the past, not for the complete past.
   d. **Correct.** Retrograde amnesia is a memory disorder that involves memory loss for a segment of the past.

17. a. Incorrect. Brain researcher Larry Squire says that most memories are probably clustered in groups of about 1,000 neurons.
   b. Incorrect. Single neurons are at work in memory. For example, some respond to faces, others to eye or hair color.
   c. **Correct.** This research has demonstrated the importance of serotonin in memory, not the importance of endorphins.
   d. Incorrect. Researchers examining the role of brain structures in memory have found that damage to the amygdala and the hippocampus cause the most serious memory deficits.

18. a. Incorrect. Bartlett's research demonstrated the effect of cultural background on memory reconstruction, not the effect of intelligence on memory reconstruction.
   b. Incorrect. Sensory memory holds information from the world in its original sensory form for only an instant, not much longer than the brief time for which one is exposed to the visual, auditory, and other sensations. Reconstructing events requires the use of memory that lasts for more than an instant.
   c. **Correct.** Bartlett found that the way an unfamiliar story was reconstructed depended upon cultural background.
   d. Incorrect. Although researchers have found that the role of the amygdala in memory is crucial, Bartlett's research did not reveal its specific function in the reconstruction of memory.

19. a. Incorrect. The method of loci and the peg method are both mnemonic techniques.
   b. Incorrect. Mnemonics are techniques that make memory more efficient. Rote memorization is rarely the most efficient technique for remembering new information.
   c. Incorrect. The method of loci and the pet method are both mnemonic techniques.
   d. **Correct.** The method of loci <u>and</u> the pet method are both mnemonic techniques.

20. a. Incorrect. Organization refers to organizing recently learned information in hierarchical form to aid memory of the information.
   b. **Correct.** Elaboration refers to improving memory by making new information more personally meaningful.
   c. Incorrect. Rote memorization does not involve memorizing for any kind of meaning, personal or otherwise.
   d. Incorrect. The peg word method involves using a set of mental pegs with numbers attached to them.

Answers to Multiple Choice Questions- Practice Test 2

1. a. Incorrect. Retaining information refers to how information is stored in memory.
   b. Incorrect. Retrieval refers to how information is found in memory.
   c. **Correct.** Encoding refers to how information is initially placed in memory.
   d. Incorrect. Maintaining information has to do with how information stays in memory.

2. a. **Correct.** Sensory memory holds information from the world in its original sensory form for only an instant, not much longer than the brief time for which one is exposed to the visual, auditory, and other sensations.
   b. Incorrect. Working memory is a limited capacity memory system in which information is retained for as long as 30 seconds.
   c. Incorrect. Long-term memory is a type of memory that holds huge amounts of information for a long period of time.
   d. Incorrect. Semantic memory is a person's general knowledge about the world. It includes "everyday" knowledge about meanings of words, famous individuals, important places, and common things. Obviously, this type of information is retained for more than an instant.

3. a. Incorrect. Maintenance rehearsal increases the length of time that information stays in working memory, not sensory memory. Information can only stay in sensory memory for an instant.
   b. **Correct.** Maintenance rehearsal is the conscious repetition of information that increases the length of time the information stays in working memory.
   c. Incorrect. Maintenance rehearsal increases the length of time that information stays in working memory, not echoic memory. Information can only stay in the auditory sensory registers of echoic memory for an instant.
   d. Incorrect. Maintenance rehearsal increases the length of time that information stays in working memory, not long-term memory.

4. a. Incorrect. The sensory registers of iconic memory store visual information.
   b. **Correct.** Echoic memory is the name given to auditory information stored in the sensory registers.
   c. Incorrect. Semantic memory is a person's general knowledge about the world. It includes "everyday" knowledge about meanings of words, famous individuals, important places, and common things.
   d. Incorrect. Memory span refers to the number of digits an individual can report back in order following a single presentation.

5. a. Incorrect. Chunking is the grouping or "packing" of information into higher-order units that can be remembered as single units. Chunking expands short-term memory by making large amounts of information more manageable. However, maintenance rehearsal also expands short-term memory.
   b. Incorrect. Iconic memory is the name given to information contained in the visual sensory registers, where it is held for only 1/4 second.
   c. Incorrect. Maintenance rehearsal is the conscious repetition of information that increases the length of time the information stays in short-term memory. However, chunking also expands short-term memory.
   d. **Correct.** Both chunking and maintenance rehearsal increase the length of time that information stays in short-term memory.

6. a. **Correct.** The phenomenological loop is one of the slave systems of the working memory. This system is specialized to process language information.
   b. Incorrect. The visuospatial scratchpad is the slave system of the working memory that processes spatial skills.
   c. Incorrect. The visuospatial scratchpad is the slave system of the working memory that is important in visualization.
   d. Incorrect. The phenomenological loop is not the executive system, but one of the slave systems of the working memory.

7. a. Incorrect. Procedural memory is not a type of declarative memory. It refers to knowledge in the form of skills and cognitive operations about how to do something.
   b. Incorrect. Episodic memory is the retention of information about the where and when of life's happenings. It is a subtype of declarative memory. But semantic memory is also a subtype of declarative memory.
   c. Incorrect. Semantic memory is a person's general knowledge about the world. It is a subtype of declarative memory. But episodic memory is also a subtype of declarative memory.
   d. **Correct.** Episodic and semantic memory are both subtypes of declarative memory.

8. a. **Correct.** Declarative memory is increasing referred to as explicit memory, and procedural memory is referred to as implicit memory.
   b. Incorrect. Episodic memory refers to information about the where and when of life. Declarative memory is increasingly referred to as explicit memory.
   c. Incorrect. Semantic memory is a person's general knowledge about the world. Declarative memory is increasingly referred to as explicit memory.
   d. Incorrect. Traditional refers to the traditional information-processing model; according to this model memory involves a sequence of three stages: sensory registers, short-term memory and long-term memory.

9. a. **Correct.** The contemporary working-memory model is Alan Baddeley's view that long-term memory often precedes working memory and that working memory uses long-term memory in flexible ways.
   b. Incorrect. The traditional model portrays memory as flowing from sensory registers to working memory to long-term memory, but not visa-versa. In this model, long-term memory can get information from short-term memory, but short-term memory cannot use long-term memory.
   c. Incorrect. The Atkinson-Shiffrin model is the same thing as the traditional model. The traditional model portrays memory as flowing from sensory registers to working memory to long-term memory, but not visa-versa. In this model, long-term memory can get information from short-term memory, but short-term memory cannot use long-term memory.
   d. Incorrect. Implicit memory refers to knowledge in the form of skills and cognitive operations about how to do something. This type of memory cannot be consciously recollected, at least not in the form of specific events or facts.

10. a. Incorrect. Elaboration, the extensiveness of information processing at any given depth in memory, is a type of effortful, rather than automatic, processing
    b. Incorrect. Developing a mental image of information to facilitate memory is a type of effortful, rather than automatic, processing.
    c. Incorrect. Organizing information to facilitate memory is a type of effortful, rather than automatic, processing.
    d. **Correct.** Elaboration, mental imagery, and organization are not automatic, but effortful, processes.

11. a. Incorrect. Network, not schema, theories suggest that our memories consist of a complex network of nodes that stand for labels and concepts.
    b. Incorrect. Schema theories do claim that long-term memory searches are not very exact, but they also suggest that we reconstruct information to fit into concepts, events, and knowledge that already exist in our minds.
    c. Incorrect. Schema theories do suggest that we reconstruct information to fit into existing schemas, but they also claim that long-term memory searches are not very exact.
    d. **Correct.** Schema theories suggest that our memory search is not very exact and that we reconstruct information.

12. a. **Correct.** The recency effect refers to better recall for items at the end of a list.
    b. Incorrect. The tip-of-the-tongue phenomenon suggests that without good retrieval cues, information encoded in memory can be difficult to find.
    c. Incorrect. The primacy effect refers to better recall for items at the beginning of a list.
    d. Incorrect. Network theories claim that our memories consist of a hierarchical network of nodes that stand for labels or concepts.

13. a. **Correct.** The primacy effect refers to superior recall for items at the beginning of a list.
    b. Incorrect. The primacy effect refers to superior recall for items at the beginning of a list.
    c. Incorrect. The primacy effect refers to superior recall for items at the beginning of a list. The recency effect refers to superior recall for items at the end of a list.
    d. Incorrect. The serial position effect refers to superior recall for items both at the beginning and end of a list. The primacy effect refers only to superior recall for items at the beginning of a list.

14. a. **Correct.** On an essay test, an individual must retrieve or recall previously learned information.
    b. Incorrect. On an essay test, an individual must do more than just identify, or recognize, learned information.
    c. Incorrect. The primacy effect refers to superior recall for items at the beginning of a list. Essay tests generally require more than remembering the beginning of a list.
    d. Incorrect. The recency effect refers to superior recall for items at the end of a list. Essay tests generally require more than remembering the end of a list.

15. a. Incorrect. Retroactive interference occurs when material learned later disrupts retrieval of information learned earlier.
    b. Incorrect. This is an example of proactive interference in which retrieval of information that was learned earlier disrupts recall of material learned later.
    c. **Correct.** Retroactive interference occurs when material learned later (in this case, French) disrupts retrieval of information learned earlier (in this case, Spanish).
    d. Incorrect. This might be the case if retroactive and proactive interference were occurring simultaneously.

16. a. **Correct.** Anterograde amnesia is a memory disorder in which the individual cannot form memories of new information or events.
    b. Incorrect. Anterograde amnesia is a memory disorder in which the individual cannot form memories of new information or events. It generally effects all new information, rather than only segments of new information.
    c. Incorrect. Anterograde amnesia only effects memory of new information. Retrograde amnesia is the memory disorder that involves memory loss of the past.
    d. Incorrect. Anterograde amnesia only effects memory of new information. Retrograde amnesia is the memory disorder that involves memory loss of the past.

17. a. Incorrect. Mishkin's research on monkeys demonstrated that the most serious memory deficits were caused by damage to the amygdala and hippocampus.
    b. Incorrect. Mishkin's research on monkeys demonstrated that the most serious memory deficits were caused by damage to the amygdala and hippocampus.
    c. Incorrect. Mishkin's research on monkeys demonstrated that the most serious memory deficits were caused by damage to the amygdala and hippocampus.
    d. **Correct.** Mishkin's research on monkeys demonstrated that the most serious memory deficits were caused by damage to the amygdala and hippocampus.

18. a. Incorrect. It is the neurobiological view, not the cultural specificity hypothesis, that addresses the effects of brain neurochemistry on memory.
    b. **Correct.** The cultural specificity hypothesis states that cultural experiences determine what is socially relevant in a person's life and, therefore, what the person is most likely to remember in general.
    c. Incorrect. The cultural specificity hypothesis does not directly address cultural influence on the duration of sensory memory.
    d. Incorrect. The cultural specificity hypothesis does not directly address cultural influence on the capacity of working memory.

19. a. **Correct.** The peg word method is an imagery technique which involves using a set of mental pegs with numbers attached to them.
    b. Incorrect. ARESIDORI stands for attention, rehearsal, elaboration, semantic processing, imagery, distinctiveness, organization, retrieval, and interest. This mnemonic involves improving memory through wordplay rather than visual images.
    c. Incorrect. Organization refers to organizing recently learned information in hierarchical form to aid memory of the information. It does not generally involve imagery.
    d. Incorrect. Elaboration refers to improving memory by making new information more personally meaningful. It does not generally involve imagery.

20. a. Incorrect. Successful students organize their study time effectively.
    b. Incorrect. You can improve academic performance by minimizing distraction and giving your full attention to the material you want to remember.
    c. **Correct.** When you elaborate the meaning of a concept to promote deep processing, you are memorizing for understanding. This strategy should not be avoided in improving academic performance.
    d. Incorrect. Cramming for tests should be avoided. When you leave your learning to the last minute, you guarantee that your learning will be shallow and short- rather than long-term.

Chapter 7 Thinking, Language, and Intelligence

Learning Objectives

After studying this chapter, you should be able to:

1. Explain the similarities and differences in the functioning of computers and cognitive processes. (p. 226)

2. Describe the process of concept formation and discuss the differences between "real-life" concepts and those often used in psychological research. (p. 228)

3. Identify the components of the ideal problem solver. (p. 230)

4. Distinguish between algorithms and heuristics. (p. 231)

5. Distinguish between inductive reasoning and deductive reasoning. (p. 233)

6. Explain critical thinking and describe common pitfalls in critically thinking about behavior. (p. 234)

7. Distinguish between convergent and divergent thinking and identify characteristics of creative thinkers. (p. 237)

8. Define the terms *language* and *infinite generativity*. (p. 240)

9. Distinguish among the following: phonology, morphology, syntax, and semantics. (p. 240)

10. Discuss the processes that occur early in the development of human language, including the holophrase hypothesis and telegraphic speech. (p. 241)

11. Discuss the issue of whether there is a critical period for language acquisition. (p. 242)

12. Describe the evidence for biological, environmental, and cultural influences on language. (p. 243)

13. State the linguistic relativity hypothesis and discuss its significance. (p. 244)

14. Describe the controversies concerning bilingual education. (p. 246)

15. Discuss the debate regarding the ability of animals to learn language. (p. 248)

16. Define intelligence. (p. 250)

17. Distinguish among Spearman's two-factor theory, Thurstone's multiple-factor theory, Sternberg's triarchic theory, and Gardner's frames of intelligence. (p. 251)

18. Describe the following components of tests: reliability, validity, standardization, and norms. (p. 254)

19. Describe widely used contemporary measures of intelligence. (p. 255)

20. Distinguish between organic and cultural-familial causes of mental retardation. (p. 258)

21. Describe the challenges faced by those with learning differences. (p. 258)

22. Identify the characteristics of "giftedness." (p. 259)

23. Discuss the heredity-environment controversy as it relates to intelligence. (p. 261)

24. Discuss the efforts to develop a culture-fair intelligence test. (p. 264)

25. Explain the use and misuse of intelligence tests. (p. 265)

Chapter 7 Outline

I. The Cognitive Revolution in Psychology
  A. Artificial Intelligence
  B. Expert Systems
II. Thinking
  A. Concept Formation
  B. Problem Solving
    1. IDEAL Method
      a. identifying problems
      b. defining problems
      c. exploring alternative approaches
      d. acting on a plan
      e. looking at the effects
    2. Additional Components Involved in Problem Solving
      a. algorithms
      b. heuristics
        (1) representative heuristic
        (2) available heuristic
      c. functional Fixedness
  C. Reasoning
    1. Inductive reasoning
      a. analogies
      b. metaphors
    2. Deductive reasoning
  D. Critical Thinking
    1. Thinking critically about behavior
    2. Critical thinking pitfalls
      a. substituting labels or names for explanations of behavior
      b. confusing correlation and causation
      c. explaining behavior with a single cause
      d. resisting coincidence as a reasonable cause
      e. ignoring evidence that conflicts with our beliefs
      f. taking too much credit for confirming predictions after-the-fact
  E. Creativity
    1. Convergent and Divergent Thinking
    2. Characteristics of creative people
      a. commitment to a persona aesthetic or style
      b. excellences in problem-finding skills
      c. willingness to take risks
      d. enthusiasm for getting feedback
      e. joy from intrinsic rather than extrinsic rewards
III. Language
  A. What is Language?
    1. Definition
    2. Infinite Generativity
    3. Phonology
    4. Morphology
    5. Syntax
    6. Semantics
  B. How Language Develops
    1. Early development
      a. holophrase hypothesis
      b. telegraphic speech
    2. Critical periods in Language development
  C. Biological, Environmental, and Cultural Influences
    1. Biological Influences
    2. Environmental Influences
    3. Cultural Influences
      a. linguistic relativity hypothesis
      b. language's role in achievement and school
  D. Do Animals have Language?
IV. Intelligence
  A. The Nature of Intelligence
    1. Binet's Concept of Mental Age
    2. Terman's Concept of Intelligence Quotient
    3. Spearman's Two-Factor Theory of Intelligence
    4. Thurstone's Multiple-Factor Theory
    5. Sternberg's Triarchic Theory
    6. Gardner's Frames of Intelligence
  B. Measuring Intelligence
    1. Reliability
    2. Validity
    3. Standardization
    4. Contemporary Intelligence Tests
      a. The Stanford Binet
      b. The Wechsler Scales
  C. Variations in Cognitive Ability
    1. Mental Retardation
      a. organic retardation
      b. cultural-familial retardation
    2. Learning Differences
    3. Giftedness
  D. Culture and Ethnicity
    1. The Heredity-environment controversy
    2. Cultural and Ethnic comparisons
    3. Culture, Intelligence, and Adaptation
  E. The Use and Misuse of Intelligence Tests

Key Terms

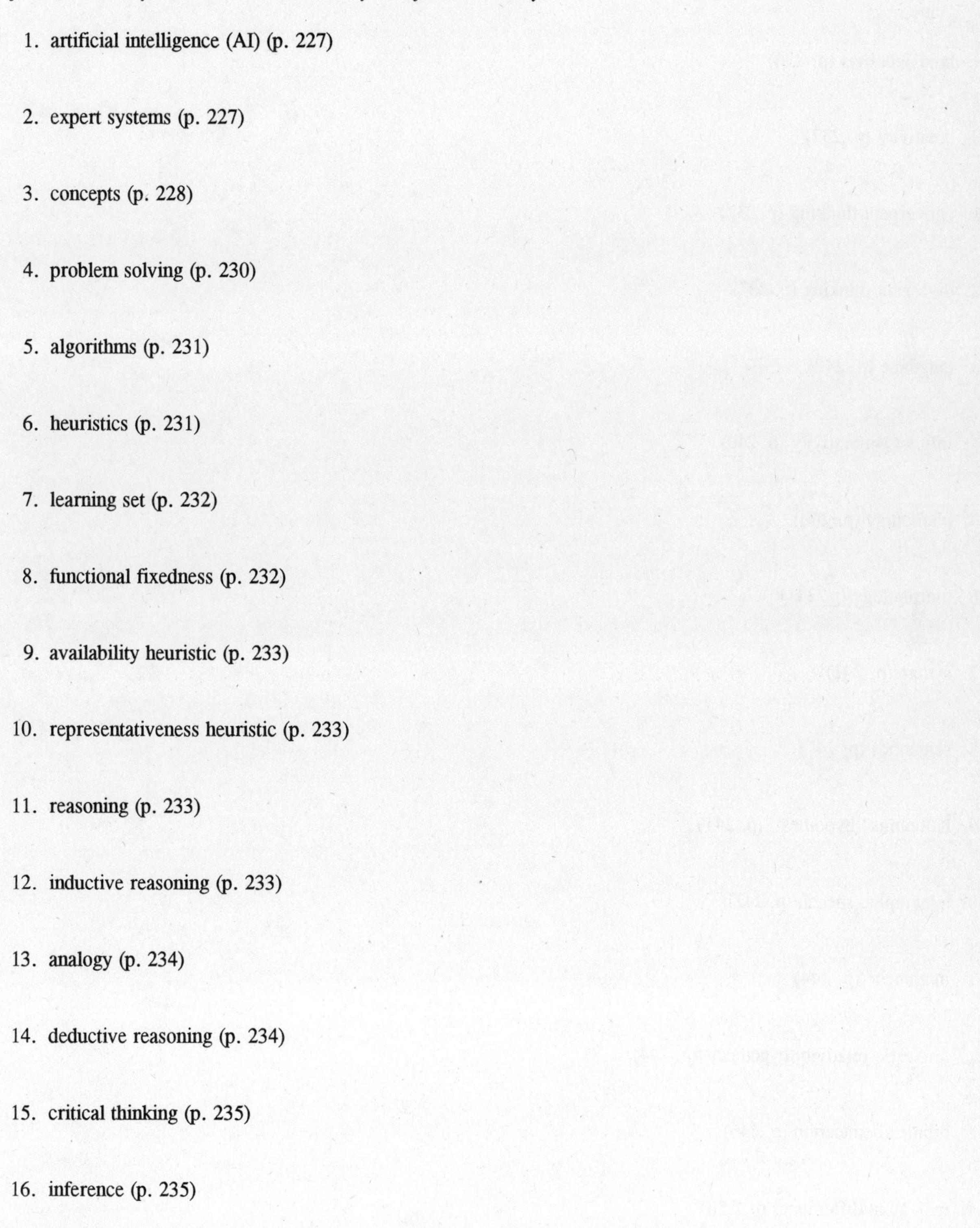

Write a brief description for each of the following terms. Where relevant, provide an original example or illustration of the term. Then, compare your answers with those provided at the end of the Study Guide chapter. Review the text for those terms you don't know and those you define incorrectly.

1. artificial intelligence (AI) (p. 227)

2. expert systems (p. 227)

3. concepts (p. 228)

4. problem solving (p. 230)

5. algorithms (p. 231)

6. heuristics (p. 231)

7. learning set (p. 232)

8. functional fixedness (p. 232)

9. availability heuristic (p. 233)

10. representativeness heuristic (p. 233)

11. reasoning (p. 233)

12. inductive reasoning (p. 233)

13. analogy (p. 234)

14. deductive reasoning (p. 234)

15. critical thinking (p. 235)

16. inference (p. 235)

17. confirmation bias (p. 236)

18. belief perseverance effect (p. 236)

19. hindsight bias (p. 236)

20. creativity (p. 237)

21. convergent thinking (p. 237)

22. divergent thinking (p. 237)

23. language (p. 240)

24. infinite generativity (p. 240)

25. phonology (p. 240)

26. morphology (p. 241)

27. syntax (p. 241)

28. semantics (p. 24`)

29. holophrase hypothesis (p. 241)

30. telegraphic speech (p. 242)

31. motherese (p. 244)

32. linguistic relativity hypothesis (p. 244)

33. bilingual education (p. 246)

34. individual differences (p. 250)

35. intelligence (p. 250)

36. mental age (p. 251)

37. intelligence quotient (IQ) (p. 251)

38. two-factor theory (p. 251)

39. multiple-factor theory (p. 251)

40. triarchic theory (p. 251)

41. reliability (p. 254)

42. test-retest reliability (p. 254)

43. inter-rater reliability (p. 255)

44. validity (p. 255)

45. content validity (p. 255)

46. criterion validity (p. 255)

47. standardization (p. 255)

48. norms (p. 255)

49. normal distribution (p. 256)

50. mental retardation (p. 257)

51. organic retardation (p. 258)

52. cultural-familial retardation (p. 258)

53. learning difference (p. 258)

54. dyslexia (p. 259)

55. gifted (p. 259)

56. culture-fair tests (p. 265)

Guided Review

The following in-depth chapter review is a challenging and comprehensive fill-in-the-blanks exercise. The answers are found near the end of the chapter. As you go through the exercise, try to resist the temptation to look at the answers until you have provided them. When you have filled in all the blanks, you will have a thorough summary of the chapter for reference and review.

The Cognitive Revolution in Psychology

Cognitive psychology seeks explanations for observable behavior that rely on mental processes and structures that cannot be directly ___(1)___.

An important factor in the growth of cognitive psychology was the development of ___(2)___. Although some ___(3)___ psychologists draw an analogy between human cognition and the functioning of computers, important differences exist. The science of creating machines capable of performing activities that require intelligence when they are performed by people is called ___(4)___ ________. Computer-based systems used to assess knowledge and make decisions in advanced skill areas are called ___(5)___ ________.

Thinking

Information in memory is manipulated and transformed through ___(6)___. Categories that are used to group objects, events, and characteristics on the basis of common properties are called ___(7)___. Concepts help make our memory more ___(8)___ and keep us from having to relearn.

An important aspect of concept formation is developing and testing ___(9)___. Eleanor Rosch believes that real-life concepts have "___(10)___ ________." She also believes that some members of a concept category are more typical than others; that is, they are more ___(11)___. Cultural experiences also affect ___(12)___ formation.

An attempt to find an appropriate way of attaining a goal, when the goal is not readily available, is called ___(13)___ ________. A model of problem solving has the acronym *IDEAL.* Step 1 involves ___(14)___ the problem. The second step involves carefully ___(15)___ the problem. Step 3 is to ___(16)___ alternative approaches. The two final steps of IDEAL problem solving involve ___(17)___ on a plan and ___(18)___ at the effects.

One procedure for solving problems that guarantees an answer to a problem, is referred to as an ___(19)___. A second approach provides rules of thumb that can suggest a solution but does not guarantee that it will work; this approach is called ___(20)___. The tendency to use the same strategy to solve different problems is referred to as a

___(21)___ ________. A related concept, ___(22)___ ________, refers to the inability to solve a problem because it is viewed only in terms of its usual functions.

Two heuristic strategies can lead to faulty reasoning. When we judge the probability of an event by the ease with which prior occurrences come to mind, we are using the ___(23)___ heuristic. When we judge the probability of an event by how well it matches a prototype, we are using the ___(24)___ heuristic.

The mental activity involved in transforming information to reach conclusions is called ___(25)___. Reasoning from the specific to the general is referred to as ___(26)___ reasoning. An inductive type of reasoning made up of four parts, where the relation between the first two is the same as the relation between the last two, is called an ___(27)___. Reasoning from the general to the specific is called ___(28)___ reasoning.

An approach to problem solving that involves grasping the deeper meaning of problems, keeping an open mind, and deciding for oneself what to believe or do is called ___(29)___ ________. An important aspect of critical thinking in psychology involves drawing conclusions from observations about behavior; these conclusions are called ___(30)___. The following represent critical thinking pitfalls: substituting labels for ___(31)___ of behavior; confusing correlation and ___(32)___; explaining behavior with a ___(33)___ cause; resisting ___(34)___ as a reasonable cause; ignoring evidence that conflicts with our ___(35)___; taking credit for confirming predictions ___(36)___ - ________ - ________. Examining only the evidence that supports our beliefs is called the ___(37)___ bias. When we cling to our beliefs even in the face of conflicting evidence, this is termed the belief ___(38)___ effect. When we produce cogent explanations or predictions after-the-fact, this is termed ___(39)___ bias.

Creativity is defined as the ability to think in ___(40)___ ways and to come up with ___(41)___ solutions to problems. One distinction is between the type of thinking that produces one correct answer, called ___(42)___ thinking, and the type that produces many answers and is associated with creativity, called ___(43)___ thinking. Creative individuals also share the following characteristics: commitment to a personal aesthetic or ___(44)___; excellence in ___(45)___ - ________ skills; willingness to take ___(46)___; enthusiasm for getting ___(47)___; and, joy from ___(48)___ rather than extrinsic rewards.

Language

A form of communication, both spoken and written, based on a system of symbols, is called ___(49)___. The ability to produce an endless number of meaningful sentences using a finite set of words and rules is called ___(50)___ ________. Language is characterized by organizational ___(51)___. Language is comprised of basic sounds, or ___(52)___. The study of the sound system of language is called ___(53)___. Meaningful strings of sounds that contain no smaller meaningful parts are called ___(54)___. The study of the rules for combining morphemes is called ___(55)___.

The way in which words are combined to form acceptable phrases and sentences is called ___(56)___. The actual meaning of words and sentences is called ___(57)___.

Infants utter their first words at ___(58)___ to ___(59)___ months. The concept that a single word can be used to imply a complete sentence is called the ___(60)___ hypothesis.

By the time children are 18 to 24 months old, they usually utter ___(61)___-________ statements, which are referred to as ___(62)___ ________.

Research, as well as the experiences of a modern-day wild child named Genie, seems to indicate there is a ___(63)___ ________ for learning language.

Both biological and cultural evolution help to explain the development of ___(64)___ ________. Strong evidence for the ___(65)___ basis of language is that children all over the world acquire language milestones about the same time and in about the same order. A type of speech that adults use in adult-child interaction, characterized by a high-pitch voice and the use of simple words, is called ___(66)___. A number of experts believe that ___(67)___ and ___(68)___ facilitate language but are not absolutely necessary.

According to the ___(69)___ ________ hypothesis, language determines the structure of our thought and shapes our basic ideas. Although the hypothesis is controversial, many researchers would agree that language can ___(70)___ thought but does not determine it.

___(71)___ education is a system for students with limited proficiency in English that instructs students in their own language while they also learn English. Among the recommendations of the National Association for Young Children for working with culturally and linguistically diverse children are these: recognize that children are strongly connected to the language of their ___(72)___; children can demonstrate their ___(73)___ and capacity in many ways; without comprehensible input, second language learning can be ___(74)___; Bilingualism does not interfere with ___(75)___ in either language or with cognitive development.

Many psychologists have wondered whether ___(76)___ can learn language. Although chimps can understand symbols, there is no strong evidence they can learn ___(77)___.

Intelligence

In the area of intelligence, psychologists are interested in studying individual ___(78)___. Intelligence is based on ___(79)___ ability, ___(80)___-________ skills, and the ability to learn from and adapt to the experiences of ___(81)___ ________. Expressions of intelligence vary from culture to culture. The concept of mental age was developed by ___(82)___. Mental age measures an individual's mental development relative to ___(83)___. In 1912 William Stern devised the term ___(84)___. It consists of a child's ___(85)___ ________ divided by a child's ___(86)___ age and multiplied by 100.

Charles Spearman's two-factor theory stated that we have a general ability, which he called ___(87)___ and a number of specific intelligences, which he called ___(88)___.

Thurstone's theory, called the ___(89)___-________ theory of intelligence, proposed the existence of seven ___(90)___ mental abilities.

A theory of intelligence developed by Sternberg is called the ___(91)___ theory of intelligence. This theory suggests that intelligence consists of three factors: the first, composed of analytical thinking and abstract reasoning, is called ___(92)___ intelligence; a second factor, involving insightful and creative thinking, is called ___(93)___ intelligence; and the third, "street smarts" and practical knowledge, is called ___(94)___ intelligence.

According to Gardner, there are seven frames or abilities in which we can have strengths or weaknesses. These are ___(95)___ skills, ___(96)___ awareness, mathematics, artistic abilities, verbal abilities, ___(97)___ abilities, and intrapersonal abilities.

___(98)___ reflects whether a test performs in a consistent manner. When reliability is measured by giving an individual the same test on two different occasions, this is called ___(99)___-________ reliability. Another reliability measure involves two raters producing judgments about the quality of test results; this is called ___(100)___-________ reliability.

The extent to which a test measures what it is intended to measure is called ___(101)___. The extent to which a test covers broadly the content it purports to cover is ___(102)___ validity. A test's ability to predict other measures or criteria of an attribute is called ___(103)___ validity.

Tests developed with uniform procedures for giving and scoring them are ___(104)___. The test constructor also develops established standards of performance called ___(105)___.

It has been found that intelligence as measured by the Stanford-Binet test approximates a ___(106)___ distribution, which means that the scores in the distribution are symmetrical, with a majority of cases falling in the middle of the possible range of scores.

In addition to the Stanford-Binet, another widely used group of individual intelligence tests is the ___(107)___ ________. These tests allow an examiner to obtain separate ___(108)___ and ___(109___ scores.

Limited mental ability, an IQ score below 70, and difficulty in adapting to everyday life are characteristic of ___(110)___ ________. The causes of mental retardation include those associated with genetic disorders or brain damage, called ___(111)___ retardation, and those with no evidence of organic retardation, referred to as ___(112)___-________ retardation.

A problematic development in specific academic skills that does not reflect overall intellectual ability is called a ___(113)___ ________. A learning difference that negatively influences the ability to read is called ___(114)___.

A person with above-average intelligence (an IQ of 120 or higher) and/or a superior talent for something is referred to as ___(115)___. Three criteria that characterize gifted children are ___(116)___, marching to a "different drummer," and a passion to ___(117)___. Terman's study of the gifted challenges the notion that they are emotionally ___(118)___ or socially ___(119)___.

Arthur Jensen has sparked debate with his thesis that intelligence is primarily ___(120)___. Jensen believes that heredity accounts for about 80 percent of intelligence. Today, most researchers agree that genetics do not determine intelligence to the extent ___(121)___ envisioned.

Although there are racial and ethnic differences among individuals' performances on intelligence tests, the evidence supporting a ___(122)___ interpretation is suspect. Intelligence is expressed differently in different cultures, and different environments require different ___(123)___. Many of the early intelligence tests were culturally

__(124)__. In response to these problems, psychologists have tried to develop __(125)__-______ tests. Two types of culture-fair tests have been devised. One type includes items that are __(126)__ to individuals from all socioeconomic and ethnic backgrounds; the other type has all the __(127)__ items removed. A test that takes into account the socioeconomic background of the child being tested is called the __(128)__. Efforts to construct a truly culture-fair intelligence test have not yet been __(129)__. To be used effectively, intelligence tests should not be relied on as the __(130)__ indicator of intelligence.

Sociocultural Worlds/Applications in Psychology

In your own words, summarize the material you have read in Sociocultural Worlds, "The Bell-Curve Controversy," and in Applications in Psychology, "How to Talk with Babies and Toddlers." Briefly describe how each of these articles relates to the information contained in the chapter.

Concept Check I

Thinking and Language

1. Inductive reasoning ____________________.
2. ________ ________ is reasoning from the general to the specific.
3. Convergent thinking ____________________.
4. ________ ________ produces many answers to the same question and is associated with creativity.
5. The holophrase hypothesis states that ____________________.
6. ________ ________ is the use of short and precise words to communicate; characteristic of young children's two- and three-word utterances.

Answers

1. is reasoning from the specific to the general; for instance, drawing conclusions about all members of a category based on observing only some of the members
2. Deductive reasoning
3. produces one correct answer and is characteristic of the kind of thinking on standardized intelligence tests
4. Divergent thinking
5. a single word can be used to imply a complete sentence, and that infants' first words characteristically are holophrastic
6. Telegraphic speech

Concept Check II

Intelligence

1. Spearman's two-factor theory ______________________.
2. ______________________ proposes that intelligence consists of componential intelligence, experiential intelligence, and contextual intelligence.
3. Gardner's frames of intelligence ______________________.
4. __________ is the extent to which a test measures what it claims to measure.
5. Standardization ______________________.
6. __________ are established standards of performance for a test.

Answers

1. proposes that individuals have both general intelligence and a number of specific intelligences
2. Sternberg's triarchic theory of intelligence
3. proposes that there are seven frames of intelligence, consisting of spatial skills, bodily awareness, mathematics, and artistic, verbal, interpersonal, and intrapersonal abilities
4. Validity
5. involves developing uniform standards for administering and scoring a test; also involves developing norms for a test
6. Norms

Multiple-Choice Questions

Practice Test 1

After answering all the multiple-choice questions in Practice Test 1, compare your answers with the answer key provided at the end of the chapter. The answer key contains a brief explanation of both the correct and incorrect answers. Each of these questions is keyed to the Learning Objectives for the chapter. If you answer any questions incorrectly, review the corresponding Learning Objective and text material before you proceed to Practice Test 2.

1. Which of the following is *true* regarding the functioning of computers and the human brain?
   a. Both computer chips and humans can develop new learning goals.
   b. In the analogy between computers and the human brain, the physical brain is the hardware and cognition is the software.
   c. In the analogy between computers and the human brain, the physical brain is the software and cognition is the hardware.
   d. Computers have been able to simulate the mind's nonlogical, intuitive nature.

LO 1

2. Which of the following is *true* regarding concept formation?
   a. Culture appears to have little effect on concept formation.
   b. Developing and testing hypotheses are essential in concept formation.
   c. Researchers suggest that concept formation makes memory more efficient.
   d. both *b* and *c*

LO 2

3. The first step in IDEAL problem solving is to
   a. explore alternatives.
   b. integrate heuristics and algorithms.
   c. define the problem.
   d. identify the problem.

LO 3

4. Joe has misplaced his car keys. He is certain they are in his apartment, but he is not sure where. In which of the following problem solving approaches is Joe using an algorithm?
   a. check to see if the car dealer has a spare key
   b. try to remember where in the apartment he has been recently
   c. start in one room of the apartment and systematically check every possible location until the keys are found
   d. check under the sofa

LO 4

5. Opinion polls, which base their predictions on a relatively small sample of people, use what type of reasoning?
   a. inductive
   b. deductive
   c. morphological
   d. conditional

LO 5

6. A conclusion drawn from an observation about behavior is a(n)
   a. inference.
   b. truth.
   c. bias.
   d. analogy.

LO 6

7. Each of the following is associated with divergent thinking *except*
   a. unusual
   b. creative
   c. one correct answer
   d. flexible

LO 7

8. Each of the following is a characteristic of language *except*
   a. a system of symbols.
   b. communication.
   c. limited generativity.
   d. rule systems.

LO 8

9. Language is made up of basic sounds called
   a. morphemes.
   b. syntax.
   c. semantics.
   d. phonemes.

LO 9

10. A 15-month-old child pounds the tray of her high chair with a cup and firmly says, "Milk." As a student of psychology, you recognize this use of language as
   a. holophrastic speech.
   b. telegraphic speech.
   c. motherese.
   d. the generative property of language.

LO 10

11. The evidence for a critical period in the learning of language is supported by which of the following?
   a. children have greater ability to recover language skills than adults
   b. Genie, the modern-day wild child
   c. There is no critical period for learning language.
   d. both *a* and *b*

LO 11

12. Which of the following provides evidence for the biological basis of language?
   a. Language development seems to be a matter of imitation and reinforcement.
   b. Children all over the world reach language milestones at about the same time developmentally.
   c. Parents reinforce grammatically incorrect language.
   d. The linguistic relativity hypothesis emphasizes the biological influence on language.

LO 12

13. According to the linguistic relativity hypothesis,
   a. language determines our thoughts.
   b. thinking determines our language.
   c. language is strongly influenced by biological factors.
   d. both *a* and *b*

LO 13

14. According to the National Association for Young Children
    a. bilingual education interferes with proficiency in language development.
    b. bilingual education interferes with proficiency in cognitive development.
    c. verbal proficiency in a second language takes two to three years to develop.
    d. children should be emotionally distanced from their home language if it is other than English.

LO 14

15. Each of the following conclusions is true regarding animals and language *except*
    a. Animals can be trained to manipulate language-like symbols.
    b. Animals can learn language with all the characteristics of human language.
    c. Animals can communicate with each other.
    d. Sea lions appear to be able to learn syntax.

LO 15

16. Which of the following is a component of the definition of intelligence?
    a. verbal ability
    b. problem-solving skills
    c. adapting to everyday experiences
    d. all of the above

LO 16

17. Each of the following is part of Sternberg's theory of intelligence *except*
    a. componential.
    b. experiential.
    c. informational.
    d. contextual.

LO 17

18. When a test measures what it is intended to measure, it is said to have
    a. validity.
    b. reliability.
    c. standardization.
    d. test-retest reliability.

LO 18

19. Which of the following intelligence tests has separate versions for adults, children and preschoolers?
    a. Stanford-Binet
    b. Wechsler Scales
    c. Triarchic intelligence tests
    d. Gardner's intelligence tests

LO 19

20. Down syndrome is associated with
    a. cultural-familial retardation.
    b. organic retardation.
    c. profound mental retardation.
    d. one missing chromosome.

LO 20

21. Individuals with learning differences
    a. have low IQ scores.
    b. often use compensating strategies.
    c. are likely to experience anxiety about their academic performance.
    d. both *b* and *c*

LO 21

22. Terman's long-term study of the gifted has found that the gifted are more likely to
    a. suffer emotional problems.
    b. become socially maladjusted.
    c. complete advanced academic degrees.
    d. die at an earlier age.

LO 22

23. According to Jensen, the influence of heredity on intelligence is about __________ percent.
    a. 20
    b. 50
    c. 80
    d. 90

LO 23

24. Efforts at developing culture-fair tests have included
    a. using questions that are familiar to people from all ethnic and socioeconomic backgrounds.
    b. removing all written questions.
    c. removing all verbal questions.
    d. both *a* and *c*

LO 24

25. Each of the following characterizes effective use of intelligence tests *except*
  a. they should be used in conjunction with other types of information
  b. they allow broad generalizations about a person's abilities
  c. they should be thought of as indicators of a person's intelligence at this point in time
  d. extreme care should be used in interpreting the scores.

LO 25

Practice Test 2

The following multiple-choice questions also are keyed to the chapter Learning Objectives. If you answer any questions incorrectly, be sure to review the corresponding Learning Objective and text material.

1. The human brain is superior to the computer at each of the following tasks *except*
  a. changing in response to the environment.
  b. engaging in intuitive thought.
  c. maintaining an awareness of itself.
  d. calculating numbers.

LO 1

2. According to Rosch, real-life concepts have
  a. fuzzy boundaries.
  b. subgoals.
  c. heuristics.
  d. algorithms.

LO 2

3. The final step in the IDEAL problem solver is
  a. looking at the effects.
  b. learning about alternative strategies.
  c. using learning sets.
  d. learning to define the problem.

LO 3

4. The problem-solving strategies that guarantee a solution to a problem are called
  a. heuristics.
  b. algorithms.
  c. learning sets.
  d. hypothesis testing.

LO 4

5. Reasoning from the general to the specific makes use of
  a. inductive reasoning.
  b. analogies.
  c. deductive reasoning.
  d. *b* and *c* above

LO 5

6. The ability to grasp the deeper meaning of problems, and to keep an open mind about approaches and perspectives is part of
  a. creativity.
  b. divergent thinking.
  c. heuristics.
  d. critical thinking.

LO 6

7. The kind of thinking associated with creativity is called
  a. divergent thinking.
  b. convergent thinking.
  c. critical thinking.
  d. inferential thinking.

LO 7

8. The ability to produce an endless number of sentences from a finite set of words and rules refers to which characteristic of language?
  a. morphology
  b. semantics
  c. syntax
  d. infinite generativity

LO 8

9. The meaning of words and sentences is called
   a. morphology.
   b. semantics.
   c. syntax.
   d. phonology

LO 9

10. Which of the following is the actual order of the development of language?
   a. babbling, holophrasic speech, telegraphic speech
   b. babbling, telegraphic speech, holophrasic speech
   c. telegraphic speech, babbling, holophrasic speech
   d. holophrasic speech, babbling, telegraphic speech

LO 10

11. The critical period for acquiring the phonological rules of languages and dialects appears to extend through
   a the first year of life.
   b. the first 5 years of life.
   c. puberty.
   d. early adulthood.

LO 11

12. Regarding the roles of imitation and reinforcement in language acquisition, many experts believe
   a. they are absolutely necessary for language acquisition.
   b. they are unimportant in language acquisition.
   c. reinforcement is far more important than imitation in language acquisition.
   d. they facilitate language but are not absolutely necessary for language acquisition.

LO 12

13. Rosch's research on the Dani of New Guinea
   a. supported the linguistic relativity hypothesis.
   b. did not support the linguistic relativity hypothesis.
   c. found that the Dani could not perceive differences between colors.
   d. found that culture determines language.

LO 13

14. Bilingual education refers to programs that teach
   a. English only to non-English speaking learners.
   b. English as well as the learner's native language.
   c. the learner's native language only.
   d. alternating time periods of English and the native language.

LO 14

15. Which of the following is *true* regarding chimpanzees' ability to use language?
   a. Evidence suggests that chimps can understand the meaning of symbols.
   b. Evidence suggests that chimps can learn syntax.
   c. Researchers agree that chimps can use language to express complex thoughts.
   d. all of the above

LO 15

16. Which of the following is *true* regarding intelligence?
   a. There is widespread agreement regarding a definition of intelligence.
   b. The way intelligence is expressed varies from culture to culture.
   c. Verbal ability and problem-solving skills are two important components of intelligence.
   d. both *b* and *c*

LO 16

17. Which of the following theories of intelligence emphasizes the importance of *g*?
   a. Spearman's two-factor theory
   b. Thurstone's multiple-factor theory
   c. Sternberg's triarchic theory
   d. Wechsler's applied theory

LO 17

18. The consistency of test scores is measured by
   a. content validity.
   b. criterion validity.
   c. test-retest reliability.
   d. standardization.

LO 18

19. Which of the following characterizes a normal distribution?
    a. It is symmetrical.
    b. The majority of the cases fall in the middle of the possible range of scores.
    c. The majority of the cases fall in the extremes of the range of scores.
    d. both *a* and *b*

LO 19

20. The majority of mentally retarded individuals fall into which category?
    a. mildly retarded
    b. moderately retarded
    c. severely retarded
    d. profoundly retarded

LO 20

21. Dyslexia is
    a. an inability to learn.
    b. an impairment that negatively influences the ability to read.
    c. an impairment that creates challenges in performing arithmetic calculations.
    d. a form of precocity.

LO 21

22. Research on gifted people has found they are
    a. more mature.
    b. more emotionally disturbed.
    c. socially maladjusted.
    d. less athletic.

LO 22

23. Jensen's research concluded that intelligence is determined
    a. mostly by environmental factors.
    b. mostly by genetic factors.
    c. equally by environmental and genetic factors.
    d. by the specific adaptational demands of one's culture.

LO 23

24. The System of Multicultural Pluralistic Assessment (SOMPA) is based on information from each of the following *except*
    a. verbal and nonverbal intelligence.
    b. social and economic background.
    c. social adjustment to school.
    d. patterns of friendship.

LO 24

25. Each of the following is a potential problem with the use of intelligence tests *except*
    a. they lead to generalizations and stereotypes
    b. the scores are thought of as unchanging throughout life
    c. they are extremely subjective
    d. they may not take into account maturational changes.

LO 25

Answers to Key Terms

1. **Artificial intelligence (AI)** is the science of creating machines capable of performing activities that require intelligence when they are performed by people.
2. **Expert systems** are computer-based systems used to assess knowledge and make decisions in advanced skill areas.
3. A **concept** is a category used to group objects, events, and characteristics on the basis of common properties.
4. **Problem solving** is an attempt to find an appropriate way of attaining a goal when the goal is not readily available.
5. An **algorithm** is a method of problem solving that guarantees an answer to a problem.
6. **Heuristics** are problem-solving rules of thumb that can suggest a solution to a problem but do not ensure that it will work.
7. A **learning set** is the strategy an individual tends to use to solve problems.
8. **Functional fixedness** is the inability to solve a problem because it is viewed only in terms of its usual functions.
9. When we use the **availability heuristic**, we judge the probability of an event by the ease with which prior occurrences come to mind.

10. The **representativeness heuristic** is the strategy of judging the probability of an event by how well it matches a prototype.
11. **Reasoning** is the mental activity of transforming information to reach conclusions.
12. **Inductive reasoning** is reasoning from the specific to the general; that is, drawing conclusions about all members of a category based on observing only some of the members.
13. An **analogy** is a type of reasoning made up of four parts; the relation between the first two parts is the same as the relation between the last two.
14. **Deductive reasoning** is reasoning from the general to the specific; that is, starting with abstract premises and deriving a conclusion.
15. **Critical thinking** involves grasping the deeper meaning of problems, keeping an open mind about different approaches and perspectives, and making decisions for oneself.
16. An **inference** is a conclusion drawn from an observation about behavior.
17. The **confirmation bias** occurs when one examines only the evidence that supports what one already believes.
18. The **belief perseverance effect** occurs when one clings to one's beliefs even in the face of contradictory evidence.
19. **Hindsight bias** refers to explanations or predictions produced after-the-fact.
20. **Creativity** is the ability to think about something in novel and unusual ways and to develop unique solutions to problems.
21. **Convergent thinking** produces one correct answer and is characteristic of the kind of thinking measured on intelligence tests.
22. **Divergent thinking** produces many different answers to the same question and is characteristic of creativity.
23. **Language** is a system of symbols used to communicate with others.
24. **Infinite generativity** is the characteristic of language that permits us to produce an endless number of meaningful sentences using a finite set of words and rules.
25. **Phonology** is the study of a language's sound system.
26. **Morphology** refers to the rules for combining morphemes; morphemes are the smallest meaningful strings of sounds that contain no smaller meaningful parts.
27. **Syntax** involves the ways in which words are combined to form acceptable phrases and sentences.
28. **Semantics** refers to the meanings of words and sentences.
29. The **holophrase hypothesis** states that a single word can be used to express a complete sentence, and that infants' first words characteristically are holophrastic.
30. **Telegraphic speech** is the use of short and precise words to communicate; it is characteristic of young children's two-and three-word sentences.
31. **Motherese** refers to the way parents and other adults often talk to infants; it involves talking in a higher-pitched voice than normal and using simple words and sentences.
32. The **linguistic relativity hypothesis,** first proposed by Whorf, suggests that language determines the structure of thinking and shapes our basic ideas.
33. **Bilingual education** refers to programs for students with limited proficiency in English that instruct students both in their own language and in English.
34. **Individual differences** are the stable, consistent ways people are different from each other.
35. **Intelligence** consists of verbal ability, problem-solving skills, and the ability to learn from and adapt to the experiences of everyday life.
36. **Mental age (MA)** is an individual's level of mental development relative to others.
37. **Intelligence quotient (IQ),** devised in 1912 by William Stern, is a person's mental age divided by chronological age, multiplied by 100.
38. **Two-factor theory** is Spearman's theory that individuals have both general intelligence (*g*) and a number of specific intelligences (*s*).
39. **Multiple-factor theory** is Thurstone's theory that intelligence consists of the following seven primary abilities: verbal comprehension, number ability, word fluency, spatial visualization, associative memory, reasoning, and perceptual speed.
40. **Triarchic theory** is Sternberg's theory that intelligence consists of componential intelligence, experiential intelligence, and contextual intelligence.
41. **Reliability** refers to how consistently a person performs on a test.

42. **Test-retest reliability** is the consistency of results when the same person is given the same test on two different occasions.
43. **Inter-rater reliability** is the extent two which two independent raters produce similar judgments about test results.
44. **Validity** is the extent to which a test measures what it is intended to measure.
45. **Content validity** is the extent to which a test covers broadly what it is purported to cover.
46. **Criterion validity** is a test's ability to predict other measures, or criteria, of an attribute.
47. **Standardization** involves developing uniform procedures for administering and scoring a test; it also involves developing norms for the test.
48. **Norms** are established standards of performance for a test.
49. A **normal distribution** is a symmetrical distribution in which most cases fall in the middle of the possible range of scores and few fall in the extremes of the range.
50. **Mental retardation** is a condition of limited mental ability, in which the individual has a low IQ and difficulty adapting to everyday life.
51. **Organic retardation** is mental retardation caused by a genetic disorder or by brain damage.
52. **Cultural-familial retardation** is mental retardation in which no evidence of organic retardation can be found.
53. A **learning difference** is a problematic development in specific academic skills that does not reflect overall intellectual ability.
54. **Dyslexia** is a learning difference that negatively influences the quality and the rate of a person's reading.
55. **Gifted** individuals are those with above-average intelligence and/or superior talent for something.
56. **Culture-fair tests** are intelligence tests that are intended to not be culturally biased.

Answers to Guided Review

1. observed (p. 226)
2. computers (p. 226)
3. cognitive (p. 226)
4. artificial intelligence (p. 227)
5. expert systems (p. 227)
6. thinking (p. 227)
7. concepts (p. 228)
8. efficient (p. 228)
9. hypotheses (p. 228)
10. fuzzy boundaries (p. 229)
11. prototypical (p. 229)
12. concept (p. 229)
13. problem solving (p. 230)
14. identifying (p. 230)
15. defining (p. 231)
16. explore (p. 231)
17. acting (p. 231)
18. looking (p. 231)
19. algorithm (p. 231)
20. heuristics (p. 231)
21. learning set (p. 232)
22. functional fixedness (p. 232)
23. availability (p. 233)
24. representative (p. 233)
25. reasoning (p. 233)
26. inductive (p. 233)
27. analogy (p. 234)
28. deductive (p. 234)
29. critical thinking (p. 235)
30. inferences (p. 235)
31. explanations (p. 236)
32. causation (p. 236)
33. single (p. 236)
34. coincidence (p. 236)
35. beliefs (p. 236)
36. after-the-fact (p. 236)
37. confirmation (p. 236)
38. perseverance (p. 236)
39. hindsight (p. 236)
40. novel (p. 237)
41. unique (p. 237)
42. convergent (p. 237)
43. divergent (p. 237)
44. style (p. 237)
45. problem-finding (p. 237)
46. risks (p. 237)
47. feedback (p. 237)
48. intrinsic (p. 237)
49. language (p. 240)
50. infinite generativity (p. 240)
51. rules (p. 240)
52. phonemes (p. 240)
53. phonology (p. 240)
54. morphemes (p. 241)
55. morphology (p. 241)
56. syntax (p. 241)
57. semantics (p. 241)
58. 10 (p. 241)
59. 13 (p. 241)
60. holophrase (p. 241)
61. two word (p. 242)
62. telegraphic speech (p. 242)
63. critical period (p. 242)
64. language skills (p. 242)
65. biological (p. 243)
66. motherese (p. 244)
67. imitation (p. 244)
68. reinforcement (p. 244)
69. linguistic relativity (p. 244)
70. influence (p. 245)
71. Bilingual (p. 246)
72. home (p. 246)
73. knowledge (p. 247)
74. difficult (p. 247)
75. proficiency (p. 247)
76. animals (p. 248)
77. syntax (p. 249)
78. differences (p. 250)
79. verbal (p. 250)
80. problem-solving (p. 250)
81. everyday life (p. 250)
82. Binet (p. 251)
83. others (p. 251)
84. IQ (p. 251)
85. mental age (p. 251)
86. chronological (p. 251)
87. *g* (p. 251)

88. *s* (p. 251)
89. multiple-factor (p. 251)
90. primary (p. 251)
91. triarchic (p. 251)
92. componential (p. 253)
93. experiential (p. 253)
94. contextual (p. 253)
95. spatial (p. 253)
96. bodily (p. 253)
97. interpersonal (p. 253)
98. Reliability (p. 254)
99. test-retest (p. 254)
100. inter-rater (p. 255)
101. validity (p. 25)
102. content (p. 255)
103. criterion (p. 255)
104. standardized (p. 255)
105. norms (p. 255)
106. normal (p. 256)
107. Wechsler scales (p. 256)
108. verbal (p. 256)
109. nonverbal (p. 256)
110. mental retardation (p. 256)
111. organic (p. 258)
112. cultural-familial (p. 258)
113. learning difference (p. 258)
114. dyslexia (p. 259)
115. gifted (p. 259)
116. precocity (p. 260)
117. master (p. 260)
118. disturbed (p. 261)
119. maladjusted (p. 261)
120. inherited (p. 261)
121. Jensen (p. 261)
122. genetic (p. 261)
123. adaptations (p. 263)
124. biased (p. 264)
125. cultural-fair (p. 265)
126. familiar (p. 265)
127. verbal (p. 265)
128. SOMPA (p. 265)
129. successful (p. 265)
130. sole (p. 266)

Answers to Multiple Choice Questions- Practice Test 1

1. a. Incorrect. Computers, at this time, are unable to develop new learning goals for themselves.
   b. **Correct.** Cognition is the series of "programs" involved in our thinking.
   c. Incorrect. According to the text, the physical brain is the hardware.
   d. Incorrect. These skills remain the province of the human mind.

2. a. Incorrect. Culture determines the kinds of concepts we are exposed to.
   b. Incorrect. Although this statement is correct, it is not the best alternative.
   c. Incorrect. Although this statement is correct, it is not the best alternative.
   d. **Correct.** Concepts allow us to avoid having to "reinvent the wheel" when we come across information.

3. a. Incorrect. Exploring alternate strategies is step 3 of the IDEAL problem-solver.
   b. This is not a step in the IDEAL problem-solver.
   c. This is step 2 of the IDEAL problem-solver.
   d. **Correct.** In this first step a problem is identified, and someone tries to do something about the problem.

4. a. Incorrect. This is a heuristic, since it represents an effort at quickly solving the problem, but does not guarantee a solution.
   b. Incorrect. This is a heuristic, since it represents an effort at quickly solving the problem, but does not guarantee a solution.
   c. **Correct.** This approach is cumbersome, but does guarantee a solution to the problem.
   d. Incorrect. This is a heuristic, since it represents an effort at quickly solving the problem, but does not guarantee a solution.

5. a. **Correct.** In this type of reasoning, conclusions are drawn about all members of a category based on observing only some members.
   b. Incorrect. This type of reasoning starts with general statements and leads to a specific conclusion.
   c. Incorrect. Morphological reasoning sounds impressive, but has no real meaning.
   d. Incorrect. Conditional reasoning may sound impressive, but it has no real meaning.

6. a. **Correct.** Inferences are an important part of critical thinking.
   b. Incorrect. The conclusion may or may not be true.
   c. Incorrect. A conclusion might reflect a bias.
   d. Incorrect. An analogy is a type of formal reasoning made up of four parts wherein the relationship between the first two parts is the same as the relationship between the second two parts.

7. a. Incorrect. That is, divergent thinking is considered unusual.
   b. Incorrect. That is, divergent thinking is considered creative.
   c. **Correct.** Divergent thinking is not the type of thinking that leads to one correct answer.
   d. Incorrect. That is, divergent thinking is considered flexible.

8. a. Incorrect. This is a characteristic of language.
   b. Incorrect. This is a characteristic of language.
   c. **Correct.** In fact, language creates infinite generativity.
   d. Incorrect. This is a characteristic of language.

9. a. Incorrect. Morphemes are the small strings of sounds that have meaning.
   b. Incorrect. Syntax refers to the way in which words are combined into phrases and sentences.
   c. Incorrect. Semantics refers to the actual meanings of words and sentences.
   d. **Correct.** Phonemes are the basic sounds of a language.

10. a. **Correct.** This refers to the idea that a single word implies a complete sentence.
    b. Incorrect. This is characteristic of two- and three-word sentences.
    c. Incorrect. This refers to the practice of talking to babies in a higher-than-normal pitch.
    d. Incorrect. This refers to the fact that a finite number of words and rules can produce an infinite number of meaningful sentences.

11. a. Incorrect. Although this statement is true, it is not the best alternative.
    b. Incorrect. Although this statement is true, it is not the best alternative.
    c. Incorrect. There is much evidence in support of a critical period in the learning of language.
    d. **Correct.** Also in support of the critical period idea is the importance of when people learn to speak a second language.

12. a. Incorrect. These are environmental influences on the acquisition of language.
    b. **Correct.** This is true despite wide variations in the language input they receive from their environments.
    c. Incorrect. Although this is true, this does not provide evidence for the biological basis of language.
    d. Incorrect. The linguistic relativity hypothesis is an argument for the influence of culture on language.

13. a. Correct. Much of the research suggests that language influences thought, but does not determine thought.
    b. Incorrect. You've got the concepts in reverse order.
    c. Incorrect. The linguistic relativity hypothesis addresses cultural, rather than biological, influences on language.
    d. Incorrect. Only one of the alternatives is correct.

14. a. Incorrect. The NAEYC does not support this statement.
    b. Incorrect. The NAEYC does not support this statement.
    c. **Correct.** According to the NAEYC, the ability to read and write proficiently can take 4 or more years.
    d. Incorrect. This is the opposite intent of the bilingual education movement.

15. a. Incorrect. Although this alternative is true, the question is asking for an *exception*.
    b. Incorrect. Although this alternative is true, the question is asking for an *exception*.
    c. **Correct.** Animals use a variety of modalities to communicate with each other.
    d. Incorrect. Although this alternative is true, the question is asking for an *exception*.

16. a. Incorrect. Although this alternative is true, it is not the best answer.
    b. Incorrect. Although this alternative is true, it is not the best answer.
    c. Incorrect. Although this alternative is true, it is not the best answer.
    d. **Correct.** The way intelligence is expressed in behavior varies from culture to culture.

17. a. Incorrect. This is the type of intelligence measured on traditional intelligence tests.
    b. Incorrect. According to Sternberg, this refers to the ability to solve familiar problems in an automatic, rote way.
    c. **Correct.** This is not one of the components of intelligence, according to Sternberg.
    d. Incorrect. According to Sternberg, this involves practical intelligence, that is, material about getting along in the world we are not taught in school.

18. a. **Correct.** Two types of validity are content validity and criterion validity.
    b. Incorrect. This is a measure of a test's consistency.
    c. Incorrect. This involves the uniform procedures for administering and scoring a test.
    d. Incorrect. This measure of reliability compares a person's test results from two different sessions in order to assess the consistency of the test.

19. a. Incorrect. This test has been standardized by giving it to thousands of children and adults.
    b. **Correct.** The test also allows for separate verbal and nonverbal IQ scores.
    c. Incorrect. According to the text, there is not yet a widely accepted way to measure the multiple forms of intelligence proposed by Sternberg.
    d. Incorrect. According to the text, there is not yet a widely accepted way to measure the multiple forms of intelligence proposed by Gardner.

20. a. Incorrect. In this type of mental retardation, there is no evidence of organic brain damage.
    b. **Correct.** This occurs when an extra chromosome is present in an individual's genetic makeup.
    c. Incorrect. Individuals with Down syndrome have a wide range of intelligence.
    d. Incorrect. In fact, Down syndrome is linked to an extra chromosome.

21. a. Incorrect. Actually, some individuals with learning difference have very high IQ scores.
    b. Incorrect. Although this alternative is true, it is not the best answer.
    c. Incorrect. Although this alternative is true, it is not the best answer.
    d. **Correct.** Although students with learning differences face challenges, these differences do not automatically predict academic failure.

22. a. Incorrect. Terman's study has not supported this myth.
    b. Incorrect. the results of Terman's study have not supported this notion.
    c. **Correct.** A much higher percentage of Terman's participants have completed advanced degrees than among the general public.
    d. Incorrect. Terman's study did not find an earlier mortality for the intellectually gifted participants.

23. a. Incorrect. According to Jensen, the influence of heredity is much higher.
    b. Incorrect. According to Jensen, the influence of heredity is higher.
    c. **Correct.** Jensen's views have sparked much controversy among researchers.
    d. Incorrect. According to Jensen, the influence of heredity is not quite this high.

24. a. Incorrect. Although this alternative is true, it is not the best answer.
    b. Incorrect. According to the text, this approach has not been tried.
    c. Incorrect. Although this alternative is true, it is not the best answer.
    d. **Correct.** Thus far, there is not a widely accepted culture-fair test.

25. a. Incorrect. Although this statement is true, the question is asking for an *exception*.
    b. **Correct.** This constitutes a *misuse* of intelligence tests.
    c. Incorrect. Although this statement is true, the question is asking for an *exception*.
    d. Incorrect. Although this statement is true, the question is asking for an *exception*.

Answers to Multiple Choice Questions- Practice Test 2

1. a. Incorrect. Although this statement is true, the question is asking for an *exception*.
   b. Incorrect. Although this statement is true, the question is asking for an *exception*.
   c. Incorrect. Although this statement is true, the question is asking for an *exception*.
   d. **Correct.** Most people's brains can't begin to compete with the calculating abilities of computers.

2. a. **Correct.** Roach contends the examples used in laboratories to study concept formation are too artificial.
   b. Incorrect. Roach is concerned with prototypes and the artificiality of the laboratory.
   c. Incorrect. Roach is concerned with prototypes and the artificiality of the laboratory.
   d. Incorrect. Roach is concerned with prototypes and the artificiality of the laboratory.

3. a. **Correct.** This involves evaluating the effectiveness of the solution.
   b. Incorrect. Exploring possible strategies is the third step.
   c. Incorrect. Learning sets can be a problem in problem solving.
   d. Incorrect. According to the IDEAL problem solver, defining the problem is the second step.

4. a. Incorrect. These may involve short-cuts in problem solving, but do not guarantee a solution.
   b. **Correct**. These involve step-by-step procedures that guarantee a solution.
   c. Incorrect. Often learn sets interfere with one's ability to solve problems.
   d. Incorrect. This approach to problem solving does not guarantee a solution.

5. a. Incorrect. Inductive reasoning is reasoning from the specific to the general.
   b. Incorrect. Analogies draw on reasoning from the specific to the general.
   c. **Correct.** Solving puzzles and riddles often involve deductive reasoning.
   d. Incorrect. Analogies are a form of *inductive* reasoning.

6. a. Incorrect. Creativity involves flexible, divergent thinking, rather than grasping the "deeper meaning."
   b. Incorrect. Divergent thinking involves flexible, creative thought, rather than grasping the "deeper meaning."
   c. Incorrect. Heuristics is a form of problem solving.
   d. **Correct.** The best ways to teach critical thinking remains a hotly debated issue.

7. a. **Correct.** This type of thinking produces many answers to the same question.
   b. Incorrect. This type of thinking produces one correct answer.
   c. Incorrect. This is the type of thinking associated with grasping the "deeper meaning."
   d. Incorrect. Inferences involve conclusions drawn from premises; this is a type of critical thinking.

8. a. Incorrect. This refers to the rules for combining the sounds of a language.
   b. Incorrect. This refers to the meaning of words and sentences.
   c. Incorrect. This refers to the way words are combined to form sentences.
   d. **Correct.** This quality makes language a highly creative enterprise.

9. a. Incorrect. This refers to the rules for combining the sounds of a language.
   b. **Correct.** Each word has a set of semantic features.
   c. Incorrect. This refers to the way words are combined to form sentences.
   d. Incorrect. This refers to the study of a language's sound system.

10 a. **Correct.** Babbling begins at 3 to 6 months.
   b. Incorrect. The last two items are out of sequence.
   c. Incorrect. Infants begin by babbling.
   d. Incorrect. Infants begin by babbling.

11. a. Incorrect. The critical period extends well beyond the first year.
    b. Incorrect. Research suggests the critical period extends well beyond the first 5 years.
    c. **Correct.** This is based on the results of research with deaf children, children with mental retardation, and people with left-hemisphere brain damage.
    d. Incorrect. The critical period appears not to extend quite that long.

12. a. Incorrect. Most experts believe these factors are important, but not absolutely essential.
    b. Incorrect. Most experts underscore the importance of imitation and reinforcement.
    c. Incorrect. Actually, research suggests parents often reinforce grammatically incorrect statements.
    d. **Correct**. Even most behaviorists today acknowledge there's more to language acquisition than reinforcement and imitation.

13. a. Incorrect. The predictions of the linguistic relativity hypothesis were not supported by Rosch's findings.
    b. **Correct.** The predictions of the linguistic relativity hypothesis were not supported by Rosch's findings.
    c. Incorrect. In fact, Rosch found the Dani were able to perceive differences in colors.
    d. Incorrect. Rosch was investigating the influence of language on thought.

14. a. Incorrect. Bilingual programs instruct students both in their native language and in English.
    b. **Correct.** Controversy continues with respect to bilingual education.
    c. Incorrect. Bilingual programs instruct students both in their native language and in English.
    d. Incorrect. There is no set formula regarding the teaching of both languages.

15. a. **Correct.** Chimps Sherman and Austin have demonstrated their abilities to understand the meaning of symbols.
    b. Incorrect. This is a major sticking point for researchers and chimps.
    c. Incorrect. There is, however, some evidence of chimps being able to learn to express some simple thoughts.
    d. Incorrect. Only one of the other alternatives is correct.

16. a. Incorrect. Unfortunately, researchers have not been able to agree about a comprehensive definition of intelligence.
    b. Incorrect. Although this alternative is true, it is not the best answer.
    c. Incorrect. Although this alternative is true, it is not the best answer.
    d. **Correct.** The two alternatives referred to by this answer are true.

17. a. **Correct.** According to Spearman, g refers to general intelligence.
    b. Incorrect. Thurstone's approach suggested there are a variety of abilities that comprise intelligence.
    c. Incorrect. This theory proposes there are three main components of intelligence.
    d. Incorrect. This theory proposes there are seven "frames" of intelligence.

18. a. Incorrect. This is the extent to which a test measures what it purports to measure.
    b. Incorrect. This is a test's ability to predict other measures of an attribute.
    c. **Correct.** This compares one person's scores from two different sessions.
    d. Incorrect. This involves the procedures for administering and scoring a test.

19. a. Incorrect. Although this answer is true, it is not the best alternative.
    b. Incorrect. Although this answer is true, it is not the best alternative.
    c. Incorrect. In fact the majority of the cases fall elsewhere.
    d. **Correct.** An example of a bell-shaped normal distribution can be found in your text on page 256.

20. a. **Correct**. This category consists of individuals with IQ scores in the range of 55 to 70.
    b. Incorrect. This group makes up about 6 percent of those with mental retardation.
    c. Incorrect. This group makes up about 3.5 percent of those with mental retardation.
    d. Incorrect. This group makes up less than 1 percent of those with mental retardation.

21. a. Incorrect. Dyslexia refers to difficulty with one specific academic skill.
    b. **Correct.** This often leads to poor performance in school.
    c. Incorrect. This is called dyscalculia.
    d. Incorrect. Dyslexia refers to difficulty with one specific academic skill.

22. a. **Correct.** This research finding may be inconsistent with some stereotypes about gifted people.
    b. Incorrect. Research has not supported this notion.
    c. Incorrect. Research has not supported this notion.
    d. Incorrect. Research has not supported this notion.

23. a. Incorrect. Jensen believes the environment accounts for a small percentage of intelligence.
    b. **Correct.** Jensen's beliefs have spawned a great deal of controversy.
    c. Incorrect. Jensen views one of these factors as being far more influential than the other.
    d. Incorrect. Jensen's views are irrespective of cultural influences.

24. a. Incorrect. Although the statement is true, the question is asking for the *exception.*
    b. Incorrect. Although the statement is true, the question is asking for the *exception.*
    c. Incorrect. Although the statement is true, the question is asking for the *exception.*
    d. **Correct.** This is not one of the factors involved in the SOMPA.

25. a. Incorrect. Although the statement is true, the question is asking for the *exception.*
    b. Incorrect. Although the statement is true, the question is asking for the *exception.*
    c. **Correct**. When administered and scored properly, intelligence tests are not subjective.
    d. Incorrect. Although the statement is true, the question is asking for the *exception.*

Chapter **8** # Human Development

Learning Objectives

After studying this chapter, you should be able to:

1. Define development. (p. 275)
2. Describe the issue of maturation vs. experience as it relates to development. (p. 276)
3. Distinguish between the continuity and discontinuity explanations of development and discuss the impact of social policy on child development. (p. 276)
4. Discuss the course of prenatal development, including the germinal, embryonic and fetal periods. (p. 278)
5. Explain the impact of different teratogens on prenatal development. (p. 280)
6. Describe the course of physical development of infants and children. (p. 282)
7. Explain Piaget's concepts of assimilation and accommodation. (p. 285)
8. Describe the challenges and achievements that occur in Piaget's sensorimotor and preoperational stages. (p. 285)
9. Discuss the characteristics of Piaget's stages of concrete operational thought and formal operational thought. (p. 287)
10. Summarize the main contributions and criticisms of Piaget's theory. (p. 289)
11. Explain Vygotsky's view of cognitive development. (p. 290)
12. List and describe the childhood stages of Erikson's socioemotional theory of development. (p. 291)
13. Discuss the process of attachment during infancy. (p. 292)

14. Distinguish among Baumrind's parenting styles: authoritarian, authoritative, neglectful, and indulgent. (p. 295)

15. Discuss cultural, social class, and ethnic variations in families. (p. 297)

16. Describe Hall's storm-and-stress view of adolescence and contrast that view with contemporary research on adolescence. (p. 298)

17. Describe the events that characterize puberty. (p. 299)

18. Describe cognitive development in adolescence and explain adolescent egocentrism. (p. 300)

19. Describe moral development according to both Kohlberg and Gilligan. (p. 301)

20. Contrast the old and new models of parent-adolescent relationships and discuss the importance of peer relationships to adolescents. (p. 304)

21. Discuss identity development in adolescence according to both Erik Erikson and James Marcia. (p. 305)

22. Identify adolescent challenges and describe the components of programs that successfully meet these challenges. (p. 308)

23. Describe the course of physical development in early to middle adulthood and in late adulthood. (p. 311)

24. Trace the changes in cognitive abilities and discuss socioemotional issues that occur as we get older. (p. 315)

25. Distinguish between Erikson's and Levinson's theories of adult personality development. (p. 317)

26. Contrast the life-events approach and the stages approach to adult development. (p. 319)

27. Define activity theory and identify the components of successful aging. (p. 320)

28. Describe the challenges that accompany death and dying. (p. 321)

Chapter 8 Outline

I. What is development?
   A. Biological, Cognitive, and Socioemotional Processes
   B. Maturation and Experience (Nature and Nurture)
   C. Continuity and Discontinuity
      1. Continuity of development
      2. Discontinuity of development
   D. Social Policy
II. Child Development
   A. Prenatal Development
      1. The course of prenatal development
         a. conception
         b. germinal period
         c. embryonic period
         d. fetal period
      2. Challenges to prenatal development
         a. teratogen
         b. Fetal alcohol syndrome
   B. Physical Development
   C. Cognitive Development
      1. Piaget's Theory
         a. Process of adaptation
            (1) assimilation
            (2) accommodation
         b. Stages of cognitive development
            (1) sensorimotor thought
            (2) preoperational thought
               (a) conservation
               (b) egocentrism
            (3) concrete operational thought
            (4) formal operational thought
         c. Piaget's contributions and criticisms
      2. Vygotsky's Theory
   D. Socioemotional Development
      1. Erikson's Theory of Socioemotional Development
         a. Trust versus Mistrust
         b. Autonomy versus Shame and Doubt
         c. Initiative versus Guilt
         d. Industry versus Inferiority
      2. Attachment
         a. imprinting
         b. secure attachment
      3. Parenting styles
         a. authoritarian parenting
         b. authoritative parenting
         c. neglectful parenting
         d. indulgent parenting
III. Adolescence
   A. Historical Beginnings and the Nature of Adolescence
   B. Physical Development
   C. Cognitive Development
      1. Piaget's ideas about adolescent cognition
      2. Moral development
         a. preconventional
         b. conventional
         c. postconventional
   D. Socioemotional Development
      1. Parent-Adolescent relationships
      2. Peers
      3. Identity development
      4. Identity statuses
         a. identity confusion
         b. identity foreclosure
         c. identity moratorium
         d. identity achievement
      5. Identity, culture, and ethnicity
   E. The Challenges of Adolescence
IV. Adult Development and Aging
   A. Periods of Adult Development
   B. Physical Development
   C. Cognitive Development
   D. Socioemotional Development
      1. Lifestyles
      2. Stage theories of adult personality development
         a. intimacy versus isolation
         b. generativity versus stagnation
         c. integrity versus despair
      3. Life events and cohorts effects
      4. Continuity-discontinuity
V. Death and Dying

Key Terms

Write a brief description for each of the following terms. Where relevant, provide an original example or illustration of the term. Then, compare your answers with those provided at the end of the Study Guide chapter. Review the text for those terms you don't know and those you define incorrectly.

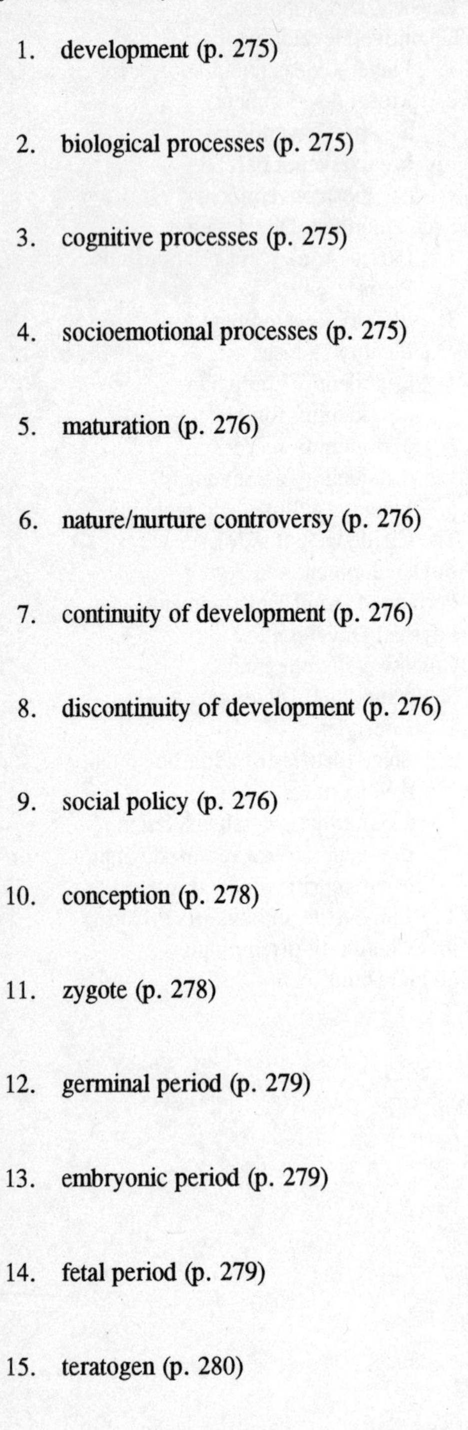

1. development (p. 275)

2. biological processes (p. 275)

3. cognitive processes (p. 275)

4. socioemotional processes (p. 275)

5. maturation (p. 276)

6. nature/nurture controversy (p. 276)

7. continuity of development (p. 276)

8. discontinuity of development (p. 276)

9. social policy (p. 276)

10. conception (p. 278)

11. zygote (p. 278)

12. germinal period (p. 279)

13. embryonic period (p. 279)

14. fetal period (p. 279)

15. teratogen (p. 280)

16. fetal alcohol syndrome (FAS) (p. 280)

17. assimilation (p. 285)

18. accomodation (p. 285)

19. sensorimotor thought (p. 285)

20. object permanence (p. 285)

21. operations (p. 286)

22. preoperational thought (p. 286)

23. conservation (p. 287)

24. egocentrism (p. 287)

25. concrete operational thought (p. 287)

26. formal operational thought (p. 288)

27. hypothetical-deductive reasoning (p. 289)

28. neo-Piagetians (p. 289)

29. zone of proximal development (ZPD) (p. 290)

30. trust versus mistrust (p. 291)

31. autonomy versus shame and doubt (p. 291)

32. initiative versus guilt (p. 291)

33. industry versus inferiority (p. 291)

34. attachment (p. 292)

35. imprinting (p. 294)

36. secure attachment (p. 295)

37. authoritarian parenting (p. 295)

38. authoritative parenting (p. 296)

39. neglectful parenting (p. 296)

40. indulgent parenting (p. 296)

41. storm-and-stress view (p. 298)

42. puberty (p. 299)

43. testosterone (p. 300)

44. estradiol (p. 300)

45. adolescent egocentrism (p. 300)

46. internalization (p. 302)

47. preconventional level (p. 302)

48. conventional level (p. 302)

49. postconventional level (p. 302)

50. justice perspective (p. 302)

51. care perspective (p. 302)

52. indentity vs. identity confusion (p. 305)

53. rites of passage (p. 308)

54. menopause (p. 312)

55. Alzheimer's disease (p. 314)

56. cognitive mechanics (p. 315)

57. cognitive pragmatics (p. 316)

58. intimacy versus isolation (p. 317)

59. generativity versus stagnation (p. 317)

60. cohorts (p. 319)

61. activity theory (p. 320)

62. integrity vs. despair (p. 321)

63. ageism (p. 320)

Guided Review

The following in-depth chapter review is a challenging and comprehensive fill-in-the-blanks exercise. The answers are found near the end of the chapter. As you go through the exercise, try to resist the temptation to look at the answers until you have provided them. When you have filled in all the blanks, you will have a thorough summary of the chapter for reference and review.

Themes and Issues in Development

Psychologists use the term development to mean a pattern of movement or change that begins at ___(1)___ and continues throughout the ___(2)___ ________. Development is the product of several processes: ___(3)___, cognitive, and ___(4)___.

The orderly sequence of changes dictated by the genetic code is called ___(5)___. Development is shaped by the interplay of maturation and ___(6)___.

The ___(7)___ of development view suggests that development involves gradual changes, whereas the ___(8)___ of development view suggests that development involves distinct stages. In this view, we pass through stages that are ___(9)___ different.

The national government's efforts at influencing the welfare of its citizens is called ___(10)___ ________. A special concern involves the high numbers of children who live in ___(11)___.

Prenatal Development and Birth

The union of a single sperm cell and an ovum is called ___(12)___, or fertilization. The fertilized egg, called a ___(13)___, receives ___(14)___-________ of its chromosomes from each parent. The first 2 weeks after conception is referred to as the ___(15)___ period; the period from 2 to 8 weeks is the ___(16)___ period. This embryonic period is marked by increasing cell ___(17)___ and the appearance of ___(18)___.

The ___(19)___ period begins 2 months after conception and lasts for about 7 months.

Scientists label any agent that causes birth defects a ___(20)___. Mothers who are heavy drinkers, for example, risk giving birth to children with ___(21)___ ________ ________. Children with this syndrome may have facial ___(22)___ or below average ___(23)___.

Dimensions of Child Development

One important reflex of newborns, in which the infant arches its back and throws back its head, is the ___(24)___ ________.

During the elementary school years, ___(26)___ development becomes smoother and more coordinated.

With regard to cognitive development, Jean Piaget stressed that children ___(27)___ construct their own cognitive world. Piaget believed that two processes underlie a child's mental construction of the world: ___(28)___ and ___(29)___. Piaget believed that we adapt in two ways: when we incorporate new information into our existing knowledge, it is called ___(30)___. When we have to adjust to new information, it is called ___(31)___. Piaget believed we pass through four stages in understanding the world. The first stage of development, which lasts from birth to about age 2, is called the stage of ___(32)___ ________. In this stage, infants realize that objects continue to exist even when they are not in sight; Piaget called this ___(33)___ ________.

According to Piaget, preschool children have trouble understanding the concept of reversibility; they cannot perform ___(34)___. Children between the ages of 2 and 7 are in a stage Piaget referred to as ___(35)___ thought. Children in this stage have not yet grasped the concept of ___(36)___, which is the recognition that a quantity stays the same even though its shape has changed. Children in this stage are also unable to distinguish between their perspective and someone else's perspective, a quality Piaget called ___(37)___. Piaget also called preoperational thought ___(38)___.

Between the ages of 7 and 11, children are in a stage Piaget called ___(39)___ ________ thought. In this stage, mental ___(40)___ are possible and intuitive thought is replaced by ___(41)___ reasoning. Important skills that characterize concrete operational thought are the ability to ___(42)___ and the ability to classify or divide things and to consider their ___(43)___.

Piaget's fourth stage of cognitive development is called ___(44)___ _______ thought. This type of thinking is abstract, idealistic and ___(45)___ . Adolescents are able to engage in ___(46)___-_______ reasoning.

Piaget is credited with helping to establish the field of ___(47)___ psychology. Critics of Piaget have raised questions in the following areas: estimates of childrens' ___(48)___ at different levels, stages, training children to reason at higher levels, and issues regarding ___(49)___ and education. A group of developmental psychologists who have elaborated on Piaget's theory are referred to as ___(50)___-_______. A theory that emphasizes the roles played by culture and social interaction was proposed by ___(51)___. An important concept in his theory refers to tasks that can be mastered only with help from adults or more-skilled children; this is referred to as the zone of ___(52)___ _______.

Erik Erikson proposed an influential theory of ___(53)___ development. Each of the eight stages in his theory confronts individuals with a ___(54)___ that must be resolved. The first year of life represents the stage of ___(55)___ versus ___(56)___. Erikson believes that the focus of the second year of life is on ___(57)___ versus ___(58)___. During the preschool years, children face the conflict of ___(59)___ versus guilt. Developing a sense of ___(60)___ increases initiative. During the elementary school years, children are challenged by industry versus ___(61)___.

In developmental psychology, ___(62)___ is a close emotional bond between an infant and its caregiver. Harlow and Zimmerman's research with infant monkeys illustrated the importance of ___(63)___ _______. Lorenz's research with goslings demonstrated the process of ___(64)___. Bowlby and Ainsworth have suggested that, in humans, attachment to the ___(65)___ during the first year provides an important foundation. ___(66)___ attached infants use caregivers as a secure base from which to explore the environment. Critics of attachment theory argue that infants are ___(67)___, that genetic and temperament characteristics are important factors, and that there is a diversity of social agents and social contexts in an infant's world.

Baumrind has proposed a classification scheme for parenting styles. She refers to a restrictive, punitive style as ___(68)___ parenting. Children are encouraged to be independent but still have limits and controls on their actions in ___(69)___ parenting. A parenting style characterized by lack of parental involvement is ___(70)___-_______ parenting. A style of parenting in which parents are highly involved with their children but place few demands on them is called ___(71)___-_______ parenting.

Researchers have found wide variation in some child-rearing practices between ___(72)___ _______. Working-class and low-income parents tend to emphasize ___(73)___ characteristics, whereas middle-class parents emphasize ___(74)___ characteristics. Ethnic minority families differ from White American families in size, structure, reliance on ___(75)___ networks, and levels of income and education.

Adolescence

G. Stanley Hall viewed adolescence as a turbulent time charged with conflict; his perspective is known as the ___(76)___-________-________ view. Although adolescents are commonly portrayed as being rebellious and self-centered, a study by Daniel Offer revealed that most adolescents are ___(77)___ human beings who are not experiencing deep emotional turmoil. Studies of adolescents around the world have found a ___(78)___ self-image in three of every four adolescents studied.

Adolescents have not experienced an improvement in health over the past 30 years. Their health problems, including suicide, homicide, and ___(79)___ ________, have been labeled "the new ___(80)___."

The rapid maturation that occurs mainly in early adolescence is called ___(81)___. During adolescence there is a dramatic increase in the hormone ___(82)___ in boys and in the hormone ___(83)___ in girls.

Recent research indicates that early maturation places girls at risk for a number of ___(84)___ problems.

According to Piaget, adolescent cognitive development involves ___(85)___ operational thought. The main characteristics are abstract, ___(86)___, and logical thinking. Adolescents are also able to engage in hypothetical-___(87)___ reasoning. Adolescent thought is also ___(88)___. The belief that others are as ___(89)___ with the adolescent as he or she is with him or herself, the belief that one is ___(90)___, and the belief that one is ___(91)___ are all components of adolescent egocentrism. Lawrence Kohlberg has identified three levels of ___(92)___ development. The first, which shows no internalization of moral values, is the ___(93)___ level. At the second level, called the ___(94)___ level, internalization is intermediate. At the highest level, called the ___(95)___ level, morality is completely internalized. Kohlberg's approach has been criticized because it doesn't adequately reflect ___(96)___ with others. Carol Gilligan's view is the ___(97)___ perspective, in contrast with Kohlberg's justice perspective. According to Gilligan, the dilemmas faced by girls at adolescence often cause them to "___(98)___" their own distinctive voices. Kohlberg's theory has also been criticized for being ___(99)___ biased.

Two prominent myths about parent-adolescent relationships are that adolescents ___(100)___ themselves from parents and that parent-adolescent relationships are intense and filled with ___(101)___. Adolescence is a time when individuals push for ___(102)___. Although conflict with parents increases during adolescence, much of it involves the everyday events of family life. These conflicts can serve a positive function of helping the adolescent make the ___(103)___ to increased autonomy.

During adolescence, especially early adolescence, there is more conformity to ___(104)___ standards than in childhood.

According to Erikson, the adolescent stage of development is characterized by identity versus ___(105)___ ________. During this stage, according to Erikson, adolescents enter a "psychological ___(106)___." This stage is also characterized by experimenting with different ___(107)___. Identity may be defined along the following dimensions: career, ___(108)___, religious, ___(109)___, achievement, sexual, ___(110)___, ethnic/cultural, intertests, personality, or ___(111)___. According to James Marcia, exploration and ___(112)___ are important in determining identity. Marcia believes there are four identity stages: confusion, ___(113)___, moratorium, and achievement.

Most ethnic minority individuals consciously confront their ethnicity for the first time in ___(114)___. In some cultures, ___(115)___ ________ ________ mark a clear distinction between childhood and adulthood.

Researchers have found that problem behaviors in adolescence are often ___(116)___. As many as ___(117)___ percent of U.S. adolescents have serious multiple-problem behaviors. Two components of programs that have been successful in addressing adolescent problems are intensive ___(118)___ attention and ___(119)___ multiagency collaboration.

Adulthood Development and Aging

Adult development is divided into three periods: early, ___(120)___, and late adulthood. According to Neugarten, we are becoming an ___(121)___-________ society.

Most people reach their peak physical performance in ___(122)___ adulthood. This is also the time when most people are the ___(123)___. As individuals enter middle adulthood, the three greatest health concerns are ___(124)___ ________, cancer, and ___(125)___.

For women, middle age is the time when ___(126)___ will occur. For the majority of women, menopause does not produce psychological or ___(127)___ problems. A widely used approach for women who are experiencing menopause is ___(128)___ replacement therapy.

Virtually all biological theories of aging assign an important role to ___(129)___. Biologists place the upper limit of the human life cycle at about ___(130)___ years. A degenerative brain disorder that impairs memory and social behavior is called ___(131)___ disease.

Although Piaget believed that adults and adolescents are cognitively the same, not all adolescents and adults reach ___(132)___ operational thought. Other psychologists believe that adolescent ___(133)___ and youthful ___(134)___ diminish in early adulthood. Memory decline in middle age is more likely when ___(135)___-________ memory is involved, when strategies such as ___(136)___ and ___(137)___ are not used, when the information has been recently acquired, when ___(138)___ rather than recognition is needed, and when the individual is in poor health. Although older adults do not think as quickly as young adults, when we consider general knowledge and ___(139)___, older adults often outperform younger adults. Although cognitive ___(140)___ are likely to decline with aging, improvement in cognitive ___(141)___ is possible into old age.

Contrary to popular opinion, only about ___(142)___ percent of Americans change careers in midlife.

Since the 1930s, the desire for a stable marriage has received competition from the desire for individual ___(143)___. The decline of marriage in the United States may be partly explained by couples who choose to not make their relationships ___(144)___, and because marriage may create financial liabilities compared with remaining single. Idealistic ___(145)___ may contribute to dissatisfaction in a marriage. Gay and ___(146)___ couples may face even more complicated choices.

According to Erikson, the stage of development that characterizes early adulthood is ___(147)___ versus isolation. In middle adulthood, the stage is called generativity versus ___(148)___.

Levinson's view of adulthood, based on interviews with middle-aged men, also emphasizes a ___(149)___ approach. Critics of Erikson's and Levinson's theories have pointed out that they are not based on ___(150)___ sound research, and they tend to describe the stages as ___(151)___.

Life events rather than ___(152)___ may account for changes in our adult lives. Some developmentalists believe that changes in our society influence how different ___(153)___ move through the life cycle.

Personality in adulthood is characterized by both ___(154)___ and ___(155)___.

According to ___(156)___ theory, older people who are more active and involved are more satisfied with life. Many elderly face prejudice, referred to as ___(157)___.

According to Baltes and his colleagues, successful aging is related to selection, ___(158)___, and compensation. According to Erikson, the crisis associated with late adulthood is integrity versus ___(159)___.

Death and Dying

According to Elisabeth Kübler-Ross, we go through the following five stages in facing death: ___(160)___ and isolation, anger, ___(161)___, depression, and ___(162)___.

___(163)___ ________ is an important factor in adjusting to the death of a spouse.

Sociocultural Worlds/Applications in Psychology

In your own words, summarize the material you have read in Sociocultural Worlds, "Caring for Children Around the World," and in Applications in Psychology, "Improving the Lives of Adolescents." Briefly describe how each of these articles relates to the information contained in the chapter.

Concept Check

Theorist	Developmental area	Concepts
1. ____________	Cognitive	Sensorimotor, preoperational, concrete operational, and formal operational
2. Vygotsky	Cognitive	____________
3. Erikson	Psychosocial	____________
4. Baumrind	Parenting styles	____________
5. ____________	Moral development	preconventional, conventional, postconventional
6. Gilligan	Moral development	____________
7. Levinson	Adult personality development	____________
8. Kübler-Ross	Death and dying	____________

Answers

1. Piaget
2. Zone of proximal development
3. Eight stages or crises, the outcomes of which will determine personality development
4. Authoritarian, authoritative, indulgent, and permissive
5. Kohlberg
6. justice perspective vs. care perspective
7. "seasons of a man's life"
8. denial, anger, bargaining, depression, and acceptance

Multiple-Choice Questions

Practice Test 1

After answering all the multiple-choice questions in Practice Test 1, compare your answers with the answer key provided at the end of the chapter. The answer key contains a brief explanation of both the correct and incorrect answers. Each of these questions is keyed to the Learning Objectives for the chapter. If you answer any questions incorrectly, review the corresponding Learning Objective and text material before you proceed to Practice Test 2.

1. Each of the following is part of the definition of development *except*
   a. a pattern of movement or change
   b. continues throughout the lifespan
   c. begins at conception
   d. ends in late adolescence

LO 1

2. A child's ability to solve math problems is provided by
   a. maturation.
   b. experience.
   c. biological inheritance
   d. all of the above

LO 2

3. To his parents, it seems that Johnny is able to think abstractly "all of a sudden." Which developmental approach are they demonstrating?
   a. continuity of development
   b. discontinuity of development
   c. the authoritative approach
   d. the interaction approach

LO 3

4. What stage of prenatal development marks the appearance of the neural tube and internal organs?
   a. the germinal period
   b. the embryonic period
   c. the fetal period
   d. the zygotic period

LO 4

5. An infant born with facial deformities and/or defective limbs has most likely been affected by which teratogen?
   a. AIDS
   b. crack cocaine
   c. alcohol
   d. marijuana

LO 5

6. Each of the following statements regarding physical development is true *except*
   a. The Moro reflex disappears at 3 or 4 months of age.
   b. After the second year, the rate of growth accelerates for most children.
   c. At birth, the brain and nervous system contain approximately 100 billion nerve cells.
   d. Dendritic connections dramatically increase between birth and 2 years of age.

LO 6

7. Little Amy screams with delight as she sees a horse. She yells to her dad, "See doggie." Dad gently corrects her, "No that's a horse." Later, Amy is able to identify a picture of a horse. According to Piaget, what process has occurred?
   a. assimilation
   b. accommodation
   c. object permanence
   d. operations

LO 7

8. According to Piaget, the realization that a ball continues to exist even when it rolls under a couch is an example of
   a. reversibility.
   b. object permanence.
   c. conservation.
   d. preoperational thought.

LO 8

9. According to Piaget, hypothetical-deductive reasoning is a characteristic of
   a. sensorimotor thought.
   b. preoperational thought.
   c. concrete operational thought.
   d. formal operational thought.

LO 9

10. Piaget's theory has been subject to criticism in each of the following areas *except*
    a. estimates of child's competence at different levels
    b. stages of development
    c. training children to reason at higher levels
    d. the notion of children as active thinkers

LO 10

11. Vygotsky's theory emphasizes
    a. the zone of proximal development.
    b. the importance of working alone in the development of skills.
    c. the importance of social influences on development.
    d. both *a* and *c*

LO 11

12. According to Erikson, the first psychosocial stage of development is called
    a. autonomy vs. shame and doubt.
    b. industry vs. inferiority.
    c. initiative vs. guilt.
    d. trust vs. mistrust.

LO 12

13. A child's mother picks him up at a day-care center. The child, who is very fearful of strangers, does not seem excited to see Mom. When Mom picks up the child, he squirms to get down. The child is demonstrating
    a. object permanence.
    b. insecure attachment.
    c. secure attachment.
    d. imprinting.

LO 13

14. A parenting style that encourages children to be independent but still places limits on their behavior is called
    a. authoritative.
    b. authoritarian.
    c. neglectful.
    d. indulgent.

LO 14

15. According to the text, working-class and low-income parents often place a high value on
    a. internal characteristics.
    b. external characteristics.
    c. the use of reasoning
    d. the use of praise.

LO 15

16. G. Stanley Hall described adolescence as a time of "storm and stress." Modern developmental psychologists
    a. agree that he was correct.
    b. find there is no more conflict with parents at this time than at any other stage in life.
    c. believe that adolescents are competent human beings and, for the most part, maintain a positive self-image.
    d. have shown that the turmoil is caused by hormonal disturbances.

LO 16

17. During puberty there is a dramatic increase in
    a. testosterone.
    b. adrenaline.
    c. estradiol.
    d. both *a* and *c*

LO 17

18. Individuals are able to engage in hypothetical-deductive reasoning after they achieve _________ thought.
    a. sensorimotor
    b. preoperational
    c. concrete operational
    d. formal operational

LO 18

19. According to Kohlberg, at what level is moral development completely internalized and not based on others' standards?
    a. preconventional
    b. conventional
    c. postconventional
    d. justice

LO 19

20. Conformity to peers is likely to peak around which grade?
    a. fourth
    b. sixth
    c. eighth
    d. twelfth

LO 20

21. The term *psychological moratorium* was used to describe adolescence by
    a. Freud.
    b. Piaget.
    c. Erikson.
    d. Kohlberg.

LO 21

22. Programs that have been successful in preventing or reducing adolescent problems provide
    a. intensive individualized attention.
    b. a high degree of parental involvement.
    c. communitywide multiagency approaches.
    d. both *a* and *c*

LO 22

23. People tend to become more concerned about their health status in
    a. early adulthood.
    b. adolescence.
    c. middle adulthood.
    d. late adulthood.

LO 23

24. Memory decline in middle age is more likely under each of the following circumstances *except*
    a. when short-term memory is involved.
    b. when recall rather than recognition is needed.
    c. when strategies such as organization and imagery are not used.
    d. when certain information is not used often.

LO 24

25. According to Levinson, the change to middle adulthood requires resolving
    a. being young versus being old.
    b. being destructive versus being constructive.
    c. being attached to others versus being separated from them.
    d. all of the above

LO 25

26. An alternative to stage theories of adult development is the __________ approach.
    a. biological changes
    b. life events
    c. lifestyles
    d. continuity

LO 26

27. According to Erikson, the final developmental stage is called
    a. generativity vs. stagnation.
    b. intimacy vs. isolation.
    c. integrity vs. despair.
    d. ageism vs. activity theory.

LO 27

28. Kübler-Ross has claimed that the stages of the dying process are
    a. applicable only in cancer patients.
    b. an optimal path toward death but not followed in a rigid sequence by all.
    c. not sequential.
    d. derived from careful experimental designs using many subjects.

LO 28

Practice Test 2

The following multiple-choice questions also are keyed to the chapter Learning Objectives. If you answer any questions incorrectly, be sure to review the corresponding Learning Objective and text material.

1. Which of the following processes are involved in development?
   a. biological processes
   b. cognitive processes
   c. socioemotrional processes
   d. all of the above

LO 1

2. Each of the following would be considered an environmental factor *except*
   a. nutrition.
   b. medical care.
   c. genetics.
   d. culture.

LO 2

3. Although development frequently seems to take place all of a sudden, it actually involves gradual change according to the
   a. continuity of development approach.
   b. discontinuity of development approach.
   c. qualitative development approach.
   d. maturational approach.

LO 3

4. During which prenatal stage does attachment to the uterine wall occur?
   a. the germinal period
   b. the embryonic period
   c. the fetal period
   d. the zygotic period

LO 4

5. Facial deformities and below-average intelligence are frequently seen in children who suffer from
   a. AIDS.
   b. "crack" addiction.
   c. fetal alcohol syndrome.
   d. nicotine addiction.

LO 5

6. Which of the following is true with regard to the development of the brain?
   a. Neurons keep reproducing until a child is 5 years old.
   b. In the first 2 years of life there is a dramatic increase in dendritic growth.
   c. At birth, the brain and nervous system contain up to 5 billion neurons.
   d. The brain of most children keeps growing new axons until the child is 8 years old.

LO 6

7. According to Piaget, when individuals incorporate new information into their existing knowledge, this process is called
   a. assimilation.
   b. accommodation.
   c. conservation.
   d. object permanence.

LO 7

8. According to Piaget, object permanence occurs in which stage of development?
   a. sensorimotor thought
   b. preoperational thought
   c. concrete operational thought
   d. formal operational thought

LO 8

9. Children are able to grasp the principle of conservation in which stage of development?
   a. sensorimotor thought
   b. preoperational thought
   c. concrete operational thought
   d. formal operational thought

LO 9

10. Each of the following describes Piaget's approach *except*
    a. Children are active thinkers.
    b. Children help manufacture their own development.
    c. Children's thinking ability proceeds in predictable steps.
    d. Children rarely proceed to formal operations without training.

LO 10

11. In contrast with Piaget's theory, Vygotsky's approach emphasizes
   a. the child as a scientist.
   b. the child working alone.
   c. the importance of the cognitive stages of development.
   d. the importance of social interaction and culture.

LO 11

12. According to Erikson, children in their elementary school years are in the developmental stage called
   a. autonomy vs. shame and doubt.
   b. industry vs. inferiority.
   c. initiative vs. guilt.
   d. trust vs. mistrust.

LO 12

13. On what basis has attachment theory been criticized?
   a. Too much importance is attributed to the attachment bond in infancy.
   b. There is not enough research to support the theory.
   c. Infants may show attachments to many people.
   d. both *a* and *c*

LO 13

14. A parenting style in which parents are highly involved with their children but place few demands on them is called
   a. authoritative.
   b. authoritarian.
   c. neglectful.
   d. indulgent.

LO 14

15. Each of the following is true regarding cultural, social class, and ethnic variations *except*
   a. Single-parent families are more common among African Americans and Latinos than among White American.
   b. The role of the extended family is stronger among ethnic minority groups.
   c. Middle-class families prize "internal characteristics" more than working-class families do.
   d. There is more joint decision making among members of ethnic minority groups.

LO 15

16. The contemporary view of adolescence sees it as a time of
   a. rebellion and crisis.
   b. decision making and evaluation.
   c. overwhelming feelings of incompetence.
   d. generally negative self-image.

LO 16

17. Which of the following is true regarding puberty?
   a. It is a time of rapid skeletal and sexual maturation.
   b. It is generally advantageous to be an early-maturing boy.
   c. Hormonal changes occur earlier in males than in females.
   d. It is generally advantageous to be an early-maturing female.

LO 17

18. Each of the following characterizes adolescent cognitive development *except*
   a. formal operational thought
   b. hypothetical-deductive reasoning
   c. problems with assimilation
   d. adolescent egocentrism

LO 18

19. Kohlberg's theory of moral development has been criticized because
   a. it does not reflect the care perspective.
   b. it does not reflect the justice perspective.
   c. it is culturally biased.
   d. both *a* and *c*

LO 19

20. Parent-adolescent conflict
   a. usually occurs in later adolescence.
   b. usually involves major issues such as drugs and delinquency.
   c. can help facilitate autonomous behavior for the adolescent.
   d. often leaves lifelong emotional scars for both parents and adolescents.

LO 20

21. According to James Marcia, an adolescent who has made a commitment to an identity before adequately exploring his or her options is in which identity status?
   a. confusion
   b. foreclosure
   c. moratorium
   d. achievement

LO 21

22. According to the text, the number of adolescents with serious multi-problem behaviors is
   a. less than 1 percent.
   b. approximately 10 percent.
   c. greater than 40 percent.
   d. unknown.

LO 22

23. Research indicates that, for the majority of women, menopause causes
   a. a variety of physical problems.
   b. psychological problems.
   c. neither physical nor psychological problems.
   d. both *a* and *b*

LO 23

24. Older adults
   a. can process information as quickly as younger adults.
   b. can maintain and improve their cognitive mechanics.
   c. score higher on IQ tests.
   d. can maintain and improve their cognitive pragmatics.

LO 24

25. According to Erikson, the two stages of early and middle adulthood consist of intimacy versus isolation and
   a. integrity versus despair.
   b. identity versus identity confusion.
   c. generativity versus despair.
   d. generativity versus stagnation.

LO 25

26. William James, who believed that our personality was set by the time we are 30 years old, favored which view of personality?
   a. continuity
   b. discontinuity
   c. stage
   d. cohort effect

LO 26

27. According to Paul Bates, successful aging is related to each of the following *except*
   a. selection
   b. retention
   c. optimization
   d. compensation

LO 27

28. According to Kübler-Ross, the first stage in facing death is
   a. denial.
   b. depression.
   c. acceptance.
   d. anger.

LO 28

Answers to Key Terms

1. **Development** is a pattern of movement or change that begins at conception and continues throughout the life cycle.
2. **Biological processes** involve changes in an individual's physical nature.
3. **Cognitive processes** involve changes in an individual's thought, intelligence, and language skills.
4. **Socioemotional processes** involve changes in an individual's relationships with others, changes in emotion, and changes in personality.
5. **Maturation** is the orderly sequence of changes dictated by the genetic code.
6. The **nature/nurutre controversy** is the debate whether development is primarily influenced by maturation or experience.
7. **Continuity of development** is gradual, cumulative change from conception to death.
8. **Discontinuity of development** is development involving qualitatively distinct stages in the life span.
9. **Social policy** is a government's course of action designed to influence the welfare of its citizens.

10. **Conception** occurs when a single sperm cell from the male penetrates the female's ovum.
11. **Zygote** refers to a fertilized egg.
12. The **germinal period** is the first 2 weeks after conception.
13. The **embryonic period** is the third through eighth weeks after conception.
14. The **fetal period** begins 2 months after conception and lasts, on the average, for 7 months.
15. A **teratogen** is any agent that causes a birth defect.
16. **Fetal alcohol syndrome (FAS)** is a cluster of abnormalities that appear in the offspring of mothers who drink alcohol heavily during pregnancy.
17. **Assimilation** occurs when individuals incorporate new information into their existing knowledge.
18. **Accommodation** occurs when individuals adjust to new information.
19. **Sensorimotor thought** is Piaget's name for the stage of development corresponding to infancy.
20. **Object permanence** is the realization that objects and events continue to exist even when they can't be seen, heard, or touched. It is considered to be a major accomplishment of the sensorimotor stage.
21. **Operations,** according to Piaget, are mental representations that are reversible.
22. **Preoperational thought** is the term Piaget gave to the 2- to 7-year-old child's understanding of the world. Children in this stage are not able to reverse mental representations.
23. **Conservation** is Piaget's term for the belief in the permanence of certain attributes of objects or situations in spite of superficial changes.
24. **Egocentrism** is the inability to distinguish between one's own perspective and someone else's perspective.
25. **Concrete operational thought** is the term Piaget gave to the 7- to 11-year-old child's understanding of the world. Children at this stage can use mental operations and logical reasoning.
26. **Formal operational thought,** according to Piaget, is the abstract, idealistic, and logical thought that appears between 11 and 15 years of age; it is Piaget's fourth stage of cognitive development.
27. **Hypothetical-deductive reasoning** is Piaget's name for the adolescent's cognitive ability to develop hypotheses, or best guesses, about how to solve problems.
28. **Neo-Piagetians** are developmentalists who have elaborated on Piaget's theory, believing that children's cognitive development is more specific in many ways than he thought.
29. The **zone of proximal development,** according to Vygotsky, refers to tasks too difficult for a child to master alone but that can be mastered with help from adults or more-skilled children.
30. **Trust versus mistrust,** which occurs during the baby's first year, is Erikson's first psychosocial stage.
31. **Autonomy versus shame and doubt,** is Erikson's second stage of development, occurring in late infancy and toddlerhood (1–3 years).
32. **Initiative versus guilt** is Erikson's third stage of development and occurs around the preschool years. In this stage, children begin to assume more responsibility for their behavior.
33. **Industry versus inferiority** is Erikson's fourth developmental stage, occurring approximately in the elementary school years.
34. **Attachment** is a close emotional bond between the infant and its caregiver.
35. **Imprinting** is the tendency for an animal to form an attachment to the first moving object it sees or hears.
36. **Secure attachment** is Ainsworth's term for attachment in which infants use the caregiver as a secure base from which to explore the environment.
37. **Authoritarian parenting** is Baumrind's term for a restrictive, punitive parenting style that exhorts the child to follow the parent's directions and to respect work and effort.
38. **Authoritative parenting** is Baumrind's term for a parenting style that encourages children to be independent but still places limits and controls on their behavior.
39. **Neglectful parenting** is a style of parenting in which parents are very uninvolved with their child's life.
40. **Indulgent parenting** is a parenting style in which parents are highly involved with their children but place few demands or controls on them.
41. The **storm-and-stress view,** suggested by G. Stanley Hall, is the concept that adolescence is a turbulent time, charged with conflict and mood swings.
42. **Puberty** is a period of rapid skeletal and sexual maturation that occurs mainly in early adolescence.
43. **Testosterone** is a hormone associated, in boys, with the development of genitals, an increase in height, and a change of voice.

44. **Estradiol** is a hormone associated, in girls, with breast, uterine, and skeletal development.
45. **Adolescent egocentrism** refers to the adolescent's belief that others are as preoccupied with the adolescent as she herself is, the belief that one is unique, and the belief that one is indestructible.
46. **Internalization** is the developmental change from behavior that is externally controlled to behavior controlled by internal, self-generated standards and principles.
47. The **preconventional level** is Kohlberg's lowest level of moral thinking, in which the individual shows no internalization of moral values; moral thinking is based on expectations of punishments or rewards from the external world.
48. The **conventional level** is Kohlberg's second level of moral thinking, in which the individual has an intermediate level of internalization; the individual abides by the standards of others.
49. In the **postconventional level,** moral development is completely internalized; this is Kohlberg's highest level of moral thinking.
50. The **justice perspective** is a theory of moral development that focuses on the rights of the individual; in this view, individuals make moral decisions independently. Kohlberg's theory is a justice perspective.
51. The **care perspective,** an approach taken by Carol Gilligan, sees people in terms of their connectedness with other people; it focuses on interpersonal communication, relationships with others, and concern for others.
52. **Identity versus identity confusion,** according to Erikson, is the stage of development in which adolescents attempt to find out who they are and where they are headed in life; it is Erikson's fifth stage of human development.
53. **Rites of passage** are ceremonies or rituals that mark an individual's transition from one staus to another.
54. **Menopause** is a time in middle age when a women's menstrual periods cease completely.
55. **Alzheimer's disease** is a degenerative, irreversible brain disorder that impairs memory and social behavior.
56. **Cognitive mechanics** are the "hardware" of the mind; these are related to speed and accuracy mental processes. Their decline with aging is likely.
57. **Cognitive pragmatics** refer to the culture-based "software" of the mind. Improvement of cognitive pragmatics into old age is possible.
58. **Intimacy versus isolation,** Erikson's sixth stage of development, occurs mainly in early adulthood. Intimacy is the ability to develop close, loving relationships.
59. **Generativity versus stagnation,** Erikson's seventh stage of development, is associated with middle adulthood. Middle-aged adults need to assist the younger generation in leading useful lives.
60. **Cohorts** are groups of people born in the same year or time period.
61. According to **activity theory,** the more active and involved older people are, the more satisfied they are with their lives and the more likely it is that they will stay healthy.
62. **Integrity versus despair,** Erikson's eighth and final stage of human development, occurs mainly in late adulthood. It is a time of looking back at what we have done with our lives.
63. **Ageism** is prejudice against people based on their age.

Answers to Guided Review

1. conception (p. 275)
2. life cycle (p. 275)
3. Biological (p. 275)
4. socioemotional (p. 275)
5. maturation (p. 276)
6. experience (p. 276)
7. continuity (p. 276)
8. discontinuity (p. 276)
9. qualitatively (p. 276)
10. social policy (p. 276)
11. poverty (p. 277)
12. conception (p. 278)
13. zygote (p. 278)
14. one-half (p. 279)
15. germinal (p. 279)
16. embryonic (p. 279)
17. differentiation (p. 279)
18. organs (p. 279)
19. fetal (p. 279)
20. teratogen (p. 280)
21. fetal alcohol syndrome (p. 280)
22. deformities (p. 281)
23. intelligence (p. 281)
24. Moro reflex (p. 282)
25. dendritic (p. 283)
26. motor (p. 283)
27. actively (p. 284)
28. organization (p. 284)
29. adaptation (p. 284)
30. assimilation (p. 285)
31. accommodation (p. 285)
32. sensorimotor thought (p. 285)
33. object permanence (p. 285)
34. operations (p. 286)
35. preoperational (p. 286)
36. conservation (p. 287)
37. egocentrism (p. 287)
38. intuitive (p. 287)
39. concrete operational (p. 287)
40. operations (p. 287)
41. logical (p. 287)
42. conserve (p. 288)
43. interrelations (p. 288)
44. formal operational (p. 288)
45. logical (p. 288)
46. hypothetical-deductive (p. 289)
47. cognitive (p. 289)
48. competencies (p. 289)
49. culture (p. 289)
50. neo-Piagetians (p. 289)
51. Vygotsky (p. 290)
52. proximal development (p. 290)
53. socioemotional (p. 291)
54. crisis (p. 291)
55. trust (p. 291)
56. mistrust (p. 291)
57. autonomy (p. 291)
58. doubt (p. 291)
59. initiative (p. 291)
60. responsibility (p. 291)
61. inferiority (p. 291)
62. attachment (p. 292)
63. contact comfort (p. 292)
64. imprinting (p. 294)
65. caregiver (p. 295)
66. Securely (p. 295)
67. resilient (p. 295)
68. authoritarian (p. 295)
69. authoritative (p. 296)
70. neglectful (p. 296)
71. indulgent (p. 296)
72. social classes (p. 297)
73. external (p. 297)
74. internal (p. 297)
75. kinship (p. 297)
76. storm-and-stress (p. 298)
77. competent (p. 299)
78. positive (p. 299)
79. substance abuse (p. 299)
80. morbidity (p. 299)
81. puberty (p. 299)
82. testosterone (p. 300)
83. estradiol (p. 300)
84. developmental (p. 300)
85. formal (p. 300)
86. idealistic (p. 300)
87. deductive (p. 300)
88. egocentric (p. 300)
89. preoccupied (p. 300)
90. unique (p. 300)
91. indestructible (p. 300)
92. moral (p. 301)
93. preconventinal (p. 302)
94. conventional (p. 302)
95. postconventional (p. 302)
96. relationships (p. 302)
97. care (p. 302)
98. silence (p. 303)
99. culturally (p. 303)
100. detach (p. 304)
101. conflict (p. 304)
102. autonomy (p. 304)
103. transition (p. 304)
104. peer (p. 304)
105. identity confusion (p. 305)
106. moratorium (p. 305)
107. identities (p. 305)
108. political (p. 305)
109. relationship (p. 305)
110. gender (p. 305)
111. physical (p. 305)
112. commitment (p. 305)
113. foreclosure (p. 306)
114. adolescence (p. 307)
115. rites of passage (p. 308)
116. interrelated (p. 308)
117. 10 (p. 308)
118. individualized (p. 310)
119. communitywide (p. 310)
120. middle (p. 311)
121. age-irrelevant (p. 311)
122. early (p. 311)
123. healthiest (p. 311)
124. heart disease (p. 311)
125. weight (p. 311)
126. menopause (p. 312)
127. physical (p. 312)
128. estrogen (p. 312)
129. genes (p. 314)
130. 120 (p. 314)
131. Alzheimer's (p. 314)
132. consolidate (p. 315)
133. logic (p. 315)
134. optimism (p. 315)
135. long-term (p. 315)
136. organization (p. 315)
137. imagery (p. 315)
138. recall (p. 315)
139. wisdom (p. 315)
140. mechanics (p. 315)
141. pragmatics (p. 316)
142. 10 (p. 316)
143. fulfillment (p. 316)
144. formal (p. 316)
145. expectations (p. 316)
146. lesbian (p. 317)
147. intimacy (p. 317)

148. stagnation (p. 317)
149. stage (p. 317)
150. empirically (p. 319)
151. crises (p. 319)
152. stages (p. 319)
153. cohorts (p. 319)
154. continuity (p. 320)
155. discontinuity (p. 320)
156. activity (p. 320)
157. ageism (p. 320)
158. optimization (p. 320)
159. despair (p. 321)
160. denial (p. 322)
161. bargaining (p. 322)
162. acceptance (p. 322)
163. Social support (p. 323)

Answers to Multiple Choice Questions- Practice Test 1

1. a. Incorrect. This *is* part of the definition of development.
   b. Incorrect. This *is* part of the definition of development.
   c. Incorrect. This *is* part of the definition of development.
   d. **Correct.** Development is thought of as a life-long process.

2. a. Incorrect. Although this is partially true, it is not the best alternative.
   b. Incorrect. Although this is partially true, it is not the best alternative.
   c. Incorrect. Although this is partially true, it is not the best alternative.
   d. **Correct.** Factors involving nature and nurture work together to help us solve problems.

3. a. Incorrect. This approach views development as a continuous, gradual change.
   b. **Correct.** This approach suggests development involves distinct stages.
   c. Incorrect. This refers to a style of parent-child interaction.
   d. Incorrect. This approach could mean just about anything!

4. a. Incorrect. This refers to the first two weeks after conception.
   b. **Correct.** This period lasts from 2 to 8 weeks after conception.
   c. Incorrect. This period begins 2 months after conception and lasts about 7 months.
   d. Incorrect. The text doesn't mention a "zygotic" period.

5. a. Incorrect. This disease does not lead to the problems described in the question.
   b. Incorrect. This disease does not lead to the problems described in the question.
   c. **Correct.** This disorder is called fetal alcohol syndrome.
   d. Incorrect. This disease does not lead to the problems described in the question.

6. a. Incorrect. Although this statement is true, the question is asking for an *untrue* statement.
   b. **Correct.** The rate of growth actually decelerates after infancy.
   c. Incorrect. Although this statement is true, the question is asking for an *untrue* statement.
   d. Incorrect. Although this statement is true, the question is asking for an *untrue* statement.

7. a. Incorrect. Amy has had to make some changes to adjust to this new information.
   b. **Correct.** Amy has made an accommodation to information that did not fit her existing schema.
   c. Incorrect. This refers to the realization that things continue to exist even if they can't be directly seen, heard or touched.
   d. Incorrect. According to Piaget, these are mental representations that are reversible.

8. a. Incorrect. This is the realization that mental operations can be reversed.
   b. **Correct.** Object permanence is achieved at about 8 months of age.
   c. Incorrect. This refers to the realizations that certain attributes remain constant in spite of superficial changes.
   d. Incorrect. This refers to the cognitive developmental stage of the 2- to 7-year-old.

9. a. Incorrect. During this first stage of cognitive development, the child is incapable of this type of reasoning.
   b. Incorrect. During this second stage of cognitive development, the child is incapable of this type of reasoning.
   c. Incorrect. During this third stage of cognitive development, the child is incapable of this type of reasoning.
   d. **Correct.** The adolescent has the skill to solve problems by forming hypotheses and then systematically testing these hypotheses.

10. a. Incorrect. This *has* been a criticism of Piaget's theory; the question is asking for an exception.
    b. Incorrect. This *has* been a criticism of Piaget's theory; the question is asking for an exception.
    c. Incorrect. This *has* been a criticism of Piaget's theory; the question is asking for an exception.
    d. **Correct.** Few take exception to Piaget's view of children as active, constructive thinkers.

11. a. Incorrect. Although this answer is correct, it is not the best alternative.
    b. Incorrect. Vygotsky emphasizes social interaction and culture.
    c. Incorrect. Although this answer is correct, it is not the best alternative.
    d. **Correct.** Vygotsky's theory emphasizes social interaction and culture.

12. a. Incorrect. This is the second of Erikson's psychosocial stages of development.
    b. Incorrect. This is the fourth stage of Erikson's psychosocial stages of development.
    c. Incorrect. This is the third of Erikson's stages of psychosocial development.
    d. **Correct.** According to Erikson, trust is built for an infant when the infant's needs are met.

13. a. Incorrect. This refers to a cognitive achievement in Piaget's sensorimotor stage.
    b. **Correct.** Attachment theorists place great emphasis on forming attachments during the first year of life.
    c. Incorrect. A securely attached infant is generally not fearful of strangers.
    d. Incorrect. This refers to the attachment tendencies of certain infant animals.

14. a. **Correct.** Some students confuse this with "authoritarian" because the spellings are similar.
    b. Incorrect. This refers to a restrictive, punitive style.
    c. Incorrect. This refers to a lack of involvement in a child's life.
    d Incorrect. This refers to a style which places few demands or restrictions on a child.

15. a. Incorrect. Such characteristics as self-control and delay of gratification are more highly valued by middle-class families.
    b. **Correct.** These include obedience and neatness.
    c. Incorrect. Research suggests this is more likely to be used by middle-class parents.
    d. Incorrect. Research suggests this is more likely to be used by middle-class parents.

16. a. Incorrect. Most believe he exaggerated the difficulties of adolescence.
    b. Incorrect. Although conflicts might increase, these involve boundary testing and acting out.
    c. **Correct.** Research supports these notions, although problems, such as health issues, continue to trouble adolescents.
    d. Incorrect. Remember that most developmental psychologists have downplayed the "storm and stress" issues of adolescence.

17. a. Incorrect. Although this answer is true, it is not the best alternative.
    b. Incorrect. This is not one of the "adolescent hormones."
    c. Incorrect. Although this answer is true, it is not the best alternative.
    d. **Correct.** These hormone concentrations increase dramatically during adolescence.

18. a. Incorrect. This is the first of Piaget's cogntive stages. Infants are more concerned with such issues as object permanence,
    b. Incorrect. This is the second of Piaget's cognitive stages. The young child is concerned with issues such as conservation.
    c. Incorrect. This is the third stage of Piaget's cognitive stages. The child is able to reason as long as the principles are applied to concrete examples.
    d. **Correct.** This is one of the major achievements of formal operational thinking.

19. a. Incorrect. This level shows no internalization of moral values.
    b. Incorrect. This level shows a moderate level of internalization.
    c. **Correct.** This is the highest level of moral thinking, according to Kohlberg.
    d. Incorrect. Justice perspective refers to theories of moral development, such as Kohlberg's, that focus on the rights of the individual.

20. a. Incorrect. Although some conformity is found in this age group, conformity is not yet at its peak.
    b. Incorrect. Although some conformity is found in this age group, conformity is not yet at its peak.
    c. **Correct.** Conformity also includes conforming to the antisocial standrads of the teen years.
    d. Incorrect. Although conformity is found in this age group, researchers suggest it has peaked at an earlier age.

21. a. Incorrect. Freud had a host of other terms to describe adolescence.
    b. Incorrect. Piaget saw the adolescent beginning to emerge as an adult thinker.
    c. **Correct.** This was meant to describe a gap between the security of childhood and the autonomy of adulthood.
    d. Incorrect. Kohlberg theory focused on moral development, at the conventional or postconventional level.

22. a. Incorrect. Although this is partially true, it is not the best alternative.
    b. Incorrect. This is not mentioned as part of successful adolescent programs.
    c. Incorrect. Although this is partially true, it is not the best alternative.
    d. **Correct.** In addition to the individualized attention, the various agencies must engage in a collaborative effort.

23. a. Incorrect. Peak performance and optimal health typically characterize early adulthood.
    b. Incorrect. Adolescents are typically more concerned with socioemotional issues than with health issues.
    c. **Correct.** The decline in physical fitness and deterioration of health lead to the concerns.
    d. Incorrect. Although people are concerned about their health staus at this point, the concern first begins at an earlier stage of life.

24. a. **Correct.** Memeory decline is more likely when *short*-term memory is involved.
    b. Incorrect. This statment is true of memory decline in middle age; the question is looking for an *exception.*
    c. Incorrect. This statment is true of memory decline in middle age; the question is looking for an *exception.*
    d. Incorrect. This statment is true of memory decline in middle age; the question is looking for an *exception.*

25. a. Incorrect. Although this answer is true, it is not the best alternative.
    b. Incorrect. Although this answer is true, it is not the best alternative.
    c. Incorrect. Although this answer is true, it is not the best alternative.
    d. **Correct.** Levinson believes this change takes about 5 years.

26. a. Incorrect. Many stage theories on based, in part, on biological changes.
    b. **Correct.** Such events might include marriage, divorce, the birth of children, and so on.
    c. Incorrect. This is not an alternative to the stage theories.
    d. Incorrect. This approach suggests that stages unfold in a gradual process.

27. a. Incorrect. This stage is associated with the challenges of middle age.
    b. Incorrect. According to Erikson, this challenge is faced in early adulthood.
    c. **Correct.** Erikson sees this life review as an important part of the final stage of development.
    d. Incorrect. This is not one of Erikson's stages of development.

28. a. Incorrect. Kübler-Ross sees her stages as applicable to all people who are dying.
    b. **Correct.** Kübler-Ross feels she has been misquoted on this issue.
    c. Incorrect. Although people may not follow the specific sequence she has outlined, she does believe the stages to be sequential.
    d. Incorrect. Kübler-Ross has made no such claim for her theory.

Answers to Multiple Choice Questions- Practice Test 2

1. a. Incorrect. Although this answer is partially true, it is not the best alternative.
   b. Incorrect. Although this answer is partially true, it is not the best alternative.
   c. Incorrect. Although this answer is partially true, it is not the best alternative.
   d. **Correct.** These processes are continuously interacting with each other.

2. a. Incorrect. Nutrition is an environmental factor.
   b. Incorrect. Medical care is an environmental factor.
   c. **Correct.** This is the "nature" component of the "nature-nurture" controversy.
   d. Incorrect. Culture is an environmental factor.

3. a. **Correct.** Development may seem to involve dramatic changes, according to this approach, but it is actually an ongoing process.
   b. Incorrect. This approach suggests development occurs in distinct stages in the life span.
   c. Incorrect. This does not support the idea of gradual change in development.
   d. Incorrect. This does not support the idea of gradual change in development.

4. a. **Correct.** This occurs the second week after fertilization.
   b. Incorrect. This period, 2 to 8 weeks after conception,marks the appearance of the neural tube.
   c. Incorrect. This period, from 2 months on, is marked by the maturation of organs.
   d. Incorrect. A zygote is a fertilized egg.

5. a. Incorrect. These symptoms are not seen in AIDS babies.
   b. Incorrect. These symptoms are not seen in "crack" babies.
   c. **Correct.** Even moderate drinking among pregnant mothers can lead to difficulties.
   d. Incorrect. These symptoms are not seen in children of mothers who are addicted to nicotine.

6. a. Incorrect. At birth, the infant has virtually all the neurons it is going to have. During the first two years of life, there is a dramatic increase in the interconnectedness of these neurons.
   b. **Correct.** The 100 billion or so neurons are busily growing connections to each other.
   c. Incorrect. The number is closer to 100 billion.
   d. Incorrect. The axons are, for the most part, fixed in number at birth.

7. a. **Correct.** According to Piaget this is a life-long process.
   b. Incorrect. This process occurs when individuals make some changes in behavior to adjust to new information.
   c. Incorrect. This ability unfolds during the concrete operational stage.
   d. Incorrect. This understanding unfolds around the eighth month of life.

8. a. **Correct.** Object permanence typically occurs at around the eighth month.
   b. Incorrect. Object permanence has occurred prior to this stage.
   c. Incorrect. Object permanence has occurred prior to this stage.
   d. Incorrect. Object permanence has occurred prior to this stage.

9. a. Incorrect. Conservation is associated with a later stage of thought.
   b. Incorrect. According to Piaget, the preoperational child does not yet have the logic to perform conservation tasks.
   c. **Correct.** During this stage the child's thinking has matured; he or she can also understand reversibility.
   d. Incorrect. Children have developed conservation skills at an earlier developmental stage.

10. a. Incorrect. Piaget did conceive of children as active thinkers; the question is asking for an *exception*.
    b. Incorrect. Piaget did believe children helped to manufacture their own development; the question is asking for an *exception*.
    c. Incorrect. This statement is consistent with Piaget's theory; the question is asking for an *exception*.
    d. **Correct.** Formal operations, in which children are now able to use abstractions in their thinking, does not require specific training.

11. a. Incorrect. This statement more closely typifies Piaget's approach.
    b. Incorrect. This is the opposite of Vygotsky's emphasis.
    c. Incorrect. This statement more closely typifies Piaget's approach.
    d. **Correct.** Vygotsky's approach reminds us children do not develop in a social vacuum.

12. a. Incorrect. This stage occurs around the age of 2.
    b. **Correct.** Children in this stage are directing their energy toward learning and mastering skills.
    c. Incorrect. This stage occurs during a child's preschool years.
    d. Incorrect. According to Erikson, this stage occurs during the first year of life.

13. a. Incorrect. Although this statement is true, it is not the best alternative.
    b. Incorrect. Much research supports the importance of attachment.
    c. Incorrect. Although this statement is true, it is not the best alternative.
    d. **Correct.** Attachment theory continues to stir controversy among developmental psychologists.

14. a. Incorrect. This is a restrictive, punitive style of parenting.
    b. Incorrect. This refers to a style that encourages the child to be independent, but places limits and controls on their behavior.
    c. Incorrect. This style describes parents uninvolved with their children's lives.
    d. **Correct.** This style is associated with a child's incompetence, especially a lack of self-control.

15. a. Incorrect. This statement is accurate, but the question is looking for an untrue statement.
    b. Incorrect. This statement is accurate, but the question is looking for an untrue statement.
    c. Incorrect. This statement is accurate, but the question is looking for an untrue statement.
    d. **Correct.** There is *less* joint decision making among members of ethnic minority parents.

16. a. Incorrect. This was the sentiment associated with Hall's "storm and stress" view.
    b. **Correct.** In this view, the adolescent is basically competent and has a postive self-image.
    c. Incorrect. The contemporary view sees the adolscent as competent.
    d. Incorrect. Adolescents have a generally positive self-image.

17. a. **Correct.** This occurs mainly in early adolescence.
    b. Incorrect. According to the text, early-maturing boys have a less positive identity development when they reach adulthood.
    c. Incorrect. On the average, hormonal changes occur earlier in girls than in boys.
    d. Incorrect. Early-maturing females are at greater risk for drug-use, delinquency, pregnancy, and so on.

18. a. Incorrect. Formal operational thought *does* characterize adolescent cognitive development.
    b. Incorrect. Hypothetical-deductive reasoning, according to Piaget, *does* characterize adolescent cognitive development.
    c. **Correct.** This is not a problem associated with adolescent cognitive development.
    d. Incorrect. According to Elkind, this *does* characterize adolescent thinking.

19. a. Incorrect. Although this statement is correct, it is not the best alternative.
    b. Incorrect. Kohlberg's theory emphasizes the justice perspective.
    c. Incorrect. Although this statement is accurate, it is not the best alternative.
    d. **Correct.** Gilligan's theory was designed to address some of Kohlberg's theoretical shortcomings.

20. a. Incorrect. Conflict with parents is more common in early adolescence.
    b. Incorrect. Most conflict involves the everyday events of family life.
    c. **Correct.** This view sees parents as important "anchors" as adolescents explore the complex world.
    d. Incorrect. The new view holds that conflicts and negotiations help prepare the adolescent for the world.

21. a. Incorrect. This is characteristic of young adolescents, who have not yet made a commitment.
    b. Correct. This may happen when adolescents are pressured to follow in a parent's "footsteps."
    c. Incorrect. This occurs while an adolescent is exploring alternatives.
    d. Incorrect. This is the outcome after adequately exploring alternative paths and making a commitment.

22. a. Incorrect. Unfortunately, the percentage is higher than this.
    b. **Correct.** This includes drug problems, school problems, sexual activity without contraception, and so on.
    c. Incorrect. Fortunately, the percentage is lower than this.
    d. Incorrect. One of the other alternatives is correct.

23. a. Incorrect. Menopause is not the negative experience for most women it was once thought to be.
    b. Incorrect. Menopause is not the negative experience for most women it was once thought to be.
    c. **Correct.** Menopause is not the negative experience for most women it was once thought to be.
    d. Incorrect. Menopause is not the negative experience for most women it was once thought to be.

24. a. Incorrect. The speed involved in processing information slows as we age.
    b. Incorrect. The "hardware" of mental processes shows decline with age.
    c. Incorrect. Part of the reason for scores dropping is related to the speed of processing information.
    d. **Correct.** The "software" of the mind can be maintained and even show improvement into old age.

25. a. Incorrect. According to Erikson, this is the final challenge of life.
    b. Incorrect. This stage is associated with adolescence.
    c. Incorrect. This is not one of Erikson's stages of development.
    d. **Correct.** This reflects the desire to have a positive influence on the next generation.

26. a. **Correct.** James's view is supported by contemporary researcher Paul Costa.
    b. Incorrect. Some psychologists believe the changes that mark child development continue into adulthood.
    c. Incorrect. James did not favor a "stage" view of personality.
    d. Incorrect. James did not describe the "cohort effect."

27. a. Incorrect. According to Bates, his is one of the key elements to succesful aging.
    b. **Correct.** According to Bates, this is not one of the keys to succesul aging.
    c. Incorrect. According to Bates, his is one of the key elements to succesful aging.
    d. Incorrect. According to Bates, his is one of the key elements to succesful aging.

28. a. **Correct.** Denial and isolation comprise the first stage in facing death.
    b. Incorrect. According to Kübler-Ross, this is the third stage in facing death.
    c. Incorrect. According to Kübler-Ross, this is the final sdtage in facing death,
    d. Incorrect. According to Kübler-Ross, this is the second stage in facing death.

Chapter **9** **Motivation and Emotion**

Learning Objectives

After studying this chapter, you should be able to:

1. Define motivation and describe the ways in which motives differ. (p. 339)

2. Describe the neurobiological perspective on motivation, including instinct theory, ethology, and drive reduction theory. (p. 331)

3. Contrast the psychoanalytic, behavioral, cognitive, humanistic and sociocultural perspectives on motivation. (p. 332)

4. Describe the role of physiological and peripheral factors in hunger, and discuss the importance of external cues, self-control and exercise in regulating hunger. (p. 335)

5. Describe hormonal and cultural factors that are involved in sexual arousal. (p. 338)

6. List and describe the four phases of the human sexual response cycle. (p. 339)

7. Describe the changes that have occurred over the last several decades in sexual attitudes and behavior. (p. 340)

8. Compare and contrast the traditional religious script, the romantic sexual script, and the double standard. (p. 342)

9. Discuss the results of research into the factors that determine an individual's sexual orientation. (p. 343)

10. Discuss sexual dysfunctions and their treatments. (p. 344)

11. List and describe the paraphilias. (p. 345)

12. Describe the results of research regarding rape and sexual harassment. (p. 345)

13. Distinguish between competence motivation and achievement motivation and explain the following, regarding achievement: attribution theory, intrinsic and extrinsic motivation, and goal-setting and planning. (p. 347)

14. Discuss cultural, ethnic, and socioeconomic variations in achievement. (p. 348)

15. Define emotion and explain the four dimensions of Plutchik's classification of emotions. (p. 353)

16. Distinguish between positive and negative affectivity, and discuss the research on the emotions of happiness and anger. (p. 353)

17. Distinguish between the James-Lange and the Cannon-Bard theories of emotion. (p. 358)

18. Discuss the role of cognition in emotions. (p. 358)

19. Explain the relationship between emotions and physiology and discuss the issues surrounding the use of polygraph tests. (p. 360)

20. Describe sociocultural influences on emotion. (p. 362)

21. Define and describe emotional intelligence. (p. 364)

Chapter 9 Outline

I. Perspectives on Motivation
   A. The Neurobiological Perspective
      1. Instinct Theory
      2. Ethology
      3. Drive-Reduction Theory
   B. The Psychoanalytic Perspective
   C. The Behavioral Perspective
   D. The Cognitive Perspective
   E. The Humanistic Perspective
   F. The Sociocultural Perspective
II. Selected Motives
   A. Hunger
      1. Physiological Factors
      2. Peripheral Factors
      3. Brain Processes
         a. ventromedial hypothalamus
         b. set point
      4. External cues
      5. Self-control and exercise
   B. Sexuality
      1. The Human Sexual Response Cycle
         a. excitement
         b. plateau
         c. orgasm
         d. resolution
      2. Sexual attitudes and behavior
      3. Homosexual Attitudes and Behaviors
      4. Psychosexual Dysfunctions
         a. incest
         b. paraphilias
      5. Rape
      6. Sexual Harassment
   C. Competence
   D. Achievement
      1. Attribution
      2. Intrinsic-Extrinsic Motivation
      3. Goal Setting

(Chapter 9 Outline continued on page 196)

III. Emotion
- A. Defining and Classifying Emotion
  1. Wheel Models
  2. Two-Dimensional Approach
     - a. positive affectivity: happiness
     - b. flow
     - c. negative affectivity: anger
- B. Theories of Emotion
  1. James-Lange Theory
  2. Cannon-Bard Theory
  3. Schachter-Singer Theory
- C. Distinguishing Emotions
  1. The Physiology of Emotion
  2. The Polygraph and Lie Detection
- D. Sociocultural Influence on Emotion
  1. The Universality of Emotional Expressions
  2. Variations in Emotional Expression
  3. Gender Influences
- E. Emotional Intelligence

Key Terms

Write a brief description for each of the following terms. Where relevant, provide an original example or illustration of the term. Then, compare your answers with those provided at the end of the Study Guide chapter. Review the text for those terms you don't know and those you define incorrectly.

1. motivations (p. 330)

2. motives (p. 330)

3. intrinsic motivation (p. 330)

4. extrinsic motivation (p. 330)

5. instinct (p. 331)

6. ethology (p. 331)

7. drive (p. 332)

8. need (p. 332)

9. drive reduction theory (p. 332)

10. homeostasis (p. 332)

11. incentives (p. 332)

12. hierarchy of motives (p. 333)

13. self-actualization (p. 333)

14. ventromedial hypothalamus (VHM) (p. 336)

15. set point (p. 337)

16. estrogens (p. 338)

17. androgens (p. 338)

18. human sexual response pattern (p. 339)

19. sexual script (p. 342)

20. traditional religious script (p. 342)

21. romantic script (p. 342)

22. double standard (p. 343)

23. bisexual (p. 343)

24. psychosexual disorders (p.344)

25. psychosexual dysfunctions (p. 344)

26. incest (p.344)

27. paraphilias (p. 345)

28. fetishism (p. 345)

29. transvestism (p. 345)

30. transsexualism (p. 345)

31. exhibitionism (p. 345)

32. voyeurism (p.345)

33. sadism (p. 345)

34. masochism (p. 345)

35. pedophilia (p. 345)

36. rape (p. 345)

37. date or acquaintance rape (p. 346)

38. competence motivation (p. 347)

39. achievement motivation (need for achievement) (p. 348)

40. attribution theory (p. 349)

41. emotion (p. 353)

42. positive affectivity (PA) (p. 353)

43. negative affectivity (NA) (p. 353)

44. Yerkes-Dodson law (p. 354)

45. flow (p. 355)

46. James-Lange theory (p. 358)

47. Cannon-Bard theory (p. 358)

48. polygraph (p. 361)

49. display rules (p. 362)

50. emotional intelligence (p. 364)

Guided Review

The following in-depth chapter review is a challenging and comprehensive fill-in-the-blanks exercise. The answers are found near the end of the chapter. As you go through the exercise, try to resist the temptation to look at the answers until you have provided them. When you have filled in all the blanks, you will have a thorough summary of the chapter for reference and review.

Perspectives on Motivation

To study why individuals behave, think, and feel the way they do is to study ___(1)___. Motives energize and ___(2)___ behavior toward solving a problem or achieving a goal. Motives differ in ___(3)___, in their origins, and in the degree to which we are ___(4)___ of them. Motivation based on our own internal needs and drives is ___(5)___ motivation; motivation based on external incentives is ___(6)___ motivation. Behaviors that have an innate, biological determinant are called ___(7)___. Throughout history psychologists have believed that much human behavior was controlled by ___(8)___. The study of the biological basis of behavior in natural habitats is called ___(9)___; it is sometimes referred to as ___(10)___ ________ theory.

A ___(11)___ is a psychological state that occurs because of a physiological need. A ___(12)___ is a deprivation that energizes a drive. One theory of motivation suggests that, as a drive becomes stronger, we are motivated to reduce it; this is the ___(13)___ ________ theory. Whereas drives pertain to a ___(14)___ state, needs involve a ___(15)___ state. The body's tendency to maintain equilibrium is called ___(16)___.

According to the psychoanalytic perspective, behavior is ___(17)___ based, and we are largely unaware of why we behave as we do. In the behavioral perspective, stimuli that motivate behavior are called ___(18)___. Behavior is energized by both ___(19)___ and ___(20)___ incentives. The cognitive perspective has created interest in self-___(21)___ goals. Bandura believes that plans and self-___(22)___ play powerful roles in motivation.

Abraham Maslow's theory, based on the humanistic perspective, uses a ___(23)___ ________ ________. The highest level of motivation, according to Maslow, is ___(24)___-________.

The sociocultural perspective reminds us to exercise caution in applying ___(25)___ theories to non-Western cultures.

Selected Motives

Peripheral factors involved in hunger include contractions of the ___(26)___ and blood ___(27)___ levels. Central factors involved in hunger involve the ___(28)___. Researchers have found that brain lesions of the ___(29)___ ________ cause animals to become hyperphagic. These animals stop gaining weight when they reach a ___(30)___ ________.

Stanley Schachter believes that an important difference between obese and normal individuals is their response to ___(31)___ cues. According to Rodin, two important factors in weight control are ___(32)___-________ and ___(33)___.

Both ___(34)___ and ___(35)___ factors are involved in our sexual arousal. Sexual behavior is influenced by ___(36)___ in our bloodstream. ___(37)___ is the main class of hormones in females, while ___(38)___ are the main class in males. In the male, the production of androgen is fairly consistent, but in females, estrogen levels vary over a ___(39)___-________ cycle. Estrogen levels are highest in females midway through the menstrual cycle, when the female is ___(40)___. Compared with other animals, in humans ___(41)___ control over sexual behavior is less dominant. For humans, ___(42)___ and cognitive factors play more important roles.

Masters and Johnson have carefully observed and measured ___(43)___ responses to sexual arousal. These responses, called the human ___(44)___ ________ ________, have four phases: excitement, ___(45)___, orgasm, and ___(46)___. In the final phase, males enter a ___(47)___ period, in which they cannot have another orgasm.

The results of a 1994 survey on sexuality indicate that Americans are more ___(48)___ sexually than previously believed.

A stereotyped pattern of role prescriptions for how individuals should sexually behave is called a sexual ___(49)___. In the traditional ___(50)___ script, sex is acceptable only within marriage. In the ___(51)___ script, sex is synonymous with love. The ___(52)___ ________, the belief that approves many sexual activities for males but not for females, still exists in many areas of sexuality.

Many experts today view sexual orientation as a continuum ranging from exclusive ___(53)___ to exclusive homosexuality. Individuals who are attracted to people of both sexes are called ___(54)___. An individuals' sexual orientation is most likely determined by a combination of ___(55)___, hormonal, ___(56)___, and environmental factors. Research has suggested that ___(57)___ hormone conditions may influence sexual orientation.

Sexual problems that are caused mainly by psychological factors are referred to as ___(58)___ disorders. Disorders that involve impairments in the sexual response cycle are called psychosexual ___(59)___. Efforts to treat psychosexual dysfunctions through traditional forms of ___(60)___ have not been successful. New treatments that focus directly on each ___(61)___ have proven more successful.

A virtually universal taboo, involving sex between close relatives, is called ___(62)___. Disorders in which the source of an individual's sexual satisfaction is an unusual object, ritual, or situation are ___(63)___. Among the paraphilias are the reliance on inanimate objects or specific body parts for sexual arousal and gratification, called ___(64)___; dressing up as the opposite sex, called ___(65)___; deriving sexual gratification from exposing one's sexual anatomy to others, called ___(66)___. A psychosexual disorder in which an individual has an overwhelming desire to be a member of the opposite sex is ___(67)___. Deriving sexual gratification from observing the sexual organs or sex acts of others, termed ___(68)___; deriving sexual gratification from inflicting pain on others, called ___(69)___; deriving sexual gratification from being subjected to physical pain, called ___(70)___; and deriving sexual gratification from children, called ___(71)___.

Although legal definitions vary from state to state, forcible sexual intercourse with a person who does not give consent is called ___(72)___. An increasing concern on college campuses is ___(73)___ or ___(74)___ rape. A woman's recovery from rape depends on her coping resources, ___(75)___ support, and the availability of professional ___(76)___.

Millions of women experience sexual ___(77)___ each year in work and educational settings. Sexual harassment is a manifestation of power and ___(78)___ of one person over another.

The motivation to deal effectively with our environment is referred to as ___(79)___ motivation. Studies of college students indicated they could not tolerate sensory deprivation beyond ___(80)___-________days. However, researchers have shown that shorter periods of sensory deprivation, such as in a water immersion tank, can lower ___(81)___ ________, and reduce chronic pain and ___(82)___.

David McClelland called our motivation to accomplish something and to reach a standard of excellence ___(83)___ motivation. We are motivated to discover the underlying causes of behavior, according to ___(84)___ theory.

Research suggests the undermining effects of extrinsic rewards are linked to the ___(85)___ of being rewarded, the salience of the reward, and the ___(86)___ of the reward.

Currently, there is much interest in studying self-___(87)___ goals. These goals may take the form of personal ___(88)___, life tasks , or personal ___(89)___.

People in the United States are often more ___(90)___ oriented than people in other countries. For studies involving ethnic minorities, ___(91)___ ________ is a better predictor of achievement than is ethnicity.

Emotion

Emotion is defined as a feeling, or ___(92)___, that involves physiological ___(93)___, conscious ___(94)___, and behavior. According to Plutchik's wheel model, emotions have four dimensions. They are positive or ___(95)___; they are primary or ___(96)___; many are ___(97)___ opposites; and they vary in ___(98)___.

According to the two-dimensional approach to classifying emotions, positive emotions, which range from high energy and excitement to calm and quiet, have ___(99)___ ________. Negatively toned emotions, such as anxiety, anger, and sadness, have ___(100)___ affectivity.

Early in this century, psychologists believed that performance was best under moderate rather than low or high levels of ___(101)___. This principle is the ___(102)___-________ Law. Although this law is often true, at times ___(103)___ or ___(104)___ arousal produces optimal performance.

Research on lottery winners has indicated that having more money does not lead to greater ___(105)___.

According to Csikszentmihalyi, flow involves optimal experiences in life and are most likely to occur when people develop a sense of ___(106)___. Flow involves a state of ___(107)___. According to Tavris, expressing and releasing anger does not help to ___(108)___ anger.

One theory of emotion holds that an individual perceives a stimulus in the environment, the body responds, and the person interprets the body's reaction as emotion; this is the ___(109)___-________ theory. According to the Cannon-Bard theory, one experiences an emotion and bodily changes ___(110)___. ___(111)___ theorists believe that both the body and thought are involved in emotion. Schachter and Singer believe that, after emotional events produce physiological and arousal, we look to the external world and then ___(112)___ the emotion.

The ___(113)___ debate centers around whether cognitive activity precedes emotions or emotions precede our thoughts.

Research has found that the emotional states of fear and anger produce different ___(114)___ responses. Recent research has focused on different ___(115)___ ________ that are associated with different moods.

A machine that tries to determine if an individual is lying by monitoring physiological changes in the body is called a ___(116)___. When polygraphs are used, accurately identifying truth or deception depends upon the ___(117)___ of the examiner and the skill of the ___(118)___ being examined.

Although much of the interest in emotion has focused on physiological and cognitive factors, emotion also takes a place in a ___(119)___ context. Ekman's research has shown that facial expressions of basic emotions are ___(120)___ across cultures. The ___(121)___ ________ for emotion, however, are not universal.

Research does not generally support the ___(122)___ stereotype regarding gender influences on emotion. However, gender does matter when considering some specific emotional experiences, the ___(123)___ in which emotion is displayed, and certain beliefs about emotion.

According to Goleman, an important factor in predicting a person's competence is emotional ___(124)___. Goleman believes emotional intelligence consists of emotional ___(125)___-________, managing emotions, reading emotions and handling ___(126)___. According to Goleman, emotional intelligence can be nurtured and ___(127)___.

Sociocultural Worlds/Applications in Psychology

In your own words, summarize the material you have read in Sociocultural Worlds, "Sex Education and Attitudes Among Youth in Holland and Sweden," and Applications in Psychology, "Flow." Briefly describe how each of these articles relates to the information contained in the chapter.

Concept Check

Models of Motivation and Emotion

Proposed by	Basic elements of theory
1. Maslow proposed that	________________.
2. Plutchik proposed that	________________.
3. The ________-__________ ______ proposed that	performance is better under conditions of moderate rather than low or high arousal.
4. The __________-__________ theory proposed that	emotional stimuli first produce bodily reactions; these reactions then produce the emotions we feel.
5. The Cannon-Bard theory proposed that	________________.
6. __________ _____ __________ proposed that	we interpret stimuli from the environment and we interpret our autonomic arousal.

Answers

1. our motives are arranged in a hierarchy from the most basic to the most personal and advanced
2. emotions have four dimensions: (1) positive or negative, (2) primary or mixed, (3) polar opposition, and (4) intensity
3. Yerkes-Dodson law
4. James-Lange theory
5. conscious emotional experience and physiological arousal occur simultaneously
6. Schachter and Singer

Multiple-Choice Questions

Practice Test 1

After answering all the multiple-choice questions in Practice Test 1, compare your answers with the answer key provided at the end of the chapter. The answer key contains a brief explanation of both the correct and incorrect answers. Each of these questions is keyed to the Learning Objectives for the chapter. If you answer any questions incorrectly, review the corresponding Learning Objective and text material before you proceed to Practice Test 2.

1. "The factors that explain why individuals behave, think, and feel the way they do" defines
   a. motivation.
   b. instinct.
   c. emotion.
   d. drive reduction theory.

LO 1

2. Drive reduction theory states the goal of drive reduction is
   a. ethological balance.
   b. homeostasis.
   c. instinct reduction.
   d. unconscious gratification

LO 2

3. Interest in self-generated goals is consistent with which perspective on motivation?
   a. psychoanalytic
   b. cognitive
   c. humanistic
   d. sociocultural

LO 3

4. Each of the following is a peripheral factor involved in hunger *except*
   a. stomach contractions
   b. blood sugar
   c. sugar receptors in the liver
   d. the ventromedial hypothalamus

LO 4

5. As we move from lower to higher animals,
   a. hormonal control over sexual behavior is less dominant.
   b. hormonal control over sexual behavior disappears.
   c. cultural factors become less important.
   d. hormonal control over sexual behavior becomes more dominant.

LO 5

6. According to Masters and Johnson, an initial increase in blood flow to the genital areas and muscle tension characterize which phase of the human sexual response cycle?
   a. the excitement phase
   b. the plateau phase
   c. orgasm
   d. the resolution phase

LO 6

7. The 1994 survey of American sexuality found most Americans
   a. are more conservative sexually than previously believed.
   b. are obsessed with sexual thoughts.
   c. refused to respond to survey questions.
   d. are interested in extramarital sex.

LO 7

8. The double standard for sexual behavior
   a. has virtually disappeared in American culture.
   b. has actually increased during the last few decades.
   c. still exists in many areas of sexuality.
   d. now applies more to females than to males.

LO 8

9. A biological factor believed to be involved in homosexuality is
   a. prenatal hormone conditions.
   b. the nutritional quality of pregnant mothers.
   c. the amount of vitamins received in infancy.
   d. the development of the limbic system.

LO 9

10. The treatment of sexual dysfunctions has been largely
    a. successful using traditional forms of psychotherapy.
    b. successful using treatments that focus directly on the dysfunction.
    c. unsuccessful regardless of the treatment.
    d. successful when they are treated as personality disorders.

LO 10

11. A paraphilia in which individuals receive sexual gratification from inflicting pain on themselves is called
    a. masochism.
    b. sadism.
    c. voyeurism.
    d. exhibitionism.

LO 11

12. Each of the following is true *except*
    a. Many rape victims subsequently experience sexual dysfunctions.
    b. The incidence of reported date rape is decreasing on college campuses.
    c. Social support is an important factor in recovery from rape.
    d. Sexual harassment is a manifestation of power and domination of one person over another.

LO 12

13. When first-graders work hard on a project in order to collect praise and gold stars from their teacher, what kind of motivation are they demonstrating?
    a. attribution motivation
    b. competence motivation
    c. extrinsic motivation
    d. intrinsic motivation

LO 13

14. A cross-cultural study of achievement orientation found that, compared with parents in industrialized countries, parents in nonindustrialized countries placed a
    a. higher value on achievement in their children.
    b. higher value on independence in their children.
    c. higher value on obedience in their children.
    d. lower value on cooperation in their children.

LO 14

15. The definition of emotion contains each of the following components *except*
    a. physiological arousal.
    b. conscious experience.
    c. unconscious experience.
    d. overt behavior.

LO 15

16. According to the Yerkes-Dodson law, your performance on an exam will be best if you are
    a. extremely aroused.
    b. minimally aroused.
    c. moderately aroused.
    d. extremely happy.

LO 16

17. According to the James-Lange theory, an environmental stimulus
    a. is perceived as emotional by the hypothalamus.
    b. triggers emotional arousal, which is labeled by the brain.
    c. is emotional because of cultural and social expectations.
    d. causes arousal if it appears threatening.

LO 17

18. According to Schachter and Singer, the specific emotion we experience depends on the
    a. rate of firing of fibers leading from the hypothalamus to the neocortex.
    b. nature of the cause of the arousal.
    c. specific pattern of heart rate, blood pressure, and skin resistance.
    d. environmental circumstances to which we attribute our arousal.

LO 18

19. Which of the following is true regarding the use of polygraph tests?
    a. The Employee Polygraph Protection Act of 1988 helped to standardize the administration of polygraph exams.
    b. The polygraph works by measuring changes in brain waves.
    c. Experts claim that the polygraph errs about one-third of the time.
    d. The skill of the examiner is not important, since the equipment is so sophisticated.

LO 19

20. Researchers have found universality in facial expressions for each of the following emotions *except*
    a. happiness.
    b. fear.
    c. anger.
    d. love.

LO 20

21. According to Goleman, a good predictor of one's competence is
    a. the ability to use display rules.
    b. the ability to repress feelings.
    c. the ability to express anger.
    d. emotional intelligence.

LO 21

Practice Test 2

The following multiple-choice questions also are keyed to the chapter Learning Objectives. If you answer any questions incorrectly, be sure to review the corresponding Learning Objective and text material.

1. The key question asked by psychologists who study motivation is
    a. When?
    b. How?
    c. Who?
    d. Why?

LO 1

2. Which of the following is occasionally referred to as "modern instinct theory"?
    a. ethology
    b. drive reduction theory
    c. homeostasis theory
    d. incentive theory

LO 2

3. The motivation to achieve self-actualization was proposed by adherents of which perspective?
    a. psychoanalytic
    b. cognitive
    c. humanistic
    d. sociocultural

LO 3

4. Blood sugar receptors that help signal hunger are located in the
    a. brain.
    b. stomach.
    c. liver.
    d. both *a* and *c*

LO 4

5. At puberty, females' ovaries begin to produce female sex hormones called
   a. androgens.
   b. testosterone.
   c. estrogen.
   d. epinephrine

LO 5

6. Which of the following is true regarding the refractory period?
   a. Only males experience a refractory period.
   b. Only females experience a refractory period.
   c. Males and females both experience a refractory period.
   d. The refractory period occurs immediately following the excitement phase.

LO 6

7. The 1994 survey of American sexuality
   a. confirmed the trend toward a more permissive sexual standard
   b. found evidence of the double standard.
   c. found most Americans to be conservative sexually.
   d. was probably less reliable than previous surveys.

LO 7

8. Sex is synonymous with love, according to the
   a. double standard.
   b. traditional religious script.
   c. romantic script.
   d. 1994 survey of sexuality.

LO 8

9. Which of the following is considered to be a factor in homosexuality?
   a. prenatal hormone conditions
   b. dominant mothers
   c. weak or absent fathers
   d. children raised by gay or lesbian parents

LO 9

10. Regarding psychosexual dysfunctions, each of the following has been successful *except*
   a. treating psychosexual dysfunctions as personality disorders
   b. directly treating the dysfunction
   c. treating premature ejaculation
   d. treating the inability to achieve orgasm in women

LO 10

11. A paraphilia in which the individual achieves sexual gratification from an inanimate object is called
   a. transvestism.
   b. exhibitionism.
   c. fetishism.
   d. voyeurism.

LO 11

12. A women's recovery from rape depends on
   a. her psychological adjustment prior to the rape.
   b. her coping abilities.
   c. social support.
   d. all of the above

LO 12

13. Psychologist David McClelland is associated with research on
   a. competence motivation.
   b. intrinsic motivation.
   c. extrinsic motivation.
   d. achievement motivation.

LO 13

14. When both ethnicity and social class are taken into account, the best predictor of achievement is
   a. race.
   b. social class.
   c. ethnicity.
   d. gender.

LO 14

15. According to Plutchik, mixing primary emotions leads to
   a. psychological difficulties.
   b. polar opposites.
   c. other emotions.
   d. negative emotions.

LO 15

16. In contrast to the Yerkes-Dodson law, when first learning a complex task, the optimal level of arousal is
   a. very high.
   b. moderate.
   c. low.
   d. no optimal level has been established.

LO 16

17. The experience of emotion and the physiological response occur simultaneously according to the
    a. Cannon-Bard theory.
    b. James-Lange theory.
    c. primacy theory.
    d. cognitive theory of emotion.

LO 17

18. The interpretation of external cues is essential to the
    a. Cannon-Bard theory.
    b. James-Lange theory.
    c. primacy debate.
    d. cognitive theory of emotion.

LO 18

19. The polygraph monitors each of the following changes in the body *except*
    a. heart rate
    b. breathing
    c. electrodermal response
    d. brain waves

LO 19

20. In Greece, the "thumbs up" sign generally means
    a. everything is fine.
    b. you are hitching a ride.
    c. you are requesting more food and drink.
    d. you are conveying an insult.

LO 20

21. Each of the following is a component of emotional intelligence except
    a. emotional self-awareness.
    b. the ability to read emotions.
    c. the ability to repress anger
    d. the ability to handle relationships.

LO 21

Answers to Key Terms

1. **Motivations** are the factors that help explain why people behave, think, and feel the way they do.
2. **Motives** energize and direct behavior toward solving a problem or achieving a goal.
3. **Intrinsic motivation** refers to motives based on internal drives and needs.
4. **Extrinsic motivation** refers to positive or negative external incentives that influence behavior.
5. An **instinct** is an innate, biological determinant of behavior.
6. **Ethology** is the study of the biological basis of behavior in natural habitats.
7. A **drive** is an aroused state that occurs because of a physiological need.
8. A **need** is a deprivation that energizes the drive to eliminate or reduce the deprivation.
9. **Drive reduction theory** states that a physiological need creates a drive that motivates the organism to satisfy the need.
10. **Homeostasis** is the body's tendency to maintain an equilibrium, or steady state.
11. **Incentives** are positive or negative stimuli or events that motivate an individual's behavior.
12. The **hierarchy of motives** is Maslow's concept that all individuals have five main needs that must be satisfied in the following sequence: physiological, safety, love and belongingness, self-esteem, and self-actualization.
13. **Self-actualization** is Maslow's term for the motivation to develop one's full potential as a human being.
14. The **ventromedial hypothalamus (VMH)** is a region of the hypothalamus that plays an important role in controlling hunger.
15. **Set point** is the weight maintained when no effort is made to gain or lose weight.
16. **Estrogens** are female sex hormones.
17. **Androgens** are male sex hormones.
18. The **human sexual response pattern,** identified by Masters and Johnson, consists of four phases: excitement, plateau, orgasm, and resolution.
19. A **sexual script** is a stereotyped pattern of role prescriptions for how individuals should sexually behave.
20. According to the **traditional religious script,** sex is accepted only within marriage.
21. According to the **romantic script,** sex is acceptable if we have developed a relationship and fallen in love.

22. **Double standard** refers to the belief that many sexual activities are acceptable for males but not for females.
23. **Bisexual** refers to individuals who are sexually attracted to people of both sexes.
24. **Psychosexual disorders** are sexual problems caused mainly by psychological problems.
25. **Psychosexual dysfunctions** are disorders that involve impairments in the sexual response cycle, either in the desire for gratification or in the inability to achieve it.
26. **Incest** refers to sex between close relatives.
27. **Paraphilias** are psychosexual disorders in which the source of an individual's sexual satisfaction is an unusual object, ritual, or situation.
28. **Fetishism** is a psychosexual disorder in which an individual relies on inanimate objects or a specific body part for sexual gratification.
29. **Transvestism** is a psychosexual disorder in which an individual obtains sexual gratification by dressing up as a member of the opposite sex.
30. **Transsexualism** refers to individuals with an overwhelming desire to become a member of the opposite sex.
31. **Exhibitionism** is a psychosexual disorder in which individuals obtain sexual gratification by exposing their sexual anatomy to others.
32. **Voyeurism** is a psychosexual disorder in which individuals obtain sexual gratification by observing the sexual organs or sexual acts of others.
33. **Sadism** is a psychosexual disorder in which the individual obtains sexual gratification by inflicting pain on others.
34. **Masochism** is a psychosexual disorder in which individuals derive sexual gratification from being subjected to physical pain, either self-inflicted or inflicted by others.
35. **Pedophilia** is a sexual disorder in which the sexual object is a child; the intimacy usually involves manipulation of the child's genitals.
36. **Rape** is forcible sexual intercourse with a person who does not give consent.
37. **Date or acquaintance rape** is coercive sex forced by someone with whom the victim is at least casually acquainted.
38. **Competence motivation** is the motivation to deal effectively with the environment, to be adept at what we attempt, and to make the world a better place.
39. **Achievement motivation** is the desire to accomplish something, to reach a standard of excellence, and to expend effort to excel.
40. According to **attribution theory,** individuals are motivated to discover the underlying causes of behavior as part of their effort to make sense out of behavior.
41. **Emotion** is feeling, or affect, that involves a mixture of arousal, conscious experience, and overt behavior.
42. **Positive affectivity (PA)** refers to the range of positive emotion.
43. **Negative affectivity (NA)** refers to emotions that are negatively toned.
44. The **Yerkes-Dodson law** states that performance is best under conditions of moderate rather than low or high arousal.
45. **Flow** involves optimal experiences in life that are most likely to occur when people have developed a sense of mastery.
46. The **James-Lange theory** of emotion states that emotion results from physiological states triggered by stimuli in the environment.
47. The **Cannon-Bard theory** of emotion states that emotion and physiological states occur simultaneously.
48. The **polygraph** is a machine that tries to determine if someone is lying, by measuring changes in the body thought to be influenced by emotional states. Examples of changes in the body include heart rate, breathing, and electrodermal response.
49. **Display rules** are sociocultural standards that determine where, when, and how emotions should be expressed.
50. **Emotional intelligence**, according to Goleman, involves emotional self-awareness, managing emotions, reading emotions, and handling relationships.

Answers to Guided Review

1. motivation (p. 330)
2. direct (p. 330)
3. intensity (p. 330)
4. conscious (p. 330)
5. intrinsic (p. 330)
6. extrinsic (p. 330)
7. instincts (p. 332)
8. instincts (p. 331)
9. ethology (p. 331)
10. modern instinct (p. 331)
11. drive (p. 332)
12. need (p. 332)
13. drive reduction (p. 332)
14. psychological (p. 332)
15. physiological (p. 332)
16. homeostasis (p. 332)
17. instinctually (p. 332)
18. incentives (p. 332)
19. positive (p. 332)
20. negative (p. 332)
21. generated (p. 333)
22. efficiency (p. 333)
23. hierarchy of motives (p. 333)
24. self-actualization (p. 333)
25. Western (p. 333)
26. stomach (p. 336)
27. sugar (p. 336)
28. brain (p. 336)
29. ventromedial hypothalamus (p. 336)
30. set point (p. 337)
31. environmental (p. 337)
32. self-control (p. 338)
33. exercise (p. 338)
34. biological (p. 338)
35. psychological (p. 338)
36. hormones (p. 338)
37. Estrogen (p. 338)
38. androgens (p. 338)
39. month-long (p. 338)
40. ovulating (p. 338)
41. hormonal (p. 338)
42. sociocultural (p. 339)
43. physiological (p. 339)
44. sexual response cycle (p. 339)
45. plateau (p. 339)
46. resolution (p. 339)
47. refractory (p. 339)
48. conservative (p. 340)
49. script (p. 342)
50. religious (p. 342)
51. romantic (p. 342)
52. double standard (p. 343)
53. heterosexuality (p. 343)
54. bisexual (p. 343)
55. genetic (p. 344)
56. cognitive (p. 344)
57. prenatal (p. 344)
58. psychosexual (p. 344)
59. dysfunctions (p. 344)
60. psychotherapy (p. 344)
61. dysfunction (p. 344)
62. incest (p. 344)
63. paraphilias (p. 345)
64. fetishism (p. 345)
65. transvestism (p. 345)
66. exhibitionism (p. 345)
67. transsexualism (p. 345)
68. voyeurism (p. 345)
69. sadism (p. 345)
70. masochism (p. 345)
71. pedophilia (p. 345)
72. rape (p. 345)
73. date (p. 346)
74. acquaintance (p. 346)
75. social (p. 346)
76. counseling (p. 346)
77. harassment (p. 346)
78. domination (p. 347)
79. competence (p. 347)
80. 2–3 (p. 347)
81. blood pressure (p. 348)
82. stress (p. 348)
83. achievement (p. 348)
84. attribution (p. 349)
85. expectation (p. 349)
86. tangibility (p. 349)
87. generated (p. 349)
88. projects (p. 350)
89. strivings (p. 350)
90. achievement (p. 350)
91. social class (p. 351)
92. affect (p. 353)
93. arousal (p. 353)
94. experience (p. 353)
95. negative (p. 353)
96. mixed (p. 353)
97. polar (p. 353)
98. intensity (p. 353)
99. positive affectivity (p. 353)
100. negative (p. 353)
101. arousal (p. 353)
102. Yerkes-Dodson (p. 354)
103. low (p. 354)
104. high (p. 354)
105. happiness (p. 355)
106. mastery (p. 355)
107. concentration (p. 355)
108. reduce (p. 356)
109. James-Lange (p. 358)
110. simultaneously (p. 358)
111. Cognitive (p. 358)
112. label (p. 358)
113. primacy (p. 360)
114. physiological (p. 360)
115. brain waves (p. 360)
116. polygraph (p. 361)
117. skill (p. 361)
118. individual (p. 361)
119. sociocultural (p. 362)
120. universal (p. 362)
121. display rules (p. 362)
122. master (p. 363)
123. context (p. 363)
124. intelligence (p. 364)
125. self-awareness (p. 364)
126. relationships (p. 364)
127. strengthened (p. 364)

Answers to Multiple Choice Questions- Practice Test 1

1. a. **Correct.** Motives are specific forces, such as hunger and achievement that energize and direct behavior.
   b. Incorrect. This refers to an innate, biological determinant of behavior.
   c. Incorrect. This refers to affect involving a mixture of arousal, conscious experience, and behavior.
   d. Incorrect. This states that a physiological need creates an aroused state that motivates behavior.

2. a. Incorrect. It sounds impressive, but it doesn't make sense.
   b. **Correct.** Homeostasis is the body's tendency to maintain an equilibrium.
   c. Incorrect. I'm not sure what this is.
   d. Incorrect. This is a Freudian-sounding term, but it doesn't apply here.

3. a. Incorrect. This approach suggests we are unaware of why we behave the way we do.
   b. **Correct.** The belief is that these goals influence a person's thought, behavior and emotional reactions.
   c. Incorrect. Maslow was a humanistic psychologist who believed self-actualization was a powerful motivating force.
   d. Incorrect. This approach reminds us of the influence culture has on motivation.

4. a. Incorrect. This *is* a peripheral factor in hunger.
   b. Incorrect. This *is* a peripheral factor in hunger.
   c. Incorrect. This *is* a peripheral factor in hunger.
   d. **Correct.** This refers to a brain process in hunger.

5. a. **Correct.** Hormonal control of sexuality in humans is less dominant than in other animals, but still influential.
   b. Incorrect. Hormonal control of sexuality in humans is less dominant than in other animals, but still influential.
   c. Incorrect. Cultural factors become more important in sexuality for humans.
   d. Incorrect. Hormonal control of sexuality in humans is less dominant than in other animals, but still influential.

6. a. **Correct.** This includes lubrication of the vagina and partial erection of the penis.
   b. Incorrect. The plateau phase is a continuation of the excitement phase.
   c. Incorrect. This stage is marked by an explosive discharge of neuromuscular tension and an intense pleasurable feeling.
   d. Incorrect. In this phase, blood vessels return to their normal size.

7. a. **Correct.** It turns out the surveys conducted by other magazines did indeed use biased samples.
   b. Incorrect. *Most* Americans are hardly obsessed with sexual thoughts.
   c. Incorrect. Most respondents answered the questions asked by the well-trained staff.
   d. Incorrect. Only a small percentage indicated they have participated in extramarital sex.

8. a. Incorrect. The double standard is still alive and well.
   b. Incorrect. the text cites no data to support this idea.
   c. **Correct.** The double standard is still reflecting and contributing to gender issues in our society.
   d. Incorrect. The double standard still reflects the wider sexual latitude society is willing to bestow on males.

9. a. **Correct.** This involves the second to fifth months after conception.
   b. Incorrect. This has not been cited as an influence on one's sexuality.
   c. Incorrect. This has not been cited as an influence on one's sexuality.
   d. Incorrect. This has not been cited as an influence on one's sexuality.

10. a. Incorrect. Treating sexual dysfunctions through traditional psychotherapy has not been particularly successful.
    b. **Correct.** This has necessitating moving away from the view of these dysfunctions as personality disorders.
    c. Incorrect. Some techniques have been highly successful.
    d. Incorrect. This view has probably held back the treatment of many sexual dysfunctions.

11. a. **Correct.** Masochists also derive sexual gratification by having others inflict pain on them.
    b. Incorrect. This refers to deriving sexual gratification by inflicting pain on others.
    c. Incorrect. This refers to deriving gratification by observing others.
    d. Incorrect. This refers to deriving sexual gratification by exposing themselves to others.

12. a. Incorrect. Although the statement is true, the question is asking for an exception.
    b. **Correct.** In fact, the incidence is *rising*.
    c. Incorrect. Although the statement is true, the question is asking for an exception.
    d. Incorrect. Although the statement is true, the question is asking for an exception.

13. a. Incorrect. Nice-sounding, but meaningless.
    b. Incorrect. This refers to the motivation to deal effectively with the environment and to make the world a better place.
    c. **Correct.** The praise and gold stars are external, or extrinsic, sources of motivation.
    d. Incorrect. This would be correct if the children worked without any external rewards.

14. a. Incorrect. The *opposite* was found in the study cited in the text.
    b. Incorrect. The *opposite* was found in the study cited in the text.
    c. **Correct.** Another attribute valued was cooperation.
    d. Incorrect. The *opposite* was found in the study cited in the text.

15. a. Incorrect. This *is* a component of emotion; the question is asking for an *exception.*
    b. Incorrect. This *is* a component of emotion; the question is asking for an *exception.*
    c. **Correct.** Emotion exists in the realm of conscious experience.
    d. Incorrect. This *is* a component of emotion; the question is asking for an *exception*

16. a. Incorrect. This law suggests you might have difficulty concentrating if you are too aroused.
    b. Incorrect. This law suggests you might be too lethargic if your arousal level is too low.
    c. **Correct.** This law states performance is best under conditions of moderate arousal.
    d. Incorrect. This law deals with levels of arousal rather than happiness.

17. a. Incorrect. This theory implies we react first; that is, emotion follows the body's reactions.
    b. **Correct.** This theory implies we react first; that is, emotion follows the body's reactions.
    c. Incorrect. This theory did not delve into cultural and social expectations.
    d. Incorrect. This theory implies we react first; that is emotion follows the body's reactions.

18. a. Incorrect. Schachter and Singer's theory is a cognitive theory.
    b. Incorrect. According to this theory our *interpretation* is all important.
    c. Incorrect. Schachter and Singer's theory is a cognitive theory.
    d. **Correct.** Schachter and Singer's theory is a cognitive theory.

19. a. Incorrect. This Act restricts most nongovernment polygraph testing.
    b. Incorrect. It works by monitoring changes in the heart, breathing and electrodermal response.
    c. **Correct.** This represents a high error rate.
    d. Incorrect. The skill of the examiner is extremely important.

20. a. Incorrect. Researchers have found universality in the facial expression of happiness.
    b. Incorrect. Researchers have found universality in the facial expression of fear.
    c. Incorrect. Researchers have found universality in the facial expression of anger.
    d. **Correct.** This is not reported as an emotion for which there is universality of facial expression.

21. a. Incorrect. Goleman did not research display rules.
    b. Incorrect. Goleman's approach is not psychoanalytic.
    c. Incorrect. This is not a predictor of one's competence, according to Goleman.
    d. **Correct.** This involves emotional self-awareness, managing emotions, reading emotions, and so on.

Answers to Multiple Choice Questions- Practice Test 2

1. a. Incorrect. Motivations are the factors that help explain why people behave, think, and feel the way they do.
   b. Incorrect. Motivations are the factors that help explain why people behave, think, and feel the way they do.
   c. Incorrect. Motivations are the factors that help explain why people behave, think, and feel the way they do.
   d. **Correct.** Motivations are the factors that help explain why people behave, think, and feel the way they do.

2. a. **Correct.** Ethology is the study of the biological basis of behavior in natural habitats.
   b. Incorrect. A drive is a psychological state that exists because of a physiological need.
   c. Incorrect. Homeostasis is not a theory; it refers to the body's tendency to maintain an equilibrium.
   d. Incorrect. Incentives are positive or negative stimuli or events that motivate a person's behavior.

3. a. Incorrect. Psychoanalytic theory claims we are largely unaware of why we do what we do.
   b. Incorrect. The cognitive perspective has most recently been concerned with self-generated goals.
   c. **Correct.** This refers to the motivation to develop one's full potential.
   d. Incorrect. This perspective reminds us of the role played by environmental and cultural factors in our motivation.

4. a. Incorrect. This answer is partially correct; it is not the best alternative.
   b. Incorrect. The blood sugar receptors are not located in the stomach.
   c. Incorrect. This answer is partially correct; it is not the best alternative.
   d. **Correct.** The sugar receptors in the liver signal the brain via the vagus nerve.

5. a. Incorrect. These are the main class of sex hormones in males.
   b. Incorrect. This is the primary androgen produced in males.
   c. **Correct.** Estrogen levels are highest when the female is ovulating.
   d. Incorrect. This is not a "sexual" hormone.

6. a. Incorrect. Both females and males experience a refractory period.
   b. Incorrect. Both females and males experience a refractory period.
   c. **Correct.** During this period, males are not able to achieve another orgasm, whereas females may be stimulated to orgasm again.
   d. Incorrect. The refractory period occurs immediately after orgasm.

7. a. Incorrect. The survey actually confirmed a trend in the opposite direction.
   b. Incorrect. The survey did not detect a double standard, although males reported thinking about sex more often than females.
   c. **Correct.** This was one of the more surprising outcomes of the survey.
   d. Incorrect. There is no evidence this survey was less reliable.

8. a. Incorrect. The double standard holds males and females to different sexual standards.
   b. Incorrect. According to this script, sex is acceptable only within marriage.
   c. **Correct.** According to this script the key issue is love, not necessarily marriage.
   d. Incorrect. The survey did not reveal that sex is synonymous with love.

9. a. **Correct.** Exposure to certain hormones in the second to fifth months after conception may be a factor.
   b. Incorrect. There is no evidence that this is a factor in homosexuality.
   c. Incorrect. There is no evidence that this is a factor in homosexuality.
   d. Incorrect. There is no evidence that this is a factor in homosexuality.

10. a. **Correct.** This has not been a successful way to treat psychosexual dysfunctions.
    b. Incorrect. This *has* been a successful way to treat sexual dysfunctions.
    c. Incorrect. This *has* been a successful way to treat sexual dysfunctions.
    d. Incorrect. This *has* been a successful way to treat sexual dysfunctions.

11. a. Incorrect. This paraphilia involves dressing up as a member of the opposite sex.
    b. Incorrect. This paraphilia involves exposing one's sexual anatomy.
    c. **Correct.** Another form of fetishism involves relying on a specific body part for sexual gratification.
    d. Incorrect. This paraphilia involves observing others, often from a hidden vantage point.

12. a. Incorrect. Although this answer is true, it is not the best alternative.
    b. Incorrect. Although this answer is true, it is not the best alternative.
    c. Incorrect. Although this answer is true, it is not the best alternative.
    d. **Correct.** Rape crisis centers can help provide much of the support.

13. a. Incorrect. This is the motivation to deal effectively with the environment. R.W. White is associated with competence motivation.
    b. Incorrect. McClelland is not associated with intrinsic motivation.
    c. Incorrect. McClelland is not associated with extrinsic motivation.
    d. **Correct.** This is also referred to as "need for achievement."

14. a. Incorrect. Research does not suggest this is the best predictor of achievement when social class and ethnicity are taken into account.
    b. **Correct.** This suggests that middle-class individuals, regardless of ethnicity, are more oriented toward than individuals from lower socioeconomic status.
    c. Incorrect. Research does not suggest this is the best predictor of achievement when social class and ethnicity are taken into account.
    d. Incorrect. Research does not suggest this is the best predictor of achievement when social class and ethnicity are taken into account.

15. a. Incorrect. Mixing primary colors does not lead to psychological difficulties.
    b Incorrect. Many of Plutchik's emotions are polar opposites, but this is not achieved by mixing primary emotions.
    c. **Correct.** The text uses the analogy of mixing primary colors to produce other colors.
    d. Incorrect. Plutchik does, however, describe emotions as being positive or negative.

16. a. Incorrect. This would be more appropriate for a well-earned task.
    b. Incorrect. This is the basic Yerkes-Dodson law; it doesn't apply to the question.
    c. **Correct.** Examples are learning to play tennis or solving an algebraic equation.
    d. Incorrect. Consider the best level of arousal for yourself as you try to learn a complex task.

17. a. **Correct.** In distinction to the James-Lange theory, this approach focused on what happens in the brain.
    b. Incorrect. This approach states that emotion results from physiological states triggered by stimuli in the environment.
    c. Incorrect. The primacy debate asks "which comes first: emotions or thoughts?"
    d. Incorrect. This theory places emphasis on our interpretation of the environment and of our reactions to the environment.

18. a. Incorrect. This approach states that emotions and physiological states occur simultaneously.
    b. Incorrect. This approach states that emotion results from physiological states triggered by stimuli in the environment.
    c. Incorrect. The primacy debate asks "which comes first: emotions or thoughts?"
    d. **Correct.** According to this approach, we interpret the external cues present and then label the emotion.

19. a. Incorrect. The polygraph *does* measure changes in the heart rate.
    b. Incorrect. The *polygraph does* measure changes in breathing.
    c. Incorrect. The polygraph *does* measure changes in electrodermal response.
    d. **Correct.** The polygraph does not measure brain waves.

20. a. Incorrect. This sign means the opposite of "everything is fine."
    b. Incorrect. You are hitching a ride for trouble with this sign.
    c. Incorrect. This sign is not likely to get you more food and drink.
    d. **Correct.** Be careful what you do with your thumb.

21. a. Incorrect. This *is* a component of emotional intelligence.
    b. Incorrect. This is a component of emotional intelligence.
    c. **Correct.** This is not a component of emotional intelligence.
    d. Incorrect. This *is* a component of emotional intelligence.

Chapter 10 Personality

Learning Objectives

After studying this chapter you should be able to:

1. Define the term *personality*. (p. 372)

2. Describe the approach to personality taken by the trait theorists, and identify the components of the five-factor model. (p. 372)

3. Distinguish between individualism and collectivism. (p. 376)

4. Discuss the basic ideas underlying the psychoanalytic perspective. (p. 379)

5. Distinguish among the Freudian concepts of id, ego and superego. (p. 379)

6. Trace the course of psychosexual development according to Freud, identifying the major events at each stage. (p. 380)

7. Distinguish among the theories of Horney, Jung, and Adler, and describe their differences from Freud's approach to psychoanalysis. (p. 382)

8. Distinguish between the behavioristic view of Skinner and the cognitive social learning approach of Bandura and Mischel. (p. 388)

9. Distinguish between the humanistic perspectives of Carl Rogers and Abraham Maslow. (p. 391)

10. Relate the differing personality approaches to the following issues: biological versus learned factors, the forces that drive personality, the consistency of personality, the role of the unconscious, and the degree of optimism or pessimism regarding human nature. (p. 395)

11. Distinguish between self-report tests and projective personality tests; identify examples of each. (p. 398)

12. Discuss the approach taken in the behavioral assessment of personality. (p. 402)

Chapter 10 Outline

I. The Nature of Personality
II. Personality Theories
    A. Trait Theories
        1. Sheldon's Somatotype Theory
            a. endomorph
            b. mesomorph
            c. ectomorph
        2. Five Factor Model
            a. neuroticism
            b. extraversion
            c. openness to experience
            d. agreeableness
            e. conscientiousness
        3. Culture and Personality Traits
        4. Evaluating Trait Explanations
    B. Psychoanalytic Theories
        1. Freud's Theory
            a. the role of the unconscious
            b. the structure of personality
                (1) id
                (2) ego
                (3) superego
            c. the development of personality
                (1) oral stage
                (2) phallic stage
                (3) latency stage
                (4) genital stage
        2. Psychoanalytic Revisionists and Dissenters
            a. Horney's Sociocultural modification
            b. Jung's depth psychology
            c. Adler's Individual Psychology
                (1) striving for superiority
                (2) compensation
                (3) overcompensation
                (4) Inferiority complex
                (5) superiority complex
        3. Evaluation of Psychoanalytic Theories
    C. Behavioral Theories
        1. Skinner's behaviorism
        2. Evaluating the behavioral theories
    D. Cognitive Social Learning Theories
        1. Mischel's findings with respect to delay of gratification
        2. Bandura's findings with respect to imitation
        3. Evaluating the Cognitive Social Learning Theory
    E. Humanistic Theories
        1. Rogers
            a. the self
            b. unconditional positive regard
            c. fully functioning person
        2. Maslow
        3. Evaluating Humanistic theories
    F. Comparing Personality Theories
        1. What is the relative importance of biological factors versus experience?
        2. What forces drive personality?
        3. How consistent or variable is personality across situations?
        4. Is the personality theory optimistic or pessimistic about human nature?
III. Personality Assessment
    A. Self-Report Tests
        1. Constructing self-report tests
        2. The MMPI
        3. The five factor personality instruments
        4. Evaluating self-report tests
    B. Projective Tests
        1. The Rorschach Inkblot Test
        2. The Thematic Apperception Test (TAT)
    C. Behavioral Assessment

Who Am I?

Match the psychologists listed below with their contribution to psychology. Answers appear at the end of the chapter.

_____ 1. Sigmund Freud
_____ 2. Karen Horney
_____ 3. Carl Jung
_____ 4. Alfred Adler
_____ 5. B. F. Skinner
_____ 6. Walter Mischel
_____ 7. Carl Rogers
_____ 8. Abraham Maslow

a. My approach to psychoanalytic theory emphasizes the collective unconscious and is referred to as depth psychology.
b. According to my approach, people have both deficiency needs and metaneeds.
c. Unconditional positive regard, empathy, and genuineness are key components in my humanistic perspective.
d. In my perspective, personality is viewed as an individual's behavior, which is determined by the external environment.
e. I founded the psychoanalytic perspective.
f. My approach to psychoanalytic theory emphasizes the uniqueness of every individual.
g. My approach to social learning is called "cognitive social learning."
h. I rejected Freud's notion that "anatomy is destiny," and I emphasized sociocultural factors.

Key Terms

Write a brief description for each of the following terms. Where relevant, provide an original example or illustration of the term. Then, compare your answers with those provided at the end of the Study Guide chapter. Review the text for those terms you don't know and those you define incorrectly.

1. personality (p. 372)

2. traits (p. 372)

3. trait theories (p. 373)

4. somatotype theory (p. 373)

5. endomorph (p. 373)

6. mesomorph (p. 373)

7. ectomorph (p. 373)

8. introversion (p. 374)

9. extraversion (p. 374)

10. five-factor model (p. 374)

11. individualism (p. 376)

12. collectivism (p. 377)

13. id (p. 379)

14. pleasure principle (p. 379)

15. ego (p. 380)

16. reality principle (p. 380)

17. defense mechanisms (p. 380)

18. superego (p. 380)

19. erogenous zones (p. 380)

20. fixation (p. 380)

21. oral stage (p. 380)

22. anal stage (p. 382)

23. phallic stage (p. 382)

24. Oedipus complex (p. 382)

25. latency stage (p. 382)

26. genital stage (p. 382)

27. collective unconscious (p. 384)

28. archetypes (p. 384)

29. individual psychology (p. 384)

30. striving for superiority (p. 385)

31. compensation (p. 385)

32. overcompensation (p. 385)

33. inferiority complex (p. 385)

34. superiority complex (p. 385)

35. reductionistic (p. 388)

36. cognitive social learning theory (p. 389)

37. situationism (p. 389)

38. delay of gratification (p. 389)

39. self-efficacy (p. 390)

40. phenomenological worldview (p. 390)

41. humanistic theory (p. 391)

42. conditional positive regard (p. 391)

43. self-concept (p. 391)

44. unconditional positive regard (p. 391)

45. Barnum effect (p. 397)

46. self-report tests (p. 398)

47. face validity (p. 398)

48. social desirability (p. 398)

49. empirically keyed tests (p. 398)

50. Minnesota Multiphasic Personality Inventory (MMPI) (p. 399)

51. projective tests (p. 400)

52. Rorschach inkblot test (p. 400)

53. Thematic Apperception Test (TAT) (p. 401)

Guided Review

The following in-depth chapter review is a challenging and comprehensive fill-in-the-blanks exercise. The answers are found near the end of the chapter. As you go through the exercise, try to resist the temptation to look at the answers until you have provided them. When you have filled in all the blanks, you will have a thorough summary of the chapter for reference and review.

The Nature of Personality/Theories of Personality

The enduring distinctive thoughts, emotions, and behaviors that characterize the way an individual with the world is what psychologists call ___(1)___.

Trait theories suggest that personality consists of broad ___(2)___ that are reflected in the ways people behave. William Sheldon's belief that different body types are associated with certain personality characteristics is called ___(3)___ theory. Sheldon's theory focused on three types: (1) the soft, round, large-stomached person who is relaxed and gregarious, called an ___(4)___; (2) the strong, athletic, muscular person who is energetic, assertive, and courageous. called a ___(5)___; and (3) the tall, thin, fragile person who is fearful, introverted and restrained, called an ___(6)___. Sheldon's theory is not widely accepted today.

In trying to establish a range of traits that make up personality, Allport sought ___(7)___ categories to describe traits. Eysenck emphasized the traits of stability-instability and ___(8)___-_________. Recent studies have revealed the existence of the big five factors of personality: neuroticism, ___(9)___, openness to ___(10)___, agreeableness and

___(11)___.

Much cross-cultural research has focused on the dichotomy of ___(12)___/_________. Some psychologists question whether it is relevant to describe entire nations as having a basic ___(13)___.

Although many consider trait approaches to be a legitimate way to describe ___(14)___ differences, trait theory has not provided ___(15)___ explanations regarding why people do what they do.

Freud was a medical doctor who developed his ideas for his theory from his work with ___(16)___ patients. When Freud began publishing his observations, some found his ideas brilliant, while others found them to be

___(17)___.

Freud believed that much more of our mind is ___(18)___ than conscious. Even trivial behaviors may have a special unconscious meaning; sometimes they slip into our behavior without our awareness, a situation known as a

___(19)___ _________.

According to Freud, personality has ___(20)___ structures. One, which is a reservoir of psychic energy and instincts and continually presses to satisfy our basic needs, is called the ___(21)___. The id works according to the ___(22)___ _________. As a child experiences the demands and constraints of society, a second personality structure called the ___(23)___ is formed. The ego tries to make the individual's pursuit of pleasure conform to social norms, a concept called the ___(24)___ _________.The ego protects us from anxiety by distorting ___(25)___. The third personality structure, the moral branch, is called the ___(26)___. The superego corresponds to our ___(27)___.

Freud believed that individuals experience pleasure in different parts of the body at different stages of development; he called these body parts ___(28)___ _________. If an individual's needs at any level of development are under- or overgratified, the result is a ___(29)___.

During the first 18 months of life, a child is in the ___(30)___ stage of development; the most pleasurable activities at this stage center around the ___(31)___.

From age 1½ to 3, the child is in the ___(32)___ stage; the child's greatest pleasure centers around the anus or ___(33)___ functions. During the next stage, the ___(34)___ stage, pleasure centers on the ___(35)___. It is during this period that the ___(36)___ _________ develops. From age 6 until puberty, the child represses all interest in sexual urge and is said to be in the ___(37)___ stage. The final stage, which begins at puberty, is the ___(38)___ stage. The source of pleasure now becomes sexual feelings for someone outside the ___(39)___.

The key objections to Freud's theory are (1) that the pervasive force behind personality is not ___(40)___, (2) the first ___(41)___ years of life are not as powerful in shaping personality, (3) the ego and ___(42)___ thought play more important roles than Freud believed, and (4) ___(43)___ factors are more important than Freud believed.

Karen Horney rejected the notion that anatomy determines ___(44)___. She suggested that the need for

___(45)___, rather than sex or aggression, was the prime human motive. She also suggested that people cope with anxiety by moving ___(46)___ people, moving ___(47)___ from people, or moving ___(48)___ people.

Jung's approach involved the belief that the roots of our personality go back to the beginning of ___(49)___ ________. Jung called this common heritage the ___(50)___ ________, and he called the impressions that common ancestral experiences made in the mind ___(51)___. Archetypes reside deep within the unconscious mind; for this reason, Jung's theory is often called ___(52)___ psychology. Two common archetypes are ___(53)___ and animus.

Adler's theory, which focused on the uniqueness of every person, is called ___(54)___ psychology. He disputed Freud's emphasis on sexual motivation, believing we can consciously monitor and ___(55)___ our lives. According to Adler, all individuals strive for ___(56)___. In order to overcome real or imagined weaknesses, we use ___(57)___. An exaggerated effort to conceal a weakness is called ___(58)___. A person who exaggerates feelings of inadequacy has an inferiority complex, whereas a person who exaggerates self-importance to mask feelings of inferiority has a ___(59)___ complex. Adler also highlighted the importance of ___(60)___ ________ in explaining personality.

Although many psychologists agree that early experiences are important determinants of personality and that personality should be studied developmentally, the main concepts of psychoanalytic theories have been difficult to ___(61)___. Other criticisms of the psychoanalytic perspective are that it overemphasizes ___(62)___ and that it has a male bias.

In contrast to the psychoanalysts, behaviorists believe that personality is ___(63)___ ________, which is determined by experiences with the environment. For B. F. Skinner, personality is a collection of ___(64)___ behaviors. Behaviorists who support Skinner's view believe consistency in behavior comes from consistent ___(65)___ experiences. Critics claim behaviorism is too ___(66)___ and suggest it is not possible to account for all behaviors using rewards and ___(67)___.

A contemporary version of behaviorism emphasizing cognition, behavior, and the environment, is called ___(68)___ ________ ________ theory. Walter Mischel believes personality varies considerably from one context to the next, a position called ___(69)___. Research supports the following: the narrower a trait the ___(70)___ likely the trait will predict behavior; some people consistently demonstrate some ___(71)___; personality traits exert a stronger influence when ___(72)___ influences are less powerful; people choose some situations and ___(73)___ others. Situationism led learning theorists to adopt a more ___(74)___ point of view. Mischel believes that ___(75)___ ________ ________ is an important factor in determining personality. Bandura believes that we acquire much behavior through the process of ___(76)___. He also emphasizes the importance of ___(77)___-________, the belief that one can master a situation and produce positive outcomes.

The cognitive social learning view is fragmented and has been criticized for being too concerned with ___(78)___ and for ignoring the ___(79)___ qualities of personality.

A view that stresses the importance of our perceptions of ourselves and our world is the ___(80)___ worldview. In this approach, reality for each person is what that individual ___(81)___. The most widely adopted phenomenological approach is the ___(82)___ perspective.

Carl Rogers, a humanistic psychologist, believed that love and praise often are not given unless we conform to ___(83)___ or social standards; thus, each of us is a victim of ___(84)___ ________ regard. Through an individual's experiences of the world, a ___(85)___ emerges. ___(86)___-________ refers to individuals' overall perceptions of their abilities, behaviors, and personality. Maladjustment results when there are large discrepancies between our experiences, our ___(87)___ self, and our ___(88)___ self. Rogers believed we should all be valued and feel accepted regardless of our behavior, a situation called ___(89)___ ________ ________. According to Rogers, humans are highly resilient and capable of becoming ___(90)___ ________.

Abraham Maslow, who called the humanistic approach the "___(91)___ ________," believed that people strive for self-actualization. A weakness of the humanistic approach is that its key concepts are very difficult to test ___(92)___.

The varying personality theories can be compared and contrasted along the following dimensions: (1) the relative importance of biological versus ___(93)___ factors; (2) the forces that ___(94)___ personality; (3) the ___(95)___ of personality across situations; (4) the influence of the ___(96)___ mind on personality; and (5) an optimistic or ___(97)___ view of human nature.

Personality Assessment

"If you make your descriptions broad enough, any person can fit the description." This is the ___(98)___ ________. The personality tests chosen for use by a psychologist frequently depend on the psychologist's ___(99)___ orientation. Also, most personality tests measure ___(100)___ characteristics. Tests that assess personality traits by asking individuals about their traits are called ___(101)___-________ tests. Although many early self-report tests were constructed using ___(102)___ ________, these assume that individuals respond honestly. However, even if an individual is honest, he or she may be giving ___(103)___ ________ answers.

Tests that select items that predict a particular criterion are called ___(104)___ ________ tests. A widely used self-report personality test used originally with individuals with mental disorders is the ___(105)___ ________ ________ ________ (MMPI). Much research has found that the MMPI is able to improve the diagnosis of ___(106)___ ________ individuals. The MMPI has been criticized for being biased in terms of ___(107)___, ethnicity, and ___(108)___. The five-factor model of personality has encouraged the development of ___(109)___-________tests to define the personality factors. Some tests present individuals with an ambiguous stimulus and then ask for a description or story. These tests are called ___(110)___ tests. A well-known projective test is the ___(111)___ ________ ________. Although many clinical psychologists use the test, researchers have found it to have low ___(112)___ and ___(113)___. Another projective test, which consists of a series of ambiguous pictures about which individuals are asked to tell a story, is the ___(114)___ ________ ________.

An assessment technique that observes an individual's behavior directly is called ___(115)___ ________.

Sociocultural Worlds/Applications in Psychology

In your own words, summarize the material you have read in Sociocultural Worlds "Freud's Theory of the Oedipus Complex: Culturally and Gender Biased," Sociocultural Worlds, "How Collectivists and Individualists Can Interact More Effectively." Briefly describe how each of these articles relates to the information contained in the chapter.

Concept Check

Major Theories of Personality

Theorist	Approach	Basic Components of Theory
1. Freud	Psychoanalytic	Emphasis on id, ego, superego; importance of displacement and identification; and five stages of personality development: oral, anal, phallic, latency, and genital.
2. Jung	Psychoanalytic	____________
3. ________	Psychoanalytic	Effort to overcome feelings of inferiority is primary emphasis.
4. Horney	________	Need for security is the prime motive for humans.
5. ________	Behaviorism	Personality is an individual's behavior, determined by the external environment.
6. Bandura and Mischel	Cognitive social learning	____________
7. ________ ________	Humanistic	Importance is placed on self, self-concept, and unconditional positive regard.
8. Maslow	________	Self-actualization, deficiency needs, and metaneeds are primary components.

Answers

2. Emphasis on archetypes; personal unconscious, and collective unconscious.
3. Adler
4. Psychoanalytic
5. Skinner
6. This theory emphasizes the role of cognitive behavior and environment in personality development.
7. Carl Rogers
8. Humanistic

Multiple-Choice Questions

Practice Test 1

After answering all the multiple-choice questions in Practice Test 1, compare your answers with the answer key provided at the end of the chapter. The answer key contains a brief explanation of both the correct and incorrect answers. Each of these questions is keyed to the Learning Objectives for the chapter. If you answer any questions incorrectly, review the corresponding Learning Objective and text material before you proceed to Practice Test 2.

1. Each of the following is part of the definition of personality *except*
   a. thoughts
   b. emotions
   c. behaviors
   d. rational

LO 1

2. Each of the following is considered one of the "big five" factors in personality *except*
   a. extroversion.
   b. neuroticism.
   c. intellect.
   d. conscientiousness.

LO 2

3. Each of the following is a component of Eysenck's personality dimensions *except*
   a. stability
   b. introversion
   c. endomorph
   d. extraversion

LO 2

4. Subordinating personal goals to preserve group integrity is a characteristic of
   a. individualism.
   b. collectivism.
   c. self-actualization.
   d. introversion.

LO 3

5. According to psychoanalytic theorists, personality is primarily shaped by
   a. unconscious processes.
   b. modeling.
   c. cognitive processes.
   d. free will.

LO 4

6. According to Freud, which part of the personality is dominated by the pleasure principle?
   a. the id
   b. the conscience
   c. the ego
   d. the superego

LO 5

7. In Freud's theory, the reality principle applies to the
   a. id.
   b. ego.
   c. superego
   d. conscience.

LO 5

8. During the Oedipus complex,
   a. the child enters the anal stage.
   b. the boy identifies with his father.
   c. the girl becomes confused about her gender identity.
   d. the genital stage begins.

LO 6

9. According to Freud, mature love relationships are possible only for those who have achieved the
   a. oral stage.
   b. phallic stage
   c. latency stage.
   d. genital stage.

LO 6

10. According to Jung, archetypes
    a. are conscious events.
    b. are responsible for hallucinations and delusions.
    c. are derived from the collective unconscious.
    d. cause inferiority and superiority complexes.

LO 7

11. The influence of birth order on personality was emphasized by
    a. Freud.
    b. Jung.
    c. Horney.
    d. Adler

LO 7

12. According to Walter Mischel, a key to understanding personality is the concept of
    a. delay of gratification.
    b. striving for superiority.
    c. unconditional positive regard.
    d. observational learning.

LO 8

13. Personality is the sum total of our behaviors, according to
    a. Skinner.
    b. Freud.
    c. Mischel.
    d. Bandura.

LO 8

14. Conditional and unconditional positive regard are important concepts in
    a. the behavioral perspective.
    b. the social learning perspective.
    c. the humanistic perspective.
    d. trait theory.

LO 9

15. Which of the following approaches regards instincts and needs as being an important determinant of personality?
    a. psychoanalysis
    b. behaviorism
    c. humanistic psychology
    d. trait psychologists

LO 10

16. Which theory of personality suggests humans have the ability to choose their behavior?
    a. psychoanalysis
    b. behaviorism
    c. humanistic psychology
    d. trait psychologists

LO 10

17. "This is a test of your imagination. I am going to show you some pictures, and I want you to tell me an interesting story about each one. What is happening, how did it develop, and how will it end?" These instructions would most likely be part of the preparation for the
    a. Thematic Apperception Test.
    b. Rorschach inkblot test.
    c. MMPI.
    d. self-report test.

LO 11

18. A widely used self-report test is the
    a. MMPI.
    b. Rorschach Inkblot Test.
    c. Thematic Apperception Test.
    d. behavioral assessment profile.

LO 11

19. A basic assumption of behavioral assessment is that
    a. the unconscious always influences behavior.
    b. personality cannot be evaluated apart from the environment.
    c. traits are consistent even in varying situations.
    d. personality is inherited.

LO 12

20. Which of the following reflects the influence of social learning theory on assessment procedures?
    a. increasing use of projective questions
    b. decreasing use of self-report tests
    c. increasing use of cognitive assessment
    d. decreasing use of cognitive assessment

LO 12

Practice Test 2

The following multiple-choice questions also are keyed to the chapter Learning Objectives. If you answer any questions incorrectly, be sure to review the corresponding Learning Objective and text material.

1. Each of the following is part of the definition of personality *except*
   a. distinctive
   b. enduring
   c. individual
   d. group

LO 1

2. Bill is curious, imaginative and somewhat unconventional. According to the five-factor model of personality, Bill would score high in
   a. openness to experience.
   b. agreeableness.
   c. conscientiousness.
   d. extraversion.

LO 2

3. Maria's friends describe her as hard-working and ambitious. According to the five-factor model of personality, she would score high in
   a. openness to experience.
   b. agreeableness.
   c. conscientiousness.
   d. extraversion.

LO 2

4. Those societies that emphasize service to the group and subordination of personal goals are said to value
   a. collectivism.
   b. individualism.
   c. self-actualization.
   d. both *a* and *c*

LO 3

5. According to the psychoanalytic perspective, personality
   a. is learned.
   b. is the result of cognition.
   c. is largely unconscious.
   d. entirely rational

LO 4

6. According to Freud, the executive branch of the personality is called the
   a. ego.
   b. superego.
   c. id.
   d. conscience.

LO 5

7. According to Freud, the source of guilt feelings is the
   a. id.
   b. ego.
   c. superego.
   d. latency stage.

LO 5

8. During what Freudian stage of development does the child focus on social and intellectual skills?
   a. the oral stage
   b. the anal stage
   c. the latency stage
   d. the genital stage

LO 6

9. According to Frued, the stage associated with the first 18 months of life is the
   a. oral stage.
   b. anal stage.
   c. latency stage.
   d. phallic stage.

LO 6

10. People cope with anxiety by either moving toward people, away from people, or against people, according to
    a. Freud.
    b. Jung.
    c. Horney.
    d. Adler.

LO 7

11. The terms "inferiority complex" and "superiority complex" are associated with the theory of
    a. Freud.
    b. Jung.
    c. Adler.
    d. Horney.

LO 7

12. An important difference between the approaches of Skinner and Mischel relates to the role of
    a. the unconscious.
    b. cognition.
    c. early childhood events.
    d. emphasis on empirical research.

LO 8

13. According to behaviorists, which of the following would be most likely to lead to a change in personality?
    a. maturation
    b. changing one's cognitions
    c. changing one's environment
    d. increasing an awareness of one's unconscious

LO 8

14. According to Rogers, acceptance of another person regardless of the person's behavior is called
    a. conditional positive regard.
    b. unconditional positive regard.
    c. self-actualization.
    d. empathy.

LO 9

15. Which personality theorists view personality pessimistically?
    a. Freudian psychoanalysts
    b. behaviorists
    c. cognitive social learning theorists
    d. humanists

LO 10

16. Which personality theory focuses on the unconscious mind?
    a. Freudian psychoanalysts
    b. behaviorists
    c. cognitive social learning theorists
    d. humanists

LO 10

17. Which type of personality test is designed to elicit the individual's unconscious feelings?
    a. self-report tests
    b. the MMPI
    c. empirically keyed tests
    d. projective tests

LO 11

18. What kinds of personality tests have been constructed in conjunction with the five-factor model of personality?
    a. projective tests
    b. self-report tests
    c. behavioral assessment
    d. apperception tests

LO 11

19. Which approach to measuring personality assumes that personality cannot be meaningfully evaluated apart from the environment?
    a. projective tests
    b. self-report tests
    c. behavioral assessments
    d. empirically keyed tests

LO 12

20. The increasing emphasis on assessing expectations, planning and memory reflects the influence of
    a. psychoanalysts.
    b. social learning theorists.
    c. humanists.
    d. trait theorists.

LO 12

Answers to Who Am I Quiz

1. e	5. d
2. h	6. g
3. a	7. c
4. f	8. b

Answers to Key Terms

1. **Personality** is the enduring thoughts, emotions, and behaviors that characterize the way an individual adapts to the world.
2. **Traits** are broad dispositions that lead people to respond in characteristic ways.
3. **Trait theories** propose that people have broad dispositions that are reflected in the basic ways they behave.
4. **Somatotype theory,** which Sheldon developed, states that an individual's body type is associated with certain personality characteristics.
5. **Endomorph** was Sheldon's term for a soft, round, large-stomached person who is relaxed, gregarious, and loves food.
6. **Mesomorph** was Sheldon's term for a strong, athletic person who is energetic, assertive, and courageous.
7. **Ectomorph** was Sheldon's term for a tall, thin, fragile person, who is fearful, introverted, and courageous.
8. **Introversion** refers to individuals who are reserved, independent and quiet.
9. **Extraversion** refers to people who are sociable, active, and fun-seeking.
10. The **five-factor model** views personality as composed of five main factors: neuroticism, extraversion, openness to experience, agreeableness, and conscientiousness.
11. **Individualism** involves giving priority to personal goals over group goals. It emphasizes values that serve the self such as feeling good, personal distinctions, and independence.
12. **Collectivism** involves giving priority to group goals over individual goals. Thus, personal goals are subordinated in order to preserve group integrity, interdependence of members, and harmonious relationships.
13. The **id** is the Freudian personality structure that consists of instincts, which are the individual's reservoir of psychic energy.
14. The **pleasure principle** is the Freudian concept that the id always seeks pleasure and avoids pain.
15. The **ego** is the Freudian personality structure that deals with the demands of reality. It is the executive branch of the personality because it makes rational decisions.
16. The **reality principle** is the Freudian concept that the ego tries to make the individual's pursuit of pleasure conform to the norms of society.
17. **Defense mechanisms** reflect unconscious methods for dealing with conflict, in which the ego distorts reality.
18. The **superego** is the Freudian personality structure that is the moral branch of the personality. It takes into account whether something is right or wrong.
19. **Erogenous zones** are those parts of the body at each stage of development that, according to Freud's theory, have especially strong pleasure-giving qualities.
20. **Fixation** is a defense mechanism that occurs when the individual remains locked in an earlier developmental stage because needs are under- or overgratified.
21. The **oral stage** is Freud's first developmental stage, in which the infant's pleasure centers on the mouth.
22. The **anal stage** occurs between the ages of 1½ and 3. The child's greatest pleasure involves the anus or the elimination functions associated with it.
23. The **phallic stage** occurs between the ages of 3 and 6. During this stage, the child's pleasure focuses on the genitals and self-stimulation.
24. In the **Oedipus complex,** according to Freud's theory, the young child develops an intense desire to replace the parent of the same sex and enjoy the affections of the opposite-sex parent.
25. The **latency stage** occurs between 6 years of age and puberty. In this stage, the child represses all interest in sexuality and develops social and intellectual skills.
26. The **genital stage** occurs from puberty throughout adulthood. This stage marks a sexual reawakening, as the source of pleasure now becomes someone outside the family.
27. **Collective unconscious,** according to Jung, is the impersonal, deepest layer of the unconscious mind shared by all human beings because of their ancestral past.
28. **Archetypes,** according to Jung, are the primordial images in every individual's collective unconscious.
29. **Individual psychology** is the name Adler gave to his theory of psychology, to emphasize the uniqueness of every individual.
30. **Striving for superiority** is the term Adler gave to the human motivation to adapt to, improve, and master the environment.

31. **Compensation** is Adler's term for the individual's effort to overcome real or imagined inferiorities or weaknesses by developing her or his abilities.
32. **Overcompensation** is Adler's term for denying rather than acknowledging a real situation, or the exaggerated effort to conceal a weakness.
33. **Inferiority complex** is Adler's term for exaggerated feelings of inadequacy.
34. **Superiority complex** is Adler's term for exaggerated self-importance used to mask feelings of inferiority.
35. **Reductionistic** refers to simplifying explanations by making behavior depend on only one or two factors.
36. **Cognitive social learning theory** is the contemporary version of social learning theory. It stresses the importance of cognition, behavior, and the environment.
37. **Situationism** is Mischel's view that personality often varies considerably from one context to another.
38. **Delay of gratification** refer to the ability to defer immediate satisfaction for a more desirable future outcome.
39. **Self-efficacy** is the belief that one can master a situation and produce positive outcomes.
40. The **phenomenological worldview** stresses the importance of our perceptions of ourselves and our world in understanding personality.
41. **Humanistic theory** stresses the capacity for personal growth, freedom to choose one's destiny and positive qualities.
42. **Conditional positive regard** is Rogers's term for the concept that love and praise are only given when an individual conforms to parental or societal standards.
43. **Self-concept,** is an individual's overall perception of her or his abilities, behavior, and personality.
44. **Unconditional positive regard** is Rogers's term of accepting, valuing, and being positive toward another person, regardless of the person's behavior.
45. The **Barnum effect,** named after circus owner P. T. Barnum, states that if you make your descriptions broad enough, any person can fit them.
46. **Self-report tests** assess personality traits by asking what their traits are; these tests are not designed to reveal unconscious personality characteristics.
47. **Face validity** is an assumption that the content of the test items are a good indicator of what the individual's personality is like.
48. **Social desirability** occurs when an individual responds according to what he or she thinks the examiner wants to hear or in a way that makes the individual look better.
49. **Empirically keyed tests** rely on the test items to predict a particular criterion: empirically keyed tests make no assumptions about the nature of the items.
50. The **Minnesota Multiphasic Personality Inventory (MMPI)** is a widely used self-report personality test. Most widely used in clinical and research settings.
51. **Projective tests** present individuals with an ambiguous stimulus and then asks them to describe it or tell a story about it.
52. The **Rorschach inkblot test** is a projective test that uses perceptions of inkblots to determine personality.
53. The **Thematic Apperception Test** is an ambiguous projective test designed to elicit stories that reveal information about an individual's personality.

Answers to Guided Review

1. personality (p. 372)
2. dispositions (p. 372)
3. somatotype (p. 373)
4. endomorph (p. 373)
5. mesomorph (p. 373)
6. ectomorph (p. 373)
7. overarching (p. 374)
8. introversion-extraversion (p. 374)
9. extraversion (p. 374)
10. experience (p. 375)
11. conscientiousness (p. 376)
12. individualism/collectivism (p. 376)
13. personality (p. 377)
14. individual (p. 377)
15. deeper (p. 377)
16. neurotic (p. 379)
17. outrageous (p. 379)
18. unconscious (p. 379)
19. Freudian slip (p. 379)
20. three (p. 379)
21. id (p. 379)
22. pleasure principle (p. 379)
23. ego (p. 380)
24. reality principle (p. 380)
25. reality (p. 380)
26. superego (p. 380)
27. conscience (p. 537)
28. erogenous zones (p. 538)
29. fixation (p. 380)
30. oral (p. 380)
31. mouth (p. 380)
32. anal (p. 382)
33. eliminative (p. 382)
34. phallic (p. 382)
35. genitals (p. 382)
36. Oedipus complex (p. 382)
37. latency (p. 382)
38. genital (p. 382)
39. family (p. 382)
40. sexuality (p. 382)
41. 5 (p. 382)
42. conscious (p. 382)
43. sociocultural (p. 384)
44. behavior (p. 382)
45. security (p. 384)
46. toward (p. 384)
47. away (p. 384)
48. against (p. 384)
49. human existence (p. 384)
50. collective unconscious (p. 384)
51. archetypes (p. 384)
52. depth (p. 384)
53. anima (p. 384)
54. individual (p. 384)
55. direct (p. 385)
56. superiority (p. 385)
57. compensation (p. 385)
58. overcompensation (p. 385)
59. superiority (p. 385)
60. birth order (p. 385)
61. test (p. 385)
62. sexuality (p. 386)
63. observable behavior (p. 388)
64. overt (p. 388)
65. environmental (p. 388)
66. reductionistic (p. 388)
67. punishments (p. 388)
68. cognitive social learning (p. 389)
69. situationsism (p. 389)
70. more (p. 389)
71. traits (p. 389)
72. situational (p. 389)
73. avoid (p. 389)
74. cognitive (p. 389)
75. delay of gratification (p. 389)
76. imitation (p. 390)
77. self-efficacy (p. 390)
78. change (p. 390)
79. enduring (p. 390)
80. phenomenological (p. 390)
81. perceives (p. 390)
82. humanistic (p. 391)
83. parental (p. 391)
84. conditional positive (p. 390)
85. self (p. 390)
86. Self-concept (p. 390)
87. real (p. 390)
88. ideal (p. 390)
89. unconditional positive regard (p. 390)
90. fully functioning (p. 391)
91. third force (p. 393)
92. scientifically (p. 394)
93. experience (p. 396)
94. drive (p. 396)
95. consistency (p. 396)
96. unconscious (p. 396)
97. pessimistic (p. 396)
98. Barnum effect (p. 397)
99. theoretical (p. 398)
100. stable (p. 398)
101. self-report (p. 398)
102. face validity (p. 398)
103. socially desirable (p. 398)
104. empirically keyed (p. 398)
105. Minnesota Multiphasic Personality Inventory (p. 399)
106. mentally disturbed (p. 399)
107. culture (p. 399)
108. gender (p. 399)
109. self-report (p. 400)
110. projective (p. 400)
111. Rorschach inkblot test (p. 400)
112. reliability (p. 401)
113. validity (p. 401)
114. Thematic Apperception Test (p. 401)
115. behavioral assessment (p. 402)

Answers to Multiple Choice Questions- Practice Test 1

1. a. Incorrect. Psychologists define personality as enduring, distinctive thoughts, emotions and behaviors that characterize the way a person interacts with the world.
   b. Incorrect. Psychologists define personality as enduring, distinctive thoughts, emotions and behaviors that characterize the way a person interacts with the world.
   c. Incorrect. Psychologists define personality as enduring, distinctive thoughts, emotions and behaviors that characterize the way a person interacts with the world.
   d. **Correct.** Rationality is not part of the definition of personality.

2. a. Incorrect. According to the five-factor model, personality consists of five main factors: neuroticism, extroversion, openness to experience, agreeableness, and conscientiousness.
   b. Incorrect. According to the five-factor model, personality consists of five main factors: neuroticism, extroversion, openness to experience, agreeableness, and conscientiousness.
   c. **Correct.** Intellect is not one of the "big five" factors in personality.
   d. Incorrect. According to the five-factor model, personality consists of five main factors: neuroticism, extroversion, oneness to experience, agreeableness, and conscientiousness.

3. a. Incorrect. Eysenck found evidence for only two dimensions of personality: stability versus instability, and introversion versus extroversion.
   b. Incorrect. Eysenck found evidence for only two dimensions of personality: stability versus instability, and introversion versus extroversion.
   c. **Correct.** Being an endomorph is not a component of Eysenck's personality dimensions. It is a term from Sheldon's somatotype theory.
   d. Incorrect. Eysenck found evidence for only two dimensions of personality: stability versus instability, and introversion versus extroversion.

4. a. Incorrect. Individualism gives priority to personal goals rather than to group goals.
   b. **Correct.** Collectivism places emphasis on values that serve the group by subordinating personal goals to preserve group integrity, the interdependence of members, and harmonious relationships.
   c. Incorrect. Self-actualization is the on-going process of fully developing one's personal potential.
   d. Incorrect. Introversion is the tendency to be reserved, independent, and quiet.

5. a. **Correct.** According to psychoanalytic theorists most of the influences on our behavior are unconscious, driven by sexual and aggressive impulses.
   b. Incorrect. Cognitive social learning theorists, such as Albert Bandura, are the ones who have pointed out the importance of modeling in personality development.
   c. Incorrect. Cognitive social learning theorists are the ones who stress the importance of cognitive processes in determining personality.
   d. Incorrect. The role of free will in personality development is stressed by humanistic theorists.

6. a. **Correct.** The id works according to the pleasure principle, the Freudian concept that the id always seeks pleasure and avoids pain.
   b. Incorrect. According to Freud's theory, the conscience is our superego and is not dominated by the pleasure principle but by morality.
   c. Incorrect. The ego is not dominated by the pleasure principle, but abides by the reality principle.
   d. Incorrect. According to Freud's theory, the superego is our conscience and is not dominated by the pleasure principle but by morality.

7. a. Incorrect. The id works according to the pleasure principle, not the reality principle.
   b. **Correct.** The ego abides by the reality principle, the Freudian concept that the ego tries to make the pursuit of individual pleasure conform to the norms of society.
   c. Incorrect. According to Freud's theory, the superego is our conscience and is not dominated by the reality principle but by morality.
   d. Incorrect. According to Freud's theory, the conscience is our superego and is not dominated by the pleasure principle but by morality.

8. a. Incorrect. The Oedipus complex is triggered during the phallic stage, not the anal stage.
   b. **Correct.** According to Freud, boys repress lustful feelings for their mother and identify with their father to resolve the Oedipus complex.
   c. Incorrect. Freud proposed that resolving the Oedipus complex clarifies gender identity.
   d. Incorrect. According to Freud, the Oedipus complex is triggered during the phallic stage, which is followed by the latent, not the genital, stage.

9. a. Incorrect. Freud believed that unresolved conflicts with parents emerge during the genital stage, and that once these conflicts are resolved, the individual becomes capable of developing a mature love relationship.
   b. Incorrect. Freud believed that unresolved conflicts with parents emerge during the genital stage, and that once these conflicts are resolved, the individual becomes capable of developing a mature love relationship.
   c. Incorrect. Freud believed that unresolved conflicts with parents emerge during the genital stage, and that once these conflicts are resolved, the individual becomes capable of developing a mature love relationship.
   d. Correct. Freud believed that unresolved conflicts with parents emerge during the genital stage, and when these conflicts are resolved, the individual becomes capable of developing a mature love relationship.

10. a. Incorrect. Archetypes are the primordial influences in every individual's collective unconscious that filter our perceptions and experiences.
    b. Incorrect. Archetypes are not responsible for altered states of consciousness.
    c. Correct. Archetypes are the primordial influences in every individual's collective unconscious that filter our perceptions and experiences.
    d. Incorrect. An inferiority complex refers to exaggerated feelings of inadequacy while a superiority complex refers to exaggerated self-importance. Neither are caused by archetypes.

11. a. Incorrect. Adler, not Freud, highlighted the importance of birth order in explaining an individual's personality.
    b. Incorrect. Adler, not Jung, highlighted the importance of birth order in explaining an individual's personality.
    c. Incorrect. Adler, not Horney, highlighted the importance of birth order in explaining an individual's personality.
    d. **Correct.** Adler highlighted the importance of birth order in explaining an individual's personality.

12. a. **Correct.** Mischel's main research area is delay of gratification, the ability to defer immediate satisfaction for a more desirable future outcome.
    b. Incorrect. Striving for superiority emphasizes the human motivation to adapt, improve, and master the environment. Adler is the one who thought that everyone strives for superiority.
    c. Incorrect. Unconditional positive regard is Rogers's, not Mischel's, term for accepting, valuing, and being positive toward another person regardless of the person's behavior.
    d. Incorrect. Bandura is the one who proposed that we acquire an extensive amount of behavior through observational learning, or imitation.

13. a. **Correct.** In Skinner's view, personality simply consists of the collection of the person's observed, overt behaviors.
    b. Incorrect. Freud would disagree with this statement. He believed that most influences on our behavior are unconscious.
    c. Incorrect. Mischel shared Skinner's belief about the importance of the environment on our behavior, but also stressed the importance of cognition.
    d. Incorrect. Bandura shared Skinner's belief about the importance of the environment on our behavior, but, like Mischel, also stressed the importance of cognition.

14. a. Incorrect. Conditional and unconditional positive regard stem from the humanistic view that, for each individual, reality is what that person perceives. The concept of multiple realities is not part of the behavioral perspective.
    b. Incorrect. Conditional and unconditional positive regard stem from the humanistic view that, for each individual, reality is what that person perceives. Although social learning theorists emphasize the important influence of different situational contexts on behavior, the influence of different personal perspectives is not a part of their theory.
    c. **Correct.** Conditional positive regard refers to making the bestowal of love or praise conditional on the individual's conformity to parental or social standards. Unconditional positive regard is the term for accepting, valuing, and being positive toward another person regardless of the person's behavior. Both terms are part of the humanistic perspective.
    d. Incorrect. Conditional and unconditional positive regard stem from the humanistic view that, for each individual, reality is what that person perceives. Trait theories emphasize particular aspects of personality rather than personal perspectives.

15. a. **Correct.** According to psychoanalytic theory, a large part of our personality operates to satisfy our instincts and needs.
    b. Incorrect. Behaviorists believe that personality is the individual's behavior, which is determined by the external environment, not internal instincts and needs.
    c. Incorrect. Humanistic psychologists believe that people are driven by a desire for personal growth, not by aggressive and sexual instincts.
    d. Incorrect. Trait psychologists propose that people have broad dispositions that are reflected in the basic ways they behave, such as whether they are outgoing and friendly or withdrawn and moody.

16. a. Incorrect.The humanistic perspective stresses a person's freedom to choose their own destiny. Psychoanalytic theory suggests that behavior is largely determined by unconscious drives.
    b. Incorrect. The humanistic perspective stresses a person's freedom to choose their own destiny. Behaviorists believe behavior is largely determined by the environment.
    c. **Correct.** Humanistic psychology stresses a person's freedom to choose their own destiny.
    d. Incorrect. Trait psychologists propose that people have broad dispositions that are reflected in the basic ways they behave, such as whether they are outgoing and friendly or withdrawn and moody.

17. a. **Correct.** Instructions for administering the Thematic Apperception Test include asking the subject to tell a story about several pictures, including events leading up to the situation described, the characters' thoughts and feelings, and how the situation turns out.
    b. Incorrect. In the Rorschach inkblot test, individual's are asked their perceptions of inkblots rather than pictures.
    c. Incorrect. The MMPI is a self-report personality test in which individuals indicate whether they agree or disagree with a series of statements.
    d. Incorrect. Self-report tests assess personality traits by asking individuals what their traits are. In this example, traits were not measured directly through self-report, but through telling a story about ambiguous stimuli. This is an example of a projective test.

18. a. **Correct.** The MMPI is the most widely used self-report personality test.
b. Incorrect. The Rorschach Inkblot test is a projective test, not a self-report measure.
c. Incorrect. The Thematic Apperception Test is a projective test, not a self-report measure.
d. Incorrect. In the behavioral assessment profile, information about an individual is obtained from an outside observer rather than through self-report.

19. a. Incorrect. Behavioral assessment emerged from the behaviorist tradition and does not stress the role of the unconscious.
b. **Correct.** Instead of removing situational influences from personality, as projective tests and self-report measures do, behavioral assessment assumes that personality cannot be evaluated apart from the environment.
c. Incorrect. Instead of removing situational influences from personality, as projective tests and self-report measures do, behavioral assessment assumes that personality cannot be evaluated apart from the environment.
d. Incorrect. Behavioral assessment emerged from the behaviorist tradition which does not emphasize the influence of genetics on personality development.

20. a. Incorrect. The influence of social learning theory has increased the use of cognitive assessment in personality evaluation.
b. Incorrect. The influence of social learning theory has increased the use of cognitive assessment in personality evaluation.
c. **Correct.** The influence of social learning theory has increased the use of cognitive assessment in personality evaluation.
d. Incorrect. The influence of social learning theory has increased the use of cognitive assessment in personality evaluation.

Answers to Multiple Choice Questions- Practice Test 2

1. a. Incorrect. Psychologists define personality as enduring, <u>distinctive</u> thoughts, emotions and behaviors that characterize the way an individual interacts with the world.
b. Incorrect. Psychologists define personality as <u>enduring</u>, distinctive thoughts, emotions and behaviors that characterize the way an individual interacts with the world.
c. Incorrect. Psychologists define personality as enduring, distinctive thoughts, emotions and behaviors that characterize the way an <u>individual</u> interacts with the world.
d. **Correct.** Psychologists define personality as enduring, distinctive thoughts, emotions and behaviors that characterize the way an individual, not a group, interacts with the world.

2. a. **Correct.** Openness to experience is the degree to which a person actively seeks out and appreciates experiences for their own sake. On the high end of the continuum, individuals show curiosity, imagination, and some unconventionality in their values.
b. Incorrect. Agreeableness is the degree to which a person compassionately connects with others.
c. Incorrect. Conscientiousness is the degree of organization, self-control, and persistence a person shows in pursuing goals.
d. Incorrect. Extroversion is the amount and intensity of preferred interpersonal interactions.

3. a. Incorrect. Openness to experience is the degree to which a person actively seeks out and appreciates experiences for their own sake.
   b. Incorrect. Agreeableness is the degree to which a person compassionately connects with others.
   c. **Correct.** Conscientiousness is the degree of organization, self-control, and persistence a person shows in pursuing goals. Conscientious people tend to be hardworking, ambitious, and driving.
   d. Incorrect. Extroversion is the amount and intensity of preferred interpersonal interactions.

4. a. **Correct.** Collectivism places emphasis on values that serve the group by subordinating personal goals to preserve group integrity, the interdependence of members, and harmonious relationships.
   b. Incorrect. Individualism gives priority to personal goals rather than to group goals.
   c. Incorrect. Self-actualization is the on-going process of fully developing one's personal potential.
   d. Incorrect. Collectivism does emphasize group service and subordination of personal goals, but self-actualization stresses, rather than subordinates, personal goals.

5. a. Incorrect. It is behaviorists who believe that personality is the individual's behavior, which is learned from the environment.
   b. Incorrect. Cognitive social learning theorists are the ones who stress the importance of cognition in determining personality.
   c. **Correct.** According to the psychoanalytic perspective, most of the influences on our behavior are unconscious.
   d. Incorrect. None of the major personality theories view personality as entirely rational.

6. a. **Correct.** The ego is called the executive branch of the personality because it makes rational decisions.
   b. Incorrect. The superego is the moral branch of the personality.
   c. Incorrect. The id is the Freudian structure of personality that consists of instincts and operates according to the pleasure principle.
   d. Incorrect. Freud called our conscience the id. It basically consists of instincts and operates according to the pleasure principle.

7. a. Incorrect. The id and ego have no morality and, therefore, do not produce guilt feelings.
   b. Incorrect. The id and ego have no morality and, therefore, do not produce guilt feelings.
   c. **Correct.** The superego is our conscience, taking into account whether something is right or wrong. The superego can produce guilt feelings when our thoughts or behavior do not live up to its ideals.
   d. Incorrect. Freud's latency stage of psychosexual development occurs approximately between 6 years of age and puberty. During this time the child represses all interest in sexuality and develops social and intellectual skills.

8. a. Incorrect. The oral stage occurs during the first 18 months of life when the child's focus centers around the mouth.
   b. Incorrect. The anal stage occurs between 1 1/2 and 3 years of age, when Freud claims the child's greatest pleasure involves the anus or the elimination functions associated with the anus.
   c. **Correct.** Freud's latency stage occurs approximately between 6 years of age and puberty. During this time the child represses all interest in sexuality and develops social and intellectual skills.
   d. Incorrect. The genital stage occurs from puberty on. This is a time of sexual reawakening when the source of sexual pleasure becomes someone outside of the family.

9. a. **Correct.** The oral stage is the term Freud used to describe development in the first 18 months of life.
   b. Incorrect. The anal stage occurs between 1 1/2 and 3 years of age.
   c. Incorrect. Freud's latency stage of psychosexual development occurs approximately between 6 years of age and puberty.
   d. Incorrect. The phallic stage occurs between the ages of 3 and 6.

10. a. Incorrect. Freud proposed that we use defense mechanisms to cope with anxiety.
b. Incorrect. Jung suggested that the roots of our behavior are tied to the collective unconscious and archetypes.
c. **Correct.** Horney suggested that people usually develop one of three strategies in their effort to cope with anxiety; moving toward people, moving away from people, and moving against people.
d. Incorrect. Adler's theory emphasized the uniqueness of every individual and proposed that everyone strives for superiority.

11. a. Incorrect. Freud emphasized the role of the unconscious in personality development.
b. Incorrect. Jung believed that the collective unconscious and primordial influences filter all of our perceptions and experiences.
c. **Correct.** Adler thought that everyone strives for superiority. Inferiority complex is the name Adler gave to exaggerated feelings of inadequacy. Superiority complex is his concept for exaggerated self-importance designed to mask feelings of inferiority.
d. Incorrect. Horney believed that the need for security is the prime motive in human existence.

12. a. Incorrect. Skinner and Mischel both deemphasize the role of the unconscious in personality development.
b. **Correct.** Cognitive social learning theorists, like Mischel agree with Skinner about personality being strongly influenced by environmental experiences. But they think Skinner went too far by ruling out cognition in understanding personality.
c. Incorrect. Skinner and Mischel both deemphasize the role of early childhood events in personality development.
d. Incorrect. Skinner and Mischel both emphasized the importance of empirical research.

13. a. Incorrect. Developmental theorists, like Freud, emphasize the role of maturation in personality change more than behaviorists.
b. Incorrect. Cognitive social learning theorists stress the importance of cognition in determining personality.
c. **Correct.** Behaviorists believe that the individual's personality can be changed by rearranging the environment.
d. Incorrect. Psychoanalysts stress the role of the unconscious in personality development.

14. a. Incorrect. Conditional positive regard refers to making the bestowal of love or praise conditional on the individual's conformity to parental or social standards.
b. **Correct.** Unconditional positive regard is the term for accepting, valuing, and being positive toward another person regardless of the person's behavior.
c. Incorrect. Self-actualization is the on-going process of fully developing one's personal potential.
d. Incorrect. Empathy is the capacity for taking another's point of view.

15. a. **Correct.** Freudian psychoanalysts emphasize conflicts, anxiety, sexual impulse and negative forces in our lives. Their approaches have been criticized for viewing personality too pessimistically.
b. Incorrect. Behaviorists' mechanistic view of personality is neither pessimistic or optimistic, but neutral.
c. Incorrect. Cognitive social learning theorists take the optimistic view that we have the ability to control our own environments.
d. Incorrect. Humanists view personality optimistically. The believe that each of us has the ability to cope with stress, to control our lives, and to achieve what we desire.

16. a. **Correct.** According to Freudian psychoanalysts, most of the influences on our behavior are unconscious, driven by sexual and aggressive impulses.
b. Incorrect. Behaviorists view personality simply as a collection of the person's observed, overt behaviors. They do not include internal traits or thoughts, like the unconscious, in their view of personality.
c. Incorrect. It was disagreement with psychanalytic ideas, like the unconscious, that launched the cognitive movement in personality theory. Cognitive social learning theorists stress the importance of cognition, behavior, and environment in determining personality.

d. Incorrect. Humanists focus on our conscious lives rather than on the unconscious.

17. a. Incorrect. Self-report tests assess personality traits by asking what they are; these tests are not designed to reveal unconscious personality characteristics.
b. Incorrect. The MMPI is a self report test. Self-report tests are not designed to reveal unconscious personality characteristics.
c. Incorrect. Empirically keyed tests are self-report tests. Self-report tests are not designed to reveal unconscious personality characteristics.
d. **Correct.** Projective tests are especially designed to elicit an individual's unconscious feelings and conflicts.

18. a. Incorrect. The popularity of the five-factor model has encouraged the development and use of self-report strategies to define personality factors.
b. **Correct.** The popularity of the five-factor model has encouraged the development and use of self-report strategies to define personality factors.
c. Incorrect. The popularity of the five-factor model has encouraged the development and use of self-report strategies to define personality factors.
d. Incorrect. The popularity of the five-factor model has encouraged the development and use of self-report strategies to define personality factors.

19. a. Incorrect. The developers of behavioral assessment believe that projective tests remove environmental forces from personality.
b. Incorrect. The developers of behavioral assessment believe that self-report tests remove environmental forces from personality.
c. **Correct.** Instead of removing situational influences from personality, as projective tests and self-report measures do, behavioral assessment assumes that personality cannot be evaluated apart from the environment.
d. Incorrect. The developers of behavioral assessment believe that empirically keyed tests remove environmental forces from personality.

20. a. Incorrect. The influence of social learning theory, not psychoanalytic theory, has increased emphasis on assessing expectations, planning, and memory.
b. **Correct**. The influence of social learning theory has increased emphasis on assessing expectations, planning, and memory.
c. Incorrect. The influence of social learning theory, not humanistic theory, has increased emphasis on assessing expectations, planning, and memory.
d. Incorrect. The influence of social learning theory, not trait theory, has increased emphasis on assessing expectations, planning, and memory.

Chapter **11** **Abnormal Psychology**

Learning Objectives

After studying this chapter, you should be able to:

1. Identify the variety of approaches used to define abnormality. (p. 408)

2. Describe the following causes of abnormal behavior: biological factors, psychological factors, and sociocultural factors. (p. 409)

3. Discuss the importance of gender, ethnicity, and socioeconomic factors in abnormal behavior. (p. 410)

4. Describe the purpose and content of the DSM-IV and the controversies surrounding its use. (p. 413)

5. Identify the following anxiety disorders: generalized anxiety, panic, phobic, obsessive-compulsive, and post-traumatic stress. (p. 415)

6. Contrast the following somatoform disorders: hypochondriasis and conversion disorder. (p. 420)

7. Distinguish among amnesia, fugue, and dissociative identity disorder. (p. 421)

8. Distinguish between the following mood disorders: major depression and bipolar disorder. (p. 423)

9 Identify the factors that are involved in suicide. (p. 426)

10. Explain the causes of mood disorders from the following perspectives: psychoanalytic, cognitive and learning, biogenetic, and sociocultural. (p. 426)

11. Discuss the characteristics of schizophrenic disorders. (p. 428)

12. Distinguish among the following types of schizophrenic disorders: disorganized, catatonic, paranoid, and undifferentiated. (p. 431)

13. Discuss the role of genetic, neurobiological, environmental, and sociocultural factors in schizophrenia. (p. 432)

14. Describe the characteristics of individuals experiencing the following personality disorders: schizotypal, obsessive-compulsive, borderline, and antisocial. (p. 433)

15. Discuss the characteristics of those experiencing substance-use disorders. (p. 435)

16. Discuss the following legal aspects of mental disorders: civil commitment, criminal commitment, insanity, and competency. (p. 436)

Chapter 12 Outline

I. Dimensions of Abnormality
  A. Defining Abnormality
    1. Statistical prevalence
    2. Maladaptiveness and Harmfulness
    3. Personal discomfort
    4. Cultural influences
  B. The Origins of Abnormal Behavior
    1. The Biological Approach
    2. The Psychological Approaches
    3. The Sociocultural Approach
  C. Prevalence Estimates
    1. Gender Prevalence
    2. Ethnicity, Socioeconomic, and Cultural Factors
    3. Interactionist Approaches
  D. Classifying Abnormal Behavior
    1. Advantages and Disadvantages of Diagnosis
    2. Using the DSM-IV
      a. Clinical disorders
      b. Personality Disorders/Developmental Problems
      c. General Medical Conditions
      d. Psychosocial and Environmental Problems
      e. Global Assessment of Functioning
    3. The Controversy Surrounding the DSM-IV
II. Diagnostic Categories of Mental Disorders
  A. Anxiety disorders
    1. Generalized Anxiety Disorder
    2. Panic Disorder
    3. Phobic Disorders
    4. Obsessive-Compulsive Disorders
    5. Post-Traumatic Stress Disorder
  B. Somatoform Disorders
    1. Hypochondriasis
    2. Conversion Disorder
  C. Dissociative Disorders
    1. Amnesia and Fugue
    2. Dissociative Identity Disorder
  D. Mood Disorders
    1. Major Depression
    2. Bipolar Disorder
    3. Suicide
    4. Explanations of Mood Disorders
      a. psychoanalytic explanations
      b. cognitive and learning explanations
      c. biogenic explanations
      d. sociocultural explanations
  E. Schizophrenic Disorders
    1. Characteristics of schizophrenic disorders
    2. Forms of schizophrenic disorders
      a. disorganized schizophrenia
      b. catatonic schizophrenia
      c. paranoid schizophrenia
      d. undifferentiated schizophrenia
    3. Explanations of Schizophrenia
      a. genetic factors
      b. neurobiological factors
      c. environmental factors
      d. sociocultural factors
  F. Personality Disorders
    1. Schizotypal Personality disorder
    2. Obsessive-compulsive personality disorder
    3. Borderline personality disorder
    4. Antisocial personality disorder
  G. Substance Use Disorders
III. Legal Aspects of Mental Disorders
  A. Commitment and Dangerousness
  B. Criminal Responsibility

Key Terms

Write a brief description for each of the following terms. Where relevant, provide an original example or illustration of the term. Then, compare your answers with those provided at the end of the Study Guide chapter. Review the text for those terms you don't know and those you define incorrectly.

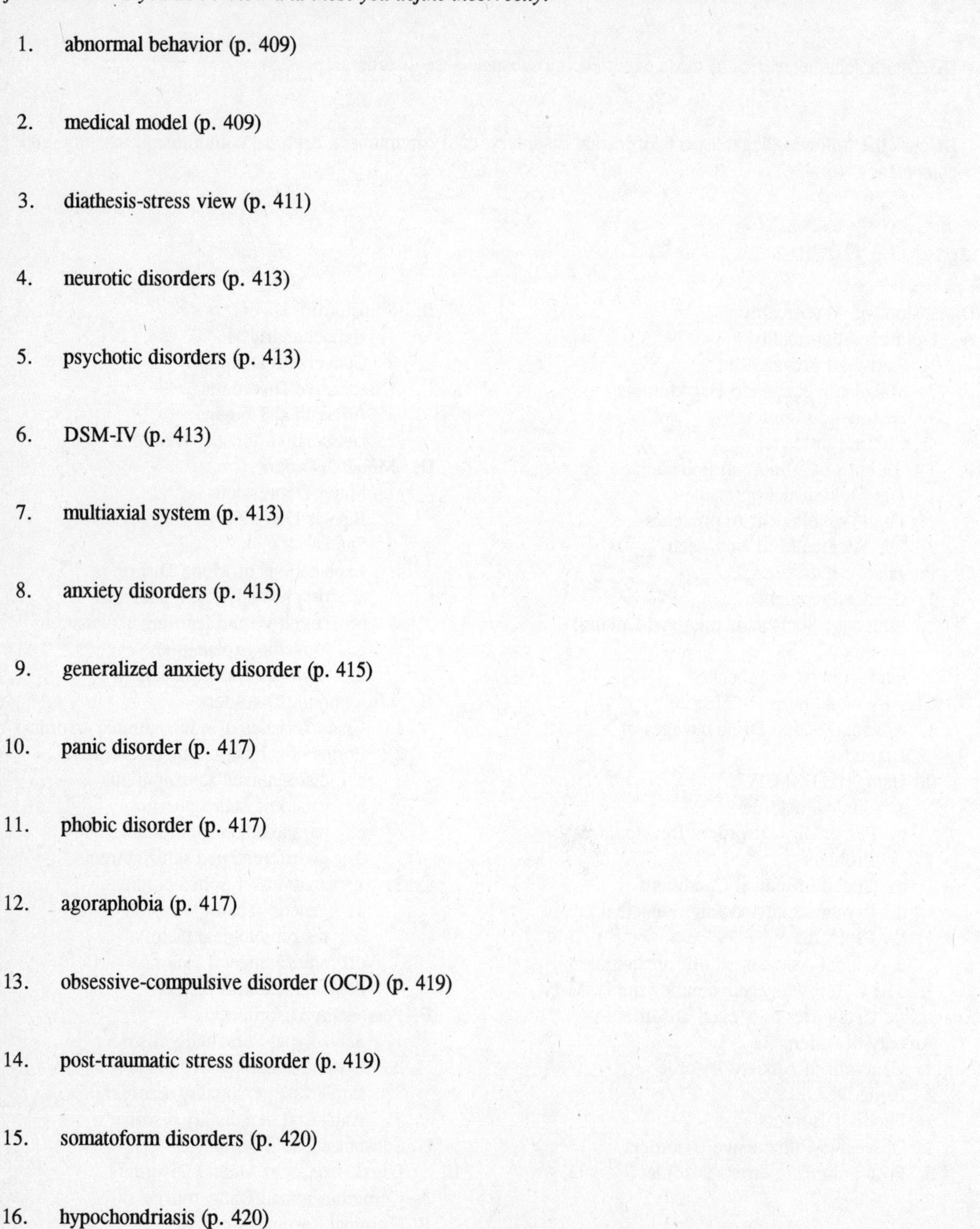

1. abnormal behavior (p. 409)

2. medical model (p. 409)

3. diathesis-stress view (p. 411)

4. neurotic disorders (p. 413)

5. psychotic disorders (p. 413)

6. DSM-IV (p. 413)

7. multiaxial system (p. 413)

8. anxiety disorders (p. 415)

9. generalized anxiety disorder (p. 415)

10. panic disorder (p. 417)

11. phobic disorder (p. 417)

12. agoraphobia (p. 417)

13. obsessive-compulsive disorder (OCD) (p. 419)

14. post-traumatic stress disorder (p. 419)

15. somatoform disorders (p. 420)

16. hypochondriasis (p. 420)

17. conversion disorder (p. 420)

18. dissociative disorders (p. 421)

19. psychogenic amnesia (p. 421)

20. fugue (p. 421)

21. dissociative identity disorder (p. 421)

22. mood disorders (p. 423)

23. major depression (p. 423)

24. bipolar disorder (p. 424)

25. learned helplessness (p. 427)

26. schizophrenic disorders (p. 428)

27. disorganized schizophrenia (p. 431)

28. catatonic schizophrenia (p. 431)

29. paranoid schizophrenia (p. 431)

30. undifferentiated schizophrenia (p. 431)

31. personality disorders (p. 433)

32. schizotypal personality disorder (p. 434)

33. obsessive-compulsive personality disorder (p. 434)

34. borderline personality disorder (p. 435)

35. antisocial personality disorder (p. 435)

36. substance-use disorder (p. 435)

37. commitment (p. 436)

38. civil commitment (p. 436)

39. criminal commitment (p. 436)

40. insanity (p. 436)

41. insanity defense (p. 436)

42. competency (p. 437)

Guided Review

The following in-depth chapter review is a challenging and comprehensive fill-in-the-blanks exercise. The answers are found near the end of the chapter. As you go through the exercise, try to resist the temptation to look at the answers until you have provided them. When you have filled in all the blanks, you will have a thorough summary of the chapter for reference and review.

Dimensions of Abnormality

A variety of factors can help define abnormality, including ___(1)___ prevalence, maladaptiveness and ___(2)___, personal ___(3)___, and ___(4)___ influences.

An approach that view\s abnormal behavior as the result of a physical malfunction of the body is the ___(5)___ approach. The forerunner of the biological approach was the ___(6)___ model. An approach that emphasizes factors like emotional turmoil and inappropriate learning is the ___(7)___ approach. Culture, ethnicity, and gender are emphasized by the ___(8)___ approach.

A random sample of residents in the United States found that more than ___(9)___ percent had experienced a mental disturbance during the previous month. One-third of the individuals reporting mental disorders had received treatment in the previous ___(10)___ months. Women had higher rates for ___(11)___ ________, and men reported higher rates for ___(12)___-________ disorders and ___(13)___ personality disorders.

One explanation for the finding that women have overall higher rates of mental disorders than men is that women are more likely to behave in ways that others label as ___(14)___ _______. Another explanation focuses on women's unequal social position and ____(15)____. A third explanation refers to the ____(16)____-________ experienced by many women.

Research suggests that individuals who live in ____(17)____ ________ neighborhoods have higher rates of mental disorder, although the research does not explain the causes. The ____(18)____ approach suggests that biological, psychological, and sociocultural factors interact to produce abnormal behavior. A model that links genetic and environmental factors to predict risk for developing psychological problems is the ____(19)____-________ model.

The first edition of the *Diagnostic and Statistical Manual of Mental Disorders* was published in ____(20)____. The current edition, ____(21)____, was published in 1994.

Classification systems for mental disorders allow psychologists to ____(22)____ with each other, allow psychologists to construct ____(23)____, and help psychologists do a better job of ____(24)____ psychological disturbances. Research suggests that a client's ____(25)____ may adversely influence the assessment and diagnosis of mental disorders. Cultural differences in behavior, historical difficulties between ethnic groups, and ethnic and social class ____(26)____ in diagnosis all contribute to the problem.

Two important terms that were included in DSM-II but not in DSM-III are ____(27)____, which consists of relatively mild mental disorders, and ____(28)____, which involves severe mental disturbances and a loss of contact with ____(29)____. These terms were dropped because the categories were too broad and ill-defined to be useful.

DSM-IV uses a five-dimensional ____(30)____ system to assess individuals. The professionals who helped to develop DSM-IV were a more ____(31)____ group than those who developed previous editions. DSM-IV is also based on more ____(32)____ data than its predecessors. Controversies surrounding the DSM-IV center on its reliance on a ____(33)____ model and its inclusion of ____(34)____ problems as mental disorders. Most health professionals in other countries adopt the International Classification of Disease guidelines established by the ____(35)____ ________ ________.

Diagnostic Categories of Mental Disorders

Disorders that are characterized by motor tension, hyperactivity, and apprehensive expectations and thoughts are called ____(36)____ disorders.

A ____(37)____ ________ ________ consists of persistent anxiety for at least 1 month, although the individual is unable to specify the reasons for the anxiety. Recurrent and sudden onset of intense apprehension or terror characterizes ____(38)____ ________. Irrational, overwhelming, and persistent fear of an object or a situation is found in ____(39)____ ________. The most common phobia is ____(40)____. Fear of social situations is called ____(41)____ phobia. Psychoanalytic theorists believe that phobias develop as ____(42)____ ________, whereas learning theorists suggest that classical conditioning and observational learning explain the development of phobias. Cross-cultural psychologists suggest that ____(43)____ factors influence phobias. Other researchers suggest a possible ____(44)____ predisposition for phobias.

Anxiety-provoking thoughts that won't go away are called ____(45)____; repetitive, ritualistic behaviors performed in a stereotyped way are ____(46)____. Although these are different problems, when they are displayed in the same individual it is referred to as ___(47)___-________ disorder.

A mental disturbance that develops through exposure to traumatic events is called ___(48)___-________ ________ disorder. Anxiety symptoms may immediately follow the trauma or be delayed by months or ___(49)___.

In some mental disturbances, the psychological symptoms take a physical form, although no evidence of a physical cause can be found. These are called ___(50)___ ________.

A somatoform disorder characterized by a pervasive fear of illness and disease is ___(51)___. In another somatoform disorder, the individual converts anxiety into a specific physical symptom, although no physiological problems can be found. This is called ___(52)___ ________.

Psychological disorders that involve sudden losses of memory or changes in identity are called ___(53)___ ________Memory loss that is due to extensive psychological stress is called ___(54)___ ________. In a ___(55)___, there is a loss of memory and the individual unexpectedly travels away from home and assumes a new identity. A dramatic but less common dissociative disorder is ___(56)___ ________ disorder. A high percentage of individuals with this disorder experienced ___(57)___ or ___(58)___ abuse in childhood.

___(59)___ disorders are characterized by wide emotional swings. A mood disorder in which an individual is deeply unhappy, demoralized, self-derogatory, and bored, is ___(60)___ ________. Depression is so widespread that it is referred to as the ___(61)___ ________ of mental disorders.

Dramatic mood swings characterize the mood disorder called ___(62)___ disorder. The rate of suicide has ___(63)___ since the 1950s in the United States. Biological factors, immediately stressful circumstances, earlier experiences, high-pressure cultures, and religious factors all appear to be involved in ___(64)___.

The suggested causes of mood disorders include early childhood experiences in the ___(65)___ perspective; self-defeating thoughts and learned helplessness in cognitive and ___(66)___ explanations; genetic inheritance and chemical changes in the brain according to ___(67)___ explanations; and sociocultural factors.

The ___(68)___ ________ are characterized by distorted thoughts and perceptions, odd communication, inappropriate emotion, abnormal motor behavior, and social withdrawal. Many schizophrenics have false beliefs, called ___(69)___; they also might hear or see things not actually there, called ___(70)___. They might communicate in incoherent, loose word associations called ___(71)___ salad.

A type of schizophrenia characterized by delusions and hallucinations that have little or no recognizable meaning is ___(72)___ schizophrenia. Bizarre motor behavior is the central feature of ___(73)___ schizophrenia. In a catatonic state, an individual may show ___(74)___ flexibility. Paranoid schizophrenia is characterized by complex, elaborate ___(75)___, particularly delusions of ___(76)___, reference, and ___(77)___. A fourth form of schizophrenia, characterized by disorganized behavior, hallucinations, delusions, and incoherence, is ___(78)___ schizophrenia.

Genetic factors are strongly implicated as a cause of schizophrenia. The more ___(79)___ similar you are to a relative who has schizophrenia, the greater your chance of becoming schizophrenic. Among neurobiological factors, possible causes include brain ___(80)___ and a malfunctioning ___(81)___ system. Some researchers continue to emphasize___(82)___ factors in schizophrenia. ___(83)___ factors are also involved; the type and incidence of schizophrenia varies from culture to culture.

When personality traits become inflexible and maladaptive, personality ___(84)___ develop. One cluster of personality disorders involves odd or ___(85)___ behaviors, a second cluster emphasizes fear and ___(86)___, and a third stresses dramatic, emotional or ___(87)___ behaviors. A personality disorder characterized by rejecting or withdrawing from others is the ___(88)___ personality disorder. Persons who have ___(89)___-compulsive personality disorder tend to be exacting, precise, and orderly. A limited tolerance of frustration and a limited ability to trust others characterize the ___(90)___ personality disorder. A life of unrepentant crime, violence, and delinquency characterizes those with ___(91)___ personality disorder.

When individuals have problems associated with drug use, they are said to have a ___(92)___-________ disorder.

Legal Aspects of Mental Disorders

The process by which an individual becomes institutionalized in a mental hospital is called ___(93)___. Commitment can be voluntary or ___(94)___. When a judge deems an individual to be at risk to self or others as a result of a mental disorder, it leads to a ___(95)___ commitment. A ___(96)___ commitment occurs when an individual who has committed a crime receives commitment to a mental health hospital rather than imprisonment.

Insanity is a ___(97)___ term that means that the individual is considered mentally disordered and incapable of being responsible for her or his actions. A plea of "innocent by reason of insanity" is referred to as the ___(98)___ ________ The appropriateness of the insanity defense remains highly ___(99)___. The ability of an individual to understand and participate in a judicial proceeding is referred to as ___(100)___.

Sociocultural Worlds/Applications in Psychology

In your own words, briefly summarize the material you have read in Sociocultural Worlds, "Women and Depression," and Applications in Psychology, "Becoming Educated About Depression." Briefly describe how this material relates to the information contained in the chapter.

Concept Check

Major Disorders

Category	Description	Examples
1. Anxiety	The person suffering from anxiety is nervous, tense, and worried.	Phobias, generalized and panic anxiety disorders, PTSD, and obsessive-compulsive disorder.
2. Somatoform disorders	The individual experiences physical health problems that have psychological rather than physical causes.	________________
3. Dissociative disorders	______________________	Amnesia, fugue, and multiple personality.
4. Mood disorders	The individual has wide emotional swings.	________________
5. Schizophrenia	______________________	Paranoid, disorganized, catatonic, and undifferentiated
6. Personality disorders	The individual has inflexible and maladaptive personality traits.	________________

Answers

2. Hypochondriasis and conversion disorder.
3. The individual has sudden alterations in cognition, characterized by a change in memory, or identity.
4. Major depression, bipolar disorder.
5. The individual experiences cognitive disorders, inappropriate emotions, and social withdrawal.
6. Schizotypal, obsessive-compulsive, borderline, antisocial.

Multiple-Choice Questions

Practice Test 1

After answering all the multiple-choice questions in Practice Test 1, compare your answers with the answer key provided at the end of the chapter. The answer key contains a brief explanation of both the correct and incorrect answers. Each of these questions is keyed to the Learning Objectives for the chapter. If you answer any questions incorrectly, review the corresponding Learning Objective and text material before you proceed to Practice Test 2.

1. Each of the following factors has been used to define abnormal behavior *except*
   a. statistical prevalence
   b. maladaptiveness
   c. being different
   d. personal discomfort

LO 1

2. The causes of abnormal behavior involve emotional turmoil, inappropriate learning, and distorted thoughts, according to the
   a. biological approach.
   b. psychological approach.
   c. medical model.
   d. sociocultural approach.

LO 2

3. Each of the following groups is at risk for mental disorders *except*
   a. ethnic minority individuals
   b. women
   c. those who live closest to the center of cities
   d. residents of suburban areas

LO 3

4. Some individuals are born with a genetic predisposition toward a particular abnormal condition according to the
   a. sociocultural approach.
   b. psychological approach.
   c. diathesis-stress model.
   d. contextual approach.

LO 3

5. The DSM-IV has been criticized for each of the following *except*
   a. It contains too many characteristics of the medical model.
   b. Many psychologists find the DSM-IV to be confusing.
   c. The focus is on pathology and on finding something wrong.
   d. It contains categories for everyday problems.

LO 4

6. Stanley was fearful of developing cancer, which was the cause of the deaths of both of his parents. He avoided any situation where someone might smoke, ate no processed meat or dairy products, and would not even speak with anyone who had been diagnosed as having cancer. Wherever he was, he constantly had thoughts of himself wasting away with cancer. Stanley's thoughts were
   a. obsessions.
   b. compulsions.
   c. a generalized anxiety disorder.
   d. a conversion disorder.

LO 5

7. Jill has a recurrent condition in which she is seized by sudden, intense apprehension and terror. She is experiencing
   a. generalized anxiety disorder.
   b. panic disorder.
   c. conversion disorder.
   d. obsessive-compulsive disorder.

LO 5

8. Mary has been changing doctors frequently and can't understand why her doctors are unable to find anything physically wrong with her. Lately she has started taking many different kinds of pills, hoping that something will help. Mary is displaying the characteristics of
   a. conversion disorder.
   b. hypochondriasis.
   c. a fugue.
   d. both *b* and *c*

LO 6

9. Each of the following is a type of dissociative disorder *except*
   a. conversion reaction.
   b. psychogenic amnesia.
   c. fugue.
   d. dissociative identity disorder

LO 7.

10. The "common cold" of mental disorders is
   a. schizophrenic disorder.
   b. depression.
   c. bipolar disorder.
   d. dissociative identity disorder.

LO 8

11. In a study of gifted men and women, each of the following were predictors of suicide *except*
   a. anxiety.
   b. instability in work and relationships.
   c. financial concerns.
   d. alcoholism.

LO 9

12. Two neurotransmitters that appear to be involved in depression are norepinephrine and
   a. dopamine.
   b. epinephrine.
   c. serotonin.
   d. acetylcholine.

LO 10

13. Each of the following characterizes a schizophrenic disorder *except*
   a. several distinct personalities
   b. hallucinations
   c. delusions
   d. bizarre motor behavior

LO 11

14. Which type of schizophrenic disorder is characterized by a "waxy flexibility"?
   a. disorganized schizophrenia
   b. catatonic schizophrenia
   c. paranoid schizophrenia
   d. undifferentiated schizophrenia

LO 12

15. Regression and withdrawal from human contact characterize
   a. disorganized schizophrenia
   b. catatonic schizophrenia
   c. paranoid schizophrenia
   d. undifferentiated schizophrenia

LO 12

16. Which of the following is true regarding genetic factors in schizophrenia?
   a. The precise mechanism by which schizophrenia is inherited is now well understood.
   b. There is no evidence of a genetic link to schizophrenia.
   c. The risk of becoming schizophrenic is 46 percent for those with an schizophrenic identical twin.
   d. The average person has a 5 percent chance of becoming schizophrenic.

LO 13

17. An individual who engages in stealing and vandalism, who cannot uphold financial obligations, and who shows no remorse after harming someone may be considered to have a(n)
   a. obsessive-compulsive personality disorder.
   b. bipolar anxiety disorder.
   c. borderline personality disorder.
   d. antisocial personality disorder.

LO 14

18. Which of the following personality disorders is an example of the odd, eccentric cluster?
   a. schizotypal
   b. obsessive-compulsive
   c. antisocial.
   d. passive-aggressive.

LO 14

19. Substance-use disorders are characterized by each of the following *except*
    a. psychological dependence.
    b. impaired social or occupational functioning.
    c. financial stress caused by the expense of the substance.
    d. physical dependence.

LO 15

20. According to the text, what must take place before a civil commitment occurs?
    a. The family must request commitment of the individual.
    b. A psychiatrist must request commitment of the individual.
    c. The individual must be judged to be dangerous to himself or herself or to others.
    d. The individual must be found insane.

LO 16

Practice Test 2

The following multiple-choice questions also are keyed to the chapter Learning Objectives. If you answer any questions incorrectly, be sure to review the corresponding Learning Objective and text material.

1. Which of the following can be used to define abnormal behavior?
    a. statistical factors
    b. maladaptiveness
    c. cultural influences
    d. all of the above

LO 1

2. The disease model of abnormal behavior was the forerunner of which contemporary approach?
    a. biological
    b. psychological
    c. sociocultural
    d. statistical

LO 2

3. Each of the following is a possible explanation for the finding that women are diagnosed and treated for mental disorders at a higher rate than men *except*
    a. Women are more likely to behave in ways that are labeled as mental disorders.
    b. Women face greater discrimination and an unequal social position.
    c. Women are often placed in a double-bind situation.
    d. Women are socialized to externalize their thoughts and feelings.

LO 3

4. The diathesis-stress model views abnormal behavior as related to
    a. genetic factors.
    b. gender factors.
    c. stress factors
    d. *a* and *c* above

LO 3

5. Each of the following is an axis on the DSM multiaxial system *except*
    a. personality disorders
    b. psychological stressors in the individual's recent past
    c. individual's current level of functioning
    d. potential cures for the individual

LO 4

6. Excessive checking, cleaning, and counting are characteristic of
    a. generalized anxiety disorder.
    b. post-traumatic stress disorder
    c. panic disorder.
    d. obsessive-compulsive disorder.

LO 5

7. Deborah is an assault victim who experiences occasional flashbacks and has difficulties with memory and concentration. Jill shows symptoms of
   a. generalized anxiety disorder.
   b. post-traumatic stress disorder
   c. panic disorder.
   d. obsessive-compulsive disorder.

LO 5

8. A somatoform disorder characterized by a pervasive fear of illness and disease is called
   a. conversion disorder.
   b. obsessive-compulsive disorder.
   c. hypochondriasis.
   d. psychogenic fugue.

LO 6

9. A disorder characterized by unexpected travel away from home and a new identity is called
   a. dissociative identity disorder.
   b. psychogenic amnesia.
   c. fugue.
   d. hypochondriasis.

LO 7

10. Extreme mood swings of either manic or depressive or both characterize
   a. bipolar disorder.
   b. dissociative identity disorder.
   c. schizophrenic disorder.
   d. post-traumatic stress disorder.

LO 8

11. Which of the following statements regarding suicide is true?
   a. Males attempt suicide more frequently than females.
   b. The suicide rate in the United States has gradually declined over the past 30 years.
   c. Females are more likely than males to succeed at suicide.
   d. Suicide accounts for 12 percent of adolescent and young adult mortality.

LO 9

12. Childhood experiences are an important determinant of depression according to which theory?
   a. psychoanalytic
   b. cognitive
   c. learning
   d. biogenetic

LO 10

13. "Word salad" refers to
   a. the rapid-fire speech that characterizes individuals in the manic state.
   b. incoherent, loose word associations that characterize schizophrenic speech.
   c. the irregular speech of catatonic schizophrenics.
   d. the rambling of an individual experiencing bipolar disorder.

LO 11

14. Delusions of reference, grandeur, and persecution characterize which type of schizophrenia?
   a. disorganized
   b. catatonic
   c. paranoid
   d. undifferentiated

LO 12

15. A schizophrenic disorder that may leave an individual in a stupor is called
   a. disorganized schizophrenia.
   b. catatonic schizophrenia.
   c. paranoid schizophrenia.
   d. undifferentiated schizophrenia.

LO 12

16. Individuals experiencing schizophrenia produce an excess of the neurotransmitter
   a. serotonin.
   b. endorphin.
   c. dopamine.
   d. acetylcholine.

LO 13

17. Which of the following characterizes antisocial personality disorder?
    a. It usually begins in middle adulthood.
    b. It affects males and females equally.
    c. Most adolescents grow out of the disorder.
    d. Those with the disorder show no remorse when harming someone.

LO 14

18. Which of the following disorders is found in the anxious, fearful cluster of personality disorders?
    a. obsessive-compulsive personality disorder
    b. borderline personality disorder
    c. antisocial personality disorder
    d. schizotypal personality disorder

LO 14

19. Substance-use disorders are characterized by
    a. pathological use.
    b. social or occupational impairment.
    c. physical dependence.
    d. any of the above

LO 15

20. Which of the following is true of the concept "innocent by reason of insanity"?
    a. *Insanity* is a psychiatric term.
    b. *Insanity* is a legal term.
    c. Being judged insane implies that an individual is not responsible for his or her actions.
    d. both *b* and *c*

LO 16

Answers to Key Terms

1. **Abnormal behavior** is behavior that is maladaptive, harmful, statistically unusual, personally distressing, and/or designated abnormal by the culture.
2. The **medical model,** or the disease model, states that abnormality is a disease or illness precipitated by internal causes.
3. The **diathesis-stress view** suggests that schizophrenia is caused by a combination of environmental stress and biogenetic disposition.
4. **Neurotic disorders** are relatively mild mental disorders in which the individual has not lost contact with reality.
5. **Psychotic disorders** are severe mental disorders marked by a loss of contact with reality.
6. **DSM-IV** refers to the Fourth Edition, of the DSM. It is the most recent major classification of mental disorders.
7. The **multiaxial system** is the system of classifying individuals used in the DSM-IV. This approach classifies individuals on five dimensions or "axes."
8. **Anxiety disorders** are characterized by motor tension, hyperactivity, and apprehensive expectations and thoughts.
9. A **generalized anxiety disorder** is characterized by persistent anxiety for at least 1 month; the individual is unable to specify the reasons for the anxiety.
10. **Panic disorder** is a recurrent anxiety disorder marked by the sudden onset of intense apprehension or terror.
11. A **phobic disorder** is characterized by an irrational, overwhelming, persistent fear of a particular object or situation.
12. **Agoraphobia** is the fear of entering unfamiliar situations, especially open or public spaces. It is the most common phobic disorder.
13. **Obsessive-compulsive disorder** is characterized by anxiety-provoking thoughts that will not cease, and/or urges to perform repetitive, ritualistic behaviors to prevent or produce some future situation.
14. **Post-traumatic stress disorder** develops through exposure to traumatic events, severely oppressive situations, severe abuse, or accidental disasters. The disorder is characterized by anxiety symptoms that immediately follow the trauma or have a delayed onset.
15. **Somatoform disorders** are mental disturbances in which psychological symptoms take a physical form, although no physical causes can be found.
16. **Hypochondriasis** is a somatoform disorder in which the individual has a pervasive fear of illness and disease.
17. **Conversion disorder** is a somatoform disorder in which the individual experiences genuine physical symptoms although no physical causes can be found.
18. **Dissociative disorders** involve a sudden memory loss or change in identity.
19. **Psychogenic amnesia** is a dissociative disorder caused by extensive psychological stress; it involves memory loss.

20. **Fugue** is a dissociative disorder in which the individual develops amnesia and unexpectedly travels away from home and assumes a new identity.
21. **Dissociative identity disorder** is a dissociative disorder in which the individual has two or more distinct personalities or selves.
22. **Mood disorders** are characterized by wide emotional swings, ranging from deeply depressed to highly euphoric and agitated. Depression can occur alone or it can alternate with mania.
23. **Major depression** is a mood disorder that is characterized by extreme mood swings; an individual with this disorder might be depressed, manic, or both.
24. **Bipolar disorder** is a mood disorder that is characterized by extreme mood swings; an individual with this disorder might be depressed, manic, or both.
25. **Learned helplessness** occurs when animals or humans are exposed to aversive stimulation, such as prolonged stress or pain, over which they have no control. The inability to avoid such aversive stimulation produces an apathetic state of helplessness. According to Seligman, this is one reason many people become depressed.
26. **Schizophrenic disorders** are severe psychological disorders characterized by distorted thoughts and perceptions, odd communication, inappropriate emotion, abnormal motor behavior, and social withdrawal.
27. In **disorganized schizophrenia** the individual experiences hallucinations and delusions that have little or no recognizable meaning.
28. **Catatonic schizophrenia** is characterized by bizarre motor behavior that sometimes takes the form of a completely immobile stupor.
29. **Paranoid schizophrenia** is characterized by delusions of reference, grandeur, and persecution.
30. **Undifferentiated schizophrenia** is characterized by disorganized behavior, hallucinations, delusions, and incoherence.
31. **Personality disorders** are psychological disorders that develop when personality traits become inflexible and thus maladaptive.
32. The person with **schizotypal personality disorder** displays distasteful behavior which leads to retreat or withdrawal from others.
33. **Obsessive-compulsive personality disorder** is characterized by anxious adjustment. Individuals with this disorder tend to be exacting, precise, and orderly.
34. **Borderline personality disorder** is in the dramatic, emotional, and erratic cluster, and the person's behavior exhibits these characteristics.
35. The **antisocial personality disorder** is characterized by criminal, delinquent, and violent behavior. These individuals regularly violate the rights of others.
36. **Substance-use disorder** is characterized by one or more of the following: pathological use, impaired social or occupational functioning due to the drug, and physical dependence.
37. **Commitment** is the process by which an individual becomes institutionalized in a mental hospital.
38. A **civil commitment** occurs when a judge deems an individual to be a risk to self or others due to a mental disorder.
39. A **criminal commitment** occurs when a crime occurs and a mental disorder is implicated in the crime.
40. The **insanity defense** is a plea of "innocent by reason of insanity," used as a legal defense in criminal trials.
42. **Competency** is an individual's ability to understand and participate in a judicial proceeding.

Answers to Guided Review

1. statistical (p. 408)
2. harmfulness (p. 408)
3. discomfort (p. 408)
4. cultural (p. 409)
5. biological (p. 409)
6. medical (p. 409)
7. psychological (p. 409)
8. sociocultural (p. 410)
9. 15 (p. 410)
10. 6 (p. 410)
11. mood disorders (p. 410)
12. substance-use (p. 410)
13. antisocial (p. 410)
14. mental disorders (p. 410)
15. discrimination (p. 411)
16. "double-bind" (p. 411)
17. poor minority (p. 411)
18. interactionist (p. 411)
19. diathesis-stress (p. 411)
20. 1952 (p. 412)
21. DSM-IV (p. 412)
22. communicate (p. 412)
23. theories (p. 412)
24. predicting (p. 412)
25. ethnicity (p. 412)
26. biases (p. 413)
27. neurotic (p. 413)
28. psychotic (p. 413)
29. reality (p. 413)
30. multiaxial (p. 413)
31. diverse (p. 414)
32. empirical (p. 414)
33. medical (p. 414)
34. everyday (p. 414)
35. World Health Organization (p. 414)
36. anxiety (p. 415)
37. generalized anxiety disorder (p. 415)
38. panic disorders (p. 417)
39. phobic disorders (p. 417)
40. agoraphobia (p. 417)
41. social (p. 418)
42. defense mechanisms (p. 418)
43. cultural (p. 418)
44. genetic (p. 418)
45. obsessions (p. 418)
46. compulsions (p. 586)
47. obsessive-compulsive (p. 418)
48. post-traumatic stress (p. 419)
49. years (p. 419)
50. somatoform disorders (p. 420)
51. hypochondriasis (p. 420)
52. conversion disorder (p. 420)
53. dissociative disorders (p. 421)
54. psychogenic amnesia (p. 421)
55. fugue (p. 421)
56. dissociative identity (p. 421)
57. sexual (p. 422)
58. physical (p. 422)
59. Mood (p. 423)
60. major depression (p. 423)
61. common cold (p. 423)
62. bipolar (p. 424)
63. tripled (p. 426)
64. suicide (p. 426)
65. psychoanalytic (p. 426)
66. learning (p. 427)
67. biogenetic (p. 428)
68. schizophrenic disorders (p. 428)
69. delusions (p. 430)
70. hallucinations (p. 430)
71. word (p. 431)
72. disorganized (p. 431)
73. catatonic (p. 431)
74. waxy (p. 431)
75. delusions (p. 431)
76. grandeur (p. 431)
77. persecution (p. 431)
78. undifferentiated (p. 431)
79. genetically (p. 432)
80. metabolism (p. 432)
81. dopamine (p. 432)
82. environmental (p. 432)
83. Sociocultural (p. 432)
84. disorders (p. 433)
85. eccentric (p. 433)
86. anxiety (p. 433)
87. erratic (p. 433)
88. schizotypal (p. 434)
89. obsessive (p. 434)
90. borderline (p. 434)
91. antisocial (p. 435)
92. substance-use (p. 435)
93. commitment (p. 436)
94. involuntary (p. 436)
95. civil (p. 436)
96. criminal (p. 436)
97. legal (p. 436)
98. insanity defense (p. 436)
99. controversial (p. 437)
100. competency (p. 437)

Answers to Multiple Choice Questions- Practice Test 1

1. a. Incorrect. This *has* been used to define abnormal behavior.
   b. Incorrect. This *has* been used to define abnormal behavior.
   c. **Correct.** Being different does not equate to being abnormal.
   d. Incorrect. This *has* been used to define abnormal behavior.

2. a. Incorrect. This approach seeks biological, chemical and genetic sources for explanations of abnormal behavior.
   b. **Correct.** Even within this approach, there is a wide variety of potential causes.
   c. Incorrect. This approach states that abnormality is a disease precipitated by internal causes.
   d. Incorrect. This approach emphasizes the roles of gender, social class, culture and so on.

3. a. Incorrect. These individuals *are* at risk for mental disorders.
   b. Incorrect. According to a 1990 survey, females are at slightly greater risk for mental disturbances than men.
   c. Incorrect. These individuals *are* at greater risk for mental disorders.
   d. **Correct.** These individuals are not at greater risk for mental disorders.

4. a. Incorrect. This approach focuses on social and cultural causes of mental disorders.
   b. Incorrect. this approach emphasizes emotional turmoil, learning and distorted thoughts as the causes of mental disorders.
   c. **Correct.** This interactionist approach emphasizes environmental stress and biogenetic predisposition.
   d. Incorrect. This is not a widely recognized approach (although it sounds sociocultural).

5. a. Incorrect. This *has* been a criticism of the DSM-IV.
   b. **Correct.** This has not been one of the widely stated criticism of the DSM-IV.
   c. Incorrect. This *has* been a criticism of the DSM-IV.
   d. Incorrect. This *has* been a criticism of the DSM-IV.

6. a. **Correct.** Anxiety-provoking thoughts that will not go away are called obsessions.
   b. Incorrect. This refers to ritualistic behaviors that often accompany obsessions.
   c. Incorrect. In this disorder, the individual is unable to specify the reasons for the anxiety.
   d. Incorrect. This is a somatoform disorder involving physical symptoms without any apparent cause.

7. a. Incorrect. This refers to persistent, rather than sudden anxiety.
   b. **Correct.** Many panic disorder sufferers do not feel anxiety all the time.
   c. Incorrect. This refers to a somatoform disorder in which there are physical symptoms with no apparent physical cause.
   d. Incorrect. This disorder is characterized by persistent thoughts and ritualistic behavior.

8. a. Incorrect. This is a somatoform disorder in which there are physical symptoms with no apparent physiological problems.
   b. **Correct.** Hypochondriasis is a difficult category to diagnose accurately; it often occurs in conjunction with other disorders, such as depression.
   c. Incorrect. A fugue is a conversion disorder in which an individual develops amnesia and establishes a new identity in a new location.
   d. Incorrect. The question does not describe an individual experiencing both of these disorder.

9. a. **Correct.** A conversion disorder is a somatoform disorder.
   b. Incorrect. This *is* a type of dissociative disorder.
   c. Incorrect. This *is* a type of dissociative disorder.
   d. Incorrect. This *is* a type of dissociative disorder.

10. a. Incorrect. Schizophrenia is a severe, but relatively rare disorder.
    b. **Correct.** This label isn't meant to suggest that depression is a mild disorder. It is meant to suggest that depression is a common disorder.

c. Incorrect. Bipolar disorder is a severe, but relatively rare disorder.
d. Incorrect. Dissociative identity disorder is an extreme, but rare, dissociative disorder.

11. a. Incorrect. Anxiety was a predictor of suicide in the study cited.
b. Incorrect. Instability was a predictor of suicide in the study cited.
c. **Correct.** This was not mentioned as a predictor in the study cited.
d. Incorrect. This was a predictor of suicide in the study mentioned.

12. a. Incorrect. Dopamine is cited as a factor in schizophrenia.
b. Incorrect. This is not mentioned as a factor in depression.
c. **Correct.** Individuals with unusually low levels of serotonin are 10 times more likely to commit suicide.
d. Incorrect. This is not mentioned as a factor in depression.

13. a. **Correct.** This characteristic of dissociative identity disorder is often confused with schizophrenia.
b. Incorrect. This *is* a characteristic of schizophrenic disorder.
c. Incorrect. This *is* a characteristic of schizophrenic disorder.
d. Incorrect. This *is* a characteristic of schizophrenic disorder.

14. a. Incorrect. Individuals with this disorder have hallucinations and delusions with little recognizable meaning.
b. **Correct.** This disorder is characterized by an immobile stupor.
c. Incorrect. This disorder is characterized by delusions of reference, grandeur and persecution.
d. Incorrect. This disorder is characterized by disorganized behavior, hallucinations, delusions, and incoherence.

15. a. **Correct.** Individuals with this disorder have hallucinations and delusions with little recognizable meaning.
b. Incorrect. This disorder is characterized by an immobile stupor.
c. Incorrect. This disorder is characterized by delusions of reference, grandeur and persecution.
d. Incorrect. This disorder is characterized by disorganized behavior, hallucinations, delusions, and incoherence.

16. a. Incorrect. Although a genetic link is suspected, the precise mechanism has yet to be determined.
b. Incorrect. There is strong suspicion of a genetic link to schizophrenia.
c. **Correct.** This is the type of data that leads to a strong suspicion of a genetic link to schizophrenia.
d. Incorrect. The average person has about a 1 percent chance.

17. a. Incorrect. A primary feature of this disorder is anxious adjustment.
b. Incorrect. This is not a type of personality disorder.
c. Incorrect. This disorder is characterized by instability, untrusting and fearful of being alone.
d. **Correct.** This is the most problematic type of disorder for society.

18. a. **Correct.** This type of disorder is associated with peculiar behavior and detachment from others.
b. Incorrect. This disorder is in the anxious, fearful cluster of personality disorders.
c. Incorrect. This disorder is in the dramatic, emotional, erratic cluster of personality disorders.
d. Incorrect. This disorder is in the anxious, fearful cluster of personality disorders.

19. a. Incorrect. This *is* a characteristic of substance use disorder.
b. Incorrect. This *is* a characteristic of substance-use disorder.
c. Correct. Although this may become an additional stress, it is not one of the characteristics of substance-use disorder.
d. Incorrect. This *is* a characteristic of substance-use disorder.

20. a. Incorrect. This is not sufficient to get an individual committed to a mental institution.
    b. Incorrect. This may occur, but is not a requirement.
    c. Correct. The evidence must be "clear and convincing."
    d. Incorrect. Civil commitment uses different criteria than "insanity."

Answers to Multiple Choice Questions- Practice Test 2

1. a. Incorrect. This answer is partially correct; one of the other alternatives is a better answer.
   b. Incorrect. This answer is partially correct; one of the other alternatives is a better answer.
   c. Incorrect. This answer is partially correct; one of the other alternatives is a better answer.
   d. **Correct.** Another factor mentioned in the text is "personal discomfort."

2. a. **Correct.** Brain processes and genetic factors are viewed as the primary causes of abnormal behavior.
   b. Incorrect. The disease model views behavior as an illness precipitated by internal causes.
   c. Incorrect. The disease model views behavior as an illness precipitated by internal causes.
   d. Incorrect. The disease model views behavior as an illness precipitated by internal causes.

3. a. Incorrect. This statement is true; women are more likely to behave in these ways.
   b. Incorrect. This statement is true; women *do* face greater discrimination.
   c. Incorrect. This statement is true; women *are* often placed in a double-bind situation.
   d. **Correct.** Women are socialized to internalize their thoughts and feelings.

4. a. Incorrect. This answer is partially correct. One of the other alternatives is a better answer.
   b. Incorrect. Gender factors are not viewed as a direct factor in abnormal behavior, according to this model.
   c. Incorrect. This answer is partially correct. One of the other alternatives is a better answer.
   d. **Correct.** This model views abnormal behavior as caused by the interaction of environmental factors and biogenetic disposition.

5. a. Incorrect. This *is* an axis on the DSM-IV multiaxial system.
   b. Incorrect. This *is* an axis on the DSM-IV multiaxial system.
   c. Incorrect. This *is* an axis on the DSM-IV multiaxial system.
   d. **Correct.** This does not constitute an axis on the DSM multiaxial model.

6. a. Incorrect. Individuals experiencing this type of anxiety are unable to specify the reasons for their anxiety.
   b. Incorrect. This disorder is characterized by anxiety symptoms related to a traumatic experience.
   c. Incorrect. This is a recurrent anxiety disorder marked by the sudden onset of intense apprehension or terror.
   d. **Correct.** Remember that obsessions refer to anxiety-provoking thoughts and compulsions refer to urges to perform behaviors, rituals, and so on.

7. a. Incorrect. Individuals experiencing this type of anxiety are unable to specify the reasons for their anxiety.
   b. **Correct.** The anxiety symptoms may be delayed by months or even by years.

c. Incorrect. This is a recurrent anxiety disorder marked by the sudden onset of intense apprehension or terror.
d. Incorrect. Obsessions refer to anxiety-provoking thoughts ,and compulsions refer to urges to perform behaviors, rituals, and so on.

8. a. Incorrect. A conversion disorder is a somatoform disorder, but the individual experiences genuine physical symptoms, even though no physiological problems can be found.
b. Incorrect. This is an anxiety disorder. Obsessions refer to anxiety-provoking thoughts, and compulsions refer to urges to perform behaviors, rituals, and so on.
c. **Correct.** This is a difficult category to accurately diagnose; it frequently occurs in conjunction with other disorders, such as depression.
d. Incorrect. This is a dissociative disorder involving amnesia and a new identity.

9. a. Incorrect. This disorder, formerly called multiple personality, is characterized by the development of two or more distinct personalities.
b. Incorrect. This is a dissociative disorder involving memory loss caused by extensive psychological stress.
c. **Correct.** This may last briefly over for several years.
d. Incorrect. This is a somatoform disorder characterized by pervasive fear of illness and disease.

10. a. **Correct.** This was formerly called manic-depressive disorder.
b Incorrect. This was formerly called multiple personality disorder.
c. Incorrect. This is a severe disorder characterized by distorted thoughts and perceptions, odd communication, inappropriate emotion, abnormal motor behavior and social withdrawal.
d. Incorrect. This anxiety disorder is a reaction to a severe trauma.

11. a. Incorrect. The reverse is true.
b. Incorrect. According to the text, the suicide rate has tripled since the 1950s.
c. Incorrect. The reverse is true.
d. **Correct.** The suicide rate begins to rise rapidly after age 15.

12. a. **Correct.** Freud viewed depression as a turning inward of aggressive instincts.
b. Incorrect. This explanation involves self-defeating and sad thoughts.
c. Incorrect. The learning approach emphasizes such factors as learned helplessness.
d. Incorrect. This explanation involves genetic inheritance and chemical changes in the brain.

13. a. Incorrect. Word salad has a different meaning.
b. **Correct.** When people with schizophrenia talk, their language often appears not to follow any rules.
c. Incorrect. Catatonic schizophrenia is characterized by bizarre motor behavior, including an immobile stupor.
d. Incorrect. Word salad has a different meaning.

14. a. Incorrect. This type of schizophrenia is characterized by delusions and hallucinations that have little or no recognizable meaning.
b. Incorrect. This type of schizophrenia is characterized by bizarre motor behavior, including an immobile stupor.
c. **Correct.** Individuals with this disorder often misinterpret random events as being directly related to their own lives.
d. Incorrect. This disorder is characterized by disorganized behavior, hallucinations, delusions and incoherence.

15. a. Incorrect. This type of schizophrenia is characterized by delusions and hallucinations that have little or no recognizable meaning.
b. **Correct.** Some individuals in this state show a waxy flexibility.
c. Incorrect. Individuals with this disorder often misinterpret random events as being directly related to their own lives.
d. Incorrect. This disorder is characterized by disorganized behavior, hallucinations, delusions and incoherence.

16. a. Incorrect. This transmitter is associated with depression.
b. Incorrect. This refers to a powerful opiate-like neurotransmitter.
c. **Correct.** Schizophrenics tend to produce an excess of dopamine.
d. Incorrect. This neurotransmitter has not been linked to schizophrenia.

17. a. Incorrect. This disorder usually begins in childhood.
b. Incorrect. This disorder is more typical of males than females.
c. Incorrect. It is a difficult disorder to treat.
d. **Correct.** Therefore, virtually any kind of antisocial behavior is possible.

18. a. **Correct.** Anxious adjustment is the primary feature.
b. Incorrect. This disorder is in the dramatic, emotional, erratic cluster of personality disorders.
c. Incorrect. This disorder is in the dramatic, emotional, erratic cluster of personality disorders.
d. Incorrect. This disorder is in the odd, eccentric cluster.

19. a. Incorrect. This answer is partially correct, however one of the other answers is a better alternative.
b. Incorrect. This answer is partially correct, however one of the other answers is a better alternative.
c. Incorrect. This answer is partially correct, however one of the other answers is a better alternative.
d. **Correct.** Biògenetic, psychological and sociocultural factors may be involved in substance-use disorder.

20. a. Incorrect. Insanity is neither a psychiatric nor a psychological term.
b. Incorrect. Although this statement is true, one of the other answers is a better alternative.
c. Incorrect. Although this statement is true, one of the other answers is a better alternative.
d. **Correct.** The appropriateness of the insanity plea remains highly controversial.

Chapter **12** **Therapies**

Learning Objectives

After studying this chapter, you should be able to:

1. Trace the history of efforts to treat mental disorders. (p. 444)

2. Define psychotherapy. (p. 446)

3. Discuss the variety of orientations to psychotherapy. (p. 446)

4. Describe the variety of mental health practitioners and settings, and discuss the importance of socioeconomic factors in obtaining psychotherapy. (p. 446)

5. Describe the following psychoanalytic techniques: free association, catharsis, interpretation, dream analysis, transference, and resistance. (p. 449)

6. Contrast the contemporary psychodyanamic therapies and the traditional Freudian approach. (p. 451)

7. Contrast the therapeutic approaches taken by person-centered therapy and Gestalt therapy. (p. 452)

8. Describe the characteristics shared by behavior therapies. (p. 453)

9. Contrast classical conditioning and operant conditioning approaches to therapy, and describe cognitive behavioral therapy. (p. 453)

10. Distinguish between rational-emotive therapy and Beck's cognitive therapy. (p. 457)

11. Identify the following group therapy approaches: family and couple therapy, personal growth groups, and self-help groups. (p. 459)

12. Discuss the community psychology movement. (p. 463)

13. Describe the results of research on the effectiveness of psychotherapy. (p. 465)

14. Discuss the concerns about factors such as gender, ethnicity, and social class in psychotherapy. (p. 467)

15. Describe the following biomedical therapies: drug therapy, electroconvulsive therapy, and psychotherapy. (p. 472)

Chapter 12 Outline

I. The Nature of Therapy
  A. Historical Viewpoint
    1. Trephining
    2. Exorcism
    3. Asylums
  B. Contemporary Practice
    1. Orientations
      a. insight therapy
      b. action therapy
      c. eclectic
    2. Practitioners and settings
    3. Access to services
    4. Ethical standards

II. Individual Therapies
  A. Psychodynamic Therapies
    1. Freud's Psychoanalysis
      a. psychoanalysis
      b. dream analysis
        (1) manifest content
        (2) latent content
        (3) transference
        (4) resistance
    2. Contemporary Psychodynamic Therapies
  B. Humanistic Therapies
    1. Person-centered therapies
      a. genuineness
      b. accurate empathy
      c. active listening
    2. Gestalt therapy
  C. Behavior Therapies
    1. Classical conditioning approaches
      a. systematic desensitization
      b. aversive conditioning
    2. Operant conditioning approaches
      a. behavior modification
      b. token economy
    3. Cognitive behavior therapies
  D. Cognitive Therapies
    1. Ellis' Rational-Emotive Therapy
    2. Beck's Cognitive Therapy

III. Systems Interventions
  A. Group Therapies
    1. Family and Couple Therapy
    2. Personal Growth Groups
    3. Self-help groups
  B. Community Psychology
    1. Primary Prevention
    2. Secondary Prevention
    3. Tertiary Prevention

IV. Is Psychotherapy Effective?
  A. Outcome Research on Effectiveness of Psychotherapy
  B. Common Themes and Specificity in Psychotherapy
  C. Gender Issues in Treatment Effectiveness
  D. Ethnicity and Social Class Issues in Treatment Effectiveness

V. Biomedical Therapies
  A. Drug Therapy
    1. Antianxiety Drugs
    2. Antidepressant drugs
    3. Antipsychotic drugs
  B. Phototherapy
  C. Electroconvulsive Therapy
  D. Psychosurgery

Key Terms

Write a brief description for each of the following terms. Where relevant, provide an original example or illustration of the term. Then, compare your answers with those provided at the end of the Study Guide chapter. Review the text for those terms you don't know and those you define incorrectly.

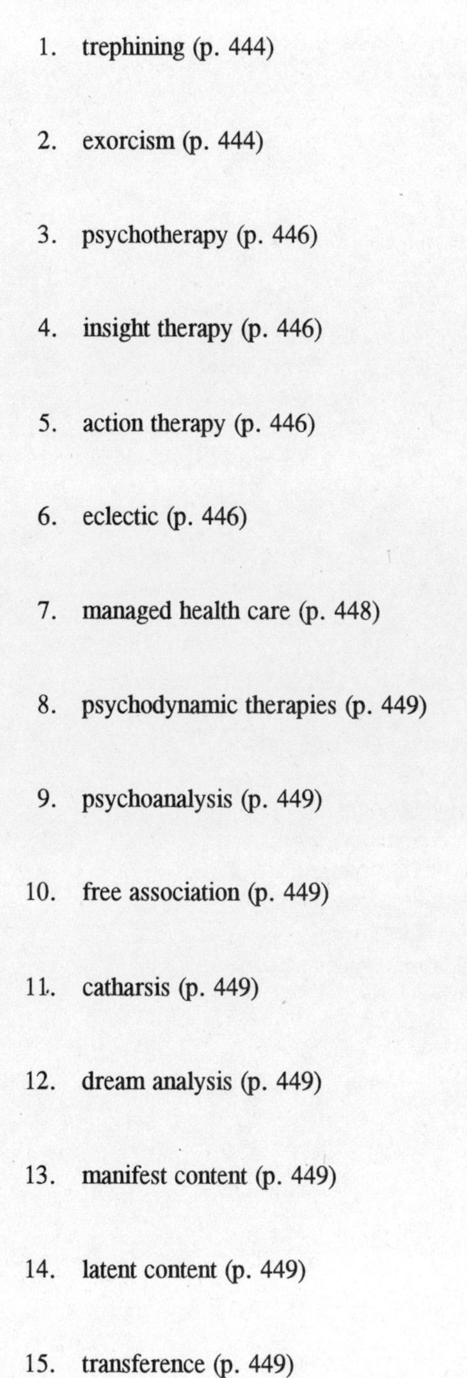

1. trephining (p. 444)

2. exorcism (p. 444)

3. psychotherapy (p. 446)

4. insight therapy (p. 446)

5. action therapy (p. 446)

6. eclectic (p. 446)

7. managed health care (p. 448)

8. psychodynamic therapies (p. 449)

9. psychoanalysis (p. 449)

10. free association (p. 449)

11. catharsis (p. 449)

12. dream analysis (p. 449)

13. manifest content (p. 449)

14. latent content (p. 449)

15. transference (p. 449)

16. resistance (p. 450)

17. humanistic psychotherapies (p. 451)

18. person-centered therapy (p. 452)

19. genuineness (p. 452)

20. accurate empathy (p. 452)

21. active listening (p. 452)

22. Gestalt therapy (p. 452)

23. behavior therapies (p. 453)

24. systematic desensitization (p. 454)

25. aversive conditioning (p. 454)

26. token economy (p. 455)

27. cognitive behavior therapy (p. 455)

28. self-efficacy (p. 456)

29. self-instructional methods (p. 456)

30. cognitive therapies (p. 456)

31. rational-emotive therapy (p. 457)

32. family therapy (p. 460)

33. couples therapy (p. 460)

34. family systems therapy (p. 460)

35. personal growth groups (p. 462)

36. encounter group (p. 462)

37. self-help groups (p. 462)

38. deinstitutionalization (p. 463)

39. primary prevention (p. 464)

40. secondary prevention (p. 464)

41. tertiary prevention (p. 464)

42. empowerment (p. 465)

43. meta-analysis (p. 465)

44. credibility (p. 471)

45. giving (p. 471)

46. biomedical therapies (p. 472)

47. antianxiety drugs (p. 472)

48. antidepressant drugs (p. 472)

49. lithium (p. 473)

50. antipsychotic drugs (p. 473)

51. tardive dyskinesia (p. 473)

52. electroconvulsive therapy (ECT) (p. 474)

53. psychosurgery (p. 475)

Guided Review

The following in-depth chapter review is a challenging and comprehensive fill-in-the-blanks exercise. The answers are found near the end of the chapter. As you go through the exercise, try to resist the temptation to look at the answers until you have provided them. When you have filled in all the blanks, you will have a thorough summary of the chapter for reference and review.

The Nature of Therapy

In ancient societies, a technique called ___(1)___ was used for mentally disabled people. In the Middle Ages, mentally disabled individuals' "evilness" was treated by ___(2)___. During the Renaissance, the mentally disabled were housed in ___(3)___.

Reform in ___(4)___ led to improved conditions in asylums. In the United States, the efforts of Dorothea Dix were instrumental in separating the mentally disabled from ___(5)___.

___(6)___ is the process mental health professionals use to work with individuals to reduce their problems and improve their adjustment. A wide variety of psychotherapeutic techniques exist today. The goal of both the psychodynamic and the humanistic therapies is to encourage insight and awareness of self; therefore, they are called ___(7)___ therapies. Therapies that promote direct changes in behavior are called ___(8)___ therapies. Most therapists use a variety of approaches to therapy; that is, they are ___(9)___. A variety of mental health professionals practice psychotherapy; these include psychologists, ___(10)___, and counselors. Psychotherapists have been criticized for preferring to work with "young, ___(11)___, verbal, ___(12)___, and successful" clients, called YAVISes, instead of "quiet, ugly, old, ___(13)___, and ___(14)___" clients, called QUOIDs. A survey of clinical psychologists indicates that clients from lower socioeconomic classes have poor prognoses for therapy, and that clinical psychologists prefer to work with clients from ___(15)___ socioeconomic classes.

A dramatic change in the way psychotherapists are paid for services has occurred recently. A system in which external reviewers approve the length and type of treatment to justify insurance reimbursement is called ___(16)___ ________ ________. A criticism of this approach is that it favors ___(17)___-________ over ___(18)___-________ therapy. Other problems include the potential violation of ___(19)___ and the costs of establishing a ___(20)___.

Ethical standards, to which licensed mental health practitioners must conform, include doing no harm to clients, protecting clients' ___(21)___, avoiding ___(22)___ relationships with clients, and staying updated.

Individual Therapies

The types of therapies that stress the importance of the unconscious mind, extensive interpretation by a therapist, and the role of the infant and childhood experiences are called ___(23)___ therapies. A well-known psychodynamic approach was developed by Freud; it is called ___(24)___. According to this approach, psychological problems can be traced to childhood experiences, often involving conflicts about ___(25)___. These conflicts are ___(26)___. Special therapeutic techniques help bring these conflicts into ___(27)___. One technique, in which the patient lies on a couch and is encouraged to talk freely, is called ___(28)___ ________. Freud thought when clients talked freely, their emotional tension could be released, a process called ___(29)___. Psychoanalysts interpret a client's dreams in the technique called ___(30)___ ________. Freud called the conscious, remembered aspects of a dream the ___(31)___ content, and he called the unconscious, symbolic aspects of a dream the ___(32)___ content.

Often, patients relate to the therapist in ways that reproduce important relationships in the patient's life, a process called ___(33)___. The client's unconscious defense strategies that prevent an analyst from understanding the client's problems are called ___(34)___. Showing up late or arguing with the psychoanalyst are examples of resistance.

An important theme in contemporary psychodynamic theories is the development of the self in ___(35)___ ________.

Clients are encouraged to understand themselves and to grow personally in the ___(36)___ psychotherapies. One type of humanistic psychotherapy, developed by Carl Rogers, is called ___(37)___-________ therapy. According to Rogers, the positive regard we receive from others has strings attached, which he refers to as ___(38)___ ________ ______ Rogers believes that therapists should create a warm and caring environment and display ___(39)___ _______ ________. Additionally, Rogers believes that therapists must not hide behind a facade; in other words, therapists must be ___(40)___ Therapists should have the ability to identify with the client, which he called ___(41)___ ________. Also, therapists should restate and support what clients say and do, a process called ___(42)___ ________.

In another type of humanistic psychotherapy, therapists question and challenge clients to help them become aware of their feelings. This approach is called ___(43)___ therapy and was founded by ___(44)___. In this technique, therapists set examples, encourage ___(45)___ between verbal and nonverbal behavior, and use ___(46)___ playing. Gestalt therapy is much more ___(47)___ than person-centered therapy.

Behavior therapies use the principles of ___(48)___ to reduce or eliminate maladaptive behavior. Two procedures deal with behaviors learned through ___(49)___ conditioning. One procedure, which treats anxiety by getting clients to relax as they visualize anxiety-producing situations, is ___(50)___ ________. Research suggests that this technique is an effective way to treat a number of ___(51)___.

A second technique that is based on classical conditioning repeatedly pairs undesirable behavior with an aversive stimulus; this is called ___(52)___ ________.

Other behavior therapy techniques make use of ___(53)___ conditioning in order to change the individual's environment; this process is often called ___(54)___ ________.

A technique that allows individuals to earn tokens that can later be exchanged for desired rewards is called a ___(55)___ ________.

A behavior therapy that helps individuals behave more adaptively by modifying their thoughts is called ___(56)___ ________ therapy. According to Bandura, the belief that one can master a situation and produce positive outcomes is important in producing ___(57)___ behavior. Bandura calls this ___(58)___-________. Cognitive behavior therapies have also emphasized teaching individuals to modify their own behavior, a technique called the ___(59)___-________ method.

A cognitive therapy based on the idea that individuals become psychologically disturbed because of their irrational and self-defeating beliefs is called ___(60)___-________ therapy. In this type of therapy, the therapist ___(61)___ the individual's self-defeating beliefs and encourages the individual to change his or her ___(62)___ system.

The cognitive therapy of Aaron Beck has focused on treating a variety of dysfunctions, especially ___(63)___.

Systems Interventions

The following features make group therapy attractive: (1) the individual receives ___(64)___ from either the group leader or group members; (2) group members realize that others are suffering also, a feature called ___(65)___; (3) group members can support one another, a feature termed ___(66)___; (4) corrective ___(67)___ of the family group; (5) development of ___(68)___ skills; and (6) ___(69)___ learning.

Group therapy with family members is called ___(70)___ therapy; therapy with couples that focuses on their relationship is called couple therapy. ___(71)___ ________ therapy stresses that an individual's psychological adjustment is related to patterns of interaction within the family. Four widely used techniques in family systems therapy are (1) ___(72)___, (2) reframing. (3) ___(73)___ ________, and (4) detriangulation.

Group therapies which focus on individuals whose lives are lacking in intimacy, intensity, and accomplishment are called ___(74)___ ________ groups. These groups have their roots in the ___(75)___ therapies. A type of group designed to promote self-understanding through candid group interaction is called an ___(76)___ group. Groups that are run on a voluntary basis and without a professional therapist are called ___(77)___-________ groups. One well-known self-help group is ___(78)___ ________.

The ___(79)___ ________ ________ was a response in the 1960s to an inadequate mental health care system. An especially important component of the community psychology movement was ___(80)___. The centers were aimed not only at treating mental disturbance, but also at ___(81)___ it from occurring.

Prevention takes place at three different levels: ____(82)____ prevention refers to efforts to reduce the number of new cases of mental disorders; ____(83)____ prevention refers to early detection and intervention; and ____(84)____ prevention refers to efforts at reducing disorders that were not prevented or arrested early in the disorder. An important component of community psychology is helping individuals develop skills they need to control their lives, which is called ____(85)____.

Is Psychotherapy Effective?

Is psychotherapy effective? One well-known study, which used a procedure called ____(86)____-________ to evaluate many other investigations, found psychotherapy to be effective. One study found the ____(87)____ therapies to be most effective in treating specific behavioral problems, whereas another found ____(88)____ therapies have been successful in treating depression. A *Consumer Reports* survey found treatment by a professional is usually effective, and long-term therapy was more effective than ____(89)____-________therapy. In certain cases, psychotherapy can actually be ____(90)____.

Frank has concluded that effective psychotherapies have the common elements of ____(91)____, mastery, and ____(92)____ ________.

In the past two decades, psychologists have become sensitive to ____(93)____ aspects of psychotherapy. Gender issues in evaluating treatment effectiveness include ____(94)____ and relatedness as therapy goals, and the effectiveness of consciousness-raising groups and feminist therapies. A problem in delivering mental health services to ethnic minority individuals is that there are relatively few ethnic minority psychotherapists. Research also suggests that ____(95)____ ________ individual are more likely than Whites to terminate therapy early.

It is useful to remember that individuals from different ____(96)____ may have different views regarding the causes and appropriate treatment of mental disorders. . According to Stanley Sue, therapists who work with ethnic minority clients should emphasize ____(97)____ and ____(98)____.

Biomedical Therapies

Treatments designed to deal with psychological problems by altering the way an individual's body functions are called ____(99)____ therapies.

A common type of biomedical therapy is ____(100)____ therapy. ____(101)____ drugs are commonly known as tranquilizers. Drugs that regulate mood are called ____(102)____ drugs. The three main classes of antidepressant drugs are ____(103)____, MAO inhibitors, and SSRI inhibitors, such as ____(104)____. A drug that is widely used to treat bipolar disorder is ____(105)____. ____(106)____ drugs are used to diminish agitation, hallucinations, and delusions. The most widely used antipsychotic drugs are the____(107)____, which are believed to block the ____(108)____ system's action in the brain. A major side effect of the neuroleptics is a neurological disorder called ____(109)____ ________.

"Shock treatment," more formally known as ____(110)____ ________ (ECT) is used to treat severe ____(111)____.

One treatment even more extreme than ECT involves removal or destruction of brain tissue to improve an individual's psychological adjustment. It is called ____(112)____.

Sociocultural Worlds/Applications in Psychology

In your own words summarize the material you have read in Sociocultural Worlds, "Therapy with African American Families," and Applications in Psychology, "Guidelines for Seeking Professional Help." Briefly describe how each of these articles relates to the information contained in the chapter.

Concept Check

Approaches to Therapy

Psychologists	Type of Therapy	Techniques
1. Freud	Psychoanalysis	Free association, catharsis, and interpretation of dreams, resistance, and transference.
2. Rogers	Humanistic (person-centered)	____________________
3. __________	Humanistic (Gestalt)	Question and challenge clients to help them become more aware of feeling.
4. Wolpe	__________ __________	This is a fear reduction method that involves relaxation, construction of a fear hierarchy, and conditioning a new response to the phobic stimulus.
5. Ellis	Rational-emotive therapy	____________________

Answers:

2. Focus is on the ability of clients to understand themselves; the therapist tries to create an emotionally supportive atmosphere; the therapist must show warmth, unconditional positive regard, and empathy.
3. Perls
4. Systematic desensitization
5. Therapist helps client learn to dispute irrational and self-defeating thoughts.

Multiple-Choice Questions

Practice Test 1

After answering all the multiple-choice questions in Practice Test 1, compare your answers with the answer key provided at the end of the chapter. The answer key contains a brief explanation of both the correct and incorrect answers. Each of these questions is keyed to the Learning Objectives for the chapter. If you answer any questions incorrectly, review the corresponding Learning Objective and text material before you proceed to Practice Test 2.

1. Hippocrates' prescription for treating depression consisted of
   a. less exercise.
   b. a spicy diet.
   c. abstinence from sex and alcohol.
   d. exorcism.

LO 1

2. Each of the following strategies is used to accomplish the goals of psychotherapy *except*
   a. talking.
   b. listening.
   c. prescribing drugs.
   d. rewarding behavior.

LO 2

3. An orientation to therapy that emphasizes direct changes in behavior is referred to as
   a. insight therapy.
   b. action therapy.
   c. systems therapy.
   d. both *b* and *c*

LO 3

4. During the early part of the twentieth century, psychotherapists practiced primarily in
   a. community mental health centers.
   b. private offices.
   c. outpatient facilities.
   d. mental hospitals.

LO 4

5. In psychoanalytic theory, a client who suddenly begins missing appointments and becomes hostile in therapy sessions is showing
   a. resistance.
   b. transference.
   c. free association.
   d. catharsis.

LO 5

6. When a patient feels he or she is falling in love with his or her psychoanalyst, Freudians would interpret this as
   a. resistance.
   b. transference.
   c. free association.
   d. catharsis.

LO 5

7. Compared with the traditional Freudian approach, modern psychodynamic therapists generally place more emphasis on
   a. the conscious mind.
   b. the transference phenomenon.
   c. current relationships.
   d. both *b* and *c*

LO 6

8. Gestalt therapy is similar to psychoanalytic therapy in that they both
   a. assume problems stem from past unresolved conflicts.
   b. assume the client can find solutions in the right atmosphere.
   c. expect resistance and transference to occur.
   d. deny the importance of dreams in understanding a person.

LO 7

9. To which type of therapist would you go if you were seeking unconditional positive regard?
   a. a person-centered therapist
   b. a psychoanalyst
   c. a Gestalt therapist
   d. a behavior therapist

LO 7

10. Behavior therapies
    a. are based on classical and operant conditioning principles.
    b. include cognitive factors.
    c. rely heavily on psychoanalytic principles.
    d. both *a* and *b*

LO 8

11. According to behavior therapists, an effective way to treat phobias is
    a. self-efficacy.
    b. aversive conditioning.
    c. a token economy.
    d. systematic desensitization.

LO 9

12. Token economies represent which approach to behavior therapy?
    a. classical conditioning
    b. cognitive behavior therapy
    c. operant conditioning
    d. rational-emotive conditioning

LO 9

13. Which approach is most likely to be concerned with irrational and self-defeating thoughts and emotional consequences?
    a. Beck's cognitive therapy
    b. Ellis's rational-emotive therapy
    c. Bandura's cognitive behavior therapy
    d. operant conditioning

LO 10

14. According to the text, each of the following is an advantage of group therapy *except*
    a. information.
    b. universality.
    c. altruism.
    d. systematic desensitization.

LO 11

15. Personal growth groups have their roots in which type of therapy?
    a. behavior therapy
    b. cognitive therapy
    c. psychoanalysis
    d. humanistic therapy

LO 11

16. Each of the following has been a goal of the community psychology movement *except*
    a. expanding the number of people treated by biomedical therapies.
    b. deinstitutionalization.
    c. prevention.
    d. reaching more people.

LO 12

17. According to the meta-analysis conducted by Smith and her associates,
    a. behavior therapies are superior to insight therapies.
    b. insight therapies are superior to behavior therapies.
    c. insight therapies were found to be surprisingly ineffective.
    d. no significant difference was found between behavior therapies and insight therapies.

LO 13

18. According to Stanley Sue, when therapists work with ethnic minority clients, they should emphasize credibility and
    a. giving.
    b. culture-bound values.
    c. cultural sensitivity.
    d. class-bound values.

LO 14

19. Electroconvulsive therapy is used in treating severe
    a. schizophrenic disorder.
    b. bipolar disorder.
    c. dissociative identity disorder.
    d. depression.

LO 15

20. Tardive dyskinesia is a potential side effect of which class of drugs?
    a. antianxiety
    b. antidepressant
    c. antipsychotic
    d. antiphobic

LO 15

Practice Test 2

The following multiple-choice questions also are keyed to the chapter Learning Objectives. If you answer any questions incorrectly, be sure to review the corresponding Learning Objective and text material.

1. Which of the following techniques has been used to rid people of "evil spirits"?
   a. trephining
   b. exercise
   c. isolation
   d. commitment to asylums

LO 1

2. The term *insight therapy* applies to both psychodynamic therapies and
   a. behavior therapies.
   b. humanistic therapies.
   c. biomedical therapies.
   d. aversive conditioning therapies.

LO 2

3. Psychodynamic therapies are generally considered to be
   a. insight therapies.
   b. action therapies.
   c. systems therapies.
   d. eclectic therapies

LO 3

4. The managed health-care approach to psychotherapy has been criticized for each of the following *except*
   a. favoring long-term treatment.
   b. favoring short-term treatment.
   c. potential confidentiality problems.
   d. creating expensive bureaucracies.

LO 4

5. A release of emotional tension associated with reliving an emotionally charged experience is called
   a. catharsis.
   b. transference.
   c. resistance.
   d. free association.

LO 5

6. A psychoanalytic therapy technique that involves having the patient say the first thing that comes to mind is called
   a. catharsis.
   b. transference.
   c. resistance.
   d. free association.

LO 5

7. Which of the following characterizes contemporary psychodynamic therapy?
   a. greater emphasis on the role of the unconscious
   b. greater emphasis on current relationships
   c. rejection of the role of early family experiences
   d. both *a* and *b*

LO 6

8. Each of the following is associated with person-centered therapy *except*
   a. genuineness.
   b. unconditional positive regard.
   c. role playing.
   d. accurate empathy.

LO 7

9. A therapist who uses a confrontational approach is most likely to be practicing
   a. person-centered therapy.
   b. Gestalt therapy.
   c. behavior therapy.
   d. psychoanalysis.

LO 7

10. The principles of operant and classical conditioning are extensively used by practitioners of
    a. psychoanalysis.
    b. Gestalt therapy.
    c. group therapy.
    d. behavior therapy.

LO 8

11. The concept of self-efficacy is associated with which approach to behavior therapy?
    a. operant conditioning
    b. classical conditioning
    c. cognitive behavior therapy
    d. person-centered therapy

LO 9

12. Matt is undergoing a form of therapy aimed at stopping his craving for alcohol. The therapist requires him to take a drug that induces nausea if he drinks alcohol. Matt is undergoing
    a. systematic desensitization.
    b. a token economy.
    c. aversive conditioning.
    d. cognitive behavior therapy.

LO 9

13. Research has supported the effectiveness of Aaron Beck's cognitive therapy in treating
    a. bipolar disorder.
    b. depression.
    c. schizophrenia.
    d. phobias.

LO 10

14. In family systems therapy, the process in which the therapist teaches family members to view individual problems as family problems is called
    a. validation.
    b. reframing.
    c. structural change.
    d. detriangulation.

LO 11

15. In family systems therapy, efforts to disentangle family conflict are often referred to as
    a. validation.
    b. reframing.
    c. structural changes.
    d. detriangulation.

LO 11

16. Community psychology efforts at early detection and intervention are referred to as
    a. primary prevention.
    b. secondary prevention.
    c. tertiary prevention.
    d. both *a* and *b*

LO 12

17. Meta-analysis on the effectiveness of different therapies has found that phobias and sexual dysfunctions were most successfully treated by
    a. behavior therapy.
    b. cognitive therapy.
    c. psychoanalysis.
    d. Gestalt therapy.

LO 13

18. Ethnic minority individuals terminate psychotherapy at a higher rate than White Americans because of
    a. the social stigma of being a mental patient.
    b. the fear of hospitalization.
    c. the availability of an alternative healer.
    d. all of the above

LO 14

19. Neuroleptics are widely used to reduce symptoms of
    a. depression.
    b. schizophrenia.
    c. bipolar disorder.
    d. dissociative identity disorder.

LO 15

20. Lithium is widely prescribed to treat the symptoms of
    a. anxiety.
    b. dissociative identity disorder.
    c. bipolar disorder.
    d. schizophrenia.

LO 15

Answers to Key Terms

1. **Trephining,** a procedure that is no longer used, involved chipping a hole in the skull to allow evil spirits to leave.
2. **Exorcism,** is a religious rite that was used during the Middle Ages and was designed to remove evil spirits from a person. It involved prayer, starvation, beatings, and various forms of torture.
3. **Psychotherapy** is the process of working with individuals to reduce their emotional problems and improve their adjustment.
4. **Insight therapy** encourages insight into and awareness of oneself.
5. **Action therapy** promotes direct behavioral changes. According to adherents of this approach, insight is not essential for change to occur.
6. **Eclectic** refers to using a variety of approaches.
7. **Managed health care** is a system in which external reviewers approve the type and length of treatment to justify reimbursement from an insurance company.
8. **Psychodynamic therapies** stress the importance of the unconscious mind, extensive interpretation by the therapist, and the role of infant and early childhood experiences.
9. **Psychoanalysis** is Freud's therapeutic technique for analyzing an individual's unconscious thought.
10. **Free association** is the psychoanalytic technique of encouraging individuals to say aloud whatever comes to mind, no matter how trivial or embarrassing.
11. **Catharsis** is the psychoanalytic term that describes clients' release of emotional tension when they relive an emotionally charged and conflicted experience.
12. **Dream analysis** is the psychoanalytic technique of interpreting a client's dream in the belief that the dream contains information about the individual's unconscious thoughts and conflicts.
13. **Manifest content** is the psychoanalytic term for the conscious, remembered aspects of a dream.
14. **Latent content** is the psychoanalytic term for the unconscious, unremembered, symbolic aspects of a dream.
15. **Transference** is the psychoanalytic term for a client's relating to an analyst in ways that reproduce important relationships in the client's life.
16. **Resistance** is the psychoanalytic term for the client's unconscious defense strategies that prevent the analyst from understanding the client's problem.
17. **Humanistic psychotherapies** encourage clients to understand themselves and to grow personally.
18. **Person-centered therapy** is a type of humanistic therapy developed by Carl Rogers. The therapist provides a warm, supportive atmosphere to improve the client's self-concept and to encourage the client to gain insight about problems.
19. **Genuineness** is the Rogerian concept of the importance of the therapist's being genuine and not hiding behind a facade when relating to a client.
20. **Accurate empathy** is Rogers's term for the therapist's ability to identify with the client.
21. **Active listening** is Rogers's term for listening to the client with total attention. Restating and supporting the client are two active listening techniques.
22. **Gestalt therapy** is a humanistic therapy developed by Perls in which the therapist questions and challenges clients to help the clients become more aware of their feelings and face their problems.
23. **Behavior therapies** use principles of learning to reduce or eliminate maladaptive behavior.
24. **Systematic desensitization** is a behavior therapy method that uses classical conditioning procedures to treat anxiety.
25. **Aversive conditioning** involves repeated pairings of the undesirable behavior with aversive stimuli to eliminate the undesirable behavior.
26. A **token economy** is a behavior modification system in which behaviors are systematically reinforced with tokens that can later be exchanged for desired rewards.
27. **Cognitive behavior therapies** help individuals change their feelings and behaviors by changing their thoughts. This approach stems both from cognitive therapy and behavior therapy.
28. **Self-efficacy** is the belief that one can master a situation and produce positive outcomes.
29. **Self-instructional methods** are cognitive behavioral techniques aimed at teaching individuals to modify their own behavior.

30. **Cognitive therapies** emphasize that a person's cognitions are the main source of abnormal behavior.
31. **Rational—emotive therapy** is based on Ellis's view that individuals become psychologically disordered because of their irrational and self-defeating beliefs.
32. **Family therapy** is a group therapy with family members.
33. **Couple therapy** is a group therapy with married or unmarried couples whose main problem is their relationship.
34. **Family systems therapy** is based on the assumption that psychological adjustment is related to patterns of interaction within the family unit.
35. **Personal growth groups** are based on humanistic therapies and emphasize personal growth and increased openness and honesty in interpersonal relations.
36. An **encounter group** is a personal-growth group designed to promote self-understanding through candid group interaction.
37. **Self-help groups** are voluntary organizations of individuals who meet regularly without a professional therapist. The goals are to discuss topics of common interest and to provide support to members.
38. **Deinstitutionalization** is the movement to transfer the treatment of mental disturbances from inpatient mental institutions to community-based facilities that stress outpatient care.
39. **Primary prevention** is a community psychology concept denoting efforts to reduce the number of new cases of mental disorders.
40. **Secondary prevention** is a prevention method, based on community psychology, involving screening for early detection of problems as well as early intervention.
41. **Tertiary prevention** is a community psychology concept denoting efforts to reduce the long-term consequences of mental health disorders that were not prevented or arrested early in the course of the disorders.
42. **Empowerment** involves helping individuals develop skills they need to improve their adaptation and circumstances.
43. **Meta-analysis** is a process for statistically analyzing diverse studies.
44. **Credibility** refers to a therapist's believability.
45. **Giving** occurs when a client receives some kind of benefit from treatment early in the therapy process.
46. **Biomedical therapies** are treatments to reduce or eliminate psychological disorders by altering the way an individual's body functions. Drug therapy is a common biomedical therapy.
47. **Antianxiety drugs,** also called tranquilizers, reduce anxiety by making the individual less excitable and more tranquil.
48. **Antidepressant drugs** help regulate mood. The three main classes of antidepressants are tricyclics, MAO inhibitors, and SSRI inhibitors.
49. **Lithium** is a drug that is widely used to treat bipolar affective disorder.
50. **Antipsychotic drugs** help diminish agitated behavior, reduce tension, decrease hallucinations and delusions, improve social behavior, and produce better sleep patterns in severely disturbed individuals, especially schizophrenics. Neuroleptics are the most widely used antipsychotic drugs.
51. **Tardive dyskinesia,** a major side effect of the neuroleptics, is a neurological disorder characterized by grotesque, involuntary movements of the face and extensive twitching of the neck, legs, and arms.
52. **Electroconvulsive therapy,** commonly called shock treatment, produces a seizure in the brain and is used to treat severely depressed individuals.
53. **Psychosurgery** is a biomedical therapy that involves the removal or destruction of brain tissue to improve an individual's psychological adjustment.

Answers to Guided Review

1. trephining (p. 444)
2. exorcism (p. 444)
3. asylums (p. 445)
4. France (p. 445)
5. criminals (p. 446)
6. Psychotherapy (p. 446)
7. insight (p. 446)
8. action (p. 446)
9. eclectic (p. 446)
10. psychiatrists (p. 446)
11. attractive (p. 447)
12. intelligent (p. 447)
13. institutionalized (p. 447)
14. different (p. 447)
15. higher (p. 448)
16. managed health care (p. 448)
17. short-term (p. 448)
18. longer term (p. 448)
19. confidentiality (p. 448)
20. bureaucracy (p. 448)
21. privacy (p. 448)
22. dual (p. 448)
23. psychodynamic (p. 449)
24. psychoanalysis (p. 449)
25. sexuality (p. 449)
26. unconscious (p. 449)
27. awareness (p. 449)
28. free association (p. 449)
29. catharsis (p. 449)
30. dream analysis (p. 449)
31. manifest (p. 449)
32. latent (p. 449)
33. transference (p. 449)
34. resistance (p. 450)
35. social contexts (p. 451)
36. humanistic (p. 451)
37. person-centered (p. 451)
38. conditions of worth (p. 451)
39. unconditional positive regard (p. 452)
40. genuine (p. 452)
41. accurate empathy (p. 452)
42. active listening (p. 452)
43. Gestalt (p. 452)
44. Perls (p. 452)
45. congruence (p. 452)
46. role (p. 452)
47. directive (p. 453)
48. learning (p. 453)
49. classical (p. 453)
50. systematic desensitization (p. 454)
51. phobias (p. 454)
52. aversive conditioning (p. 454)
53. operant (p. 455)
54. behavior modification (p. 455)
55. token economy (p. 455)
56. cognitive behavior (p. 455)
57. adaptive (p. 455)
58. self-efficacy (p. 456)
59. self-instructional (p. 456)
60. rational-emotive (p. 457)
61. disputes (p. 457)
62. belief (p. 457)
63. depression (p.457)
64. information (p. 460)
65. universality (p. 460)
66. altruism (p. 460)
67. recapitulation (p. 460)
68. social (p. 460)
69. interpersonal (p. 460)
70. family (p. 460)
71. Family systems (p. 460)
72. validation (p. 460)
73. structural change (p. 461)
74. personal growth (p. 462)
75. humanistic (p. 462)
76. encounter (p. 462)
77. self-help (p. 462)
78. Alcoholics Anonymous (p. 462)
79. community psychology movement (p. 463)
80. deinstitutionalization (p. 463)
81. preventing (p. 463)
82. primary (p. 464)
83. secondary (p. 464)
84. tertiary (p. 464)
85. empowerment (p. 465)
86. meta-analysis (p. 465)
87. behavior (p. 466)
88. cognitive (p. 466)
89. short-term (p. 466)
90. harmful (p. 466)
91. expectations (p. 466)
92. emotional arousal (p. 466)
93. sociocultural (p. 467)
94. autonomy (p. 467)
95. ethnic minority (p. 470)
96. cultures (p. 470
97. credibility (p. 741)
98. giving (p. 741)
99. biomedical (p. 472)
100. drug (p. 472)
101. Antianxiety (p. 472)
102. antidepressant (p. 472)
103. tricyclics (p. 472)
104. Prozac (p. 472)
105. lithium (p. 473)
106. Antipsychotic (p. 473)
107. neuroleptics (p. 473)
108. dopamine (p. 473)
109. tardive dyskinesia (p. 473)
110. electroconvulsive therapy (p. 473)
111. depression (p. 473)
112. psychosurgery (p. 473)

Answers to Multiple Choice Questions- Practice Test 1

1. a. Incorrect. Hippocrates prescribed more exercise for depressed mood.
   b. Incorrect. Hippocrates prescribed a bland diet for treating depression.
   c. **Correct.** Hippocrates prescribed rest, exercise, a bland diet, and abstinence from sex and alcohol as a cures for depressed mood.
   d. Incorrect. Exorcism is a religious rite that involves prayer, starvation, beatings, and various forms of torture. It was not prescribed by Hippocrates.

2. a. Incorrect. Psychologists use a number of strategies to accomplish the goals of psychotherapy including, talking, interpreting, listening, rewarding, and modeling.
   b. Incorrect. Psychologists use a number of strategies to accomplish the goals of psychotherapy including, talking, interpreting, listening, rewarding, and modeling.
   c. **Correct.** Psychotherapy does not include biomedical treatment, such as drugs or surgery.
   d. Incorrect. Psychologists use a number of strategies to accomplish the goals of psychotherapy including, talking, interpreting, listening, rewarding, and modeling.

3. a. Incorrect. Insight therapy encourages insight into and awareness of oneself as the critical focus of therapy.
   b. **Correct.** Action therapy promotes direct changes in behavior.
   c. Incorrect. In systems therapy, the assumption is that psychological adjustment is related to patterns of interaction within the family unit.
   d. Incorrect. Action therapy does promote direct changes in behavior, but systems therapy does not always focus on direct changes.

4. a. Incorrect. During the first part of the 20th century, psychotherapists primarily practiced in mental hospitals. Today, it would be more likely that someone seeking counseling or psychotherapy would go to a community health center.
   b. Incorrect. During the first part of the 20th century, psychotherapists primarily practiced in mental hospitals. Seeing a psychotherapist in a private office is a more recent practice.
   c. Incorrect. During the first part of the 20th century, psychotherapists primarily practiced in mental hospitals. Receiving psychotherapy at an outpatient clinic is much more common practice today.
   d. **Correct.** During the first part of the 20th century, psychotherapists primarily practiced in mental hospitals.

5. a. **Correct.** Showing up late or missing sessions, arguing with the psychoanalyst, or faking free associations are examples of resistance.
   b. Incorrect. Transference is the psychoanalytic term for the client's relating to the analyst in ways that reproduce or relive important relationships in the client's life.
   c. Incorrect. Free association is the technique of encouraging individuals to say aloud whatever comes to mind, no matter how trivial or embarrassing.
   d. Incorrect. Catharsis is the psychoanalytic term for clients' release of emotional tension when they relive an emotionally charged and conflicted experience.

6. a. Incorrect. Resistance is the psychoanalytic term for a client's unconscious defense strategies that prevent the analyst from understanding the client's problems.
   b. Correct. Transference is the psychoanalytic term for the client's relating to the analyst in ways that reproduce or relive important relationships in the client's life. A client might interact with an analyst as if the analyst were a parent or lover, for example.
   c. Incorrect. Free association is the technique of encouraging individuals to say aloud whatever comes to mind, no matter how trivial or embarrassing.
   d. Incorrect. Catharsis is the psychoanalytic term for clients' release of emotional tension when they relive an emotionally charged and conflicted experience.

7. a. Incorrect. Modern psychodynamic therapists place more emphasis on the conscious mind than traditional psychoanalysts, but they also place more emphasis on current relationships.
   b. Incorrect. Modern psychodynamic therapists place more emphasis on the conscious mind and current relationships, rather than transference.
   c. Incorrect. Modern psychodynamic therapists place more emphasis on current relationships than traditional psychoanalysts, but they also place more emphasis on the conscious mind.
   c. **Correct.** Modern psychodynamic therapists place more emphasis on the conscious mind <u>and</u> current relationships.

8. a. **Correct.** Gestalt therapists and psychoanalytic therapists agree that psychological problems originate in unresolved past conflicts.
   b. Incorrect. It is person-centered therapists who assume that the client can find solutions in the right atmosphere.
   c. Incorrect. It is only psychoanalytic therapists who expect resistance and transference to occur, not Gestalt therapists.
   d. Incorrect. Gestalt and psychoanalytic therapists both acknowledge, rather than deny, the importance of dreams in understanding a person.

9. a. **Correct.** Person-centered therapists use unconditional positive regard. In using this technique, they try to avoid disapproving of what a client says or does.
   b. Incorrect. Unconditional positive regard is not a strategy used by psychoanalysts.
   c. Incorrect. Unconditional positive regard is not a strategy used by Gestalt therapists.
   d. Incorrect. Behavior therapists do not use unconditional positive regard as part of their therapies.

10. a. **Correct.** Behavior therapies use principles of learning, such as classical and operant conditioning, to reduce or eliminate maladaptive behavior.
    b. Incorrect. It is cognitive therapies that emphasize cognitive factors.
    c. Incorrect. Freudian, rather than behavioral, therapists rely heavily on psychoanalytic principles.
    d. Incorrect. Behavior therapies are based on classical and operant conditioning principles, but do not include cognitive factors.

11. a. Incorrect. Self-efficacy is an aspect of cognitive behavior therapy, rather than behavior therapy. It is the belief that one can master a situation and produce positive outcomes.
    b. Incorrect. Aversive conditioning is used to treat such things as smoking and drinking, rather than phobias.
    c. Incorrect. Token economies are implemented in places like institutions for the mentally retarded and homes for delinquents. They are not generally used to treat people with phobias.
    d. **Correct.** Behavior therapists have found systematic desensitization to be an effective way to treat phobias.

12. a. Incorrect. Token economies are based on operant conditioning, not classical conditioning.
    b. Incorrect. Token economies represent a behavioral approach, not a cognitive behavior approach.
    c. **Correct.** Token economies are based on operant conditioning techniques.
    d. Incorrect. Token economies represent a behavioral approach. Rational-emotive conditioning comes from the cognitive approach.

13. a. Incorrect. Although they are similar, Ellis's rational-emotive therapy focuses more on irrational and self-defeating thoughts and emotional consequences than Beck's cognitive therapy.
    b. **Correct.** Ellis's rational-emotive therapy asserts that people become psychologically disordered because of their beliefs, especially those that are irrational and self-defeating.
    c. Incorrect. Bandura's cognitive behavior therapy is more concerned with self-efficacy than with irrational and self-defeating thoughts and emotional consequences.
    d. Incorrect. Operant conditioning focuses more on the consequences of behavior than on irrational and self-defeating thoughts.

14. a. Incorrect. Receiving information about problems from group leaders or group members is one of the advantages of group therapy.
    b. Incorrect. Universality is an advantage of group therapy. Group therapy often helps individuals develop the sense that they are not the only persons having such frightening and unacceptable impulses.
    c. Incorrect. Developing a sense of altruism by giving other member support and advise is one of the advantages of group therapy.
    d. **Correct.** Systematic desensitization is a behavioral technique used to treat individuals with phobias. It is generally not an advantage of group therapy.

15. a. Incorrect. Personal growth groups have their roots in humanistic therapy, not in behavioral therapy.
    b. Incorrect. Personal growth groups have their roots in humanistic therapy, not in cognitive therapy.
    c. Incorrect. Personal growth groups have their roots in humanistic therapy, not in psychoanalytic therapy.
    d. **Correct.** Personal growth groups have their roots in humanistic therapy; they emphasize personal growth and increased openness and honesty in interpersonal relations.

16. a. **Correct.** Expanding the number of people treated by biomedical therapies is not a goal of the community psychology movement.
    b. Incorrect. Deinstitutionalization, the movement to transfer the treatment of mental disabilities from inpatient mental institutions to community-based facilities, is a goal of the community psychology movement.
    c. Incorrect. Providing resources that help prevent disorders as well as treat them is a goal of the community psychology movement.
    d. Incorrect. Outreach is another goal of the community psychology movement. Rather than expecting people with mental or emotional problems to make an appointment at a mental health center, mental health care workers go to community locations.

17. a. Incorrect. This meta-analysis found that no specific type of therapy was better than any other for any problem.
    b. Incorrect. This meta-analysis found that no specific type of therapy was better than any other for any problem.
    c. Incorrect. This meta-analysis found that no specific type of therapy was better than any other for any problem.
    d. **Correct.** This meta-analysis found that no specific type of therapy was better than any other for any problem.

18. a. **Correct.** According to Stanley Sue, when working with ethnic minority clients, therapists should emphasize two processes: credibility and giving. Giving refers to clients' receiving some kind of benefit from treatment early in the therapy process.
    b. Incorrect. When using a specific approach based on a client's cultural background, it is sometimes difficult for a therapist to deal with diversity and individual differences within a cultural group.
    c. Incorrect. Cultural sensitivity is not one of the processes recommended by Stanley Sue.

d. Incorrect. Class-bound values is not one of the processes recommended by Stanley Sue.

19. a. Incorrect. Electroconvulsive therapy is used in treating severe depression, not severe schizophrenia.
    b. Incorrect. Electroconvulsive therapy is used in treating severe depression, not severe bipolar disorder.
    c. Incorrect. Electroconvulsive therapy is used in treating severe depression, not severe dissociative identity disorder.
    d. **Correct.** Electroconvulsive therapy is used in treating severe depression.

20. a. Incorrect. Tardive dyskinesia is a potential side effect of antipsychotic, not antianxiety, drugs.
    b. Incorrect. Tardive dyskinesia is a potential side effect of antipsychotic, not antidepressant, drugs.
    c. **Correct.** Tardive dyskinesia is a potential side effect of antipsychotic drugs. It is a neurological disorder characterized by grotesque, involuntary movements of the facial muscles and mouth, as well as extensive twitching of the neck, arms, and legs.
    d. Incorrect. Tardive dyskinesia is a potential side effect of antipsychotic, not antiphobic, drugs.

Answers to Multiple Choice Questions- Practice Test 2

1. a. Correct. Trephining is a procedure that involves chipping a hole in the skull to allow the evil spirits to escape.
   b. Incorrect. Hippocrates prescribed exercise, among other things, as a cure for depressed mood.
   c. Incorrect. Although isolation has been used to treat people with mental disorders, it was trephining that was used to rid people of "evil spirits".
   d. Incorrect. During the renaissance, people were placed in asylums to protect them from the exploitation they experienced on the streets, not to rid them of "evil spirits".

2. a. Incorrect. Behavior therapies are considered to be action, rather than insight, therapies.
   b. **Correct.** Psychodynamic therapies and humanistic therapies are both considered to be insight therapies.
   c. Incorrect. Insight therapy is a type of psychotherapy, not a type of biomedical therapy.
   d. Incorrect. Aversive conditioning, because it comes from the behavioral tradition, is an action therapy, rather than an insight therapy.

3. a. **Correct.** Psychodynamic therapies are considered to be insight therapies. Insight therapies encourage insight into an awareness of oneself as the critical focus of therapy.
   b. Incorrect. Action therapies promote direct changes in behavior. Psychodynamic therapies are considered to be insight, not action, therapies.
   c. Incorrect. Psychodynamic therapies focus on the individual. In systems therapy, the assumption is that psychological adjustment is related to patterns of interaction among all family members, rather than a single individual.
   d. Incorrect. Psychodynamic therapy would be only one of the approaches used by an eclectic therapist.

4. a. **Correct.** The emphasis on cost management of the managed health-care approach has been criticized for favoring short- over long-term treatment.
   b. Incorrect. The emphasis on cost management of the managed health-care approach has been criticized for favoring short- over long-term treatment.
   c. Incorrect. The managed health-care approach has been criticized for potential confidentiality problems. Both clients and therapists report discomfort with the potential violation of confidentiality when reporting therapy details to a third party.
   d. Incorrect. The managed health-care approach has been criticized for creating expensive bureaucracies. Some research suggests that the bureaucracy involved in setting up the system may absorb the savings that were supposed to be gained.

5. a. **Correct.** Catharsis is the psychoanalytic term for clients' release of emotional tension when they relive an emotionally charged and conflicted experience.
   b. Incorrect. Transference is the psychoanalytic term for the client's relating to the analyst in ways that reproduce or relive important relationships in the client's life.
   c. Incorrect. Resistance is the psychoanalytic term for a client's unconscious defense strategies that prevent the analyst from understanding the client's problems.
   d. Incorrect. Free association is the technique of encouraging individuals to say aloud whatever comes to mind, no matter how trivial or embarrassing.

6. a. Incorrect. Catharsis is the psychoanalytic term for clients' release of emotional tension when they relive an emotionally charged and conflicted experience.
   b. Incorrect. Transference is the psychoanalytic term for the client's relating to the analyst in ways that reproduce or relive important relationships in the client's life.
   c. Incorrect. Resistance is the psychoanalytic term for a client's unconscious defense strategies that prevent the analyst from understanding the client's problems.
   d. **Correct.** Free association is the technique of encouraging individuals to say aloud whatever comes to mind.

7. a. Incorrect. Contemporary psychodynamic therapists give greater emphasis to the role of the conscious, not the unconscious.
   b. **Correct.** Contemporary psychodynamic therapists accord more power to current relationships in understanding a client's problems.
   c. Incorrect. Contemporary psychodynamic therapists still emphasize the importance of early family experiences.
   d. Incorrect. Contemporary psychodynamic therapy does place more emphasis on current relationships, but does not place greater emphasis on the unconscious.

8. a. Incorrect. Genuineness, the Rogerian concept of the importance of the therapist's being genuine, is associated with person-centered therapy.
   b. Incorrect. Person-centered therapists use unconditional positive regard. In using this technique, they try to avoid disapproving of what a client says or does.
   c. **Correct.** Role playing is a technique used in group therapy.
   d. Incorrect. Person-centered therapists use accurate empathy to try to identify with the client.

9. a. Incorrect. Person-centered therapists do not generally use a confrontational approach with their clients.
   b. **Correct.** Gestalt therapy is a humanistic therapy in which the therapist questions and confronts clients to help them become more aware of their feelings and face their problems.
   c. Incorrect. Behavioral therapists do not generally use a confrontational approach.
   d. Incorrect. Therapists using psychoanalysis do not generally use a confrontational approach.

10. a. Incorrect. Psychoanalysts use techniques based on Freudian theory, not the principles of operant and classical conditioning.
    b. Incorrect. Gestalt therapy is based on the principles of Freudian and humanistic theory, rather than the principles of operant and classical conditioning.

c. Incorrect. Group therapy is sometimes based on behavioral therapy, but it can also be based on humanistic or cognitive therapy, among others.
d. **Correct.** The principles of operant and classical conditioning are extensively used by practitioners of Behavior therapy.

11. a. Incorrect. Self-efficacy is associated with cognitive behavior therapy, not operant conditioning.
b. Incorrect. Self-efficacy is associated with cognitive behavior therapy, not classical conditioning.
c. Correct. Cognitive behavioral therapy tries to help individuals behave more adaptively by modifying their thoughts. Self-efficacy, the belief that one can master a situation and produce positive outcomes, is associated with cognitive behavior therapy.
d. Incorrect. Self-efficacy is associated with cognitive behavior therapy, not person-centered therapy.

12. a. Incorrect. Systematic desensitization is a method of behavior therapy that treats anxiety by associating deep relaxation, rather than nausea, with successive visualizations of increasingly intense anxiety-producing situations.
b. Incorrect. A token economy is a behavior modification system in which behaviors are reinforced with tokens that can be exchanged later for desired rewards.
c. **Correct.** Matt is undergoing aversive conditioning. Aversive conditioning is an approach to behavior therapy that involves repeated pairings of an undesirable behavior (in this case, drinking) with aversive stimuli (in this case, a drug that induces nausea) to decrease the behavior's rewards so that the individual will stop doing it.
d. Incorrect. Matt is undergoing aversive conditioning which is a type of behavioral therapy, not a type of cognitive behavior therapy.

13. a. Incorrect. Results from a large scale, national study support the belief that Beck's cognitive therapy is an effective treatment for depression, not bipolar disorder.
b. **Correct.** Results from a large scale, national study support the belief that Beck's cognitive therapy is an effective treatment for depression.
c. Incorrect. Results from a large scale, national study support the belief that Beck's cognitive therapy is an effective treatment for depression, not schizophrenia.
d. Incorrect. Results from a large scale, national study support the belief that Beck's cognitive therapy is an effective treatment for depression, not phobias.

14. a. Incorrect. Validation, in family systems therapy, is the process in which the therapist expresses an understanding and acceptance of each family member's feelings and beliefs and, thus, validates the person.
b. **Correct.** When a family systems therapist uses reframing, he or she teaches the family to cast problems as family problems rather than an individual's problems.
c. Incorrect. Structural change is the process in which the family systems therapist tries to restructure the coalitions in a family.
d. Incorrect. When using detriangulation, a family systems therapist tries to disentangle family conflict.

15. a. Incorrect. Validation, in family systems therapy, is the process in which the therapist expresses an understanding and acceptance of each family member's feelings and beliefs and, thus, validates the person.
b. Incorrect. When a family systems therapist uses reframing, he or she teaches the family to cast problems as family problems rather than an individual's problems.
c. Incorrect. Structural change is the process in which the family systems therapist tries to restructure the coalitions in a family.
d. **Correct.** When using detriangulation, a family systems therapist tries to disentangle family conflict.

16. a. Incorrect. Primary prevention is a community psychology concept, borrowed from the public health field, that describes efforts to reduce the number of new cases of mental disorders.
    b. **Correct.** Secondary prevention is a community psychology concept in which screening for early detection of problems, as well as early intervention, is carried out.
    c. Incorrect. Tertiary prevention is a community psychology concept that describes efforts to reduce the long-term consequences of mental health disorders that were not prevented or arrested early in the course of the disorder.
    d. Incorrect. Community psychology efforts at early detection and intervention are referred to as secondary prevention only, not as primary and secondary prevention.

17. a. **Correct.** This meta-analysis found that behavior therapies have been most successfully in treating specific behavioral problems, such as phobias and sexual dysfunctions.
    b. Incorrect. This meta-analysis found that cognitive therapy is most effective in treating depression.
    c. Incorrect. This meta-analysis found that behavior, not psychoanalytic, therapies are the most successful in treating phobias and sexual dysfunctions.
    d. Incorrect. This meta-analysis found that behavior, not Gestalt, therapies are the most successful in treating phobias and sexual dysfunctions.

18. a. Incorrect. The social stigma of being a "mental patient", fear of hospitalization, conflict between their own belief system and the beliefs of modern mental health practitioners, and the availability of an alternate healer are all reasons ethnic minority individuals terminate therapy early.
    b. Incorrect. The social stigma of being a "mental patient", fear of hospitalization, conflict between their own belief system and the beliefs of modern mental health practitioners, and the availability of an alternate healer are all reasons ethnic minority individuals terminate therapy early.
    c. Incorrect. The social stigma of being a "mental patient", fear of hospitalization, conflict between their own belief system and the beliefs of modern mental health practitioners, and the availability of an alternate healer are all reasons ethnic minority individuals terminate therapy early.
    d. **Correct.** The social stigma of being a "mental patient", fear of hospitalization, conflict between their own belief system and the beliefs of modern mental health practitioners, and the availability of an alternate healer are all reasons ethnic minority individuals terminate therapy early.

19. a. Incorrect. Neuroleptics are widely used to reduce the symptoms of schizophrenia, not depression.
    b. **Correct.** Neuroleptics are widely used to reduce the symptoms of schizophrenia.
    c. Incorrect. Neuroleptics are widely used to reduce the symptoms of schizophrenia, not bipolar disorder.
    d. Incorrect. Neuroleptics are widely used to reduce the symptoms of schizophrenia, not dissociative identity disorder.

20. a. Incorrect. Lithium is widely prescribed to treat the symptoms of bipolar disorder, not anxiety.
    b. Incorrect. Lithium is widely prescribed to treat the symptoms of bipolar disorder, not dissociative identity disorder.
    c. **Correct.** Lithium is widely prescribed to treat the symptoms of bipolar disorder.
    d. Incorrect. Lithium is widely prescribed to treat the symptoms of bipolar disorder, not schizophrenia.

Chapter 13 Health, Stress and Coping

Learning Objectives

After studying this chapter, you should be able to:

1. Define health psychology, behavioral medicine, and psychoneuroimmunology. (p. 483)

2. Describe the effects of exercise on physical and mental health. (p. 484)

3. Describe the importance of proper nutrition to good health. (p. 485)

4. Discuss the causes of obesity and describe the results of research on dieting. (p. 487)

5. Distinguish between anorexia nervosa and bulimia. (p. 489)

6. Identify and describe the techniques used to help people quit smoking. (p. 490)

7. Discuss the prevalence of misinformation about sexual matters. (p. 491)

8. Identify and describe the various sexually transmitted diseases. (p. 493)

9. Discuss governmental efforts to promote health. (p. 495)

10. Identify the roles played by ethnicity and gender in health and life expectancy. (p. 495)

11. Describe the difficulties in defining the term *stress*. (p. 496)

12. Identify the stages of Selye's general adaptation syndrome. (p. 497)

13. Explain the importance of cognitive factors in stress. (p. 498)

14. Describe the Type A behavior pattern. (p. 499)

15. Identify the personality style called *hardiness*. (p. 499)

16. Describe the components of overload, conflict and frustration. (p. 500)

17. Describe the impact of life events and daily hassles on our lives. (p. 501)

18. Explain the following sociocultural factors in stress: acculturation, socioeconomic status, and gender. (p. 503)

19. Contrast problem-focused coping and emotion-focused coping. (p. 506)

20. Discuss the advantages of optimism and positive thinking. (p. 506)

21. Describe efforts to control stress with social support and with stress management techniques such as meditation, relaxation and biofeedback. (p. 508)

Chapter 13 Outline

I. Relating Health and Psychology
   A. Historical Background
   B. Contemporary Approaches
      1. Health Psychology
      2. Behavioral Medicine
      3. Psychoneuroimmuniology
II. Promoting Health
   A. Regular Exercise
   B. Proper Nutrition
      1. Nutritional Standards
      2. Obesity
      3. Dieting
      4. Anorexia Nervosa and Bulimia
   C. Freedom From Smoking
      1. Nicotine substitutes
      2. stimulus control
      3. aversive conditioning
      4. going "Cold Turkey"
   D. Making Sound Sexual Decision
      1. Sexual knowledge
      2. Contraception
      3. Sexually Transmitted Diseases
      4. Prevention issues
III. Understanding Stress
   A. Biological Factors
      1. The Nervous System
      2. The General Adaptation Syndrome
   B. Cognitive Factors
   C. Personality Factors
      1. Type A Behavior Pattern
      2. Hardiness
   D. Environmental Factors
      1. Overload, Conflict, and Frustration
      2. Life Events and Daily Hassles
   E. Sociocultural Factors
      1. Acculturation and Acculturative Stress
      2. Socioeconomic Status
      3. Gender
IV. Coping Strategies
   A. Problem-Focused Coping
      1. Problem-focused coping
      2. Emotion-focused coping
      3. Avoidance strategies
   B. Optimism and Positive Thinking
   C. Social Support
   D. Assertive Behavior
   E. Stress Management
   F. Multiple Coping Strategies

Key Terms

Write a brief description for each of the following terms. Where relevant, provide an original example or illustration of the term. Then, compare your answers with those provided at the end of the Study Guide chapter. Review the text for those terms you don't know and those you define incorrectly.

1. health psychology (p. 483)
2. behavioral medicine (p. 483)
3. psychoneuroimmunology (p. 483)
4. aerobic exercise (p. 484)
5. set point (p. 488)
6. basal metabolism rate (BMR) (p. 488)
7. anorexia nervosa (p. 489)
8. bulimia (p. 489)
9. sexually transmitted diseases (STDs) (p. 493)
10. AIDS (p. 493)
11. stress (p. 496)
12. general adaptation syndrome (GAS) (p. 497)
13. eustress (p. 497)
14. cognitive appraisal (p. 498)
15. Type A behavior pattern (p. 499)
16. hardiness (p. 499)

17. overload (p. 500)

18. burnout (p. 500)

19. approach/approach conflict (p. 501)

20. avoidance/avoidance conflict (p. 501)

21. approach/avoidance conflict (p. 501)

22. frustration (p. 501)

23. acculturation (p. 503)

24. acculturative stress (p. 503)

25. assimilation (p. 503)

26. integration (p. 503)

27. separation (p. 503)

28. marginalization (p. 503)

29. feminization of poverty (p. 505)

30. coping (p. 506)

31. problem-focused coping (p. 506)

32. emotion-focused coping (p. 506)

33. avoidance strategies (p. 506)

34. social support (p. 508)

35. stress management programs (p. 510)

36. meditation (p. 510)

37. transcendental meditation (TM) (p. 510)

38. biofeedback (p. 512)

Guided Review

The following in-depth chapter review is a challenging and comprehensive fill-in-the-blanks exercise. The answers are found near the end of the chapter. As you go through the exercise, try to resist the temptation to look at the answers until you have provided them. When you have filled in all the blanks, you will have a thorough summary of the chapter for reference and review.

Relating Health and Psychology

Health psychology is a multidimensional approach to health that emphasizes ___(1)___ factors, lifestyle, and the nature of the ___(2)___-________ delivery system. Closely related is the field of ___(3)___ ________, which attempts to combine medical and behavioral knowledge to reduce illness and promote health. One of the main areas of interest is the relation between ___(4)___ and illness.

The field that explores the relationships between psychological factors, the nervous system, and the immune system is called ___(5)___.

Promoting Health

Sustained exercise, such as jogging, swimming, or cycling, that stimulates heart and lung activity is called ___(6)___ exercise. The main focus of exercise has been on preventing ___(7)___ ________. Exercise also produces positive benefits for ___(8)___-________, and reduces anxiety and ___(9)___.

Researchers have linked poor nutrition, in the form of high fat and ___(10)___ intake, to increased risk for certain diseases. Cross-cultural research strongly suggests that varying ___(11)___ practices in different cultures have an important effect on health. Estimates are that ___(12)___ percent of men and ___(13)___ percent of women in the U.S. are overweight. The ___(14)___ component of obesity has been explored by researchers. The weight that one maintains when no effort is made to gain or lose weight is called the ___(15)___ ________. An important factor in one's set point is the amount of stored ___(16)___ in one's body. The ___(17)___ metabolism rate, the minimal amount of energy an individual uses in a resting state, is another factor in weight. Strong evidence of the influence of the environment is the ___(18)___ of the rate of obesity since 1900.

One advantage of exercise in a weight loss program is that it can actually lower the body's ___(19)___ ________ for weight. Although some diets seem to produce favorable long-term results, the frequency with which these results occur is open to question. Empirical evidences suggests a link between frequent weight cycling, sometimes called "___(20)___-________ dieting" and chronic disease

An eating disorder that involves the relentless pursuit of thinness through starvation is called ___(21)___ ________. An eating disorder characterized by binging and purging is called ___(22)___. A common characteristic of bulimics is ___(23)___.

Although the adverse consequences of smoking have been highly publicized, smoking is still widespread because it is ___(24)___ and ___(25)___. Four methods that have been used to help smokers abandon their habit include the use of ___(26)___ substitutes, stimulus control, ___(27)___ conditioning, and going "cold turkey."

Citizens in the U.S. are not very knowledgeable about sex. Among adolescents there is much ___(28)___ about sexual matters. The inconsistent use of ___(29)___ has led to the U.S. having the highest adolescent pregnancy rate in the industrialized world.

Diseases that are contracted primarily through sex are called ___(30)___ ________ ________ (STDs). A common STD in the United States is ___(31)___, which is caused by a bacterium. Gonorrhea can be successfully treated in the early stages with ___(32)___ drugs. Another sexually transmitted disease caused by a bacterium is ___(33)___. Treatment with ___(34)___ is successful if begun while the disease is in its early stages. The most common of all bacterial STDs in the U.S. is ___(35)___.

A sexually transmitted disease caused by a virus is genital ___(36)___. Although there is no known cure for herpes, drugs can help reduce ___(37)___. A sexually transmitted disease caused by the human immunodeficiency virus is ___(38)___. According to experts, AIDS can be transmitted only by ___(39)___ contact, the sharing of needles, ___(40)___ transfusions, or other contact with an infected person's blood, or sexual fluids. A survey of college students indicated that ___(41)___ about sexual behavior is widespread.

Seven out of the ten leading causes of death in the United States are associated with the ___(42)___ of good health behaviors. Many experts believe that the next major step to improve general health in the United States will be ___(43)___, not medical. Among the health objectives established by the federal government for the year 2000 are the development of ___(44)___ services, health promotion, cleaner air and water, and efforts to meet the health needs of ___(45)___ populations.

Gender and ___(46)___ play roles in life expectancy and health. ___(47)___ ________ have a higher mortality rate than Whites, for most of the leading causes of death.

Understanding Stress

Stress is the response of individuals to the circumstances and events, called ___(48)___, that threaten them and tax their coping abilities.

Selye calls the body's reaction to stress the ___(49)___ ________ ________. The GAS consists of three stages: (1) the body enters a state of shock in the ___(50)___ stage, (2) an all-out effort is made to combat stress in the ___(51)___ stage, and (3) wear and tear on the body increase in the ___(52)___ stage. According to Selye, not all stress is bad. The positive features of stress are called ___(53)___.

Lazarus calls individuals' interpretations of their lives and their determination of whether they have the resources to cope with the events ___(54)___ ________. According to Lazarus, in ___(55)___ appraisal, people interpret whether an event involves harm, threat, or challenge. In ___(56)___ appraisal, they evaluate their resources and determine how to cope with the event.

A cluster of characteristics—being excessively competitive, hard-driven, impatient, and hostile—that are thought to be related to the incidence of heart disease is called ___(57)___ ________ behavior.

A personality style characterized by a sense of commitment, control, and a perception of problems as being challenges is called ___(58)___.

When stimuli become so intense that we can no longer cope with them, we experience ___(59)___.

A hopeless, helpless feeling brought on by relentless work-related stress is called ___(60)___. Burnout usually occurs as a result of a ___(61)___ ________ of stress rather than from one or two incidents. Burnout is also a problem with ___(62)___ ________.

Conflicts in which an individual must choose between two attractive stimuli or circumstances are called ___(63)___/________ conflicts. Conflicts in which an individual must choose between two unattractive stimuli or circumstances are called ___(64)___/________ conflicts. A conflict in which a single stimulus or circumstance has both positive and negative characteristics is called an ___(65)___/________ conflict. Another stress-producing circumstance, in which a person cannot reach a desired goal, is called ___(66)___.

Significant ___(67)___ ________ have been proposed as a major source of stress. A widely used scale to measure life events and their possible impact on illness is the ___(68)___ ________ ________ ________. People who experience clusters of significant life events are more likely to become ___(69)___. Psychologists are increasingly considering the nature of ___(70)___ ________ and their effects on stress.

The cultural change that results from continuous, firsthand contact between two distinct cultural groups is called ___(71)___. ___(72)___ ________ refers to the negative consequences of acculturation.

___(73)___ occurs when individuals relinquish their cultural identity and move into the larger society. In contrast, ___(74)___ implies the maintenance of cultural integrity and the movement to become part of the larger culture. Self-imposed withdrawal from the larger culture is called ___(75)___, but when it is imposed by the larger society, it is referred to as ___(76)___. ___(77)___ refers to the process in which groups are put out of contact with both their traditional society and the dominant society. Two adaptive outcomes of acculturative stress are ___(78)___ and ___(79)___

Poverty creates considerable stress for individuals and families; ___(80)___ ________ families are disproportionately among the poor. Poverty is also related to threatening and uncontrollable ___(81)___ ________, such as crime and violence.

With regard to gender, studies suggest that ___(82)___ women are healthier than ___(83)___ women. Women experience more ___(84)___ between roles and more overload than men do.

Far more women than men live in poverty. This has been termed the ___(85)___ of poverty.

Coping Strategies

According to Lazarus, individuals who cope with stress by facing their problems and trying to solve them engage in ___(86)___-________ coping, whereas those who cope with stress in an emotional, defensive manner engage in ___(87)___-________ coping.

Individuals who keep stress out of awareness are using ___(88)___ strategies. Researchers have emphasized that an effective way to deal with stress is a positive feeling of ___(89)___. According to Seligman, the key to optimism is to challenge ___(90)___-________ thoughts. According to Ellis, the key to optimism is to ___(91)___ ________ to negative thoughts.

Information from others that one is loved and cared for is referred to as ___(92)___ ________. An effective strategy for coping with stress involves learning to act ___(93)___.

Programs designed to teach individuals how to appraise stressful events and to develop skills for coping with stress are called ___(94)___ ________ programs. A technique that incorporates exercises to attain bodily or mental control and well-being is called ___(95)___. A popular form of meditation derived from an ancient Indian technique that involves the use of a mantra is ___(96)___ meditation. According to some researchers, a technique as effective as meditation is ___(97)___. A process in which individuals' muscular or visceral activities are monitored so they can learn to voluntarily control their physiological activities is called ___(98)___. ___(99)___ coping strategies are often better than a single strategy.

Sociocultural Worlds/Applications in Psychology

In your own words, summarize the material you have read in Sociocultural Worlds, "The Acculturative Stress of Ethnic Minority Individuals," and Applications in Psychology, "The Value of Sexual Skepticism." Briefly describe how each of these articles relates to the information contained in the chapter.

Concept Check

Trait or behavior pattern	Characteristics
1. General adaptation syndrome	______________________.
2. Type A behavior pattern	______________________.
3. Hardiness	______________________.
4. Emotion-focused coping	______________________.
5. _________-_________ _________	Coping with stress by facing problems and trying to solve them.

Answers:

1. Reactions to stress are characterized by the stages of alarm, resistance, and exhaustion
2. Being excessively competitive, hard-driven, impatient, and hostile; this is believed to be related to increased probability of heart disease
3. A sense of commitment, control, and a perception of problems as challenges
4. Coping with stress in an emotional, defensive manner
5. Problem-focused coping

Multiple-Choice Questions

Practice Test 1

After answering all the multiple-choice questions in Practice Test 1, compare your answers with the answer key provided at the end of the chapter. The answer key contains a brief explanation of both the correct and incorrect answers. Each of these questions is keyed to the Learning Objectives for the chapter. If you answer any questions incorrectly, review the corresponding Learning Objective and text material before you proceed to Practice Test 2.

1. The field of health psychology emphasizes
   a. psychological factors.
   b. lifestyle.
   c. the health-care delivery system.
   d. all of the above

LO 1

2. According to the text, each of the following is true of exercise *except*
   a. The risk of heart attack can be cut significantly with moderate exercise.
   b. Aerobic activity can be achieved without exercising.
   c. Exercise provides mental health benefits.
   d. Aerobic exercise stimulates heart and lung activity.

LO 2

3. The results of animal research and of cross-cultural research demonstrate a link between diet and
   a. stress.
   b. heart disease.
   c. certain types of cancer.
   d. depression.

LO 3

4. According to research, effective diet programs contain which of the following?
   a. very low-calorie diets
   b. intensive education
   c. behavior modification
   d. an exercise component

LO 4

5. Anorexia nervosa primarily affects
   a. females during adolescence and early adulthood.
   b. males during adolescence and early adulthood.
   c. middle-aged females.
   d. middle-aged males.

LO 5

6. According to the text, light cigarette smokers have more success than heavier smokers with
   a. nicotine substitutes.
   b. stimulus control.
   c. aversive conditioning.
   d. going "cold turkey".

LO 6

7. Adolescents in the United States
   a. are surprisingly well-informed about sexual matters.
   b. are knowledgeable about sexual matters pertaining to their own sex.
   c. believe in much sexual mythology.
   d. are far more cautious sexually than previous generations of adolescents.

LO 7

8. Each of the following sexually transmitted diseases is caused by bacteria *except*
   a. syphilis.
   b. herpes.
   c. gonorrhea.
   d. chlamydia.

LO 8

9. Many public health professionals predict that the next major advance in improving the general health of Americans will be primarily
   a. medical.
   b. from increased immunization.
   c. from increased ability to identify microorganisms.
   d. behavioral.

LO 9

10. Each of the following is true *except*
    a. Males are at greater risk for death than females.
    b. African Americans have a higher mortality than Whites for every leading cause of death.
    c. The health care system generally treats men's health care issues more seriously than women's health care issues.
    d. African American women are more vulnerable to health problems than any other ethnic women.

LO 10

11. The term *stress* was initially reinterpreted from
    a. biology.
    b. chemistry.
    c. physics.
    d. astronomy.

LO 11

12. According to the general adaptation syndrome, in which state does a person exert an all-out effort to combat stress?
    a. alarm
    b. resistance
    c. exhaustion
    d. oral

LO 12

13. According to Lazarus, in primary appraisal, people assess whether an event involves each of the following *except*
    a. fear.
    b. harm.
    c. threat.
    d. challenge.

LO 13

14. Each of the following is characteristic of the Type A behavior pattern *except*
    a. hostility.
    b. competitiveness.
    c. impatience.
    d. a general sense of satisfaction with life.

LO 14

15. The personality style referred to as "hardiness" is characterized by each of the following *except*
    a. sense of commitment.
    b. perception of problems as challenges.
    c. competitiveness
    d. sense of control.

LO 15

16. Jane is experiencing stress. Both of her boyfriends have asked her out for the same night. Assuming she is equally attracted to both, which source of stress is Jane experiencing?
    a. approach-avoidance conflict
    b. approach-approach conflict
    c. avoidance-avoidance conflict
    d. burnout

LO 16

17. According to the Social Readjustment Scale,
    a. only negative events cause stress.
    b. all stressors cause approximately the same amount of stress.
    c. both positive and negative events can cause stress.
    d. the score an individual receives is an excellent predictor of future health.

LO 17

18. A process in which groups are put out of psychological and cultural contact with both their traditional society and the dominant society is called
    a. integration.
    b. marginalization.
    c. separation.
    d. negative acculturation.

LO 18

19. Emotion-focused coping involves
    a. using defense mechanisms.
    b. facing your troubles and trying to solve them.
    c. a rational approach to solving problems.
    d. positive thinking.

LO 19

20. According to Seligman, the key to becoming more optimistic is to
    a. change your lifestyle.
    b. challenge self-defeating thoughts.
    c. seek social support.
    d. avoid stress.

LO 20

21. A process involving the use of instruments to learn to control physiological activities is called
    a. problem-focused coping.
    b. meditation.
    c. biofeedback.
    d. the relaxation response.

LO 21

Practice Test 2

The following multiple-choice questions also are keyed to the chapter Learning Objectives. If you answer any questions incorrectly, be sure to review the corresponding Learning Objective and text material.

1. Psychoneuroimmunologists study the relationship between psychological factors and
    a. the nervous system.
    b. stress.
    c. the immune system.
    d. all of the above.

LO 1

2. Research suggests each of the following mental health benefits from regular exercise *except*
    a. improved self-concept
    b. increased IQ
    c. reduced depression
    d. reduced anxiety

LO 2

3. Many researchers believe the high fat intake in the diet of Americans and the low fat intake in the diet of the Japanese are important factors the countries' different rates of
   a. strokes.
   b. cancer.
   c. heart disease.
   d. diabetes.

LO 3

4. Each of the following is an advantage of exercise as a weight-loss technique *except*
   a. It lowers the body's set point.
   b. It raises the metabolic rate for several hours after exercising.
   c. It burns up calories.
   d. It decreases the sensation of hunger.

LO 4

5. Bulimics
   a. starve themselves.
   b. are often depressed.
   c. are as likely to be male as female.
   d. are most prevalent among middle-aged women.

LO 5

6. Smoking cigarettes
   a. is positively reinforcing.
   b. is negatively reinforcing.
   c. releases neurotransmitters.
   d. all of the above

LO 6

7. The results of a national assessment of basic sexual knowledge indicated that most Americans were
   a. surprisingly knowledgeable about sexual matters.
   b. surprisingly ignorant about many sexual matters.
   c. most knowledgable about sexual matters related to their own sex.
   d. most knowledgeable about sexual matters related to the other sex.

LO 7

8. For which of the following sexually transmitted diseases does no cure currently exist?
   a. gonorrhea
   b. syphilis
   c. herpes
   d. chlamydia

LO 8

9. Men are four times more likely than women to die from
   a. homicide.
   b. suicide.
   c. accidents.
   d. heart disease.

LO 9

10. Women are at greater risk than men for death from
    a. suicide.
    b. heart disease.
    c. homicide.
    d. none of the above

LO 10

11. Stress-related symptoms are estimated to account for what proportion of visits to family doctors?
    a. one-tenth
    b. one-third
    c. one-half
    d. two-thirds

LO 11

12. According to Selye, shock occurs in what stage of the general adaptation syndrome?
    a. alarm stage
    b. resistance stage
    c. exhaustion stage
    d. eustress stage

LO 12

13. Lazarus suggests that in secondary appraisal individuals
    a. evaluate their resources for dealing with stress.
    b. determine how to use their resources to cope with stress.
    c. engage in the use of defense mechanisms.
    d. both *a* and *b*

LO 13

14. A component of the Type A behavior pattern that has been linked to heart disease is
    a. hostility.
    b. aggressiveness.
    c. perfectionism.
    d. competitiveness.

LO 14

15. A sense of control and a perception of problems as being challenges are components of
    a. the Type-A behavior pattern.
    b. primary appraisal.
    c. hardiness.
    d. multiple buffers of stress.

LO 15

16. You take a break from studying and find yourself staring into the refrigerator. You would love to snack on that leftover pizza, but ``Oh, those calories!'' The stress you are experiencing is called
    a. approach/approach conflict.
    b. avoidance/avoidance conflict.
    c. approach/avoidance conflict.
    d. burnout.

LO 16

17. Each of the following was found to be a frequent daily hassle for college students *except*
    a. wasting time.
    b. roommate problems.
    c. being lonely.
    d. worries about high achievement standards.

LO 17

18. According to the text, the healthiest, least stressful adaptation to acculturation is
    a. integration.
    b. marginalization.
    c. separation.
    d. assimilation.

LO 18

19. Which of the following is true regrading coping strategies?
    a. Problem-focused coping guarantees a favorable solution to the stress.
    b. Problem-focused coping involves the use of defensive appraisal.
    c. Emotion-focused coping may involve avoidance.
    d. Avoidance strategies are useful to individuals' adjustment.

LO 19

20. According to Ellis, a good way to become optimistic is to
    a. seek social support.
    b. learn to relax.
    c. avoid stressful situations.
    d. dispute negative thoughts.

LO 20

21. Which of the following relaxation techniques involves the use of a mantra?
    a. biofeedback
    b. transcendental meditation
    c. the relaxation response
    d. assertiveness training

LO 21

Answers to Key Terms

1. **Health psychology** is a multidimensional approach to health that emphasizes psychological factors, lifestyle, and the nature of the health-care delivery system.
2. **Behavioral medicine** attempts to combine medical and behavioral knowledge to reduce illness and promote health.
3. **Psychoneuroimmunology** is the field that explores the relationship between psychological factors, the nervous system, and the immune system.
4. **Aerobic exercise** is sustained exercise, such as jogging, swimming, or cycling, that stimulates heart and lung activity.
5. **Set point** is the weight a person maintains when no effort is made to gain or lose weight.
6. The **basal metabolism rate (BMR)** is the minimum amount of energy an individual uses in a resting state.
7. **Anorexia nervosa** is an eating disorder that involves the relentless pursuit of thinness through starvation.
8. **Bulimia** is an eating disorder in which the individual follows a binge-and-purge pattern.
9. **Sexually transmitted diseases** are diseases contracted primarily though sexual behavior.
10. **AIDS** is an STD that is caused by the human immunodeficiency virus.

11. **Stress** is the response of individuals to the circumstances and events, called stressors, that threaten them and tax their coping abilities.
12. The **general adaptation syndrome** is Selye's concept that describes the common effects on the body when demands are placed on it. The body reacts in three stages: alarm, resistance, and exhaustion.
13. **Eustress** is Selye's term that describes the positive features of stress.
14. **Cognitive appraisal** is Lazarus's concept of individuals' interpretations of events in their lives and their determination of whether they have the resources to effectively cope with the events.
15. **Type A behavior pattern** is a cluster of characteristics, such as excessive competitiveness, impatience, and hostility, thought to be related to the incidence of heart disease.
16. **Hardiness** is a personality style characterized by a sense of commitment, control, and perception of problems as being challenges.
17. **Overload** is the occurrence of stimuli so intense that the person cannot cope with them.
18. **Burnout** is a hopeless, helpless feeling brought on by relentless work-related stress. It involves physical and emotional exhaustion, including chronic fatigue and low energy.
19. An **approach/approach conflict** is one in which the individual must choose between two attractive stimuli or circumstances.
20. An **avoidance/avoidance conflict** is one in which the individual must choose between two unattractive stimuli or circumstances.
21. An **approach/avoidance conflict** is one involving a single stimulus or circumstance that has both negative and positive characteristics.
22. **Frustration** refers to any situation in which a person cannot reach a desired goal.
23. **Acculturation** refers to cultural change resulting from continuous firsthand contact between two distinctive cultural groups.
24. **Acculturative stress** refers to the negative consequences of acculturation.
25. **Assimilation** occurs when individuals relinquish their cultural identity and move into the larger society.
26. **Integration** is maintenance of cultural identity as well as movement to become an integral part of the larger culture.
27. **Separation** is self-imposed withdrawal from the larger culture.
28. **Marginalization** is the process by which groups are put out of cultural and psychological contact with both their traditional society and the lager, dominant society.
29. The **feminization of poverty** refers to the fact that more women than men live in poverty.
30. **Coping** involves managing taxing circumstances, expending effort to solve life's problems, and seeking to master or reduce stress.
31. **Problem-focused coping** involves squarely facing one's troubles and trying to solve them.
32. **Emotion-focused coping** involves responding to stress in an emotional manner, especially using defensive appraisal.
33. **Avoidance strategies** are responses that individuals use to keep stressful circumstances out of awareness so that they do not have to deal with them.
34. **Social support** is information and feedback from others that one is loved and cared for, esteemed and valued, and included in a network of communication and mutual obligation.
35. **Stress management programs** teach individuals how to appraise stressful events, how to develop skills for coping with stress, and how to use these skills in their everyday lives.
36. **Meditation** is the system of thought and form of practice that incorporates exercises to attain bodily or mental control and well-being, as well as enlightenment.
37. **Transcendental meditation,** a popular form of meditation in the United States, involves a mantra, which is a resonant sound that is repeated mentally or aloud to help focus attention.
38. **Biofeedback** is the process where, by monitoring one's muscular or visceral activities with instruments, an individual can learn to voluntarily control the physiological activities.

Answers to Guided Review

1. psychological (p. 483)
2. health-care (p. 483)
3. behavioral medicine (p. 483)
4. stress (p. 483)
5. psychoneuroimmunology (p. 483)
6. aerobic (p. 484)
7. heart attacks (p. 484)
8. self-concept (p. 485)
9. depression (p. 485)
10. cholesterol (p. 485)
11. nutritional (p. 487)
12. 31 (p. 487)
13. 24 (p. 487)
14. genetic (p. 487)
15. set point (p. 488)
16. fat (p. 488)
17. basal (p. 488)
18. doubling (p. 488)
19. set point (p. 488)
20. yo-yo (p. 489)
21. anorexia nervosa (p. 489)
22. bulimia (p. 489)
23. depression (p. 490)
24. addictive (p. 490)
25. reinforcing (p. 490)
26. nicotine (p. 490)
27. aversive (p. 491)
28. misinformation (p. 491)
29. contraception (p. 491)
30. sexually transmitted diseases (p. 493)
31. gonorrhea (p. 493)
32. antibacterial (p. 493)
33. syphilis (p. 493)
34. penicillin (p. 493)
35. chlamydia (p. 493)
36. herpes (p. 493)
37. symptoms (p. 493)
38. AIDS (p. 493)
39. sexual (p. 493)
40. blood (p. 493)
41. lying (p. 494)
42. absence (p. 495)
43. behavioral (p. 495)
44. preventive (p. 495)
45. special (p. 495)
46. ethnicity (p. 495)
47. African Americans (p. 495)
48. stressors (p. 496)
49. general adaptation syndrome (p. 497)
50. alarm (p. 497)
51. resistance (p.497)
52. exhaustion (p. 497)
53. eustress (p. 497)
54. cognitive appraisal (p. 498)
55. primary (p. 498)
56. secondary (p. 498)
57. Type A (p. 499)
58. hardiness (p. 499)
59. overload (p. 500)
60. burnout (p. 500)
61. gradual accumulation (p. 500)
62. college students (p. 500)
63. approach/approach (p. 501)
64. avoidance/avoidance (p. 501)
65. approach/avoidance (p. 501)
66. frustration (p. 501)
67. life events (p. 501)
68. Social Readjustment Rating Scale (p. 501)
69. ill (p. 501)
70. daily hassles (p. 502)
71. acculturation (p. 503)
72. Acculturative stress (p. 503)
73. Assimilation (p. 503)
74. integration (p. 503)
75. separation (p. 503)
76. segregation (p. 503)
77. Marginalization (p. 503)
78. integration (p. 503)
79. assimilation (p. 503)
80. ethnic minority (p. 503)
81. life events (p. 503)
82. employed (p. 505)
83. nonemployed (p. 505)
84. conflict (p. 505)
85. feminization (p. 505)
86. problem-focused (p. 506)
87. emotion-focused (p. 506)
88. avoidance (p. 506)
89. optimism (p. 507)
90. self-defeating (p. 507)
91. talk back (p. 507)
92. social support (p. 508)
93. assertively (p. 508)
94. stress management (p. 510)
95. meditation (p. 510)
96. transcendental (p. 510)
97. relaxation (p. 511)
98. biofeedback (p. 512)
99. Multiple (p. 512)

Answers to Multiple Choice Questions- Practice Test 1

1. a. Incorrect. This answer is partially correct; one of the other answers is a better alternative.
   b. Incorrect. This answer is partially correct; one of the other answers is a better alternative.
   c. Incorrect. This answer is partially correct; one of the other answers is a better alternative.
   d. **Correct.** Behavioral medicine is a closely related field.

2. a. Incorrect. This statement is true.
   b. **Correct.** Aerobic exercise is sustained exercise that stimulates heart and lung activity.
   c. Incorrect. This statement is true.
   d. Incorrect. This statement is true.

3. a. Incorrect. This link was not demonstrated by cross-cultural and animal research.
   b. Incorrect. Although research has established links between diet and heart disease, this is not the research discussed in the text.
   c. **Correct.** Important links have been established between diet and certain types of cancer.
   d. Incorrect. Although there may be links between these two factors, this is not the research described in the text.

4. a. Incorrect. "Starvation" diets are seldom effective in the long run.
   b. Incorrect. Nutrition education is always useful and important, but is not mentioned in the text as a component of most effective diet programs.
   c. Incorrect. Behavior modification can be a useful strategy for dieting, but the text mentions a specific component found in most successful diet programs.
   d. **Correct.** One reason exercise is important is that it can lower the body's set point for weight.

5. a. **Correct.** Many are from middle- and upper-income families.
   b. Incorrect. Wrong gender.
   c. Incorrect. Wrong age group.
   d. Incorrect. Wrong gender and age group.

6. a. Incorrect. The text does not mention how light smokers fare with nicotine substitutes.
   b. Incorrect. The text does not mention how light smokers fare with stimulus control.
   c. The text does not mention how light smokers fare with aversive conditioning.
   d. **Correct.** In this approach, one stops smoking without making any major lifestyle changes.

7. a. Incorrect. Research suggests adolescents believe much mythology about sexual matters.
   b. Incorrect. No evidence is presented in the text in support of this statement.
   c. **Correct.** For example a survey found a majority of adolescents believed that pregnancy risk is greatest during menstruation.
   d. Incorrect. No evidence is presented in the text in support of this statement.

8. a. Incorrect. Syphilis *is* caused by a bacteria.
   b. **Correct.** Herpes is caused by a virus; there is no known cure for herpes.
   c. Incorrect. Gonorrhea *is* caused by a bacteria.
   d. Incorrect. Chlamydia *is* caused by a bacteria.

9. a. Incorrect. Predictions are that improvements will be from areas other than medical.
   b. Incorrect. Immunization is an important health goal, but researchers believe improvement in American health will come from a different area.
   c. Incorrect. Predictions are that improvements will be from a different area.
   d. **Correct.** This underscores the fact that lifestyle and personal habits play a key role in health.

10. a. Incorrect. This statement is true.
    b. **Correct.** According to the text, African Americans have a higher mortality in 13 of 15 categories.
    c. Incorrect. This statement is true.
    d. Incorrect. This statement is true.

11. a. Incorrect. The term *stress* initially came from a different field.
    b. Incorrect. The term *stress* initially came from a different field.
    c. **Correct.** The analogy was drawn between humans and objects, such as metals.
    d. Incorrect. The term *stress* initially came from a different field.

12. a. Incorrect. In this stage, the body enters a temporary state of shock.
    b. **Correct.** In this stage, the body can fight off infection with remarkable efficiency.
    c. Incorrect. In this stage the body's resources have been depleted.
    d. Incorrect. This is not a stage in the general adaptation syndrome.

13. a. **Correct.** According to Lazarus, this is not one of the components of primary appraisal.
    b. Incorrect. This *is* one of the interpretations considered in primary appraisal.
    c. Incorrect. This *is* one of the interpretations considered in primary appraisal.
    d. Incorrect. This *is* one of the interpretations considered in primary appraisal.

14. a. Incorrect. This *is* one of the characteristics of the Type A behavior pattern.
    b. Incorrect. This *is* one of the characteristics of the Type A behavior pattern.
    c. Incorrect. This *is* one of the characteristics of the Type A behavior pattern.
    d. **Correct.** A sense of satisfaction with life is not one of the characteristics of the Type A behavior pattern.

15. a. Incorrect. This *is* one of the characteristics of hardiness.
    b. Incorrect. This *is* one of the characteristics of hardiness.
    c. **Correct.** This is not one of the characteristics of hardiness.
    d. Incorrect. This *is* one of the characteristics of hardiness.

16. a. Incorrect. This refers to situations in which the same situation is simultaneously attractive and unattractive.
    b. **Correct.** Jane must choose between two attractive circumstances.
    c. Incorrect. This would apply if Jane had to choose between two equally unattractive alternatives.
    d. Incorrect. Burnout usually refers to work-related stress.

17. a. Incorrect. The Scale implies both positive and negative events can cause stress.
    b. Incorrect. The Scale indicates that different stressors cause different amounts of stress.
    c. **Correct.** For example, both holidays and death of a spouse are items on the Scale.
    d. Incorrect. The Scale has been found to be ineffective at predicting future health problems.

18. a. Incorrect. This refers to maintaining cultural integrity as well as moving into the larger society.
    b. **Correct.** This often leads to feelings of alienation and a loss of identity.
    c. Incorrect. This is self-imposed withdrawal from the larger culture.
    d. Incorrect. This term is not used in the text.

19. a. **Correct.** This type of coping involves responding to stress in an emotional manner.
    b. Incorrect. This describes problem-focused coping.
    c. Incorrect. This describes problem-focused coping.
    d. Incorrect. This describes a good coping strategy.

20. a. Incorrect. Seligman takes a more cognitive view in developing optimism.
    b. **Correct.** Ellis believes we need to dispute negative thoughts.
    c. Incorrect. Seligman takes a more cognitive view in developing optimism.
    d. Incorrect. Seligman takes a more cognitive view in developing optimism.

21. a. Incorrect. This coping strategy involves squarely facing one's problems.
    b. Incorrect. This refers to a system of thought and practice leading to control, well-being and enlightenment.
    c. **Correct.** Biofeedback employs the principle of reinforcement.
    d. Incorrect. some researchers believe relaxation provides the same basic benefits as meditation.

Answers to Multiple Choice Questions- Practice Test 2

1. a. Incorrect. This answer is partially correct; one of the other answers is a better alternative.
   b. Incorrect. This answer is partially correct; one of the other answers is a better alternative.
   c. Incorrect. This answer is partially correct; one of the other answers is a better alternative.
   d. **Correct.** Researchers have found important connections between psychological factors and the immune system.

2. a. Incorrect. This *is* a benefit from regular exercise.
   b. **Correct.** The text does not cite evidence showing increased IQ as a result of exercise.
   c. Incorrect. This *is* a benefit from regular exercise.
   d. Incorrect. This *is* a benefit from regular exercise.

3. a. Incorrect. This is not the health factor cited in the text.
   b. **Correct.** There is impressive evidence concerning the link between nutrition and certain types of cancer.
   c. Incorrect. This is not the health factor cited in the text.
   d. Incorrect. This is not the health factor cited in the text.

4. a. Incorrect. This *is* an advantage of exercise.
   b. Incorrect. This *is* an advantage of exercise.
   c. Incorrect. This *is* an advantage of exercise.
   d. **Correct.** The text does not cite this ans an advantage of exercise.

5. a. Incorrect. Bulimics engage in a binge-and-purge cycle.
   b. **Correct.** Anti-depression medications are often used in treating bulimia.
   c. Incorrect. Bulimics are more likely to be female.
   d. Incorrect. Bulimia is most prevalent among traditional-age college women.

6. a. Incorrect. This answer is partially correct; one of the other answers is a better alternative.
   b. Incorrect. This answer is partially correct; one of the other answers is a better alternative.
   c. Incorrect. This answer is partially correct; one of the other answers is a better alternative.
   d. **Correct.** Nicotine is now widely recognized as an addictive drug.

7. a. Incorrect. Based on the survey, Americans can not be accused of being "surprisingly knowledgeable."
   b. **Correct.** According to the text, Americans know more about their cars than about their bodies.
   c. Incorrect. This is not mentioned in the text.
   d. Incorrect. This is not mentioned in the text.

8. a. Incorrect. A cure exists, but it should be treated promptly.
   b. Incorrect. A cure exists, but it should be treated promptly.
   c. **Correct.** Herpes is caused by a virus; no cure exists, although symptoms can usually be controlled.
   d. Incorrect. Chlamydia can be treated with antibiotics.

9. a. **Correct.** This actively contributes to the greater mortality for males.
   b. Incorrect. Approximately twice as many men die from suicide.
   c. Incorrect. Approximately twice as many men die from accidents.
   d. Incorrect. Approximately twice as many men die from heart disease.

10. a. Incorrect. Approximately twice as many men die from suicide.
   b. Incorrect. Approximately twice as many men die from heart disease.
   c. Incorrect. Approximately four times as many men die from homicide.
   d. **Correct.** Men are at greater risk for all the listed causes of death.

11. a. Incorrect. The proportion is considerably higher.
   b. Incorrect. The proportion is considerably higher.
   c. Incorrect. The proportion is higher.
   d. **Correct.** Thus, stress-related symptoms takes up a considerable amount of time for most physicians.

12. a. **Correct.** During this brief stage, resistance falls below its normal limits.
   b. Incorrect. During this stage, the body can fight off infection efficiently.
   c. Incorrect. During this stage, the body's efforts are overwhelmed.
   d. Incorrect. This is not a stage in the general adaptation syndrome.

13. a. Incorrect. This answer is partially correct; one of the other answers is a better alternative.
   b. Incorrect. This answer is partially correct; one of the other answers is a better alternative.
   c. Incorrect. This is associated with emotion-focused coping.
   d. **Correct.** The nature of the secondary appraisal depends upon the primary appraisal.

14. a. **Correct.** A related factor is turning anger inward.
   b. Incorrect. Aggressiveness is a Type A behavior pattern, but it has not been directly linked to heart disease.
   c. Incorrect. Perfectionism is a Type A behavior pattern, but it has not been linked to heart disease.
   d. Incorrect. Competitiveness is a Type A behavior pattern, but it has not been directly linked with heart disease.

15. a. Incorrect. The Type A behavior pattern does not usually enjoy a sense of control.
   b. Incorrect. This is the first step of cognitive appraisal, according to Lazarus.
   c. **Correct.** Another characteristic is a sense of commitment.
   d. Incorrect. The question refers to a single "buffer" of stress.

16. a. Incorrect. This refers to conflict between two attractive stimuli or circumstances.
   b. Incorrect. This refers to conflict between two unattractive alternatives.
   c. **Correct.** That leftover pizza is simultaneously attractive and unattractive. Eat an apple instead!
   d. Incorrect. This may apply to your feelings about school, not about the pizza.

17. a. Incorrect. This *was* found to be a frequent daily hassle.
   b. **Correct.** This was not mentioned as a frequent daily hassle.
   c. Incorrect. This *was* found to be a frequent daily hassle.
   d. Incorrect. This *was* found to be a frequent daily hassle.

18. a. **Correct.** According to the text, selecting from both cultures may help to provide the base for effective coping.
   b. Incorrect. This often leads to feelings of alienation and a loss of identity.
   c. Incorrect. This may lead to conflict with those who seek assimilation.
   d. Incorrect. Assimilation implies some loss of culture.

19. a. Incorrect. No coping mechanism can guarantee a favorable solution.
   b. Incorrect. Emotion-focused coping involves using defensive appraisal.
   c. **Correct.** Emotion-focused coping involves the use of defense mechanisms.
   d. Incorrect. Avoidance strategies are generally harmful.

20. a. Incorrect. Ellis favors a more cognitive approach to becoming optimistic.
    b. Incorrect. Ellis favors a more cognitive approach to becoming optimistic.
    c. Incorrect. Ellis favors a more cognitive approach to becoming optimistic.
    d. **Correct.** Ellis believes we should talk back to negative thoughts.

21. a. Incorrect. This approach makes use of electronic equipment.
    b. **Correct.** The mantra helps one to focus attention.
    c. Incorrect. This approach generally encourages focusing on breathing.
    d. Incorrect. This is not a relaxation technique.

Chapter **14** **Social Psychology**

Learning Objectives

After studying this chapter, you should be able to:

1. Define social perception. (p. 518)

2. Discuss the processes by which we form impressions of others. (p. 518)

3. Explain the process of social comparison; identify and describe four impression management techniques. (p. 519)

4. Explain attribution theory and the fundamental attribution error. (p. 520)

5. Define attitudes and describe the relationship between attitudes and behavior. (p. 521)

6. Distinguish between cognitive dissonance theory and Bem's self-perception theory. (p. 522)

7. Identify and describe the four components of a persuasive message. (p. 524)

8. Describe the results of Milgram's "shocking" experiments on obedience. (p. 527)

9. Distinguish between norms and roles. (p. 530)

10. Define conformity and identify the factors that contribute to conformity. (p. 531)

11. Describe the circumstances under which groupthink and deindividuation occur, and discuss the ways in which cults attract members. (p. 532)

12. Contrast the "great person" theory and the situational theory of leadership and discuss the ways in which the minority can influence the majority. (p. 534)

13. Discuss the main factors in interpersonal attraction; identify the components of friendship and love. (p. 536)

14. Identify the characteristics of lonely individuals. (p. 540)

15. Identify the following aspects of altruism: reciprocity and social exchange; contrast altruism and egoism. (p. 542)

16. Explain the bystander effect; describe the circumstances under which the bystander effect is less likely to occur. (p. 544)

Chapter 14 Outline

- I. Social Cognition
  - A. Social Perception
    - 1. Impression Formation
    - 2. Social Comparison
    - 3. Impression Management
  - B. Attribution
    - 1. Internal attributions
    - 2. External attributions
    - 3. Fundamental attribution error
  - C. Attitudes and Behavior
    - 1. Predicting Behavior from Attitudes
    - 2. Behavior's Influence on Attitudes
    - 3. Festinger's Cognitive Dissonance Theory
    - 4. Bem's Self-Perception Theory
- II. Social Influence
  - A. Interpersonal Influence
    - 1. Persuasion
      - a. the communicator (source)
      - b. the Medium
      - c. the Message
      - d. the Target
    - 2. Obedience
  - B. Influence in Groups
    - 1. The nature of groups
      - a. norms
      - b. roles
    - 2. Conformity
    - 3. Groupthink
    - 4. Deindividuation
    - 5. Leadership
      - a. great person theory
      - b. situational theory
    - 6. Majority-Minority Influence
- III. Interpersonal Relationships
  - A. Attraction
    - 1. Consensual validation
    - 2. Physical attraction
  - B. Friendship
  - C. Romantic Love
  - D. Companionate Love
  - E. Loneliness
  - F. Altruism
    - 1. Social exchange theory
    - 2. Bystander effect

Key Terms

Write a brief description for each of the following terms. Where relevant, provide an original example or illustration of the term. Then, compare your answers with those provided at the end of the Study Guide chapter. Review the text for those terms you don't know and those you define incorrectly.

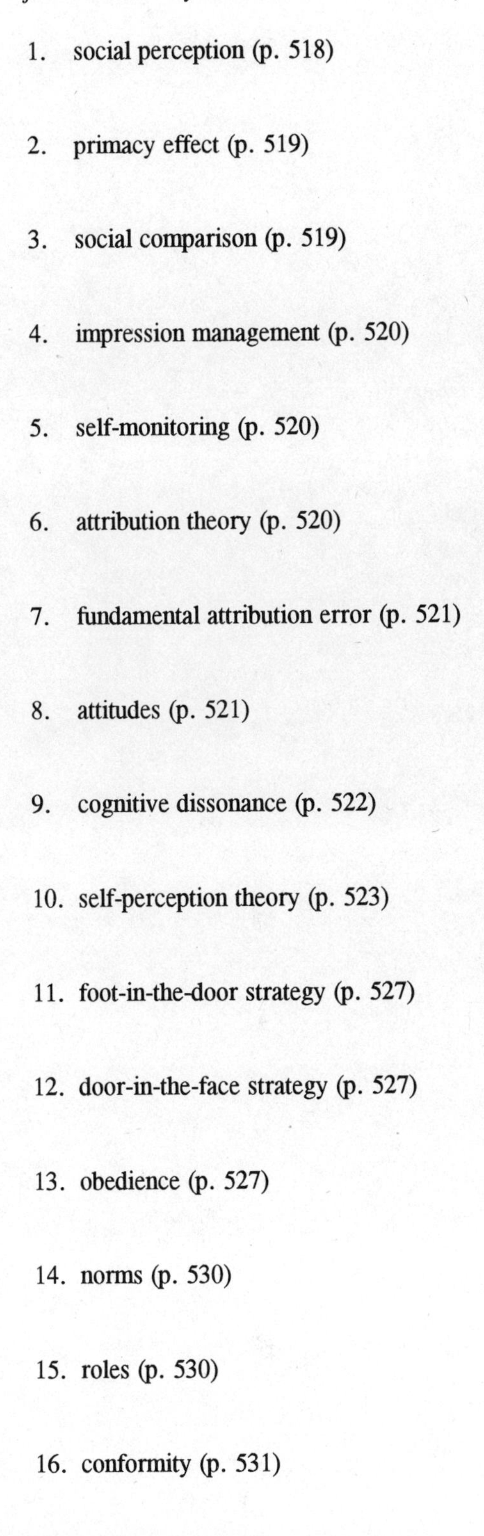

1. social perception (p. 518)

2. primacy effect (p. 519)

3. social comparison (p. 519)

4. impression management (p. 520)

5. self-monitoring (p. 520)

6. attribution theory (p. 520)

7. fundamental attribution error (p. 521)

8. attitudes (p. 521)

9. cognitive dissonance (p. 522)

10. self-perception theory (p. 523)

11. foot-in-the-door strategy (p. 527)

12. door-in-the-face strategy (p. 527)

13. obedience (p. 527)

14. norms (p. 530)

15. roles (p. 530)

16. conformity (p. 531)

17. groupthink (p. 532)

18. deindividuation (p. 533)

19. great person theory (p. 534)

20 situational theory of leadership (p. 534)

21. consensual validation (p. 536)

22. matching hypothesis (p. 536)

23. friendship (p. 537)

24. romantic love (p. 538)

25. affectionate love (p. 538)

26. triangular theory of love (p. 539)

27. altruism (p. 542)

28. social exchange theory (p. 543)

29. egoism (p. 544)

30. bystander effect (p. 544)

31. diffusion of responsibility (p. 544)

Guided Review

The following in-depth chapter review is a challenging and comprehensive fill-in-the-blanks exercise. The answers are found near the end of the chapter. As you go through the exercise, try to resist the temptation to look at the answers until you have provided them. When you have filled in all the blanks, you will have a thorough summary of the chapter for reference and review.

Social Cognition

The judgments we form about the qualities of others are called ___(1)___ ________. When we form impressions of others, those impression are both ___(2)___ and ___(3)___. First impressions are often enduring; psychologists refer to this as the ___(4)___ ________.

A process in which individuals evaluate their thoughts, feelings, behaviors, and abilities in relation to other people is called ___(5)___ ________. Festinger's social comparison theory suggests that when no ___(6)___ norms are available to evaluate our opinions and abilities, we compare ourselves with ___(7)___.

The process in which individuals strive to present themselves in a favorable light is called ___(8)___ ________. Four recommended impression management strategies are to use behavioral matching, ___(9)___ to situational expectations, show appreciation of others, and use positive nonverbal ___(10)___. Individuals' attention to the impressions they make on others is called ___(11)___-________.

We are motivated to discover the causes of behavior as part of our interest in making sense of the behavior, according to ___(12)___ ________. One important distinction relating to attribution is whether we attribute the causes of our behavior to the environment, called ___(13)___ ________, or to our personality, referred to as ___(14)___ ________. Our tendency to overestimate the importance of traits and underestimate the importance of situations in seeking explanations of a person's behavior is called the ___(15)___ ________ ________.

Beliefs and opinions that predispose individuals to behave in certain ways are ___(16)___. Psychologists have been interested in the relationship between attitudes and ___(17)___.

Ample evidence exists that indicates changes in behavior precede changes in ___(18)___. One explanation is that we have a need for cognitive ___(19)___. This view is central to Festinger's concept of ___(20)___ ________. This concept suggests that we are motivated to reduce the discomfort caused by discrepancies between ___(21)___ and ___(22)___.

Some psychologists believe that the dissonance view relies too heavily on ___(23)___ factors. Bem's theory, called ___(24)___-________ theory, suggests that individuals make inferences about their attitudes by perceiving their own ___(25)___.

Social Influence

Social psychologists believe that persuasion involves four components: the source, the ___(26)___, the message, and the ___(27)___. Among important communicator characteristics are ___(28)___, credibility, and ___(29)___.

A second component involved in persuasion is the ___(30)___. The average American will have watched ___(31)___ hours of television by the time he or she graduates from high school.

A third factor is the ___(32)___. Generally, messages that are ___(33)___ are more persuasive. ___(34)___ is widely used to make us feel good about messages.

When an individual starts with a small request and then requests progressively more, the strategy is called the ___(35)___-________-________-________ strategy. In contrast, a strategy of making the strongest request first and then presenting a weaker request is called the ___(36)___-________-________-________ strategy.

A final factor is the ___(37)___. Two audience factors that determine the persuasiveness of a communication are ___(38)___ and gender.

Behavior that complies with the explicit demands of an individual in authority is ___(39)___. In Milgram's classic experiment, participants obeyed even though they believed they were ___(40)___ someone. Milgram's research raises important questions regarding ___(41)___ in psychology experiments.

All groups have rules that apply to all members; these are called ___(42)___. Some rules govern only certain positions in the group; these are ___(43)___.

When individuals adopt the attitudes or behavior of others because of real or imagined pressure from others, it is referred to as ___(44)___. The power of conformity was demonstrated by Asch's study on judgments of ___(45)___ ________and by Zimbardo's study of social roles in a mock ___(46)___.

Sometimes group members seek to maintain harmony and unanimity among the group members; this may lead to ___(47)___, in which individual differences of opinion are stifled. A state of reduced self-awareness, weakened self-restraint against impulsive actions, and apathy about negative social evaluation is referred to as ___(48)___. One explanation of deindividuation is that the group offers ___(49)___. Losing the boundaries of the self is characteristic of ___(50)___.

Some individuals have certain traits that are best suited for leadership positions, according to the ___(51)___ _______ theory. The ___(52)___ theory of leadership argues that as the needs of a group change, the traits needed in a leader also change. Many psychologists believe that leadership is determined by some combination of ___(53)___ characteristics, skills, and ___(54)___ influences.

Although in most group decision making the majority wins, when the minority presents its views consistently and confidently, its views are more likely to be heard; this approach has been labeled ___(55)___.

Interpersonal Relationships

An essential condition for a close relationship to develop is ___(56)___. We like to associate with people who are ___(57)___ to us. Forming close relationships with others similar to ourselves is rewarding because it provides consensual ___(58)___ of our own attitudes and behaviors.

According to the ___(59)___ ________, we tend to select partners who are close to our own level of attractiveness.

___(60)___ is a close relationship that involves enjoyment, acceptance, trust, intimacy, respect, mutual assistance, understanding, and spontaneity. Romantic love is also referred to as ___(61)___ love or Eros. It often predominates in the ___(62)___ part of a love relationship. Romantic love is the main reason we get ___(63)___, and is especially important among ___(64)___ students. According to Berscheid, romantic love is about ___(65)___ percent sexual desire. Affectionate love is also called ___(66)___ love. It is characterized by a desire to have the other person near, and by deep, caring___(67)___ for the other person. While the early stages of love are characterized by romantic passion, that ultimately gives way to ___(68)___. Sternberg's triangular theory of love incudes these three dimensions: ___(69)___, intimacy, and ___(70)___.

Loneliness is associated with an individual's gender, attachment history, self-esteem, and ___(71)___ skills. Males and females attribute their loneliness to different sources.

An unselfish interest in helping someone else is called ___(72)___. Two important psychological aspects of altruism are ___(73)___ and social ___(74)___. Reciprocity encourages us to "do unto others as we would have them to unto us." According to ___(75)___ ________ theory, individuals should benefit those who benefit them.

Some psychologists argue that ___(76)___ has never been demonstrated. Others suggest an important distinction between altruism and ___(77)___. As with all behavior, altruism is influenced by characteristics of the ___(78)___.

Individuals who observe an emergency are less likely to help when someone else is present, according to the ___(79)___ ________. The tendency to feel less responsible and act less responsible in the presence of others is called ___(80)___ ________ ________. Bystanders are less likely to intervene when the situation might lead to personal ___(81)___when helping takes ___(82)___, when a situation is ambiguous, when the individuals are related, when a victim is drunk or of a different ___(83)___ ________, and when bystanders have no history of being victimized themselves.

Sociocultural Worlds/Applications in Psychology

In your own words, summarize the material you have read in Sociocultural Worlds, "The Gender Gap in Politics," and Applications in Psychology, "Resisting Social Influence." Briefly describe how each of these articles relates to the information contained in the chapter.

Concept Check

Term	Definition
1. Social perception	______________________.
2. ________ ________	Individuals are motivated to discover the underlying causes of behavior.
3. Cognitive dissonance	______________________.
4. ________-________ ________	Bem's theory, stressing that individuals make inferences about their attitudes by perceiving their behavior.
5. ________ ________ ________ ____ ________	Individuals have certain traits that are best suited for leadership positions.
6. Situational theory of leadership	______________________.
7. ________	A state of reduced self-awareness, weakened self-restraints against impulse, and apathy about negative social evaluation.

Answers

1. Judgment about the qualities of individuals, based on our impressions of others, our self-knowledge from perceiving others, and so on
2. Attribution theory
3. Festinger's concept that refers to an individual's motivation toward consistency and away from inconsistency
4. Self-perception theory
5. Great person theory of leadership
6. The needs of groups change over time, and a leader in one set of circumstances will not necessarily be the one who becomes a leader in other circumstances
7. Deindividuation

Multiple-Choice Questions

Practice Test 1

After answering all the multiple-choice questions in Practice Test 1, compare your answers with the answer key provided at the end of the chapter. The answer key contains a brief explanation of both the correct and incorrect answers. Each of these questions is keyed to the Learning Objectives for the chapter. If you answer any questions incorrectly, review the corresponding Learning Objective and text material before you proceed to Practice Test 2.

1. Each of the following is a component of social perception *except*
   a. developing impressions of others
   b. gaining self-knowledge from our perceptions of others
   c. presenting ourselves to others to influence them
   d. deindividuation

LO 1

2. Our perceptions of others are usually organized as continuous blocks of information, although they may have been obtained over a long period of time. This quality is referred to as
   a. unified.
   b. integrated.
   c. implicit.
   d. individuated.

LO 2

3. According to Festinger and others, our most accurate social comparisons occur when we compare ourselves with those who are
   a. similar to us in terms of background.
   b. different from us in terms of background.
   c. both similar and different in terms of background.
   d. highly successful in life.

LO 3

4. People are interested in discovering the causes of behavior, according to
   a. attribution theory.
   b. self-perception theory.
   c. cognitive dissonance.
   d. social perception theory.

LO 4

5. Each of the following is part of the definition of attitudes *except*
   a. beliefs.
   b. opinions.
   c. facts.
   d. predisposition to behave.

LO 5

6. According to cognitive dissonance theory, dissonance,
   a. is a goal we all seek.
   b. helps to improve relationships with others.
   c. is an extremely rare event.
   d. creates discomfort.

LO 6

7. Each of the following is a key component of a persuasive message *except*
   a. the source.
   b. the message.
   c. the channel.
   d. the urgency of the appeal.

LO 7

8. In Milgram's "shocking" research, it was discovered that obedience decreased
   a. as people were paid more to participate.
   b. when the authority figure was perceived to be legitimate.
   c. when the authority figure was close by.
   d. when the victim was made to seem more human.

LO 8

9. A rule that applies to all members of a group is a(n)
   a. role.
   b. norm.
   c. standard.
   d. group demand.

LO 9

10. In Asch's experiment on estimating line length, he was surprised to find participants conforming to incorrect answers
    a. none of the time.
    b. 35 percent of the time.
    c. 60 percent of the time.
    d. 90 percent of the time.

LO 10

11. The tendency for groups to stifle dissent in the interest of group harmony refers to
    a. ethnocentrism.
    b. social identity.
    c. groupthink.
    d. deindividuation.

LO 11

12. Cults practice each of the following social psychology principles *except*
    a. deindividuation.
    b. group norms.
    c. groupthink.
    d. minority influence.

LO 12

13. According to the great person theory of leadership,
    a. a good leader in one circumstance will not necessarily be a good leader in another circumstance.
    b. leaders have certain traits that are best suited for leadership positions.
    c. a combination of personality characteristics and the situation helps determine who will become a leader.
    d. leaders are born, not made.

LO 12

14. The majority normally exerts its influence by
    a. normative pressure.
    b. informational pressure.
    c. creating deindividuation.
    d. both *a* and *b*

LO 12

15. Each of the following is true *except*
    a. In relationships, "birds of a feather flock together."
    b. Romantic love is important to college students.
    c. We tend to develop relationships with others who are close to our own level of attractiveness.
    d. Physical attractiveness remains the key ingredient to relationships over the long run.

LO 13

16. Each of the following is a component of Sternberg's triangular theory of love *except*
    a. passion.
    b. infatuation.
    c. intimacy.
    d. commitment.

LO 13

17. Loneliness is associated with each of the following variables *except* an individual's
    a. gender.
    b. attachment history.
    c. income.
    d. self-esteem.

LO 14

18. Sue helps Jim tune up his car. Later, Sue says to Jim, "Remember when I helped you with your car? You owe me one. I really need your help with a plumbing problem at my apartment." This could be an example of
    a. reciprocity.
    b. social exchange.
    c. egoism.
    d. any of the above

LO 15

19. Altruism increases the chances of survival of one's genes according to
    a. social exchange theory.
    b. evolutionary psychologists.
    c. major world religions.
    d. normative expectations.

LO 15

20. Research suggests that bystander intervention is less likely in each of the following *except*
    a. when intervention might led to personal harm.
    b. when a situation is ambiguous.
    c. when the bystander has a history of victimization.
    d. when the victim is drunk rather than disabled.

LO 16

Practice Test 2

The following multiple-choice questions also are keyed to the chapter Learning Objectives. If you answer any questions incorrectly, be sure to review the corresponding Learning Objective and text material.

1. Our judgment about the personal qualities of others is known as
    a. attribution.
    b. social perception.
    c. social influence.
    d. altruism.

LO 1

2. "First impressions are lasting impressions" according to
    a. the primacy effect.
    b. the latency effect.
    c. attribution theory.
    d. the theory of social comparison.

LO 2

3. According to the text, which of the following is a good impression management strategy?
    a. Don't copy what another person is doing.
    b. Be your own person—don't conform to situational norms.
    c. Don't flatter people—they will see right through it.
    d. Try to influence others' perceptions by using positive nonverbal cues.

LO 3

4. Laura attributes her success in sales to the fact that she works hard, knows her products well, and is aggressive. Her explanation involves
    a. external attributions.
    b. internal attributions.
    c. both external and internal attributions.
    d. cognitive dissonance.

LO 4

5. Which of the following is *true* regarding the relationship between attitudes and behavior?
    a. It is easy to predict attitudes by observing behavior.
    b. It is easy to predict behavior if attitudes are known.
    c. The connection between attitudes and behavior may vary with the situation.
    d. Attitudes are always formed before behavior.

LO 5

6. Self-perception theory
    a. suggests that individuals are motivated to reduce inconsistencies.
    b. helps explain persuasion and obedience.
    c. suggests that individuals make inferences about their attitudes by perceiving their behavior.
    d. both *a* and *c*

LO 6

7. According to social psychologists, each of these characteristics can help a communicator change people's attitudes *except*
    a. power.
    b. attractiveness.
    c. similarity.
    d. intelligence.

LO 7

8. Which of the following is *true* regarding Milgram's research on obedience?
   a. Milgram's experiment caused severe physical pain to the "learners."
   b. Milgram's research failed to debrief participants.
   c. Milgram found surprisingly high levels of obedience.
   d. Milgram found vastly different results when he conducted his research in a more natural environment.

LO 8

9. The expectations that govern behavior for people in a particular position in a group are called
   a. values.
   b. laws.
   c. roles.
   d. norms.

LO 9

10. During Zimbardo's Stanford prison experiment,
   a. little change occurred among the guards.
   b. little change occurred among the prisoners.
   c. dramatic changes in behavior occurred in some prisoners and guards.
   d. dramatic changes occurred, but only after 10 days.

LO 10

11. When behavior becomes deindividuated,
   a. it leads to reduced self-awareness.
   b. individuals become increasingly concerned about negative social evaluation.
   c. group members are motivated to maintain harmony and to stifle dissent.
   d. both *a* and *b*

LO 11

12. Each of the following characterizes cult practices *except*
   a. conformity to stringent group norms
   b. simplistic solutions to complex problems
   c. options to leave the cult at any time
   d. promises of loving acceptance or future salvation

LO 12

13. Which of the following best describes the situational theory of leadership?
   a. Dan's personality characteristics make him the best leader regardless of the situation.
   b. In some situations, Dan will be particularly effective as a leader.
   c. Dan is a born leader.
   d. With proper training, Dan can be turned into a leader.

LO 12

14. The minority can exert influence by using
   a. groupthink.
   b. deindividuation.
   c. normative pressure.
   d. informational pressure.

LO 12

15. Ken and Barbie have a love relationship characterized by passion, intimacy, and commitment. According to Sternberg, this is called
   a. a temporary situation.
   b. infatuation.
   c. consummate love.
   d. affectionate love.

LO 13

16. The early stage of a love relationship is described as
   a. companionate love.
   b. romantic love.
   c. consummate love.
   d. intimate love.

LO 13

17. Research on loneliness suggests that
   a. women are more likely than men to blame themselves for being lonely.
   b. men are more likely than women to blame themselves for being lonely.
   c. men and women are equally likely to blame themselves for being lonely.
   d. loneliness does not appear to be related to the quality of one's relationship with one's parents.

LO 14

18. Jim spends all day volunteering with others to pick up roadside garbage. That evening, he confides to a roommate that his motivation to volunteer was to impress his girlfriend. Jim's behavior is an example of
    a. reciprocity.
    b. social exchange.
    c. altruism.
    d. egoism.

19. According to evolutionary psychologists, altruism
    a. increases the likelihood our genes will survive.
    b. is based on the teachings of the world's great religions.
    c. is motivated purely by egoism.
    d. is a disruptive force in society.

LO 15

20. Which of the following factors is *true* regarding the bystander effect?
    a. The diffusion of responsibility is an important factor.
    b. We tend to look to others for clues.
    c. People are more likely to get involved when others are present.
    d. both *a* and *b*

LO 16

Answers to Key Terms

1. **Social perception** is our judgment about the qualities of individuals. It involves the process of forming impressions of others, gaining self-knowledge from the perception of others and presenting ourselves to others to influence their perceptions.
2. The **primacy effect** implies that first impressions are lasting impressions.
3. **Social comparison** is the process by which individuals evaluate their thoughts, feelings, behaviors, and abilities in relation to other people.
4. **Impression management** is the process by which individuals strive to present themselves in a favorable light.
5. **Self-monitoring** refers to the attention individuals pay to the impressions they make on others and the degree to which they fine-tune their behavior accordingly.
6. **Attribution theory** states that individuals are motivated to discover the underlying causes of behavior.
7. The **fundamental attribution error** states that observers tend to overestimate the importance of traits and underestimate the importance of situations when they seek to explain a person's behavior.
8. **Attitudes** are beliefs and opinions that can predispose individuals to behave in certain ways.
9. **Cognitive dissonance,** a concept developed by Festinger, refers to an individual's motivation to move toward consistency and away from inconsistency.
10. **Self-perception theory,** developed by Bem, stresses that individuals make inferences about their attitudes by perceiving their behavior.
11. **Foot-in-the-door strategy** involves making the weakest point or a smaller request initially, saving the strongest point until the end.
12. **Door-in-the-face strategy** involves making the strongest point first, then making a weaker "concessionary" demand at the end.
13. **Obedience** is behavior that complies with the explicit demands of an individual in authority.
14. **Norms** are rules that apply to all members of a group.
15. **Roles** are rules and expectations that govern certain positions in the group.
16. **Conformity** occurs when individuals adopt the attitudes or behavior of others because of real or imagined pressure from others.
17. **Groupthink** is the motivation of group members to maintain harmony and unanimity in decision making, thus suffocating differences of opinion.
18. **Deindividuation** is the loss of identity as an individual and the development of group identity in group situations that promote arousal and anonymity.

19. The **great person theory** says that some individuals have certain traits that are best suited for leadership positions.
20. The **situational theory of leadership** states that the needs of the group change from time to time, and that a person who serves well in a leadership role in one circumstance will not necessarily be an effective leader in a different circumstance.
21. **Consensual validation** helps explain why people are attracted to others who are similar to them. Our own attitudes and behavior are supported when someone else's attitudes and behavior are similar to ours; that is, they validate our attitudes and opinions.
22. The **matching hypothesis** states that, while we might prefer a more attractive person in the abstract, in the real world we end up choosing someone who is close to our own level of attractiveness.
23. **Friendship** is a form of close relationship involving enjoyment, acceptance, trust, intimacy, mutual respect, mutual assistance, openness, understanding, and spontaneity.
24. **Romantic love,** also called passionate love or Eros, has strong components of sexuality and infatuation, and it often predominates the early part of a love relationship.
25. **Affectionate love,** also called companionate love, occurs when individuals desire to have the other person near, and have a deep, caring affection for the person.
26. The **triangular theory of love** is Sternberg's theory that suggests love has three main components: passion, intimacy, and commitment.
27. **Altruism** is an unselfish interest in helping someone else.
28. **Social exchange theory** states that individuals should benefit those who benefit them, or that, for a benefit received, an equivalent benefit should be returned at some point.
29. **Egoism** is an attitude in which one does something beneficial for another person for any of the following reasons: to ensure reciprocity, to present oneself as powerful, competent, or caring, or to avoid social censure or self-censure for failing to live up to normative expectations.
30. The **bystander effect** states that individuals who observe an emergency are less likely to help when others are present, as compared to when they are the lone observer.
31. **Diffusion of responsibility** is the tendency to feel less responsibility in the presence of others.

Answers to Guided Review

1. social perceptions (p. 518)
2. unified (p. 519)
3. integrated (p. 519)
4. primacy effect (p. 519)
5. social comparison (p. 519)
6. objective (p. 519)
7. others (p. 519)
8. impression management (p. 520)
9. conform (p. 520)
10. cues (p. 520)
11. self-monitoring (p. 520)
12. attribution theory (p. 520)
13. external causes (p. 521)
14. internal causes (p. 521)
15. fundamental attribution error (p. 521)
16. attitudes (p. 521)
17. behavior (p. 522)
18. attitudes (p. 522)
19. consistency (p. 522)
20. cognitive dissonance (p. 522)
21. attitudes (p. 522)
22. behavior (p. 522)
23. internal (p. 522)
24. self-perception (p. 523)
25. behavior (p. 523)
26. medium (p. 525)
27. target (p. 527)
28. expertise (p. 524)
29. trustworthiness (p. 525)
30. medium (p. 525)
31. 20,000 (p. 525)
32. message (p. 525)
33. frightening (p. 526)
34. Music (p. 527)
35. foot-in-the-door (p. 527)
36. door-in-the-face (p. 527)
37. target (p. 527)
38. age (p. 527)
39. obedience (p. 527)
40. hurting (p. 527)
41. ethics (p. 527)
42. norms (p. 530)
43. roles (p. 530)
44. conformity (p. 531)
45. line length (p. 531)
46. prison (p. 531)
47. groupthink (p. 532)
48. deindividuation (p. 533)
49. anonymity (p. 533)
50. cults (p. 533)
51. great person (p. 534)
52. situational (p. 534)
53. personality (p. 534)
54. situational (p. 534)
55. informational pressure (p. 535)
56. familiarity (p. 536)
57. similar (p. 536)
58. validation (p. 536)
59. matching hypothesis (p. 536)
60. Friendship (p. 537)
61. passionate (p. 538)
62. early (p. 538)
63. married (p. 538)
64. college (p. 538)
65. 90 (p. 538)
66. companionate (p. 538)
67. affection (p. 538)
68. affection (p. 538)
69. passion (p. 539)
70. commitment (p. 539)
71. social (p. 540)
72. altruism (p. 542)
73. reciprocity (p. 543)
74. exchange (p. 543)
75. social exchange (p. 543)
76. altruism (p. 543)
77. egoism (p. 544)
78. situation (p. 544)
79. bystander effect (p. 544)
80. diffusion of responsibility (p. 544)
81. harm (p. 544)
82. time (p. 544)
83. ethnic group (p. 544)

Answers to Multiple Choice Questions- Practice Test 1

1. a. Incorrect This *is* a component of social perception.
   b. Incorrect This *is* a component of social perception.
   c. Incorrect This *is* a component of social perception.
   d. **Correct.** This refers to a reduced state of awareness brought on by group influences.

2. a. **Correct.** Impressions are also integrated.
   b. Incorrect. The organization of perception described in the question refers to a different quality.
   c. Incorrect. This is not a quality referring to the organization of perception.
   c. Incorrect. This does not describe the organization of perception described in the question.

3. a. **Correct.** Festinger believes this process allows us to obtain an accurate appraisal or ourselves.
   b. Incorrect. Festinger believes just the opposite to be the case.
   c. Incorrect. Festinger believes comparing ourselves to those with different backgrounds does not lead to accurate self-appraisals.
   d. Incorrect. Festinger believes this might lead to inaccurate self-appraisals.

4. a. **Correct.** According to this approach, it is important to people to make sense out of their behavior.
   b. Incorrect. This theory states that people make inferences about their attitudes by perceiving their behavior.
   c. Incorrect. This theory states that people are motivated to reduce dissonance caused by inconsistent thoughts.
   d. Incorrect. This is defined as our judgments about the qualities of others.

5. a. Incorrect. This is part of the definition of attitudes.
   b. Incorrect. This is part of the definition of attitudes.
   c. **Correct.** Attitudes consist of beliefs and opinions.
   d. Incorrect. Beliefs and opinions create predispositions to behave.

6. a. Incorrect. Dissonance creates discomfort.
   b. Incorrect. Dissonance is uncomfortable, and usually leads to behavior change or attitude change.
   c. Incorrect. Dissonance is not extremely rare.
   d. **Correct.** According to Festinger, dissonance motivates us to become more consistent.

7. a. Incorrect. This answer is partially correct; one of the other alternatives is a more complete answer.
   b. Incorrect. This answer is partially correct; one of the other alternatives is a more complete answer.
   c. Incorrect. This answer is partially correct; one of the other alternatives is a more complete answer.
   d. **Correct.** This is not mentioned as a key component of a message.

8. a. Incorrect. This did not decrease obedience.
   b. Incorrect. This did not decrease obedience.
   c. Incorrect. This did not decrease obedience.
   d. **Correct.** Thus, the immediate environment was found to have some influence on the degree of obedience.

9. a. Incorrect. Roles apply to certain positions in a group.
   b. **Correct.** All groups have these norms.
   c. Incorrect. This is not the term applied to rules for all members of a group.
   d. Incorrect. This term is not mentioned in the text.

10. a. Incorrect. Asch found a considerably higher rate of conforming.
    b. **Correct.** Groups place powerful pressure on us to conform.
    c. Incorrect. Asch did not find rates of conforming to be this high.
    d. Incorrect. Asch did not find rates of conforming to be this high.

11. a. Incorrect. This is the tendency of group members to believe the way they do things is the best way.
    b. Incorrect. This is not related to the stifling of dissent.

c. **Correct.** Groupthink is a process implicated in a number of dramatic group errors.
d. Incorrect. This is a reduced state of self-awareness influenced by group membership.

12. a. Incorrect. Cults use deindividuation.
b. Incorrect. Cults use group norms.
c. Incorrect. Cults use groupthink.
d. **Correct.** The text does not mention cults' use of minority influence.

13. a. Incorrect. According to this theory, some people have the skills, and others just do not.
b. **Correct.** These traits include being assertive, cooperative, decisive, dominant, and so on.
c. Incorrect. This describes the situational theory of leadership.
d. Incorrect. This theory does, have specify a certain number of traits that make them best suited for leadership positions.

14. a. Incorrect. This answer is partially true; one of the other alternatives is a better answer.
b. Incorrect. This answer is partially true; one of the other alternatives is a better answer.
c. Incorrect. This is not of the ways in which the majority normally exerts its influence.
d. **Correct.** Those who fail to go along with the majority face rejection.

15. a. Incorrect. Evidence *does* support this idea.
b. Incorrect. Evidence *does* support this idea.
c. Incorrect. Evidence *does* support this idea.
d. **Correct.** Evidence suggests that companionate love eventually replaces physical attractiveness and romantic love.

16. a. Incorrect. This *is* one component of Sternberg's theory.
b. **Correct.** Sternberg's theory does not include infatuation as a component.
c. Incorrect. This *is* one component of Sternberg's theory.
d. Incorrect. This *is* one component of Sternberg's theory.

17. a. Incorrect. Loneliness *is* associated with gender.
b. Incorrect. Loneliness *is* associated with an individual's attachment history.
c. **Correct.** Loneliness *is not* associated with an individual's income.
d. Incorrect. Loneliness *is* associated with an individual's self-esteem.

18. a. Incorrect. This answer is partially true; one of the other alternatives is a better answer.
b. Incorrect. This answer is partially true; one of the other alternatives is a better answer.
c. Incorrect. This answer is partially true; one of the other alternatives is a better answer.
d. **Correct.** It is difficult to judge Sue's initial motivation to help.

19. a. Incorrect. Social exchange theory is concerned with equivalent benefits rather than survival of genes.
b. **Correct.** Evolutionary psychologists view the survival of our genes as a major motivation behind much of our behavior.
c. Incorrect. Religions are more concerned with preservation of morality and social order than with the preservation of our genes.
d. Incorrect. Normative expectations are not directly concerned with the preservation of our genes.

20. a. Incorrect. This *does* make bystander intervention less likely.
b. Incorrect. This *does* make bystander intervention less likely.
c. **Correct.** Bystander intervention is less likely when the victim has *no* prior history of victimization.
d. Incorrect. This *does* make bystander intervention less likely.

Answers to Multiple Choice Questions- Practice Test 2

1 a. Incorrect. This refers to the desire to know why people do the things they do.
b. **Correct.** This involves forming impressions of others, how we gain self-knowledge from the perception of others, and how we present ourselves to others.
c. Incorrect. this refers to understanding the way people influence each other.
d. Incorrect. this refers to an unselfish interest in helping someone else.

2. a. **Correct.** We tend to pay less attention to subsequent information about people.
b. Incorrect. This is not mentioned in the text.
c. Incorrect. This states that individuals are motivated to discover the underlying causes of behavior as part of their interest in making sense of their behavior.
d. Incorrect. This refers to the process in which we evaluate our thoughts, feelings, behavior and abilities in relation to other people.

3. a. Incorrect. Behavioral matching suggests that being a copycat can be a good strategy.
b. Incorrect. You need to be conformist to manage impressions.
c. Incorrect. Flattery and appreciation, if sincere, are good impression management strategies.
d. **Correct.** Nodding and/or smiling can be effective.

4. a. Incorrect. External attributions involve environmental, situational factors. Laura is taking the credit herself.
b. **Correct.** Laura is suggesting her internal attributes account for her success.
c. Incorrect. Laura's attributions tend to focus on one type of attribution.
d. Incorrect. Laura seems quite certain about the reasons for her success, and is not experiencing any dissonance.

5. a. Incorrect. Behavior doesn't always accurately provide information about attitudes.
b. Incorrect. Attitude doesn't always accurately provide information about behavior.
c. **Correct.** Psychologists refer to this as the demands of the situation.
d. Incorrect. Behavior may occur before attitudes are formed.

6. a. Incorrect. This describes cognitive dissonance theory.
b. Incorrect. This theory attempts to explain attitudes and behavior.
c. **Correct.** This theory was proposed by Daryl Bem.
d. Incorrect. Inconsistencies between attitudes and behavior are part of Festinger's cognitive dissonance theory.

7. a. Incorrect. Power *can* help a communicator change people's attitudes.
b. Incorrect. Attractiveness *can* help a communicator change people's attitudes.
c. Incorrect. Similarity *can* help a communicator change people's attitudes.
d. **Correct.** Intelligence is not mentioned as one of the characteristics that can help a communicator change people's attitudes.

8. a. Incorrect. Participants were deceived into thinking the learner was experiencing pain.
b. Incorrect. Milgram's research did include debriefing.
c. **Correct.** Approximately two-thirds of participants complied.
d. Incorrect. The results did not change when the situation was presented under different circumstances.

9. a. Incorrect. These are not expectations that govern behavior for a particular position.
b. Incorrect. This is a general set of legislated norms.
c. **Correct.** Every group prescribes roles.
d. Incorrect. These are rules that apply to all members of a group.

10. a. Incorrect. Dramatic changes were observed among the guards.
b. Incorrect. Dramatic changes were observed among the prisoners.
c. **Correct.** Changes occurred so dramatically and so rapidly, the experiment had to be terminated after 6 days.
d. Incorrect. The changes occurred during the first few days.

11. a. **Correct.** Self-restraints against impulsive actions also are weakened.
    b. Incorrect. Individuals become apathetic about negative social evaluation.
    c. Incorrect. This refers to groupthink.
    d. Incorrect. Only *one* of those answers is correct.

12. a. Incorrect. This *does* typify cult practice.
    b. Incorrect. This *does* typify cult practice.
    c. **Correct.** Cults typically do not provide this option for members.
    d. Incorrect. This *does* typify cult practice.

13. a. Incorrect. This refers to the "great person" theory of leadership.
    b. **Correct.** This implies that situational demands make a good leader in one situation, but not necessarily in all situations.
    c. Incorrect. This is not consistent with the situational theory of leadership.
    d. Incorrect. This is not consistent with the situational theory of leadership.

14. a. Incorrect. Groupthink is not a minority influence technique.
    b. Incorrect. Deindividuation refers to the loss of identity that occurs in some group settings.
    c. Incorrect. Normative pressure is a technique that can be used by the majority.
    d. **Correct.** The minority can be influential if it presents its position confidently, consistently and nondefensively.

15. a. Incorrect. Sternberg has a fancier name for Ken and Barbie's relationship.
    b. Incorrect. According to Sternberg, infatuation is characterized by a high degree of passion, but low in intimacy and commitment.
    c. **Correct.** Sternberg calls this the strongest, fullest type of love.
    d. Incorrect. This relationship is low in passion.

16. a. Incorrect. This is also called companionate love, marked by deep, caring affection.
    b. **Correct.** This is also called passionate love.
    c. Incorrect. According to Sternberg, this is high in passion, intimacy and commitment.
    d. Incorrect. Intimacy is an element in Sternberg's triangular theory of love.

17. a. Incorrect. According to the text, the reverse is true.
    b. **Correct.** According to the text, women are more likely to blame external factors.
    c. Incorrect. One of the genders is more likely to blame themselves.
    d. Incorrect. Loneliness *is* related to this variable.

18. a. Incorrect. Reciprocity implies an interest in deriving a future benefit. Jim's volunteering apparently was motivated by other desires.
    b. Incorrect. This approach states that individuals should benefit those who benefit them. Jim's motivation for helping apparently lies elsewhere.
    c. Incorrect. Altruism is an *unselfish* interest in helping others. Not in Jim's case.
    d. **Correct.** Egoism applies if Jim's motivation was to impress his girlfriend.

19. a. **Correct.** Evolutionary psychologists thus view altruism as having an ulterior motive.
    b. Incorrect. Evolutionary psychologists are more interested in genetic explanations for behavior.
    c. Incorrect. Evolutionary psychologists are more interested in genetic explanations for behavior.
    d. Incorrect. They view altruism as a predictable, important part of human behavior.

20. a. Incorrect. This answer is partially correct; one of the other alternatives is a more complete answer.
    b. Incorrect. This answer is partially correct; one of the other alternatives is a more complete answer.
    c. Incorrect. Research suggests the opposite is true.
    d. **Correct.** Research has uncovered many of the variables that comprise the bystander effect.

Chapter 15 Human Commonality and Diversity

Learning Objectives

After studying this chapter, you should be able to:

1. Define and describe the distinguishing features of both *culture* and *ethnicity*. (p. 550)
2. Discuss the individualism/collectivism dichotomy in the study of basic traits of cultures. (p. 551)
3. Discuss the relationship between stereotypes, prejudice, ethnocentrism, and racism. (p. 552)
4. Contrast assimilation and pluralism. (p. 555)
5. Describe the use of superordinate goals, the jigsaw classroom, and intimate contact in improving interethnic relations. (p. 556)
6. Define the term *gender*. (p. 560)
7. Explain the biological and social influences on the development of gender identity. (p. 560)
8. Distinguish between cognitive developmental theory and gender schema theory. (p. 562)
9. Discuss the results of research regarding gender similarities and differences. (p. 563)
10. Describe traditional gender roles and gender stereotypes, and discuss the consequences of sexism. (p. 567)
11. Identify both androgyny and gender-role transcendence and describe contemporary women's and men's issues. (p. 570)
12. Define *religion* and identify the following components: beliefs, practices, feeling, knowledge, and outcomes. (p. 575)

13. Distinguish between intrinsic and extrinsic religious orientation, and identify the stages in developing religious commitment. (p. 577)

14. Describe the following varieties of religious experience: mystical experience and spiritual well-being. (p. 578)

Chapter 15 Outline

I. Culture and Ethnicity
   A. The Nature of Culture and Ethnicity
   B. Individualism and Collectivism
   C. Work and Achievement
   D. Stereotyping, Prejudice, and Ethnocentrism
   E. Improving Interethnic Relations
      1. Superordinate Goals
      2. Intimate Contact
II. Gender
   A. Developing Gender Identity
      1. Biological Influences
      2. Social Influences
         a. identification theory
         b. social Learning theory of gender
      3. Cognitive Influences
         a. cognitive developmental theory
         b. gender schema theory
   B. Gender Comparisons
      1. Physical/Biological
      2. Cognitive
      3. Socioemotional
   C. Gender Expectations and Stereotypes
      1. Traditional Gender Roles
      2. Sexism
      3. Androgyny
      4. Gender Role Transcendence
      5. Women's Issues
      6. Male Role Strain
III. Religion
   A. The Nature and Scope of Religion
   B. Religious Orientation
      1. Intrinsic religious orientation
      2. Extrinsic religious orientation
   C. Developing Religious Commitment
      1. Intuitive-Projective Faith
      2. Mythical-Lyrical Faith
      3. Synthetic-Conventional Faith
      4. Individualistic-Reflective Faith
      5. Conjunctive Faith
      6. Universalizing Faith
   D. Varieties of Religious Experience
      1. Mystical Experience and Conversion
      2. Spiritual Well-Being
      3. Religion and Prejudice

Key Terms

Write a brief description for each of the following terms. Where relevant, provide an original example or illustration of the term. Then, compare your answers with those provided at the end of the study guide chapter. Review the text for those terms you don't know or define incorrectly.

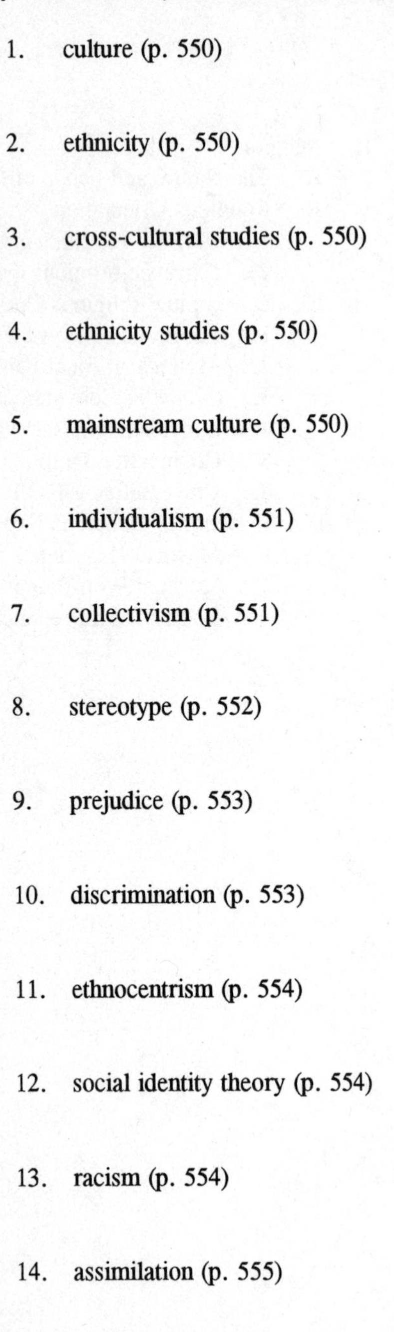

1. culture (p. 550)

2. ethnicity (p. 550)

3. cross-cultural studies (p. 550)

4. ethnicity studies (p. 550)

5. mainstream culture (p. 550)

6. individualism (p. 551)

7. collectivism (p. 551)

8. stereotype (p. 552)

9. prejudice (p. 553)

10. discrimination (p. 553)

11. ethnocentrism (p. 554)

12. social identity theory (p. 554)

13. racism (p. 554)

14. assimilation (p. 555)

15. pluralism (p. 556)

16. gender (p. 560)

17. androgen (p. 560)

18. estrogen (p. 561)

19. identification theory (p. 562)

20. social learning theory of gender (p. 562)

21. cognitive developmental theory of gender (p. 562)

22. schema (p. 563)

23. gender schema (p. 563)

24. gender schema theory (p. 563)

25. rapport talk (p. 565)

26. report talk (p. 565)

27. gender stereotypes (p. 567)

28. sexism (p. 569)

29. androgyny (p. 570)

30. gender-role transcendence (p. 571)

31. feminist (p. 571)

32. religion (p. 576)

33. intrinsic religious motivation (p. 577)

34. extrinsic religious motivation (p. 577)

35. religious conversion (p. 578)

Guided Review

The following in-depth chapter review is a challenging and comprehensive fill-in-the-blanks exercise. The answers are found near the end of the chapter. As you go through the exercise, try to resist the temptation to look at the answers until you have provided them. When you have filled in all the blanks, you will have a thorough summary of the chapter for reference and review.

Culture and Ethnicity

The behavior patterns, beliefs, and other products of a particular group of people that are passed on from generation to generation defines ___(1)___. Ethnicity is based on ___(2)___ heritage, nationality characteristics, race, religion, and language. The comparison of one culture with one or more other cultures is the area called ___(3)___-________ studies. Ethnicity studies focus on both universal and ___(4)___ behaviors. In complex cultures, individuals who practice the dominant set of values and expectations are part of the ___(5)___ culture. Ethnic groups whose members are extremely similar are ___(6)___.

According to Brislin, identity is transmitted from generation to generation primarily by ___(7)___, teachers and community leaders. Many cultural and ethnic practices become " ___(8)___ ________" to group members, although they may be puzzling to outsiders. According to Campbell and his colleagues, members of cultures tend to believe that the events and occurrences of their culture is " ___(9)___" and correct, and what happens in other cultures is " ___(10)___" and incorrect. Members also feel proud of their cultural group and feel ___(11)___ toward other cultural groups.

Cultures that emphasize personal goals rather than group goals value___(12)___, while those cultures that emphasize service to the group and subordination of personal goals stress ___(13)___. Many ___(14)___ cultures are described as individualistic; many ___(15)___ cultures are described as collectivistic. Many of psychology's basic tenets developed in ___(16)___ cultures. Some psychologists believe it is unreasonable to describe an entire nation of people as having a ___(17)___ ________. The United States is considered an ___(18)___-oriented culture with a strong ___(19)___ ethic.

An oversimplified generalization about a groups' characteristics is a ___(20)___. An unjustified negative attitude toward an individual because of the individual's membership in a group is called ___(21)___. When prejudice leads to differences in treatment based on the individual's membership in a group, it is called ___(22)___.

The tendency to favor one's group over other groups is referred to as ___(23)___. A theory that explains prejudice and conflict between groups is called ___(24)___ ________ theory. This theory suggests that, when individuals are assigned to a group, they invariably think of the group as an ___(25)___-________.

Racism occurs when the members of one group believe the members of another race or ethnic group are ___(26)___. People who claim to be without prejudice but act in ways that reveal bias, it is called ___(27)___ ________. Programs designed to help ethnic minorities reach full equality, such as affirmative action and school ___(28)___, remain controversial.

The absorption of an ethnic minority group into the dominant group is called ___(29)___. This often means the loss of some or all of the behavior and values of the ___(30)___ ________ group. The coexistence of distinct ethnic and cultural groups is called ___(31)___.

Sherif found that promoting in-groupness at a summer camp for boys created ___(32)___ between two groups. Positive relations between the two groups were created when the groups were required to carry out cooperative, ___(33)___ tasks. This cooperative strategy was applied in a classroom setting called the ___(34)___ ________. Research has also suggested that interethnic relations can be improved by ___(35)___ contact.

Gender

Human cells normally contain 46 ___(36)___, arranged in pairs. The 23rd pair may have two X chromosomes, which produces a ___(37)___, or one X and one Y chromosome, which produces a ___(38)___. Male sex organs begin to differ from female sex organs when the Y chromosome triggers secretion of ___(39)___. Low levels of androgen in a female embryo allow the development of ___(40)___ sex organs. Insufficient androgens in the male embryo or excessive androgens in the female embryo results in a ___(41)___. Recent case study reports support the idea that differentiation is already taking place ___(42)___ ________.

According to Freud, gender and sexual behavior are ___(43)___, Freud sought to explain the process of gender development with his ___(44)___ theory.

According to the behaviorists, gender development occurs through ___(45)___, imitation, ___(46)___, and punishment. This approach is called the ___(47)___ ________ ________ of gender. According to the cognitive developmental theory of gender, children's gender typing occurs after they have developed a concept of ___(48)___. This approach suggests that when children conceive of themselves as female or male, they organize their world on the basis of ___(49)___. A second cognitive approach, called ___(50)___ ________ theory, states that an individual is internally motivated to conform to gender-based standards and stereotypes.

A growing consensus among researchers suggests that differences between the sexes have often been ___(51)___. When examining differences between the sexes, it is important to remember that the differences are ___(52)___; there is considerable ___(53)___ between the sexes; and differences may be due to a combination of biological and ___(54)___ factors. Females are ___(55)___ likely than males to develop physical or mental disorders. Although cognitive differences are either small or nonexistent, males, on average, outperform females on math and ___(56)___ tasks. Males are more active and ___(57)___ than females. According to Tannen, women prefer to engage in ___(58)___ talk, and men prefer to engage in ___(59)___ talk. Males and females also differ in their ___(60)___ behavior.

According to evolutionary psychology, gender differences are found in those areas in which males and females have faced different ___(61)___ problems.

The broad categories, exaggerated generalizations and/or false beliefs about males and females are referred to as ___(62)___ ________. According to a study of college students in many different countries, stereotyping of males and females is ___(63)___. Men and women perceive themselves to be more similar in countries that are more ___(64)___. Prejudice and discrimination based on one's sex is called ___(65)___. Sexism can be obvious or ___(66)___. An endorsement of traditional gender roles and a characterization of females as being less competent than men are components of ___(67)___-________sexism. Denial that discrimination still exists and antagonism toward women's demands constitute ___(68)___ sexism.

The presence of desirable masculine and feminine characteristics in the same individual is referred to as ___(69)___. According to the Bem sex-role inventory, an androgynous individual has a high degree of feminine, (also referred to as ___(70)___) traits as well as a high degree of masculine (also referred to as ___(71)___) traits. A person who does not score high on feminine or masculine traits is referred to as ___(72)___. The belief that an individual's competence should not be conceptualized on the basis of femininity, masculinity or androgyny, but on a "person" basis is called gender role ___(73)___.

Individuals who believe women and men should be accorded the same rights are ___(74)___. Many feminist scholars believe psychology has portrayed behavior with a "male ___(75)___" theme. Feminist thinkers believe it is important for women to maintain their competency in relationships, but to be ___(76)___-________ also. A special concern involves the racism and sexism experienced by women of ___(77)___.

According to Joseph Pleck, the male role is contradictory and inconsistent, leading to male ___(78)___-________. Among the areas contributing to male role-strain are health, ___(79)___-________ relationships, and male-male relationships. Significant concerns exist regarding the experiences of males of ___(80)___.

Religion

Around the world the overwhelming majority of people are involved in or affected by religion and express a believe in ___(81)___. Generally, ___(82)___ show a stronger interest in religion than do men. Religion is the belief system that individuals use to ___(83)___ and ___(84)___ guide their behavior. A person's religion involves their beliefs, ___(85)___, feelings, ___(86)___, and outcomes.

Those who experience internal religious motives have an ___(87)___ religious orientation, whereas those with external motives have an ___(88)___ religious orientation.

According to Fowler, individuals go through six stages as they develop religious commitment: intuitive-projective faith, ___(89)___-________ faith, synthetic-conventional faith, ___(90)___-________ faith, conjunctive faith, and ___(91)___ faith.

Both dispositional and ___(92)___ factors contribute to profound religious experiences. People who change their belief systems regarding religion have experienced a religious ___(93)___. Although a stereotype suggests that religion is a "crutch" for the weak, researchers have found that many religious individuals are

___(94)___. Allport found that people who attend church are more prejudiced than non-churchgoers; he labeled this the ___(95)___ ________. He found, however, that ___(96)___ churchgoers were relatively low in prejudice, whereas sporadic attenders were more prejudiced.

Sociocultural Worlds/Applications in Psychology

In your own words, summarize the material you have read in Sociocultural Worlds, "Women's Struggle for Equality: An International Journey," and in Applications in Psychology, "Improving the Lives of African American and Latino Youth." Briefly describe how each of these articles relates to the information contained in the chapter.

Concept Check

Concept	**Meaning**
1. Gender	________________
2. Gender roles	________________
3. Gender identity	________________
4. Androgyny	________________
5. Gender-role transcendence	________________

Answers

1. The sociocultural dimension of being male or female
2. Sets of expectations that prescribe how females and males should think, feel, and act
3. The sense of being male or female; part of one's self-concept
4. The presence of desirable feminine and masculine characteristics in one individual
5. The belief that one's competence should be conceptualized not on the basis of masculinity, femininity, or androgyny but on a personal basis

Multiple-Choice Questions

Practice Test 1

After answering all the multiple-choice questions in Practice Test 1, compare your answers with the answer key provided at the end of the chapter. The answer key contains a brief explanation of both the correct and incorrect answers. Each of these questions is keyed to the Learning Objectives for the chapter. If you answer any questions incorrectly, review the corresponding Learning Objective and text material before you proceed to Practice Test 2.

1. Each of the following is a feature of culture *except*
   a. It is made up of ideals, values, and assumptions about life.
   b. It is transmitted from generation to generation.
   c. Mainstream ideas rarely predominate for more than one or two generations.
   d. Many practices become second nature to members of the culture.

LO1

2. Which of the following describes an individualistic culture?
   a. personal goals come first
   b. group integrity is important
   c. personal goals are subordinated
   d. interdependence is emphasized

LO2

3. The statement, "All used car salespeople are untrustworthy," reflects (a)
   a. prejudice.
   b. stereotype.
   c. ethnocentrism.
   d. both *a* and *b*

LO 3

4. Each of the following is associated with social identity theory *except*
   a. positive self-image.
   b. personal identity.
   c. mutual understanding.
   d. in-groups.

LO 3

5. When two or more distinct groups are able to coexist in the same society, this is referred to as
   a. assimilation.
   b. ethnocentrism.
   c. social identity.
   d. pluralism.

LO 4

6. Research on improved interethnic relations has underscored the importance of each of the following *except*
   a. assimilation.
   b. superordinate goals
   c. the jigsaw classroom.
   d. intimate contact.

LO 5

7. According to the text, what type of term is *gender*?
   a. biochemical
   b. genetic
   c. academic
   d. sociocultural

LO 6

8. The Freudian view of gender identity is referred to as
   a. gender schema theory.
   b. the social learning theory of gender.
   c. identification theory.
   d. the cognitive developmental theory of gender.

LO 7

9. The concept of gender constancy is central to
   a. gender schema theory.
   b. the social learning theory of gender.
   c. identification theory.
   d. the cognitive developmental theory of gender.

LO 8

10. When interpreting research regarding gender differences and similarities, each of the following applies *except*
    a. differences may not be statistically significant.
    b. results are often presented for averages.
    c. not all differences are biologically based.
    d. most differences involve little overlap between the sexes.

LO 9

11. According to Tanner, females are more likely to
    a. engage in rapport talk.
    b. engage in report talk.
    c. help in a dangerous situation.
    d. turn anger into aggressive action.

LO 9

12. Each of the following characterizes modern sexism *except*
    a. endorsement of traditional gender roles.
    b. denial that discrimination exists.
    c. antagonism toward women's demands.
    d. lack of support for policies designed to help women.

LO 10

13. According to traditional gender roles, which traits are males expected to display?
    a. nurturant
    b. expressive
    c. instrumental
    d. androgynous

LO 10

14. Feminist writers such as Jean Baker Miller believe women have demonstrated competency in
    a. self-motivation.
    b. relationships.
    c. cognitive skills.
    d. self-determination.

LO 11

15. The Bem Sex Role inventory is used to assess
    a. gender-role transcendence.
    b. sexism.
    c. androgyny.
    d. gender adjustment.

LO 11

16. Each of the following is true with regard to religious practices *except*
    a. In response to a recent survey, a majority of Americans said they attend religious services.
    b. About 9 percent of Americans surveyed said they had no religion at all.
    c. Males have shown a consistently stronger interest in religion.
    d. A majority of the world' peoples are either involved in religion or have their lives affected by religion in significant ways.

LO 12

17. Each of the following statements characterizes an intrinsic religious motivation *except*
    a. "My main interest in religion is due to the great business contacts I've made at church."
    b. "My religious beliefs carry over to all aspects of my life."
    c. My unshakable religious beliefs are the primary motivation for all that I do."
    d. "My religious motives lie deeply within."

LO 13

18. Which stage of religious commitment does Fowler believe few people reach?
    a. universalizing faith
    b. individualistic-reflective
    c. intuitive-projective
    d. mythical-lyrical

LO 13

19. Among the situational factors that have been explored in relation to religious experiences are
    a. ingesting hallucinogenic drugs.
    b. developing a preparatory mental set.
    c. underwater immersion.
    d. all of the above.

LO 14

20. According to the Allport, the "grand paradox" refers to
    a. conversion following mystical experiences.
    b. high levels of unhappiness among frequent churchgoers.
    c. those with neither extrinsic nor intrinsic religious orientations.
    d. high levels of prejudice among churchgoers.

LO 14

Practice Test 2

1. According to Campbell and his colleagues, people in all cultures display the following tendencies *except*
   a. feeling proud of their group.
   b. feeling hostile toward other groups.
   c. viewing customs of all cultures as equally valid.
   d. believing in ways that favor their cultural group.

LO 1

2. Which of the following describes a collectivist culture?
   a. The United States
   b. personal goals are subordinated
   c. priority is given to personal goals
   d. personal distinction is emphasized

LO 2

3. The phrase "absent-minded professor" reflects
   a. a prejudice.
   b. the faculty at your college.
   c. a stereotype.
   d. either *a* or *c* above

LO 3

4. Tajfel's social identity theory provides an explanation for
   a. prejudice.
   b. ethnocentrism.
   c. conflict between groups.
   d. all of the above.

LO 3

5. When an ethnic minority group is absorbed into the dominant group, this is referred to as
   a. assimilation.
   b. ethnocentrism.
   c. social identity.
   d. pluralism.

LO 4

6. Research on the jigsaw classroom has found that it helps improve each of the following *except*
   a. self-esteem.
   b. academic performance.
   c. bilingual skills.
   d. interethnic perceptions.

LO 5

7. According to the text, the sociocultural dimension of being male or female is referred to as
   a. sex.
   b. gender.
   c. gender schema.
   d. sexual identification.

LO 6

8. Gender development is best explained by the processes of observation, imitation, rewards, and punishments according to
   a. gender schema theory.
   b. social learning theory.
   c. identification theory.
   d. the cognitive developmental theory of gender.

LO 7

9. Categorizing information on the basis of culturally defined gender roles is central to
   a. gender schema theory.
   b. social learning theory.
   c. identification theory.
   d. the cognitive developmental theory of gender.

LO 8

10. Which of the following is true regarding differences between males and females?
    a. When angered, males are more aggressive than females.
    b. Females and males experience different emotions.
    c. Wide-ranging differences in verbal skills exist between males and females.
    d. both *a* and *c*

LO 9

11. According to Maccoby and others, a consistent difference between men and women involves which of the following skills?
    a. verbal
    b. linguistic
    c. visuospatial
    d. comprehension

LO 9

12. Which of the following groups is most likely to perceive similarity between the sexes?
    a. men in less developed countries
    b. women in less developed countries
    c. men in more highly developed countries
    d. women in more highly developed countries

LO 10

13. According to traditional gender roles, which traits are females expected to display?
    a. aggressive
    b. expressive
    c. instrumental
    d. androgynous

LO 10

14. According to Joseph Pleck, men's health and relationship issues are involved in
    a. androgyny.
    b. gender role transcendence.
    c. sexism.
    d. male role strain

LO 11

15. According to Joseph Pleck, gender-role transcendence
    a. is a merging of masculinity and femininity.
    b. should replace the notion of androgyny.
    c. encourages us to think of people as people.
    d. both *b* and *c*

LO 11

16. Each of the following is true *except*
    a. Women show more interest in religion than men.
    b. A majority of people in the U.S. and in India believe in God.
    c. Most Americans claim they do not attend religious services.
    d. About two-thirds of people around the world are involved in or affected by religion.

LO 12

17. According to Fowler's theory, individuals are capable of taking full responsibility for their religious beliefs in the stage called
    a. conjunctive faith.
    b. synthetic-conventional faith.
    c. individualistic-reflective faith.
    d. mythical-lyrical faith.

LO 13

18. According to Fowler, individuals become more aware of opposing viewpoints on religion in which stage?
    a. universalizing faith
    b. conjunctive faith
    c. intuitive-projective faith
    d. mythical-lyrical faith

LO 13

19. Research has suggested relationships between religious involvement and
    a. middle-age competence.
    b. happiness.
    c. mental disorders.
    d. both *a* and *b*

LO 14

20. Each of the following characterizes those with intrinsic religious motivation *except*
    a. a greater sense of competence and control than those with an extrinsic motivation.
    b. less worry and guilt than those with an extrinsic motivation.
    c. fewer physical illnesses than those with an extrinsic motivation.
    d. higher levels of prejudice than those with an extrinsic motivation.

LO 14

Answers to Key Terms

1. **Culture** refers to the behavior patterns, beliefs, and all other products of a group of people that are passed on from generation to generation.
2. **Ethnicity** is based on cultural heritage, nationality, race, religion, and language.
3. **Cross-cultural studies** compare one culture with one or more other cultures.
4. **Ethnic studies** focus on both universal and distinctive behaviors across ethnic groups.
5. **Mainstream culture** refers to the dominant set of expectations and values.
6. **Individualism** is a cultural trait that gives priority to personal goals rather than to group goals.
7. **Collectivism** is a cultural trait that emphasizes serving the group by subordinating personal goals.
8. A **stereotype** is a generalization about a group's characteristics that does not consider any individual variation.
9. **Prejudice** is an unjustified attitude toward an individual based on the individual's membership in a group.
10. **Discrimination** refers to the enactment of prejudices to limit opportunities to an out-group or enhance privileges to an in-group.
11. **Ethnocentrism** is the tendency to favor one's own group over other groups.
12. **Social identity theory**, proposed by Tajfel, states that when individuals are assigned to a group, they invariably think of the group as an "in-group" for them. This occurs because individuals want to have a positive self-image.
13. **Racism** occurs when the members of one race or ethnic group believe the members of another race or ethnic group are inferior.
14. **Assimilation** occurs when individuals relinquish their cultural identity and move into larger society.
15. **Pluralism** refers to the coexistence of distinct ethnic and cultural groups in the same society.
16. **Gender** is the sociocultural dimension of being male or female.
17. **Androgen** refers to the main class of male sex hormones.
18. **Estrogen** refers to the main class of female sex hormones.
19. **Identification theory** is a theory that stems from Freud's view that the preschool child develops a sexual attraction to the parent of the opposite sex; this attraction is renounced at age 5 or 6. The child then identifies with the same-sex parent, unconsciously adopting this parent's behavior.
20. **Social learning theory of gender** suggests that children's gender development occurs through observation and imitation of gender-related behavior, and through rewards and punishments they experience for gender-appropriate and gender-inappropriate behavior.
21. **Cognitive developmental theory of gender** suggests that children's gender typing occurs after they have developed a concept of gender.
22. A **schema** is a cognitive structure that organizes and guides an individual's perceptions.
23. A **gender schema** is a cognitive structure that organizes an individual's world in terms of female and male.
24. **Gender schema theory** states that children's attention and behavior are guided by an internal motivation to conform to gender-based sociocultural standards and stereotypes.
25. **Rapport talk**, according to Tannen, is the language of conversation, a style preferred by women.
26. **Report talk** is designed to give information. According to Tannen, it is a style preferred by men.
27. **Gender stereotypes** are broad categories and generalizations regarding males and females.
28. **Sexism** refers to prejudice and discrimination based on one's sex.
29. **Androgyny** is the presence of desirable feminine and masculine traits in the same individual.
30. **Gender-role transcendence** is the belief that one's competence should be based on an individual basis, rather than based on one's gender.
31. A **feminist** believes that women and men should have the same rights.
32. **Religion** is a belief system that individuals use to morally and spiritually guide their behavior.
33. **Intrinsic religious motivation** refers to religious motives that lie within the person.
34. **Extrinsic religious motivation** refers to using the religion for nonreligious ends.
35. **Religious conversion** is a change from having no beliefs to accepting a religious system, or changing from one belief system to another.

Answers to Guided Review

1. culture (p. 550)
2. cultural (p. 550)
3. cross-cultural (p. 550)
4. distinctive (p. 550)
5. mainstream (p. 550)
6. homogeneous (p. 550)
7. parents (p. 551)
8. second nature (p. 551)
9. natural (p. 551)
10. unnatural (p. 551)
11. hostility (p. 551)
12. individualism (p.551)
13. collectivism (p. 551)
14. Western (p. 551)
15. Eastern (p. 551)
16. individualistic (p. 551)
17. basic personality (p. 551)
18. achievement (p. 552)
19. work (p. 552)
20. stereotype (p. 552)
21. prejudice (p. 553)
22. discrimination (p. 553)
23. ethnocentrism (p. 554)
24. social identity (p. 554)
25. in-group (p. 554)
26. inferior (p. 554)
27. unconscious racism (p. 554)
28. desegregation (p. 555)
29. assimilation (p. 555)
30. ethnic minority (p. 556)
31. pluralism (p. 556)
32. competition (p. 556)
33. superordinate (p. 556)
34. jigsaw classroom (p. 557)
35. intimate (p. 557)
36. chromosomes (p. 560)
37. female (p. 560)
38. male (p. 560)
39. androgen (p. 560)
40. female (p. 560)
41. hermaphrodite (p. 561)
42. in utero (p. 561)
43. instinctual (p. 561)
44. identification (p. 562)
45. observation (p. 562)
46. rewards (p. 562)
47. social learning theory (p. 562)
48. gender (p. 562)
49. gender (p. 562)
50. gender schema (p. 563)
51. overstated (p. 563)
52. averages (p. 564)
53. overlap (p. 564)
54. environmental (p. 564)
55. less (p. 564)
56. visuospatial (p. 564)
57. aggressive (p. 565)
58. rapport (p. 565)
59. report (p. 565)
60. helping (p. 565)
61. adaptive (p. 566)
62. gender stereotypes (p. 567)
63. pervasive (p. 567)
64. developed (p. 568)
65. sexism (p. 569)
66. subtle (p. 569)
67. old-fashioned (p. 569)
68. modern (p. 569)
69. androgynous (p. 570)
70. expressive (p. 570)
71. instrumental (p. 571)
72. undifferentiated (p. 571)
73. transcendence (p. 571)
74. feminists (p. 571)
75. dominant (p. 571)
76. self-motivated (p. 571)
77. color (p. 572)
78. role-strain (p. 572)
79. male-female (p. 572)
80. color (p. 572)
81. God (p. 575)
82. women (p. 575)
83. morally (p. 576)
84. spiritually (p. 576)
85. practices (p. 576)
86. knowledge (p. 577)
87. intrinsic (p. 577)
88. extrinsic (p. 577)
89. mythical-lyrical (p. 577)
90. individualist-reflective (p. 577)
91. universalizing (p. 578)
92. situational (p. 578)
93. conversion (p. 578)
94. competent (p. 578)
95. grand paradox (p. 579)
96. regular (p. 579)

Answers to Multiple Choice Questions-Practice Test 1

1. a. Incorrect. This *is* a feature of culture.
   b. Incorrect. This *is* a feature of culture.
   c. **Correct.** Mainstream ideas typically predominate for many generations.
   d. Incorrect. This *is* a feature of culture.

2. a. **Correct.** Independence is one of the values of a n individualistic culture.
   b. Incorrect. This feature is characteristic of a collectivist culture.
   c. Incorrect. This feature is characteristic of a collectivist culture.
   d. Incorrect. This feature is characteristic of a collectivist culture.

3. a. Incorrect. This answer is true, however one of the other answers is a better alternative.
   b. Incorrect. This answer is true, however one of the other answers is a better alternative.
   c. Incorrect. Ethnocentrism refers to the tendency to favor one's own group over other groups.
   d. **Correct.** The statement reflects both stereotyped thinking and prejudicial thinking.

4. a. Incorrect. This *is* associated with social identity theory.
   b. Incorrect. This *is* associated with social identity theory.
   c. **Correct.** Social identity theory explains prejudice and conflict rather than mutual understanding.
   d. Incorrect. This *is* associated with social identity theory.

5. a. Incorrect. This refers to the absorption of one group into the more dominant group.
   b. Incorrect. This refers to the tendency to favor one's group over other groups.
   c. Incorrect. This refers to the identity provided by group membership.
   d. **Correct.** Many people feel caught between the desire for assimilation and the desire for pluralism.

6. a. **Correct.** This is not associated with improved interethnic relations.
   b. Incorrect. According to the text, this *is* associated with improved interethnic relations.
   c. Incorrect. According to the text, this *is* associated with improved interethnic relations.
   d. Incorrect. According to the text, this *is* associated with improved interethnic relations.

7. a. Incorrect. There are biochemical influences on one's gender identity, but the term does not refer to biochemistry.
   b. Incorrect. There are genetic influences on one's gender, but the term does not refer to genetics.
   c. Incorrect. It is not only an academic term.
   d. **Correct.** It is defined as "the sociocultural dimension of being male or female."

8. a. Incorrect. This refers to a cognitive theory.
   b. Incorrect. This refers to a social learning approach, emphasizing imitation, rewards and punishments.
   c. **Correct.** Freud's theory remains controversial.
   d. Incorrect. This refers to a cognitive theory.

9. a. Incorrect. This theory states that we are motivated to conform to gender-based sociocultural standards and stereotypes.
   b. Incorrect. this approach emphasizes imitation, rewards, and punishment in the formation of gender behavior.
   c. Incorrect. This is Freud's theory.
   d. **Correct.** This theory states that once children consistently think of themselves as male or female, they organize their world on the basis of gender.

10. a. Incorrect. Differences often are *not* statistically significant.
    b. Incorrect. Results often *are* presented for averages.
    c. Incorrect. Indeed, not all differences *are* biologically based.
    d. **Correct.** Most differences involve *significant* overlap between the sexes.

11. a. **Correct.** According to Tanner, this is the language of conversation.
    b. Incorrect. This type of talk, designed to convey information, is characteristic of males.
    c. Incorrect. Males are more likely to help in a dangerous situation.
    d. Incorrect. Males are more likely to engage in this behavior.

12. a. **Correct.** This is characteristic of old-fashioned sexism.
    b. Incorrect. This *is* characteristic of modern sexism.
    c. Incorrect. This *is* characteristic of modern sexism.
    d. Incorrect. This *is* characteristic of modern sexism.

13. a. Incorrect. This is a traditionally feminine gender role.
    b. Incorrect. This is a traditionally feminine gender role.
    c. **Correct.** Androgynous people have a high degree of both expressive and instrumental traits.
    d. Incorrect. Androgynous people have a high degree of both expressive and instrumental traits.

14. a. Incorrect. Miller believes that women have demonstrated competency in other areas.
    b. **Correct.** Miller believes women should use these skills as a springboard to the development of self-determination.
    c. Incorrect. Women certainly have demonstrated competency in this area; but Miller has emphasized other competencies.
    d. Incorrect. Miller believes this competency needs to be more fully developed.

15. a. Incorrect. This is not measured by the Bem Inventory.
    b. Incorrect. This is not measured by the Bem Inventory.
    c. **Correct.** this refers to a high degree of desirable feminine and masculine traits in the same individual.
    d. Incorrect. This is not measured by the Bem Inventory.

16. a. Incorrect. This statement is true.
    b. Incorrect. This statement is true.
    c. **Correct.** Females have demonstrated a consistently stronger interest in religion.
    d. Incorrect. This statement is true.

17. a. **Correct.** This demonstrates an extrinsic religious motivation.
    b. Incorrect. This does typify an intrinsic religious motivation.
    c. Incorrect. This does typify an intrinsic religious motivation.
    d. Incorrect. This does typify an intrinsic religious motivation.

18. a. **Correct.** In this stage, individuals achieve a sense of unity with all beings.
    b. Incorrect. This stage is associated with late adolescence and early adulthood.
    c. Incorrect. This is the first stage in Fowler's theory, associated with early childhood.
    d. Incorrect. This stages is associated with elementary school years.

19. a. Incorrect. Although this answer is partially true; one of the other answers is a better alternative.
    b. Incorrect. Although this answer is partially true; one of the other answers is a better alternative.
    c. Incorrect. Although this answer is partially true; one of the other answers is a better alternative.
    d. **Correct.** Others include being deprived of sensory experiences.

20. a. Incorrect. The grand paradox is not related to conversion issues.
    b. Incorrect. In fact, churchgoers do not show high levels of unhappiness.
    c. Incorrect. The grand paradox relates to other issues.
    d. **Correct.** Allport determined that regular churchgoers were relatively low in prejudice toward ethnic groups.

Answers to Multiple Choice Questions- Practice Test 2

1. a. Incorrect. This *is* a tendency of people in all cultures.
   b. Incorrect. This *is* a tendency of people in all cultures.
   c. **Correct.** People tend to perceive *their* cultural customs as universally valid.
   d. Incorrect. This *is* a tendency of people in all cultures.

2. a. Incorrect. The U.S. is an individualistic culture.
   b. **Correct.** The preservation of group integrity is an important value in collectivist cultures.
   c. Incorrect. Priority is given to group goals in collectivist cultures.
   d. Incorrect. Just the opposite is true in collectivist cultures.

3. a. Incorrect. This answer is partially correct; another alternative is more complete.
   b. Incorrect. *Hopefully* incorrect.
   c. Incorrect. This answer is partially correct; another alternative is more complete.
   d. **Correct.** The statement may reflect either a prejudice or a stereotype.

4. a. Incorrect. This answer is partially correct; another alternative is more complete.
   b. Incorrect. This answer is partially correct; another alternative is more complete.
   c. Incorrect. This answer is partially correct; another alternative is more complete.
   d. **Correct.** This theory states that when individuals are assigned to a group they think of the group as an in-group for them.

5. a. **Correct.** This often implies the loss of some or all of the behavior or values of the ethnic minority group.
   b. Incorrect. This is the tendency to favor one's own group over other groups.
   c. Incorrect. This theory states that when individuals are assigned to a group they think of that group as an in-group for themselves.
   d. Incorrect. This refers to the coexistence of distinct cultural and ethnic groups in the same society.

6. a. Incorrect. Research suggests the jigsaw classroom does help improve self-esteem.
   b. Incorrect. Research suggests the jigsaw classroom does help improve academic performance.
   c. **Correct.** The jigsaw classroom does not improve bilingual skills.
   d. Incorrect. Research suggests the jigsaw classroom does help improve interethnic perceptions.

7. a. Incorrect. One's sex is biologically determined.
   b. **Correct.** Thus one's gender and one's sex are not always identical.
   c. Incorrect. This refers to a cognitive structure that helps organize the world in terms of female and male.
   d. Incorrect. This term sounds as though it might have been derived from Freud's identification theory.

8. a. Incorrect. Gender schema refers to a cognitive organization of the world.
   b. **Correct.** Modeling is another process important to this approach.
   c. Incorrect. This is Freud's theory on gender development.
   d. Incorrect. This theory states children's gender typing occurs after they have developed a concept of gender.

9. a. **Correct.** This theory states that gender schemas help a person to organize their world in terms of male and female.
   b. Incorrect. This theory focuses on such environmental factors as imitation, modeling and rewards for gender-appropriate behavior.
   c. Incorrect. This is Freud's theory on gender development.
   d. Incorrect. This theory states that children begin the process of gender typing once they have developed a concept of gender.

10. a. **Correct.** This is true especially when aggressive male action is culturally approved.
    b. Incorrect. Both genders experience the same range of emotions.
    c. Incorrect. Some slight differences have been uncovered, but the similarities seems to outweigh the differences.
    d. Incorrect. Only one of those alternatives is correct.

11. a. Incorrect. Research suggests differences here have virtually disappeared.
    b. Incorrect. The text suggests verbal differences have virtually disappeared.
    c. **Correct.** Another areas showing some consistent difference is in math.
    d. Incorrect. The text does not address this skill.

12. a. Incorrect. People who less in less developed countries are more likely to perceive differences.
    b. Incorrect. People who live in less developed countries are more likely to perceive differences.
    c. Incorrect. Try the other gender.
    d. **Correct.** As sexual equality increases, stereotypes will likely diminish.

13. a. Incorrect. Traditionally, women have been expected to be passive.
    b. **Correct.** Sensitivity and nurturance are other traits traditionally associated with being female.
    c. Incorrect. This has traditionally been a male trait.
    d. Incorrect. This refers to the simultaneous presence of masculine and feminine traits in the same person.

14. a. Incorrect. This refers to the simultaneous presence of masculine and feminine traits in the same person.
    b. Incorrect. This is the belief that it is best to look beyond issues of femininity and masculinity and to focus on an individual's competence.
    c. Incorrect. This refers to differential treatment on the basis of one's sex.
    d. **Correct.** According to Pleck, strain is evident in male-female and in male-male relationships.

15. a. Incorrect. Gender role transcendence takes us beyond gender roles.
    b. Incorrect. This answer is partially true, but another alternative is more complete.
    c. Incorrect. This answer is partially true, but another alternative is more complete.
    d. **Correct.** According to this view, people should be judged on the basis of competence rather than gender.

16. a. Incorrect. This statement is true.
    b. Incorrect. This statement is true.
    c. **Correct.** In fact, about 60 percent of Americans claim to attend religious services.
    d. Incorrect. This statement is true.

17. a. Incorrect. This stage is associated with middle adulthood.
    b. Incorrect. This stage is associated with early adolescence. Little exploration of alternative ideologies has occurred.
    c. **Correct.** This stage is associated with late adolescence, or early adulthood.
    d. Incorrect. This stages is associated with the elementary school years.

18. a. Incorrect. This stage is associated with achieving a sense of unity with all being.
    b. **Correct.** This stage is associated with middle adulthood.
    c. Incorrect. This stage is associated with early childhood. Fantasy and reality are the same in this stage.
    d. Incorrect. This stage is associated with the literal interpretation of religious stories. It is associated with elementary school years.

19. a. Incorrect. This answer is partially correct; another alternative is a better answer.
    b. Incorrect. This answer is partially correct; another alternative is a better answer.
    c. Incorrect. No relationship has been established between religious involvement and mental disorders.
    d. **Correct.** These data help to dispel the notion of religion as a "crutch" for the weak.

20. a. Incorrect. Those with intrinsic religious motivation do report a greater sense of competence and control.
b. Incorrect. Those with intrinsic religious motivation do report less worry and guilt.
c. **Correct.** This is not reported in the text.
d. Incorrect. Those with intrinsic religious motivation were less likely to be prejudiced toward ethnic groups.

Chapter **16** **Applied Psychology**

Learning Objectives

After studying this chapter, you should be able to:

1. Define *applied psychology* and *industrial/organizational psychology*. (p. 586)

2. Identify the following dimensions of industrial psychology: job analysis, selection, performance appraisal, and training. (p. 587)

3. Discuss the following dimensions of organizational psychology: job satisfaction, motivation, communication, and organizational changes. (p. 589)

4. Describe the goals of human factors (engineering) psychology. (p. 594)

5. Identify the field of environmental psychology and distinguish between density and crowding. (p. 596)

6. Identify the field of forensic psychology. (p. 599)

7. Discuss the results of research regarding the characteristics of defendants and juries. (p. 600)

8. Explain how the media and pretrial publicity can affect jury verdicts. (p. 600)

9. Identify and describe the legal topics about which psychologists testify as expert witnesses. (p. 601)

10. List and describe the techniques sports psychologists use to help athletes improve their performances. (p. 602)

11. Identify the field of educational psychology. (p. 604)

12. Discuss the role played by educational psychologists in identifying exceptional learners and in developing learner-centered principles. (p. 605)

Chapter Outline

I. What is Applied Psychology?
II. Industrial/Organization Psychology
   A. Industrial Psychology
      1. Job Analysis
      2. Selection
      3. Performance Appraisal
      4. Training
   B. Organizational Psychology
      1. Job Satisfaction
      2. Motivation
      3. Communication
      4. The Changing Places and Faces of Organizations
      5. Gender and Ethnicity
   C. Human Factors (Engineering) Psychology
III. Environmental Psychology
   A. Noise
   B. Density and Crowding
   C. Changing Environmentally Damaging Behavior
IV. Forensic Psychology
   A. Characteristics of Defendants and Juries
   B. The Jury System in Action
      1. The Media and Pretrial Publicity
      2. Making Judgments and Decisions
   C. Psychologists as Expert Witnesses
      1. Insanity Defense
      2. Competency to stand trial
      3. Civil commitment
      4. Psychological damages in civil cases
      5. Negligence and product liability
      6. Class action suits
      7. Guardianship and Conservatorship
      8. Child custody
V. Sport Psychology
   A. Improving Sports Performance
      1. Emphasize the process rather than the outcome
      2. Use deep breathing and muscle relaxation
      3. Use cognitive restructuring and positive self-talk
      4. Use visualization
   B. Enjoying Sports Participation
VI. Educational Psychology
   A. Socioeconomic Status, Ethnicity, and Schools
   B. Exceptional Learners
   C. Learner-Centered Psychological Principles
      1. The nature of learning
      2. Goals of learning
      3. The Construction of knowledge and thinking
      4. Contexts of learning
      5. Motivational and emotional influences on learning

Key Terms

Write a brief description for each of the following terms. Where relevant, provide an original example or illustration of the term. Then, compare your answers with those provided at the end of the study guide chapter. Review the text for those terms you don't know or define incorrectly.

1. applied psychology (p. 586)
2. industrial/organizational (I/O) psychology (p. 587)
3. industrial psychology (p. 587)
4. organizational psychology (p. 589)
5. human factors (engineering) psychology (p. 594)
6. environmental psychology (p. 596)
7. density (p. 598)
8. crowding (p. 598)
9. forensic psychology (p. 599)
10. sports psychology (p. 602)
11. educational psychology (p. 604)
12. exceptional learners (p. 605)
13. inclusion (p. 605)

Guided Review

The following in-depth chapter review is a challenging and comprehensive fill-in-the-blanks exercise. The answers are found near the end of the chapter. As you go through the exercise, try to resist the temptation to look at the answers until you have provided them. When you have filled in all the blanks, you will have a thorough summary of the chapter for reference and review.

What is Applied Psychology?/Industrial/Organizational Psychology

The name given to the field that uses psychological principles to improve the lives of humans and to solve human problems is ___(1)___ psychology. The branch of psychology that focuses on the workplace is called ___(2)___/________ psychology. There are three components of I/O psychology: industrial psychology, ___(3)___ psychology and ___(4)___ factors psychology.

The branch of I/O psychology that focuses on personnel and human resource management is called ___(5)___ psychology. A process that helps to determine which candidates to hire and how to train and evaluate employees is called ___(6)___ ________. Application blanks, psychological tests interviews and work samples are examples of personnel ___(7)___ tools. Currently, there is interest in determining whether tests based on the "___(8)___ ________" personality factors can predict job success. Two other industrial psychology functions are ___(9)___ appraisal and training.

The field of I/O psychology that focuses on the social and group influences in an organization is ___(10)___ psychology. Among the areas of concern of organizational psychologists are job ___(11)___, employee ___(12)___, and communication.

An anticipated change to the workplace is a shift from ___(13)___-producing to ___(14)___-producing jobs. The fastest growing and highest paying jobs will be those requiring the most ___(15)___ and training. Organizational changes include ___(16)___, and the expansion of businesses into ___(17)___ operations.

A subtle barrier that prevents women and minorities from moving up the management ladder is called the "___(18)___ ________." Women are advancing the fastest in "cutting edge" industries like ___(19)___, finance, and advertising.

The subdivision of I/O that focuses on machine design and the environments in which humans function is called ___(20)___ ________ psychology. Human factors engineers help to decide what kinds of ___(21)___ to use on machinery.

Environmental Psychology/ Forensic Psychology

Environmental psychology is the study of transactions between people and the ___(22)___ ________. An environmental factor that has considerable influence on behavior is ___(23)___. Noise is more annoying when it occurs at ___(24)___ intervals and when we have no ___(25)___ over it.

The actual number of people per unit area is referred to as ___(26)___. The psychological experience that others are too close is ___(27)___. Crowding is more stressful when people perceive they have little or no ___(28)___.

Suggestions for increasing awareness of environmentally damaging behavior include arousing ___(29)___ ________ and getting people to understand their behavior is not ___(30)___ ________.

The field of forensic psychology applies psychological principles to the ___(31)___ system. Forensic psychologists study the characteristics of defendants and ___(32)___. They have found that people are more likely to be convicted if they are from ___(33)___-income, ___(34)___ educated and ___(35)___ minority backgrounds. Likewise, jurors who are white, older, better educated, of higher social status and politically conservative are ___(36)___ likely to convict and recommend ___(37)___ sentences. Forensic psychologists have determined that two reasons why juries may not always reach the right verdict have to do with the ___(38)___ and with ___(39)___ publicity. Forensic psychologists also try to determine which factors influence the ___(40)___ in a trial. Forensic psychologists also serve as ___(41)___ witnesses in a trial.

Sport Psychology/Educational Psychology

The field that applies psychology's principles to improving sport performance and enjoying sports participation is called ___(42)___ psychology. Among the techniques used by sport psychologists to improve sports performance are: emphasizing ___(43)___ rather than outcome, using deep breathing and ___(44)___ relaxation, using cognitive restructuring and positive ___(45)___-________, and using ___(46)___. Sport psychologists also emphasize ___(47)___ of participation in sports.

The field that applies psychological concepts to teaching and learning is called ___(48)___ psychology. Educational psychologists conduct ___(49)___, consult with school ___(50)___, counsel ___(51)___ and work directly with ___(52)___. A special concern involves the difficulties experienced in school by children from ___(53)___-income and ___(54)___ minority backgrounds. Students who require additional services to meet their individual needs are referred to as ___(55)___ learners. A trend today is to educate exceptional learners in regular classrooms, a practice called ___(56)___. Among the learner-centered issues advocated by educational psychologists are principles addressing the nature of ___(57)___, the goals of learning, the ___(58)___ of knowledge and thinking, the ___(59)___ of learning, and motivational and ___(60)___ influences on learning.

Sociocultural Worlds/Applications in Psychology

In your own words, summarize the material you have read in Sociocultural Worlds, "Nenko Management in Japan," and Applications in Psychology, "Schools for Thought." Briefly describe how each of these articles relates to the information contained in the chapter.

Concept Check

Applied Psychology

Field	Specializes in
1. Industrial psychology	______________.
2. Organizational psychology	______________.
3. Engineering psychology	______________.
4. Environmental psychology	______________.
5. Forensic psychology	______________.
6. Sport psychology	______________.
7. Educational psychology	______________.

Answers

1. the subdivision of I/O psychology that involves personnel and human resource management.
2. the subdivision of I/O psychology that examines the social and group influences in an organization.
3. also called engineering psychology, this subdivision of I/O psychology focuses on improving the safety and efficiency of machines and the environment.
4. studies the transactions between people and their physical environments.
5. applies psychological concepts to the legal system.
6. applies psychological principles to improving sport performance and to the enjoyment of sport participation.
7. applies psychological concepts to teaching and to learning.

Multiple-Choice Questions

Practice Test 1

After answering all the multiple-choice questions in Practice Test 1, compare your answers with the answer key provided at the end of the chapter. The answer key contains a brief explanation of both the correct and incorrect answers. Each of these questions is keyed to the Learning Objectives for the chapter. If you answer any questions incorrectly, review the corresponding Learning Objective and text material before you proceed to Practice Test 2.

1. Each of the following is an example of applied psychology *except*
   a. sport psychology.
   b. forensic psychology.
   c. industrial psychology.
   d. basic research.

LO 1

2. According to the text, virtually all other personnel functions stem from
   a. job analysis.
   b. employee selection.
   c. performance appraisal.
   d. employee training.

LO 2

3. The "big five factors" are currently used in
   a. job analysis.
   b. selection of employees.
   c. performance appraisal.
   d. training.

LO 2

4. Each of the following represents a future trend in the United States workplace *except*
   a. increasing service-producing jobs.
   b. increasing need for educational preparation.
   c. increasing numbers of ethnic minority individuals.
   d. leveling off or decreasing numbers of women.

LO 3

5. The "glass ceiling" has prevented women and ethnic minorities from
   a. getting hired.
   b. receiving adequate training.
   c. receiving adequate employee benefits.
   d. moving into management positions.

LO 3

6. According to the text, if information has a "half-life" of 5 years, it means
   a. workers will forget half the information in 5 years.
   b. half of what workers know will be obsolete in 5 years.
   c. in 10 years, workers will know nothing.
   d. in 2-1/2 years, workers will need to be retrained.

LO 3

7. Each of the following is true of human factors psychology *except*
   a. It is often referred to as engineering psychology.
   b. It focuses on the design of machines used by workers.
   c. It focuses on the safety and the efficiency of the environment.
   d. It focuses on employee selection.

LO 4

8. Which of the following strategies do the authors suggest in order to encourage people to take better care of our planet?
   a. increased penalties for polluters
   b. arouse awareness of cognitive dissonance
   c. better education
   d. more tangible rewards for decreasing pollution

LO 5

9. Forensic psychologists apply psychological concepts to
   a. computers.
   b. the legal system.
   c. leisure activities.
   d. health-related issues.

LO 6

10. Each of the following characteristics makes a defendant more likely to be convicted *except*
    a. low income
    b. poor education
    c. unattractive
    d. younger

LO 7

11. According to researchers, the more information people receive from the media about a trial, the more likely they are to
    a. believe the defendant is guilty.
    b. believe the defendant is innocent.
    c. have incorrect information about the defendant.
    d. acquit the defendant.

LO 8

12. Psychologists may be called upon to serve as expert witnesses in which of the following?
    a. insanity defense
    b. competency to stand trial
    c. child custody
    d. all of the above

LO 9

13. Sport psychologists use each of the following techniques *except*
    a. emphasis on process rather than outcome
    b. emphasis on outcome rather than process
    c. use of deep breathing
    d. use of positive self-talk

LO 10

14. According to Comer, inner-city and ethnic minority students will benefit from
    a. rigorous academic standards.
    b. a less demanding curriculum.
    c. inclusion.
    d. creating a family-like school environment.

LO 11

15. Each of the following is true of learner-centered principles *except*
    a. they move the focus from the teacher to the student
    b. they move the emphasis from the student to the teacher
    c. they encourage students to set goals
    d. they encourage integrating new knowledge with existing knowledge

LO 12

Practice Test 2

The following multiple-choice questions also are keyed to the chapter Learning Objectives. If you answer any questions incorrectly, be sure to review the corresponding Learning Objective and text material.

1. The branch of industrial-organizational psychology that involves human resources management is
    a. industrial psychology.
    b. organizational psychology.
    c. human factors psychology.
    d. environmental psychology.

LO 1

2. Each of the following is an important function of industrial psychology *except*
    a. job analysis
    b. performance appraisal
    c. job satisfaction
    d. job training

LO 2

3. The term *personnel psychology* is increasingly used to identify
    a. industrial psychology.
    b. organizational psychology.
    c. human factors psychology.
    d.. applied psychology.

LO 2

4. What happens to levels of job satisfaction as employees grow older?
    a. it increases
    b. it decreases for females, but not for males
    c. it remains constant
    d. it decreases for males, but not for females

LO 3

5. The National Association of College Employers listed each of the following as important employee skills *except*
    a. oral communication skills
    b. computer skills
    c. interpersonal skills
    d. teamwork skills

LO 3

6. An implication of the "half-life" of information is that workers need
    a. more vacations.
    b. better communication skills.
    c. better health benefits.
    d. continuing education.

LO 3

7. If you were interested in improving the design of a computer keyboard to reduce user fatigue, you would most likely seek the services of a(n)
   a. industrial psychologist.
   b. organizational psychologist.
   c. human factors psychologist.
   d. environmental psychologist.

LO 4

8. Children who are repeatedly exposed to high levels of noise were found to have each of the following characteristics *except*
   a. poor reading skills
   b. easily distracted
   c. better concentration skills
   d. higher blood pressure

LO 5

9. Who is most likely to employ a forensic psychologist?
   a. a computer firm
   b. a lawyer
   c. a physician
   d. an athlete

LO 6

10. Jurors are more likely to vote for a conviction when they have each of the following characteristics *except*
    a. older
    b. politically conservative
    c. better educated
    d. male

LO 7

11. The information broadcast by the media about a defendant
    a. usually implies the defendant is innocent.
    b. usually implies the defendant is guilty.
    c. is severely limited by law.
    d. is usually balanced in terms of implying innocence or guilt.

LO 8

12. In which of the following situations are psychologists called upon to help determine a defendant's mental state at the time a crime was committed?
    a. civil commitment
    b. insanity defense
    c. competency to stand trial
    d. class action suits

LO 9

13. Which of the following is a technique used by sport psychologists?
    a. cognitive restructuring
    b. deep breathing for relaxation
    c. positive self-talk
    d. all of the above

LO 10

14. Educational psychologists believe exceptional learners can benefit by
    a. inclusion.
    b. educating them exclusively outside the regular classroom.
    c. using resource rooms.
    d. *a* and *c* above

LO 11

15. Each of the following is consistent with "learner-related principles" *except*
    a. learning benefits from intrinsic motivation
    b. learning should take place without regard to the context in which it occurs
    c. learning improves when students set goals
    d. learning benefits when it is actively constructed

LO 12

Answers to Key Terms

1. **Applied psychology** is the field that uses psychological principles to improve the lives of humans and to solve human problems.
2. **Industrial/organizational psychology** is the branch of psychology that focuses on the workplace, both on the workers and on the organization that employs them.
3. **Industrial psychology** focuses on personnel and human resource management.
4. **Organizational psychology** examines the social and group influences within an organization.
5. **Human factors psychology** focuses on the design of machines that workers use and on the environments in which humans function.
6. **Environmental psychology** studies the transactions between people and their environments.
7. **Density** is the number of people per unit area.
8. **Crowding** is the psychological experience that people are too close.
9. **Forensic psychology** is the area that applies psychological concepts to the legal system.
10. The goals of **sport psychology** are to improve sport performance and enjoyment of sport participation.
11. **Educational psychology** is the field that applies psychological concepts to teaching and learning.
12. **Exceptional learners** are students who require additional services to meet their individual needs.
13. **Inclusion** is the principle of educating exceptional learners in the regular classroom.

Answers to Guided Review

1. applied (p. 586)
2. industrial/organizational (p. 587)
3. organizational (p. 587)
4. human (p. 587)
5. industrial (p. 587)
6. job analysis (p. 587)
7. selection (p. 587)
8. big five (p. 587)
9. performance (p. 588)
10. organizational (p. 589)
11. satisfaction (p. 589)
12. motivation (p. 589)
13. goods (p. 591)
14. service (p. 591)
15. education (p. 593)
16. downsizing (p. 593)
17. international (p. 593)
18. glass ceiling (p. 593)
19. computers (p. 593)
20. human factors (p. 594)
21. displays (p. 594)
22. physical environment (p. 596)
23. noise (p. 596)
24. irregular (p. 596)
25. control (p. 596)
26. density (p. 598)
27. crowding (p. 598)
28. control (p. 598)
29. cognitive dissonance (p. 599)
30. socially acceptable (p. 599)
31. legal (p. 599)
32. juries (p. 600)
33. low (p. 600)
34. poorly (p. 600)
35. ethnic (p. 600)
36. more (p. 600)
37. harsher (p. 600)
38. media (p. 600)
39. pretrial (p. 600)
40. verdict (p. 600)
41. expert (p. 601)
42. sport (p. 602)
43. process (p. 602)
44. muscle (p. 602)
45. self-talk (p. 602)
46. visualization (p. 603)
47. enjoyment (p. 603)
48. educational (p. 604)
49. research (p. 604)
50. administrators (p. 604)
51. teachers (p. 604)
52. students (p. 604)
53. low (p. 604)
54. ethnic (p. 604)
55. exceptional (p. 605)
56. inclusion (p. 605)
57. learning (p. 605)
58. construction (p. 606)
59. contexts (p. 606)
60. emotional (p. 607)

Answers to Multiple Choice Questions- Practice Test 1

1. a. Incorrect. This *is* an example of applied psychology.
   b. Incorrect. This *is* an example of applied psychology.
   c. Incorrect. This *is* an example of applied psychology.
   d. **Correct.** Basic research is concerned with deriving knowledge from research; applied psychologists use this knowledge to solve human problems and improve the lives of people.

2. a. **Correct.** This process helps top determine who to hire and how to train and evaluate workers.
   b. Incorrect. This functions is derived from another personnel function.
   c. incorrect. This function is derived from another personnel function.
   d. Incorrect. This function is derived from another personnel function.

3 a. Incorrect. The big five factors are based on personality factors.
   b. **Correct.** Two measures being used are the Revised NEO Personality Inventory and the Hogan Personality Inventory.
   c. Incorrect. The big five factors are based on personality factors.
   d. Incorrect. The big five factors are based on personality factors.

4. a. Incorrect. This *does* represent a future trend.
   b. Incorrect. This *does* represent a future trend.
   c. Incorrect. This *does* represent a future trend.
   d. **Correct.** The number of women entering the workforce is expected to continue to grow.

5. a. Incorrect. The expression "glass ceiling" doesn't relate to getting hired.
   b. Incorrect. This expression doesn't relate to training.
   c. Incorrect. The expression doesn't relate to receiving benefits.
   d. **Correct.** This relates to the subtle barrier that keeps minorities and women from moving up the organizational ladder.

6. a. Incorrect. The expression "half-life" in this context doesn't refer to forgetting.
   b. **Correct.** This reminds us about the need for continuing education throughout one's career.
   c. Incorrect. Hopefully, this is not true.
   d. Incorrect. This is not what is meant by a "half-life".

7. a. Incorrect. Human factors psychology *is* often referred to as engineering psychology.
   b. Incorrect. Human factors psychology *does* focus on the design of machines.
   c. Incorrect. Human factors psychology *does* focus on safety and efficiency issues.
   d. **Correct.** This is the focus of industrial psychology.

8. a. Incorrect. Although this technique is used, it is not one the suggestions in the text.
   b. **Correct.** Help people understand that they are not practicing what they may be preaching with regard to environmental issues.
   c. Incorrect. Although this technique is used, it is not one of the suggestions from the text.
   d. Incorrect. Although this technique is sometimes used, it is not one of the suggestions from the text.

9. a. Incorrect. the design of computer keyboards would be a function of human factors psychology.
   b. **Correct.** This includes selection of juries, expert witness testimony, and so on.
   c. Incorrect. This is the arena of sport psychology.
   d. incorrect. This is the area of behavioral medicine.

10. a. Incorrect. This characteristic *does* make a defendant more likely to be convicted.
   b. Incorrect. This characteristic *does* make a defendant more likely to be convicted.
   c. Incorrect. This characteristic *does* make a defendant more likely to be convicted.
   d. **Correct.** Age is not mentioned as a factor in the likelihood of conviction.

11. a. **Correct.** Thus, pretrial publicity can make it difficult to receive a fair trial.
    b. Incorrect. The opposite is actually true.
    c. Incorrect. The information from the media usually points toward the defendant's guilt.
    d. Incorrect. The information from the media usually points toward the defendant's guilt.

12. a. Incorrect. This is partially true; another answer is a better alternative.
    b. Incorrect. This is partially true; another answer is a better alternative.
    c. Incorrect. This is partially true; another answer is a better alternative.
    d. **Correct.** Other functions may include psychological damages in civil cases, civil commitment, class action suits, and so on.

13. a. Incorrect. Sport psychologists *do* emphasize process.
    b. **Correct.** Sport psychologists emphasize process over outcome.
    c. Incorrect. Sport psychologists *do* emphasize deep breathing as a way to control anxiety.
    d. Incorrect. Sport psychologists *do* emphasize positive self-talk as a way to minimize negative thinking.

14. a. Incorrect. This is not Comer's main emphasis.
    b. Incorrect. This is not what Comer maintains.
    c. Incorrect. This is not what Comer maintains.
    d. **Correct.** Comer emphasizes stronger parental involvement.

15. a. Incorrect. This *is* a focus of learner-centered principles.
    b. **Correct.** Learner-centered principles move the emphasis in the opposite direction.
    c. Incorrect. This *is* a focus of learner-centered principles.
    d. Incorrect. This *is* a focus of learner-centered principles.

Answers to Multiple Choice Questions- Practice Test 2

1. a. **Correct.** This includes job analysis, employee selection, performance appraisal, and training.
   b. Incorrect. This branch explores the social and group influences on an organization.
   c. Incorrect. This branch is sometimes referred to as engineering psychology.
   d. Incorrect. This branch studies the transactions between people and the physical environment.

2. a. Incorrect. This *is* a function of industrial psychology.
   b. Incorrect. This *is* a function of industrial psychology.
   c. **Correct.** This is an organizational psychology function.
   d. Incorrect. This *is* a function of industrial psychology.

3. a. **Correct.** This is due to the emphasis on personnel and human resources management.
   b. incorrect. This branch focuses on the social and group influences within the organization.
   c. Incorrect. This is frequently referred to as engineering psychology.
   d. Incorrect. This term applies to the overall field that includes industrial/organizational psychology, human factors psychology, forensic psychology, and so on.

4. a. **Correct.** Satisfaction increases steadily until at least age 60.
   b. Incorrect. The text does not cite data on gender differences.
   c. Incorrect. Levels of job satisfaction do change with age.
   d. Incorrect. The text does not cite data on gender differences with regard to levels of job satisfaction.

5. a. Incorrect. This *was* listed as an important skill by the National Association of College Employees.
   b. **Correct.** This was not among the important skills listed.
   c. Incorrect. This *was* listed as an important skill by the National Association of College Employees.
   d. Incorrect. This *was* listed as an important skill by the National Association of College Employees.

6. a. Incorrect. This may be true, but is not an implication of the "half-life" of information.
   b. Incorrect. This may be true, but is not an implication of the "half-life" of information.
   c. Incorrect. This may be true, but is not an implication of the "half-life" of information.
   d. **Correct.** Continuing education and retraining are the only ways to keep up with our rapidly changing world.

7. a. Incorrect. These psychologists specialize in employee selection, job analysis, and so on.
   b. Incorrect. These psychologists specialize in social and group dynamics within an organization.
   c. **Correct.** This field is also referred to as engineering psychology.
   d. Incorrect. These psychologists study the transactions between people and their physical environments.

8. a. Incorrect. This characteristic was found in children exposed to high levels of noise.
   b. Incorrect. This characteristic was found in children exposed to high levels of noise.
   c. **Correct.** This was not found among children exposed to high levels of noise.
   d. Incorrect. This characteristic was found in children exposed to high levels of noise.

9. a. Incorrect. Forensic psychologists apply psychological concepts to the legal system.
   b. **Correct.** Forensic psychologists apply psychological concepts to the legal system.
   c. Incorrect. Forensic psychologists apply psychological concepts to the legal system.
   d. Incorrect. Forensic psychologists apply psychological concepts to the legal system.

10. a. Incorrect. According to the text, jurors with this characteristic *are* more likely to vote for a conviction.
    b. Incorrect. According to the text, jurors with this characteristic *are* more likely to vote for a conviction
    c. Incorrect. According to the text, jurors with this characteristic *are* more likely to vote for a conviction
    d. **Correct.** The text does not mention gender as a juror variable.

11. a. Incorrect. The information usually implies guilt.
    b. **Correct.** The source of the information usually is the police, the district attorney, and so on.
    c. Incorrect. In an open society, there is much information provided about defendants.
    d. Incorrect. The information is seldom balanced.

12. a. Incorrect. This issue relates to whether a defendant presents an immediate danger or threat to self or others.
    b. **Correct.** They might also judge the degree to which a defendant is responsible for the crime.
    c. Incorrect. This is the issue regarding whether a defendant is capable of understanding the legal proceedings.
    d. Incorrect. In this regard psychologists may testify about whether people are being discriminated against.

13. a. Incorrect. This answer is partially true; another answer is a better alternative.
    b. Incorrect. This answer is partially true; another answer is a better alternative.
    c. Incorrect. This answer is partially true; another answer is a better alternative.
    d. **Correct.** Sport psychologists also encourage athletes to use visualization and to emphasize the process over the outcome.

14. a. Incorrect. This answer is partially correct; another answer is a better alternative.
    b. Incorrect. This is not consistent with the beliefs of most educational psychologists.
    c. Incorrect. This answer is partially correct; another answer is a better alternative.
    d. **Correct.** The current thinking emphasizes both inclusion and the use of resource rooms.

15. a. Incorrect. This *is* consistent with learner-related principles.
    b. **Correct.** These principles hold learning is influenced by its contexts.
    c. Incorrect. This *is* consistent with learner-related principles.
    d. Incorrect. This *is* consistent with learner-related principles.